ORDNANCE
GUIDE TO THE
WATERWAYS

1: SOUTH

Series editor: David Perrott

Nicholson

An Imprint of Bartholomew
A Division of HarperCollins*Publishers*

Also available in this series:

Nicholson/Ordnance Survey Guide to the Waterways 2. Central
Nicholson/Ordnance Survey Guide to the Waterways 3. North
Nicholson/Ordnance Survey Guide to the River Thames
Nicholson/Ordnance Survey Guide to the Broads & Fens
Nicholson/Ordnance Survey Inland Waterways Map of Great Britain

The indication of a towpath in this book
does not necessarily imply a public right
of way. If you are in any doubt, check
before you proceed with the latest published Ordnance Survey Map.
Pathfinder Series (2½ in to 1 mile scale or
1:25 000). These OS walker and rambler maps show the
countryside in great detail, including rights
of way in England and Wales.
Landranger Series (1¼ in to 1 mile scale or
1:50 000). This OS series covers the country
in 204 sheets and is ideal for detailed
exploring by car or on foot.

First published in 1983 by
Nicholson
77–85 Fulham Palace Road
Hammersmith, London W6 8JB
and
Ordnance Survey,
Romsey Road, Maybush,
Southampton SO9 4DH

5th edition 1991
Reprinted 1992
© Text, Nicholson 1991

Nicholson
An Imprint of Bartholomew
A Division of HarperCollins*Publishers*

The series editor gratefully acknowledges the help
given by British Waterways and their staff. Thanks
is also due to CAMRA representatives and branch
members for their help in recommending real ale pubs.

Research: Jane Bruton, Jane and Jonathan Mosse

Cover photograph: Derek Pratt

Typeset by Rowland Phototypesetting Limited,
Bury St Edmunds, Suffolk
Printed in Great Britain by
HarperCollinsManufacturing Glasgow

Ordnance Survey ISBN 03190 0250 0
Nicholson ISBN 07028 1259 5

83/5/512

INTRODUCTION

The canals and navigable rivers of Britain were built as a system of new trade routes at a time when roads were virtually non-existent. After their boom period in the late 18th and early 19th centuries, they gradually declined in the face of fierce competition from the new railway companies, and large-scale commercial carrying ended by the time of the Second World War, when many of the routes had slipped into decay and ruin. It is true that in a few areas goods continue to be carried profitably to this day, but for the majority of canals it was the new traffic of pleasure boats that provided the impetus for rescue and restoration.

The founding of the Inland Waterways Association by L. T. C. Rolt and Robert Aickman in 1946 brought together enthusiasts from all over the country who were to campaign to save and restore these 2000 miles of navigable waterways that are so much a part of our history. During the past few years an amazing transformation has taken place. British Waterways, local councils, and IWA volunteers working with various job creation schemes have tidied up great lengths of town and city canal, and much of the dereliction that was once commonplace has been replaced with gardens and parkland. The completion of the restoration of the Kennet & Avon Canal in 1990 is the most recent achievement, and one of the most remarkable.

There is something for everyone in the canals: engineering feats like aqueducts, tunnels and flights of locks (all of which amazed a world that had seen nothing like it since Roman times); the brightly decorated narrowboats which used to throng the waterways; the wealth of birds, animals and plants on canal banks; the mellow, unpretentious architecture of canalside buildings like pubs, stables, lock cottages and warehouses; and the sheer beauty and quiet isolation that is a feature of so many canals.

A special feature of this guide is the many new or expanded pub entries, giving details of real ales as recommended by CAMRA. So use this book to discover the waterways for yourself; it is one of five volumes covering the South, Centre and North of England and Wales; the rivers Thames and Wey, and the Basingstoke Canal; and the Norfolk Broads, Ouse, Nene and Middle Level Navigations. A full-colour Nicholson/Ordnance Survey *Inland Waterways Map* is also available to help you plan your route.

CONTENTS

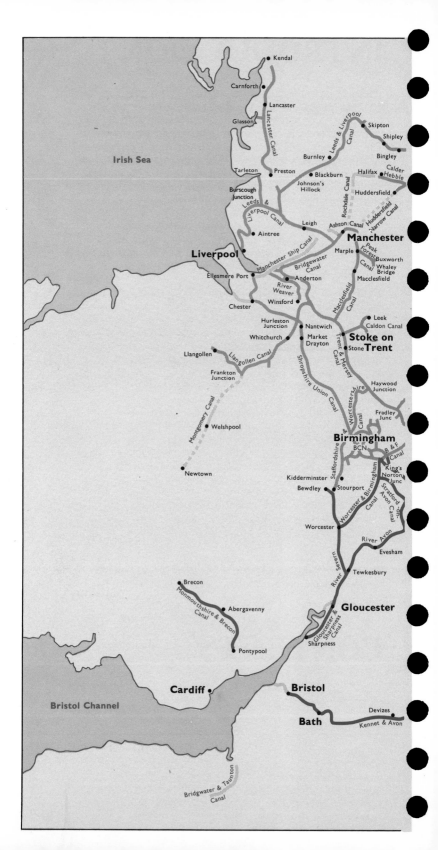

Waterways Map showing Nicholson Guide Areas

Waterways covered in this guide
Waterways covered in other guides in the series
Other Waterways
Waterways unnavigable at present time

HOW TO USE THIS GUIDE

The maps are drawn at a scale of 2 inches to 1 mile. Adjacent to each map section is a description of the countryside and places of interest together with a commentary on the course of the canal or river. Details of the boatyards and pubs marked are also given, adjacent to each map, and are arranged in order from the top of the page to the bottom.

Symbols and abbreviations used in the text:

Ⓑ	Boatyard or boatyard services
Ⓡ	Refuse disposal
Ⓢ	Sewage or 'Elsan' disposal
Ⓦ	Water
Ⓟ	Petrol
Ⓓ	Diesel
Ⓔ	Electric boat recharging
●	Public house
✕	Restaurant
!	Licensed to sell alcohol
L	Open for lunch
D	Open for dinner
EC	Early closing
MD	Market day
BW	British Waterways
IWA	Inland Waterways Association
NT	National Trust

Symbols used on maps:

Ⓑ	Boatyard or boatyard services
●	Public house
R	Refuse disposal
S	Sewage or 'Elsan' disposal point
W	Water point

Locks, with number and 'rise'. The symbol points uphill.

Staircase locks.

Bridge and its number. Many are named.

Tunnel – often described in the text.

Aqueduct – often described in the text.

Winding hole – turning point for boats longer than the ordinary width of the canal (it's pronounced as in the wind that blows). Canal junctions are also good places to 'wind'.

Weir.

Scale and north point
The strip maps are drawn at 2 inches to 1 mile. North is indicated on each map.

Navigational notes
These appear where necessary to point out potential hazards, navigational limits or other vital information.

Boatyards
Services listed are those usually available; do not, however, expect a hire base to stop what they are doing on fleet 'turn around' day (usually Saturday) to help you – *they will be extremely busy*. Any other day you are sure to be made to feel welcome. Remember also that moorings get filled very quickly, so do not assume that there will be space for your boat. Always ask.

A feature of these guides is the 'milestone' which appears on every map thus:

This performs many useful functions. It reminds you of your direction of travel – in this example **up** the page is towards Napton, **down** the page is towards Oxford; it denotes distances and indicates the number of locks between the milestone and strategic points (usually junctions) along the waterway – in this example, Napton is 22¼ miles (M) with 22 locks (L) from the 'milestone', and Oxford is 27 miles and 17 locks from the milestone. By deducting the miles and locks on one milestone from those on the next, distances from page to page can be accurately estimated. Using the 'lock-miles' system (see **Planning a cruise**, page 13) the time your journey will take can be calculated, and with a little experience based on your speed of travel and lock operation, your own time formula can be arrived at.

Where this device occurs on a map it simply means that the actual route of the waterway would not fit neatly onto the page, so the cartographer has 'bent' the map, using two north points. The navigator on the water, or the walker on the bank, will notice nothing amiss. Distances in this book should be measured along the thick blue line only, not including these gaps.

LOCKS AND THEIR USE

The different locks and their attendant machinery are a source of endless fascination for all waterway users. Understanding why they are there and the principle upon which they work will help you in their use.

A lock is a device for transporting craft from a higher water level to a lower level, or vice versa, for example when a canal crosses a range of hills. It consists of a box with gates at each end, and a separate means of letting water in at the top (higher level) and out at the bottom (lower level). This is controlled by paddles. These paddles may simply open and shut holes in the gates (gate paddles), or they may open and shut underground culverts (ground paddles). A windlass (carried on the boat) is used to wind the paddles open and shut. Whilst locks differ in detail, the following instructions will apply in the case of the vast majority of *narrow* canal locks. Some extra points regarding wide locks are covered later.

A typical narrow lock

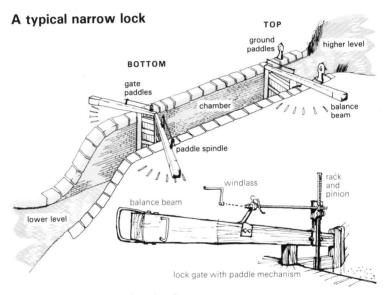

lock gate with paddle mechanism

How to go through a lock

PRELIMINARIES

Stop the boat well outside the lock and secure it. If members of your crew can get off the boat before the lock (at the narrow point under a bridge for example) and run ahead to prepare the lock, this will save time.

GOING UP IN A LOCK (LOCKING UP)

Lock empty – ie water at lower level

Open bottom gate(s)
Drive boat in
Close gate(s)
Check bottom paddles closed
Keep boat near to the bottom of lock
Open top paddles to fill lock
Open top gate(s) when lock is full
Drive boat out
Close top gate(s)
Close top paddles

Lock full – ie water at higher level

Check top gate(s) and paddles closed
Open bottom paddles to drain lock
Open bottom gate(s)
Drive boat in
Close bottom gate(s) and paddles
Keep boat near to the bottom of lock
Open top paddles to fill lock
Open top gate(s) when lock is full
Drive boat out
Close top gate(s)
Close top paddles

GOING DOWN IN A LOCK (LOCKING DOWN)

Lock full – ie water at higher level

Open top gate(s)
Drive boat in
Close top gate(s)
Check top paddles closed
Keep boat near to the bottom of the lock
Open bottom paddles to empty lock
Open bottom gate(s)
Drive boat out
Close bottom gates and paddles

Lock empty – ie water at lower level

Check bottom gate(s) and paddles closed
Open top paddles to fill lock
Open gate(s)
Drive boat in
Close top gate(s) and paddles
Keep boat near to the bottom of the lock
Open bottom paddles to empty lock
Open bottom gate(s)
Drive boat out
Close bottom gate(s) and paddles

If you have to drain or fill a lock in order to enter it, make sure there is no boat approaching that could usefully use the lock before you. Always try to conserve water, which is being continually passed down the canal from its summit and thus requires constant replenishment at a higher level.

SOME GENERAL DOS AND DON'TS AT LOCKS

Do not leave your windlass slotted onto the paddle spindle – if something slips it could be thrown off and cause injury.

Always leave all gates and paddles closed when you leave, but look out for notices which may give other instructions for the proper operation of a particular lock.

Always wind the paddles down – letting them drop is bad practice, and causes damage.

Beware of protrusions in the side walls of the lock chamber that may damage the boat, and don't use fenders in narrow locks – they may jam.

When opening and closing lock gates, keep to the landward side of the balance beam.

Don't rush around at locks, especially in wet weather, when the sides are slippery. Never jump across partly opened gates.

Always make the safety of the crew and boat your prime concern and remember that if things do start to go wrong, you can stop everything by closing the paddles.

There is no reason why your children, wearing buoyancy aids and properly supervised, should not help at locks – it is all part of the fun, after all – but impress upon them the potential dangers, and establish some common-sense rules. You have no authority over other people's children, and their participation should be discouraged. Great difficulties could ensue should they be injured in any way.

Beware of fierce top gate paddles, especially in wide locks.

Don't leave your windlass behind; hundreds are lost this way each year.

WIDE LOCKS

Taking a narrowboat (7ft beam) through a wide lock (14ft) can present special difficulties, especially when locking up. If all the top paddles were to be opened fully at the same time, the boat would be buffeted considerably. The diagram below illustrates one method of ensuring a smooth passage. The stern line held ashore will provide added security.

Locking up in a wide lock
(a suggested technique)

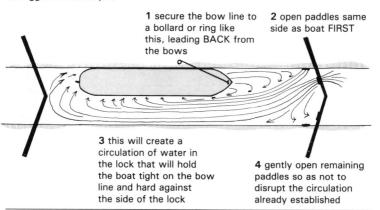

1 secure the bow line to a bollard or ring like this, leading BACK from the bows

2 open paddles same side as boat FIRST

3 this will create a circulation of water in the lock that will hold the boat tight on the bow line and hard against the side of the lock

4 gently open remaining paddles so as not to disrupt the circulation already established

STAIRCASE LOCKS

Where the top gates of one lock are the bottom gates of the next. Usually there is a board nearby giving operating instructions – read it carefully and make sure you understand it before you start. And remember: in a narrow staircase you can't pass a boat coming the other way.

Even young children can help, if properly supervised, but you must make sure life jackets are worn all the time when near the water. *David Perrott.*

GENERAL CRUISING INFORMATION

The majority of the waterways covered in this book are controlled by British Waterways. All craft using BW canals must be licensed and those using BW rivers must be registered. Charges are based on the length of the boat and a canal craft licence covers all the navigable waterways under BW's control. Permits for permanent mooring on the canals are also issued by BW. Apply in each case to the British Waterways Offices listed on page 203 or to:

Customer Services,
British Waterways,
Greycaine Road,
Watford,
WD2 4JR.
(0923 226422).

Other river navigation authorities relevant to this book are mentioned where appropriate.

Getting afloat

There is no better way of discovering the joys of canals than by getting afloat. The best thing is to hire a boat for a week or a fortnight from one of the boatyards on the canals (each boatyard has an entry in the text, and most of them offer craft for hire; brochures may be easily obtained from such boatyards). Or, go on one of the trip boats for a couple of hours, or longer. The notes on page 13 will help you plan a cruise.

General cruising

Most canals are saucer-shaped in section and so are deepest in the middle. Very few have more than 3–4ft of water and many have much less. Try to keep to the middle of the channel except on bends, where the deepest water is on the *outside* of the bend. When you meet another boat, the rule is to keep to the right, slow down, and aim to miss the approaching boat by a couple of yards: do not steer right over to the bank or you will most likely run aground. The deeper the draught of the boat, the more important it is to keep in the middle of the deep water, and so this must be considered when passing other boats. If you meet a loaded working boat, keep right out of the way. Working boats should always take precedence, for their time is money. If you meet a boat being towed from the bank, pass it on the outside rather than intercept the towing line. When overtaking, keep the other boat on your starboard, or right, side.

Speed

There is a general speed limit of 4 mph on most British Waterways canals. This is not just an arbitrary limit: there is no need to go any faster, and in many cases it is impossible to cruise even at this speed. Canals were not built for motor boats, and so the banks are easily damaged by excessive wash and turbulence. Erosion of the banks makes the canal more shallow, which in turn makes running aground a more frequent occurrence. So keep to the limits and try not to aggravate the situation. It is easy to see when a boat is creating excessive turbulence by looking at the wash – if it is 'breaking' or causing large waves, you are going too fast and should slow down.

Slow down also when passing moored craft, engineering works and anglers.

Slow down when there is a lot of floating rubbish on the water: old planks and plastic bags may mean underwater obstacles that can damage a boat or its propeller if hit hard. Try to drift over obvious obstructions in neutral.

Slow down when approaching blind corners, narrow bridges and junctions.

Running aground

The effective end of commercial traffic on the narrow canals has resulted in canals being shallower than ever. Running aground is a not uncommon event, but is rarely serious, as the canal bed is usually soft. If you run aground, try first of all to pull the boat off by gently reversing the engine. If this fails, use the pole as a lever against the bank or some solid object, in combination with a tow rope being pulled from the bank. Do not keep revving the engine in reverse if it is obviously having no effect. Another way is to get your crew to rock the boat from side to side while using the pole or mooring lines. If all else fails, lighten your load; make all the crew leave the boat except the helmsman, and then it will often float off quite easily.

Remember that if you run aground once, it is likely to happen again as it indicates a particularly shallow stretch – or that you are out of the channel. If you are continually bumping the bottom in a shallow stretch, it may be that you are going too fast, causing the boat to 'dig in' at the back. Going slower may make things more comfortable.

In a town you may run aground on sunken rubbish; this is most likely to occur near bridges and housing estates. Use the same methods, but be very careful as these hard objects can easily damage your boat or propeller.

Remember that winding holes are often silted up – do not go further in than you have to.

Mooring

All boats carry metal stakes and a mallet. These are used for mooring when there are no rings or bollards in sight, which is usually the case. Generally speaking you may moor anywhere to BW property but there are certain basic rules. Avoid mooring anywhere that could cause an obstruction to other boats; do not moor on a bend, in a winding hole or a narrow stretch, do not moor abreast boats already moored. Never moor in a lock, and do not be tempted to tie up in a tunnel or under a bridge if it is raining. Pick a stretch where there is a reasonable depth of water at the bank, otherwise the boat may bump and scrape the canal bed – an unpleasant sensation if you are trying to sleep. For reasons of peace and quiet and privacy it is best to moor away from main roads and railway lines.

Never stretch your mooring lines across the towpath; you may trip someone up and face a claim for damages.

There is no need to show a riding light at night, except on major rivers and busy commercial canals.

Beware of mooring at unrecognised sites in cities – you may attract the unwelcome attention of vandals.

So long as you are sensible and keep to the rules, mooring can be a pleasant gesture of individuality.

Knots

A simple and easy way of securing a rope to a bollard or mooring stake is to use a couple of round turns and a half hitch or two made with a loop and pulled tight. This can be released quickly by pulling the loose end, which will have been left tidily coiled.

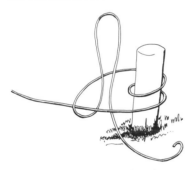

When leaving a mooring, coil all the ropes up again. They will then be out of the way, but ready if needed in a hurry. Many a sailor has fallen overboard after tripping on an uncoiled rope.

Fixed bridges

At most bridges the canal becomes very narrow, a means of saving building costs developed by the engineers. As a result, careful navigation is called for if you are to avoid hitting either the bridge sides with the hull, or the arch with the cabin top. As when entering a lock, the best way to tackle 'bridgeholes' is to slow down well in advance and aim to go straight through, keeping a steady course. Adjustments should be kept to a minimum for it is easy to start the boat zig-zagging, which will inevitably end in a collision. One technique is to gauge the width of the approaching bridgehole relative to the width of the boat, and then watch one side only, aiming to miss that side by a small margin – say 6in; the smaller you can make the margin, the less chance you have of hitting the other side of the bridge. If you do hit the bridge sides when going slowly it is not likely to do much damage;

it will merely strengthen your resolve to do better next time.

Moveable bridges

Swing and lift bridges are an attractive feature of some canals and cannot be ignored as they often rest only 2 or 3ft above the water. They are moved by being swivelled horizontally, or raised vertically. Operation is usually manual, although some have gearing to ease the movement. There are one or two mechanised versions; these have clear instructions at control points. Before operating any bridge make sure that approaching road traffic is aware of your intention to open the bridge. Use protective barriers if there are any and remember to close the bridge again after you.

Some lift bridges are *very unstable*, and could close while your boat is passing underneath, with disastrous consequences. For this reason it is prudent to have your strongest (or heaviest) crew member hold it open until the boat is clear. Many swing bridges are very heavy to operate, and require two strong people to move them. Keep your crew off the sides of the boat when you are negotiating narrow bridges – they could easily be knocked off and seriously injured.

Tunnels

Many people consider a canal incomplete without one or two tunnels, and certainly they are an exciting feature of any trip. Nearly all are easy to navigate, although there are a few basic rules:

Make sure your boat has a good headlight in working order and *always* use it.

If it is a narrow tunnel (ie 7ft) make sure there is no boat coming the other way *before* you enter. Craft of 7ft beam can pass in some wide tunnels – slow right down when you meet to lessen the almost inevitable bump.

In most tunnels the roof drips constantly, especially under ventilation shafts. Put on a raincoat and some form of hat before going in.

A notice on the tunnel portal will give its length, in yards, and will say whether unpowered craft are permitted to use it.

Where there are restrictions on time of entry, and one-way systems, these must be adhered to. To meet head on half way through a long narrow tunnel would create great difficulties.

Care of the engine

Canal boats are generally powered by either diesel, petrol or two-stroke engines. If you have a hire craft, the boatyard will give you instructions for your daily maintenance, which will no doubt include some or all of the following:

Every day before starting off, you should:

Check the oil level in the engine.
Check the fuel level in the tank.

If your engine is water-cooled, check that the filter near the intake is clean and weedfree. Otherwise the engine will over-heat, which could cause serious damage.

Check the level of distilled water in the battery, and ensure that it is charging correctly.

Lubricate any parts of the engine, gearbox or steering that need daily attention.

Check that the propeller is free of weeds, wire, plastic bags and any other rubbish. The propeller and the water filter should be checked whenever there is any suspicion of obstruction or overheating – which may mean several times a day.

Pump the bilges every day.

If there is a stern gland greaser, screw it down a turn at the end of each day's cruising.

When navigating in shallow water, keep in mind the exposed position of the propeller. If you hit any underwater obstruction put the engine into neutral immediately. When running over any large floating object put the engine into neutral and wait for the object to appear astern before re-engaging the drive.

Fuel

Petrol engines and petrol/oil outboards are catered for by some boatyards and all road-side fuel stations. Running out is inconvenient; remember you may have to walk several miles carrying a heavy can.

Diesel-powered craft, and narrowboats in particular, can usually cruise for over two weeks before needing to be refilled. Those using diesel-powered hire craft rarely need to be concerned about fuel. Those with their own boats, however, should bear in mind that boatyards are few and far between on some parts of the network, and should a diesel-powered boat run out of fuel, the system will need to be bled before the engine can run again. Most boatyards sell marine diesel (indicated ⒟ in the text), which is cheaper than the road fuel.

Electrically powered boats

These are becoming increasingly popular on the inland waterways, in view of their quietness and lack of environmental pollution. Indicated ⒠ under the **BOATYARD** heading are those establishments known to offer recharging facilities – polite enquiry by electric boat users will certainly reveal more. If you are lucky enough to be using this form of power, please note the following:

All boats using this information are assumed to have a battery charger on board and 50 metres of cable fitted with standard 13 amp terminals.

It is essential for the safety of the boater, the owner of the supply and the general public that a proper residual current circuit breaker (RCD) be carried by the boat and fitted between the boat's cable and the supply unless the supply is already so protected. The RCD must be tested for correct operation before battery charging starts.

Water

Fresh water taps occur irregularly along the canals, usually at boatyards, BW depots, or by lock cottages. These are marked on the maps in the guide. Ensure that there is a long water hose on the boat (BW taps have a ½-inch slip-on hose connection). Fill up every day.

Lavatories

Some canal boats are fitted with chemical lavatories which have to be emptied from time to time. Never empty them over the side or tip them into the bushes. Use the sewage disposal points marked on the map ⒮ (for which you will need a BW key) or those located at boatyards. Many boats now have pump-out toilets, which must be emptied with a special machine – usually at boatyards and indicated in the text. This symbol at the canalside indicates just such a 'pump-out station' (although not all boatyards with the facility display it). Expect to have to pay.

Some BW depots and boatyards have lavatories for the use of boat crews; again, you may need your BW key.

Litter

Some canals are in a poor state today because they have long been misused as unofficial dumps for rubbish, especially in towns. Out of sight is only out of mind until some object is tangled round your propeller. So keep all rubbish until you can dispose of it at a refuse disposal point, indicated ⒭ on the map, or at a boatyard equipped to deal with it.

By-laws

Although no-one needs a 'driving licence' to navigate a boat, boat users should remember that they have certain responsibilities to others on the waterways and should abide by the Waterways Code (available from BW offices). Prospective navigators are advised to obtain a copy of the by-laws relevant to the waterways on which they are to travel.

Stoppages

Although BW and other navigation authorities plan their maintenance for the winter months, it often becomes necessary to carry out repairs during the cruising season. Many of the structures on the canal system are beginning to show their age (especially the tunnels) and repairs are a lengthy and costly affair, sometimes resulting in stoppages lasting many years. A long dry spell can lower water levels and restrict lock operation, and a canal embankment can, of course, breach at any time.

To avoid disappointment it is wise to check that your planned route is clear before you set off, and that there are no time restrictions on locks that may upset your schedule. Those using hire craft may be able to get this information from their boatyard, although some are surprisingly lax. It is best to check for yourself by ringing the BW Area Offices (listed at the end of this book) or the relevant navigation authority. News of any last minute stoppages is available on 'Canalphone', as a recorded message. Ring 071-723 8486 for the North and Midlands, or 071-723 8487 for the South and Midlands. Check before you go.

PLANNING A CRUISE

It is wise when planning a cruise to establish a means of calculating the time it takes to travel any given length of canal. This ensures that you can reliably work out whether you will reach a shop or pub before closing time. And of course for those who have hired their boat, it is vital to return to the starting point on time.

The time taken to navigate any canal depends, of course, on the average cruising speed of your boat and the amount of time it takes to negotiate the locks along the way. Remember that there is in any case an overall legal speed limit of 4 mph on all canals. In practice, 3 mph is a realistic canal cruising speed for most boats and 2 mph is the maximum which can be achieved on shallow canals, such as the Peak Forest.

To the uninitiated, 3 mph may sound an unbearably slow rate of progress through the countryside; but a few hours of gentle cruising on a fine day is usually enough to convert most people to this pace. For only by proceeding at walking pace can you appreciate the peace and beauty of the countryside, watch the bird life, and see the scurry of voles, rats and other creatures as they suddenly notice the slowly approaching boat.

The length of time taken to work through a lock depends on several things: whether the lock is full or empty, wide or narrow, deep or shallow. It depends on the number and size of the paddles that control the sluices, on the presence or otherwise of other boats near the lock, and of course on the number and competence of the boat crew. Most people take between 10–20 minutes on average to work through a typical lock – or, to put it another way, they may take as long to get through a lock as they would have taken to travel another mile at 3 mph. Herein lies a basis for a simple method of estimating time required to travel along a given length of canal: take the number of miles to be travelled and add the number of locks to be negotiated on the way. This gives the number of 'lock-miles'. Divide this by three, and the result is the approximate length of time it will take, in hours. Thus if you intend to travel 30 miles, and there are 12 locks along the way, the calculation is as follows: 30 + 12 divided by 3 (mph) = 14 hours. So this particular journey will take you around 14 hours, assuming your average cruising speed to be 3 mph and assuming you take about 20 minutes to get through each lock (if they are all narrow locks in good condition then you may well better this time). The length of

your journey and the number of locks can easily be calculated using the 'milestones' that appear on every map in this series of guides. To refine the system, simply tailor it more closely to the actual cruising speed of your boat and the efficiency of your lock-operating technique.

An excellent fortnight's trip, for example, would be the circuit formed by the River Soar and Trent & Mersey, Coventry, Oxford and Grand Union (Leicester section) canals. This is 152 miles and 100 locks long (about 84 hours' cruising time), and takes you through some of the very best parts of Leicestershire. You will see the Foxton staircase locks, Braunston Tunnel, the delightful canal village of Shardlow and have time to explore the lock-free Ashby Canal (22 miles long – 2 days there and back) or the meandering course of the unspoilt Market Harborough arm, 5 miles long.

For just a one-week holiday, a good round trip with plenty of contrasts could encompass the Staffs & Worcs north of Aldersley Junction, the Trent & Mersey from Great Haywood to Fradley, the Coventry to Fazeley Junction, the Birmingham & Fazeley to Farmers Bridge and returning along the Birmingham Canal Main Line. With 75 miles and 79 narrow locks, this should take no more than 50 hours' cruising time. You will enjoy the old locks and bridges of the Staffs & Worcs as it follows the pretty valleys of the rivers Penk and Sow, culminating at Tixall Wide. After a visit to Shugborough Hall you continue past the eccentric footbridge at Drayton Manor before starting the long climb to Farmers Bridge. There's a choice of routes on the Birmingham Canal Main Line to complete the circuit.

These are just two examples of the many circular cruising routes available – a glance at the planning map on pages 4 and 5 will reveal many more. Of course, there is also much to be said for a straight out and back cruise – it will all look different when you are coming the other way, and you can arrange to re-visit that favourite pub again. The whole secret is to *allow plenty of time*, for shopping, for exploring and for gentle cruising. Many a holiday has been spoilt by becoming a race against time. The most comprehensive source of information for planning a waterways cruise is Nicholson's *The Ordnance Survey Inland Waterways Map of Great Britain*.

See also 'Stoppages' in the **General Cruising Information** *section.*

The Three Locks, Soulbury, on the Grand Union. *David Perrott.*

RIVER AVON

Maximum dimensions

Length: 70′
Beam: 13′ 6″
Draught: 3′ 6″
Headroom: 8′ (at normal levels)

Lower Avon Navigation Trust
(Tewkesbury to Evesham Lock)
Mill Wharf, Mill Lane, Wyre Piddle,
Pershore, Worcs. Tel: (0386) 552517.
Upper Avon Navigation Trust
(Evesham Lock to Alveston Sluice)
Avon House, Harvington, Evesham, Worcs.
Tel: (0386) 870526.

Mileage

Avon Lock, TEWKESBURY to:
Pershore Lock: 14½
Evesham Lock: 25¾
Bidford Bridge: 32¾
Tramway Bridge, STRATFORD: 42¼
Alveston Sluice: 45½

Locks: 17

Rising at Welford on the Leicestershire and Northamptonshire boundary and joining the River Severn at Tewkesbury, the River Avon was first made navigable to Stratford by William Sandys of Fladbury during the period 1636–39, with plans to extend eventually to Warwick.

In 1717 the ownership of the river was split into the Upper and Lower Avon, the dividing line being Workman Bridge, Evesham; following several changes in ownership, the Upper river was purchased by the Great Western Railway in 1863. By refusing tolls they avoided the obligation to maintain the river and as a result within 10 years it was in a ruinous state. In 1875 all traffic on the Upper Avon had ceased.

Although deteriorating gradually, the Lower Avon did remain navigable to Pershore until it was bought, for £1500, by C. D. Barwell in 1950. At this time the Lower Avon Navigation Trust was formed and restoration began, with navigation being restored to the Bridge Inn, Offenham by June 1964. In July of that year, the southern section of the Stratford-on-Avon Canal from Kingswood Junction to Stratford was also re-opened, making the restoration of the Upper Avon the next logical step. But with no right of access to the river, a non-effective navigation authority, all but two of the weirs collapsed and the locks in complete ruin, it seemed an all but impossible task.

Under the leadership of David Hutchings MBE the Upper Avon Navigation Trust was formed in 1965, and in 1969 work began. An appeal was made to raise £300,000 and eventually over a third of this sum was given by one anonymous donor. Despite enormous difficulties, the Upper river was officially opened by HM Queen Elizabeth the Queen Mother on 1 June 1974. A truly magnificent achievement for private initiative and volunteer labour.

Cruising on the Avon

This is a river navigation, and as such can present problems to those more accustomed to the still waters of the canals. Just 36 hours of summer rain can put sufficient 'fresh' water into the river to make passage hazardous – the 'pull' upstream of the weirs increases, cross-currents below the weirs become fierce and the water 'piles up' as it rushes through narrow bridge-holes. *When this happens, all boats must moor up out of the main stream and wait for the level to return to normal.* If you are in any doubt, phone your hire company or seek expert advice.

All the locks on the river are wide locks, and those on the Upper Avon demonstrate considerable ingenuity in the recycling of gates and paddle gear from other canals and rivers – as a consequence some of the locks are difficult to operate, and require a good deal of physical strength. Do not believe that a cruise on this part of the river will necessarily be restful.

Finally, those accustomed to the cosy informality and 'go as you please' atmosphere of the narrow canals will not be impressed by the plethora of 'Private' and 'No Mooring' notices. Many landowners and local authorities have yet to come to terms with the river, especially the Upper river, as a navigation, and boaters can begin to feel distinctly unloved. Many villages are sited back from the river, away from the floods, and the scenery is generally that of quiet water-meadows with prolific bird life. However, those who plan their journey carefully and avoid the crowded summer peak period will find much to enjoy.

The Lower and Upper Navigation Trusts are charities operated almost entirely by volunteers. Boat crews can help them to keep down their costs by observing their rules and requests. They should also be acquainted with the relevant by-laws, and ensure that their craft is equipped with such items as an anchor made off to a chain and warp, a bow fender and so on. Remember also:

Power gives way to sail.
Maximum speed – Lower Avon 6 mph, Upper Avon 4 mph.
Watch out for anglers, and slow down.
Keep off private land.
Keep well away from weirs and slow down when approaching locks or blind corners.
Moor only at recognised sites, moor economically, and be prepared to 'breast up' (moor side by side) where this does not obstruct traffic.
Moorings are *very* limited and marked **M** on the maps.

Tewkesbury

The River Avon joins the Severn some 600 yards below Mythe Bridge. A short distance upstream past Healing's Mill, which still receives grain by barge from time to time, is the attractive Avon Lock, mechanised and with a resident lock keeper (0684 292129). Continuing upstream through the narrow navigation arch of King John's Bridge (built circa 1200 and widened in 1964) the river widens, passing a marina on its way into open farmland and water-meadows, a reach extensively used by the local sailing clubs. There is no longer a ferry at Twyning, and moorings are limited to those of the attractive Fleet Inn, where a lane beside the pub leads to the small village.

Navigational note
Craft entering the Avon from the Severn should be wary of a shallow spit projecting south west from the north bank at the junction of the two rivers. When approaching from upstream on the Severn, do not cut the corner but steer close to the south side of the junction. Craft leaving the Avon and wishing to proceed upstream on the Severn should not turn north until Mythe Bridge can be seen in its entirety.
Craft navigating between the Severn and the Avon Lock should steer a course close to the Town Quay and Healing's Mill, thus avoiding the mudbank opposite. Note that Avon Lock is operated by a resident lock keeper – do not disturb him outside of his usual operating times, which are posted by the lock. Keep your craft clear of the lock wall nearest the lock house, as there are three metal bosses that stand proud of the wall, and may catch your boat when ascending or descending.
When entering the Avon from the lock, and when passing through the centre arch of King John's Bridge, visibility is restricted, and great care should be taken.

Tewkesbury
Glos. EC Thur. MD Wed, Sat. All services. An historic town at the junction of the rivers Avon and Severn, with many attractive and ancient buildings to see, chief among these being, of course, the Abbey. One of the more unusual aspects of Tewkesbury is the great number of tiny alleys leading off the main street that is the backbone of the town. These alleys yield tempting views of discreet cottages, gardens, back walls and private yards. One of these – Baptist Chapel Court – leads to the old chapel, built around 1655. This tiny, simple building and its little burial ground reflect well the modest aspirations of the minority Baptist movement. There are many other buildings of great interest throughout Tewkesbury, chiefly of the timbered variety, with overhanging gables. Some have curious names like 'House of the Nodding Gables' and 'Ancient Drudge'. There is also a liberal scattering of historic pubs, notably the Hop Pole Inn (associated with Dickens' *Pickwick Papers*) and the Bell hotel, an Elizabethan building which was Abel Fletcher's home in the book *John Halifax, Gentleman*.
Tewkesbury Abbey This superb building is cathedral-like in proportions and is generally reckoned to be one of the finest Norman churches in the country. It is contemporary with Gloucester Cathedral, and has the same type of vast cylindrical arches the length of the nave. This massive scale is repeated throughout the building: the beautifully decorated central tower, 46ft square and over 130ft high, is the largest Norman tower in existence. The recessed arch that frames the mighty west window is over 60ft high. The Abbey's interior is no less splendid than the exterior, and contains interesting monuments, notably the Despencer and Beauchamp tombs. The Abbey, which was completed in about 1120, was part of a Benedictine monastery until this was threatened with dissolution by King Henry VIII in 1539. The townspeople bought the Abbey – for £453 – to save it from demolition, and it became the town's parish church.

The Abbey Cottages Church Street. The most unusual buildings in Tewkesbury must surely be the row of medieval shops near the Abbey. These 25 cottages were rescued from dereliction and threatened demolition when it was realised that they are unique in this country. As built, in about 1450, they were made of wattle and daub in a heavy timber framework. The ground floor consisted of trodden earth, the windows had no glass, and there was no chimney in the roof – the smoke from the fireplace escaped through a hole under the eaves. The shutters covering the big window facing the street folded down to form a shop counter. One of the houses has been restored to this original state and may be visited: the others have been modified to provide pleasantly discreet modern houses. This restoration won a Civic Trust award.
Tewkesbury Museum Barton Street. A small museum in a delightfully irregular timber-framed house. Displays of local history, costumes and furniture. Also a large model of the Battle of Tewkesbury. *Open weekdays during the summer.*
Barton Fair takes place in Tewkesbury every *10 October* except when that date falls on a Sunday. One of the oldest fairs in the country, it used to be held at the monastery gate.
Tewkesbury Steam Fair and Organ Festival every *July*, in the meadows by the Avon. This is becoming an important event on steam enthusiasts' calendars, attracting increasing numbers of cherished traction engines, steam rollers and miscellaneous fairground machinery every year.
Battle of Tewkesbury 4 May 1471 The last decisive battle in the Wars of the Roses, fought to the south of the town, where the Lancastrians, under Queen Margaret's commanders Somerset, Wenlock and Devonshire were defeated by Edward IV's Yorkists under Edward, Gloucester and Hastings.
Tourist Information Centre (0684) 295027.

BOATYARDS

Ⓑ **The Tewkesbury Yacht Marina** Bredon Road, Tewkesbury. (0684 293737).
R S W P D E Pump-out, gas, overnight mooring, long-term mooring, winter storage, slipway, gantry, chandlery, books and maps, boat sales, engine repairs, toilets, showers.
Ⓑ **Telestar Pleasure Cruisers** 185 Queen's Road, Tewkesbury. (0684 294088). On the Mill Avon by Abbey Mill. Cruiser hire, day boat hire. BW & Avon licences.

MOORING

See also Boatyards and Pubs. Overnight moorings on Mill Avon by Healing's Mill (fee).

PUBS

There are many pubs and hotels in Tewkesbury, including:
🍺 **Bell** Church Street. 12thC inn opposite the Abbey.
🍺 **Berkeley Arms** Church Street. 17thC.
🍺 **Olde Black Bear** High Street. Said to be the oldest inn in Gloucestershire.
🍺 **Riverside** On the Mill Avon. Mooring by arrangement.
🍺✕ **Royal Hop Pole Hotel** On the Mill Avon near Abbey Mill. (0684 293236). Lunch and dinner, mooring by arrangement.
🍺 **Fleet Inn** Twyning. Riverside with gardens, overnight mooring by arrangement.
🍺 **Village Inn** Twyning.

River Avon at Tewkesbury. *Derek Pratt.*

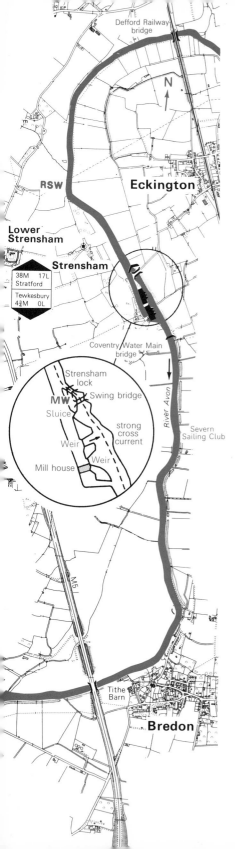

Bredon

A ½ mile above Twyning, the M5 motorway crosses the flood plain on a high embankment, beyond which is the village of Bredon, where the fine 14thC Tithe Barn can be seen from the river. There are many moored cruisers and tidy gardens making the river-front attractive and interesting. The river is wide to Strensham Lock, and is used extensively by the unusually named Severn Sailing Club. Below the lock a pipe bridge carries the Coventry Water Main over the navigation, and beyond this the weir spills into the river, creating a very strong cross current when there is 'fresh' water in the river. The lock is operated by a resident lock keeper (0386 750355) who lives in the old Mill House. A limited number of moorings are available by arrangement with him, and you may buy an ice cream here. The river now starts to meander around Eckington village, passing under a railway bridge carrying the main Exeter to Newcastle upon Tyne line before reaching Eckington Bridge, a many-arched and irregular 16thC structure, still in good condition.

Bredon
Hereford & Worcs. PO, stores. A substantial and attractive village with many fine timbered buildings. Close to the river is a 14thC Tithe Barn (National Trust), 124ft long and once one of the best preserved in the country, where grain – paid as taxes to the church – was once stored. Severely damaged by fire, it has now been rebuilt. The Church of St Giles has a vaulted Norman porch, and dates from c1180 – it was mentioned by John Masefield in 'All the land from Ludlow Town to Bredon Church's spire'. Bredon Hill, which dominates the river for several miles, rises to 961ft some 3 miles to the north east – it is said that eight or more counties can be seen from its summit on a fine day. On the southern slope is an 18thC castellated folly, Bell's Castle, and on the top is a 2ndC BC hill fort containing Parson's Folly, a prominent tower built late 18thC. The hill was celebrated in A. E. Housman's *A Shropshire Lad.*
Strensham
Hereford & Worcs. Birthplace of Samuel Butler (1612–1680), verse satirist and secretary to Judge Thomas Jeffrey, who lived in the 16thC house by the well-sited Church of St Phillip and St James, which has a painted gallery and two fine brasses of the Russells, once the Lords of the Manor. The key is kept at the farm.
Eckington
Hereford & Worcs. PO, stores. A dormitory village of little interest except for Holy Trinity Church, which dates from the 12thC, and three pubs. Walk from Strensham Lock or Eckington Bridge.

MOORING

Overnight mooring by prior arrangement with the lock keeper at Strensham (0386 750355).

PUBS

- Royal Oak Bredon.
- Fox & Hounds Bredon. (0684 72377). Thatched 15thC inn with garden and restaurant.
- Crown Inn Eckington.
- Bell Inn Eckington.
- Anchor Inn Cotheridge Lane, Eckington. Wadworths real ale.

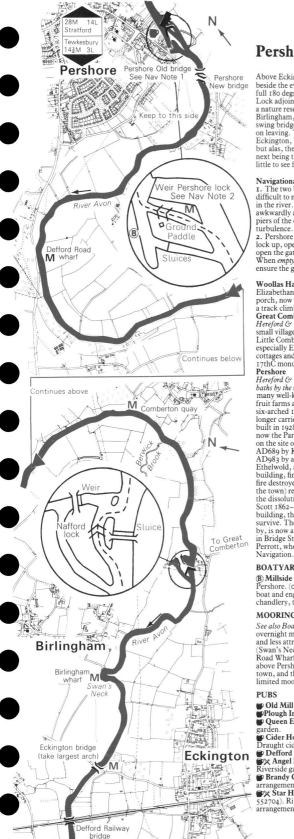

Pershore

Above Eckington Bridge, the river meanders beside the ever-present Bredon Hill, turning a full 180 degrees at the Swan's Neck. Nafford Lock adjoins the wilderness of Nafford Island, a nature reserve, and a path leads from here to Birlingham, 1 mile to the north west. The swing bridge across the lock must be left closed on leaving. The path over the sluice leads to Eckington, Woollas Hall and Great Comberton but alas, there are no moorings by the lock, the next being those at Comberton Quay. There is little to see from the river until Pershore.

Navigational notes
1. The two bridges at Pershore are extremely difficult to navigate when there is 'fresh' water in the river. The navigable arches align awkwardly and the current rushes around the piers of the old bridge, causing considerable turbulence.
2. Pershore Lock. When *filling* the chamber to lock up, open the ground paddle first, then open the gate paddle when it is submerged. When *emptying* the chamber to lock down, ensure the ground paddle is closed.

Woollas Hall A mile south of Nafford Lock. Elizabethan manor house with a three-storey porch, now divided into flats. Beyond the hall, a track climbs to the summit of Bredon Hill.
Great Comberton
Hereford & Worcs. Stores. One of the timeless small villages which surround Bredon Hill – Little Comberton, Bricklehampton and especially Elmley Castle, with its half-timbered cottages and Church of St Mary containing fine 17thC monuments are worth visiting.
Pershore
Hereford & Worcs. All services, and swimming baths by the river. A busy market town with many well-kept Georgian buildings, set among fruit farms and market gardens. The fine six-arched 14thC bridge over the Avon no longer carries traffic – a three-arched structure built in 1928 now takes the load. The Abbey, now the Parish Church of Holy Cross, was built on the site of a wooden building erected in AD689 by King Oswald. This was replaced in AD983 by a new building commissioned by Ethelwold, and again by a later Norman building, finally consecrated in 1239. In 1288 a fire destroyed part of the Abbey (and much of the town) resulting in much rebuilding before the dissolution in 1539. Restoration was by Scott 1862–65. Of the original Norman building, the nave, crossing and transepts survive. The Church of St Andrew, very close by, is now a community centre. Perrott House in Bridge Street was built in 1760 by George Perrott, when he purchased the Lower Avon Navigation.

BOATYARDS
Ⓑ **Millside Boatyard** 37a Bridge Street, Pershore. (0386 552849). W P D Slipway, gas, boat and engine repairs, long-term mooring, chandlery, toilets, winter storage.

MOORING
See also Boatyards and Pubs. There are good overnight moorings above Eckington Bridge, and less attractive ones at Birlingham Wharf (Swan's Neck), Comberton Quay and Defford Road Wharf. The Recreation Ground moorings above Pershore Lock are convenient for the town, and thus very popular. There is also limited mooring below the lock.

PUBS
🍺 **Old Mill** Elmley Castle. Food, garden.
🍺 **Plough Inn** Elmley Castle. Own brew cider.
🍺 **Queen Elizabeth** Elmley Castle. Food, garden.
🍺 **Cider House** Woodmancote, Defford. Draught cider, no beer.
🍺 **Defford Arms** Garden.
🍺✕ **Angel Inn** Pershore. (0386 552046). Riverside garden. Mooring by arrangement.
🍺 **Brandy Cask** Pershore. Mooring by arrangement.
🍺✕ **Star Hotel** Bridge Street, Pershore. (0386 552704). Riverside garden. Mooring by arrangement.

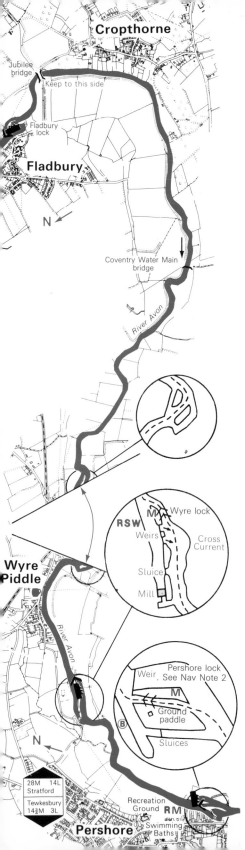

Wyre Piddle

The reach between the locks at Pershore and Wyre Piddle is the shortest on the navigation, being just 1 mile. Wyre Mill, called by the traveller Charles Showell 'the ugliest, of which the Avon is ashamed' is now used by the Lower Avon Navigation Trust as a sailing and social club. The lock is diamond-shaped, the last of its kind on the river. Approaching from downstream the weir creates a strong cross current, especially after prolonged rain. Wyre Piddle (the Piddle Brook runs behind the village) spreads around the outside of a wide bend, with gardens down to the river, and the Anchor Inn providing a useful mooring for patrons. The villages then skirt the flood plain of the Avon, and there is little to see except for the wild life – those interested in herons will be particularly pleased. Beyond the Coventry Water Main Bridge the village of Cropthorne sits on higher ground to the south east. Below Jubilee Bridge are the remains of the last flash lock on the river, dismantled in 1961.

Wyre Piddle
Hereford & Worcs. PO, stores. A main road village with no public mooring. The church has a Norman chancel arch and font, and an early English bellcote.
Cropthorne
Hereford & Worcs. Store. An attractive village of thatch and timbers on the 'Spring blossom route'. Much local fruit and vegetable produce is sold from small roadside stalls in this area.

MOORING

See also Pubs and Restaurants. There are overnight moorings in the weir stream at Wyre Lock.

PUBS AND RESTAURANTS

🍺✕ **Anchor Inn** Wyre Piddle. (0386 552799). Bar meals and restaurant, large riverside garden and the only mooring for the village, by arrangement only.
🍺 **New Inn** Cropthorne.

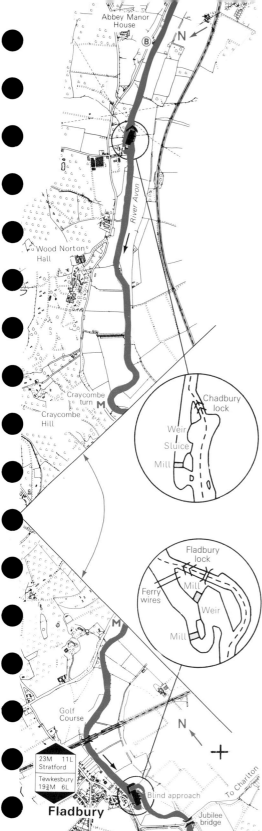

Fladbury

The approach channel below Fladbury Lock is
extremely narrow and steep sided, with
restricted vision. The lock walls narrow
towards the base and this should be borne in
mind when two craft lock down together. The
beautiful Fladbury Mill overlooks the weir – it
was in use as recently as 1930, and ferry wires,
difficult to see from upstream, stretch across
the weir stream. On the north side, beyond the
railway bridge carrying the main London to
Worcester line, is Evesham golf course. Above
Craycombe Turn are extensive woodlands,
while to the south lie the inevitable
water-meadows, with few buildings or roads
near the river. There is another handsome mill
at Chadbury Lock, which was restored in
1952–53, the first major project carried out by
the Lower Avon Navigation Trust, who were
helped by the Royal Engineers. Beyond the
lock, the river passes the Abbey Manor House,
and a boatyard, before passing through
Evesham in a wide loop.

Fladbury
Hereford & Worcs. PO, stores. A picturesque
village of half-timbered houses and cottages
around a square, once the home of William
Sandys, who began making the Avon navigable
in 1636. The Church of St John Baptist has a
fine 14thC rib-vaulted porch and contains some
fine brasses to John Throckmorton and his
wife. About 1 mile to the north east is
Craycombe House, built c1791 by George
Byfield for George Perrott (*see Pershore page 19*)
and later restored by the author Francis Brett
Young, who lived here from 1932 until he went
to South Africa after the Second World War.
Wood Norton Above the north bank below
Chadbury Lock. Once the seat of the Duc
d'Aumale and later the Duc d'Orleans,
pretender to the throne of France, it now
houses an engineering school run by the BBC,
who have built some incongruous modern
buildings to accompany the mansion.
Abbey Manor House 1 mile above Chadbury
Lock, on the north bank, c1840. An obelisk in
the grounds overlooks the site of the Battle of
Evesham, 4 August 1265, when Simon de
Montfort and his rebel barons were defeated by
the Royalists under Prince Edward, resulting in
some 4000 deaths. Another memorial, the
Leicester Tower, built c1840, is visible in the
woodland.

BOATYARDS
Ⓑ **Sankey Marine** Worcester Road, below the
Abbey Manor House, Evesham. (0386 442338).
ⓌⓅⒹ Gas, overnight mooring, long-term
mooring, winter storage, slipway, chandlery,
books and maps, boat sales, engine sales and
repairs, toilets, showers. Restaurant and bar at
weekends.

MOORING
See also Boatyards. Overnight mooring available
at Craycombe Turn.

PUBS
🍺 **Anchor** Fladbury.
🍺 **Chequers** Fladbury.
🍺 **Gardener's Arms** The Green, Charlton.

Evesham

Care should be taken approaching Hampton
Ferry, where a wire stretches across the river –
this will be lowered when the ferry man hears
three long blasts of your hooter. Above the
ferry to the west is Clarke's Hill, where the
monks of Evesham once grew vines. Beyond
the A435 road bridge the Abbey Public Park
opens out to the north, with riverside gardens
giving way to the borough moorings and
Workman Gardens to the east, below the
handsome Workman Bridge, built in 1856.
After passing through the centre arch of the
bridge, you will see the lock to the left past the
old mill stream. This marks the boundary
between the Lower and Upper Navigation.
There is a resident lock keeper here (0386
6511), who lives in an unusual triangular house
built in 1972 to span the chamber of an earlier
lock. He has a small shop and sells Lower Avon
Navigation Trust licences. Lock open
*09.00–18.00 Easter–May, 09.00–20.00
May–Sep, 09.00–18.00 Oct–Nov, 10.00–16.00
Nov–Easter.* Craft should keep well away from
the weir above the lock, passing close to the
boatyard on the opposite bank. The river is
then once again in open country, entering the
Vale of Evesham, a major fruit and vegetable
growing area. The wooden bridge at Offenham
no longer exists but a cable ferry operates by
the Bridge Inn, and a lookout should be kept
for this obstruction.

Evesham
Hereford & Worcs. EC Wed. All services. A
town which owes the major part of its
prosperity to the fruit and vegetable growing in
the Vale of Evesham – in the spring a mass of
blossom, and in the autumn rich in local
produce. All that remains of the once-
important Benedictine abbey, founded in
AD714 by Bishop Egwin and dissolved by
Henry VIII in 1539, is the fine timbered
gatehouse, a detached bell tower (1533) and a
few ruins. Close by there are elegant Georgian
buildings and half-timbered houses, Booth Hall
(late 15thC) being a fine example. Close to the
bell tower are two notable churches – St
Lawrence (16thC) and All Saints (12thC). There
is an annual regatta on *Spring Bank
Holiday*, rowing boats can be hired and an
ex-Thames steamer, the *Gaiety*, does trips.
Tourist Information Centre The Almonry
Museum, Abbey Gate, Evesham. (0386
446944).
Offenham
Hereford & Worcs. EC Sat. PO, tel, stores.
Twelve centuries ago this was the headquarters
of Offa, King of Mercia; today it is one of the
few English villages to possess a maypole. The
village has grown considerably, and of the
original Church of St Mary and St Milburga
only the tower remains.

BOATYARDS

Ⓑ **Evesham Marina** Kings Road, Evesham.
(0386 47813). Ⓡ Ⓦ Ⓓ Pump-out, gas,
narrowboat hire, overnight mooring, long-term
mooring, winter storage, slipway, crane, books
and maps, boat building, boat sales, engine
repairs.

MOORING

See also Boatyards and Pubs. There is a single
overnight mooring, for a fee, below the A435
bridge on the south side, and extensive borough
moorings by Workman Gardens, for a fee.
Weir Meadow Caravan Park, between
Workman Bridge and the lock, has overnight
moorings with full facilities for craft up to 24ft
long. By arrangement, ring (0386) 442417.

PUBS AND RESTAURANTS

🍺 **Cider Mill** Hampton.
Plenty of pubs in Evesham.
🍺✗ **Northwich Arms Hotel** Waterside,
Evesham. (0386 40322). Grill and Buttery.
Moorings opposite, by arrangement.
🍺✗ **Evesham Hotel** Coopers Lane, Evesham.
(0386 765566).
Garden, moorings opposite.
🍺 **Swan** Port Street, Evesham. Snacks,
garden.
🍺✗ **Bridge Inn** by the ferry, Offenham. (0386
446565). Mooring by arrangement.

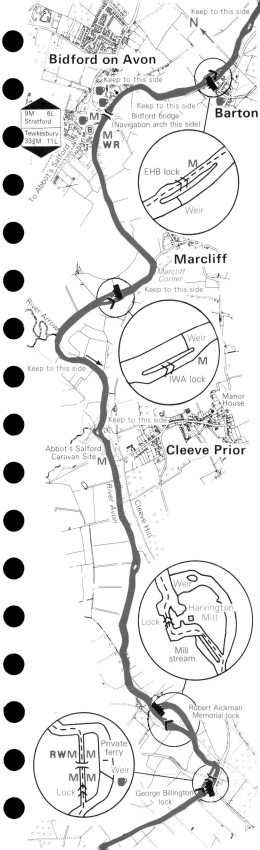

Bidford-on-Avon

George Billington Lock is the first of the new
Upper Avon locks, built in the winter of 1969.
The unusual flood-proof lock keeper's hut, the
'Offenham light' is a more recent addition. The
new lock cut joins the river at right angles, and
care should be exercised when rejoining the
main course. Robert Aickman Memorial Lock
soon follows, overlooked by Harvington Mill,
disused since the turn of the century. The
original Robert Aickman Lock was the first to
be built on the restored Upper Avon, but was
re-sited in 1982 due to erosion and silting of the
original course. The steep ridge of Cleeve Hill
closes from the south to a virtual cliff at the
water's edge below Cleeve Prior. The river
now heads north away from Marcliff Hill,
entering Warwickshire and approaching
Bidford-on-Avon.

Navigational note
The navigation arch of Bidford Bridge is to the
far right when heading upstream.

Middle Littleton
Hereford & Worcs. Walk east from the Fish &
Anchor Inn to see the tithe barn thought to
have been built by John de Ombersley, Abbot
of Evesham from 1367 to 1377. Nearby is the
17thC manor house and St Nicholas's Church.
Harvington
Hereford & Worcs. PO, stores. A typical
timbered Worcestershire village.
Cleeve Prior
Hereford & Worcs. PO, stores. The manor
house (private) is a handsome 16thC building,
standing in well-kept grounds with a fine
display of yews. The Church of St Andrew still
retains some Norman and Early English work.
Bidford-on-Avon
Warwicks. PO, stores, bank. The irregularly-
arched bridge was built in 1482 by the monks of
Alcester, near the site of a Roman ford which
was finally removed in 1970. A new bypass has
brought peace to this pleasant village of old
timbered buildings, amongst which is the
solidly built former Falcon Inn – Shakespeare is
said to have taken part in a drinking contest
here. The Church of St Lawrence, by the river,
dates from 1276, but was restored in 1835.

BOATYARDS

Ⓑ **Bidford Boats** Riverside House, 4 The
Pleck, Bidford-on-Avon. (0789 773205). Ⓢ Ⓦ
Narrowboat hire, overnight mooring,
long-term mooring, winter storage, slipway,
boat sales, minor engine repairs.

MOORING

See also Pubs. There are free overnight
moorings at George Billington Lock. Overnight
moorings are available, for a fee, at Abbots
Salford Caravan Site (unfortunately on the
opposite bank to Cleeve Prior), and at IWA
Lock (free). The public moorings at Bidford
are very good, but limited in number. There is
a single mooring available at Bell Court on the
town side, and more at Bidford Boats, both for
a fee. Upstream, at Barton, there are free
overnight moorings in the lock cut.

PUBS AND RESTAURANTS

🛥 **Fish & Anchor Inn** George Billington Lock.
Food, gardens. A private ferry crosses the weir
stream from the moorings.
🛥✗ **Golden Cross** Harvington. (0789 772420).
Smart, comfortable modernised pub offering
good value bar food *lunchtime and evening*, and
Whitbread, Durham and Flowers real ales.
Restaurant open *D and Sun L.* Garden, B&B.
🛥✗ **White Lion Hotel** Bidford-on-Avon.
(0789 773309). Comfortable hotel next to the
bridge, serving Everards real ale and *lunchtime*
bar meals. Restaurant meals *L & D.* Garden.
🛥 **Anglo Saxon** High Street, Bidford-on-
Avon. Flowers real ale in a basic village local
near the bridge.
🛥 **Pleasure Boat** High Street, Bidford-on-
Avon. Riverside pub offering Ansells real ale
and food *lunchtime and evening.*
🛥✗ **Cottage of Content** Barton. (0789
772279). A picturesque 15thC pub with a
riverside garden. Flowers real ale, bar snacks
and restaurant meals (*L & D*). Live music on
Sat evening.

Map labels:

N ←

RS WM
Luddington lock

Weir

Luddington

Keep to this side

Weston-on-Avon

3M 2L
Stratford

Tewkesbury
39¾M 15L

Binton bridges
(Navigation channel this side)

M

Welford-on-Avon

Keep to this side

Keep to this side

Weir

M

WA Cadbury lock

River Avon

Hillborough Manor

Weir

M

Pilgrim lock

Navigation channel this side

Welford-on-Avon

Proceeding upstream, craft should follow the
narrower right-hand channel below Bidford
Grange – there were once two mills and a lock
here, but now nothing remains. Beyond is the
new Pilgrim Lock, built in the winter of 1970.
The river flows through attractive meadowland,
and pleasant orchards announce the village of
Welford-on-Avon and W. A. Cadbury Lock,
completed in July 1971. The river meanders
round the village, passing a once-fine Victorian
house inappropriately adorned with a modern
chimney, before the multi-arched Binton
Bridges, the former mill and the Four Alls pub
are reached. Weston-on-Avon lies to the south
on a very attractive stretch of deep water with
many trees lining the banks. Luddington Lock
was built in spring 1971 – there are overnight
moorings here, but a sign informs 'sorry, no
shop, no pub'.

Hillborough Manor Private. It is thought that
Charles II fled here in September 1651 after
being defeated by Cromwell at Worcester.
Welford-on-Avon
Warwicks. PO, tel, stores. The Church of St
Peter is of Norman and early English origin,
situated in the older and more attractive part of
what is now a desirable commuter village.
There is a maypole, and several pubs. Weston-
on-Avon lies a short distance to the east and can
be reached by what is, in part, a riverside walk;
visit the Church of All Saints, itself by the
river.
Luddington
Warwicks. It is thought that Shakespeare may
have been married here, in a church now
replaced by a more recent building.

MOORING
See also Pubs. There are free overnight
moorings at Pilgrim Lock, W. A. Cadbury
Lock, Welford (no access to village), and below
Binton Bridges (access to Welford) for a fee.
There are also free overnight moorings above
Luddington Lock.

PUBS
Four Alls Binton Bridges. (0789 756228).
A smart riverside pub and restaurant with a
garden, serving Flowers real ale. Its name, in
the stained glass of the public bar, is explained
thus:

> A King I rule over all
> A parson I pray for all
> A soldier I fight for all
> A farmer I pay for all

Overnight mooring by arrangement. (A
similarly named pub, the 'Five-Alls', is situated
in Chepstow.) W
Bell Welford-on-Avon. A comfortable
beamed pub in the village centre. Flowers real
ale, bar snacks and children's room.
Shakespeare Inn Chapel Street, Welford-
on-Avon. A popular local housing the village
library. Flowers real ale, bar snacks, and a large
garden with a children's play area and barbecue
facilities.

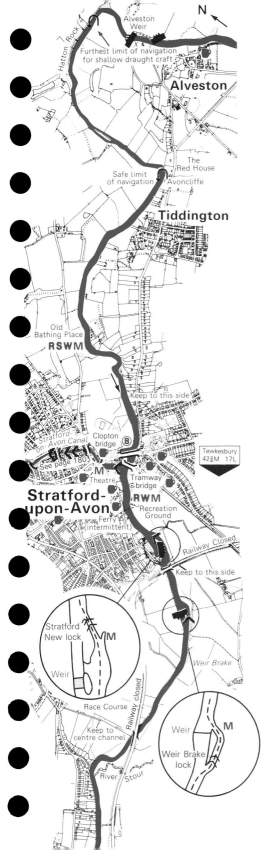

Stratford-upon-Avon

The River Stour joins the Avon from the south.
The disused railway bridge here once carried
the line from Stratford to Gloucester. Weir
Brake Lock, which takes its name from the
wooded bank to the south east of the river, was
completed early in 1973; the weir was
completed a few months later. Immediately
beyond the disused Stratford to London
railway bridge is the very deep Stratford New
Lock, reinforced by a series of rectangular steel
girder frames to overcome the high ground
pressures and overlooked by a monument to
celebrate the reopening of the navigation. On
sunny summer weekends the lockside and
bridge is thick with gongoozlers enjoying the
river, the boats and the extensive parkland. A
block of flats now stands on the site of the old
Lucy's Mill. Above the lock the river throngs
with cruisers, trip boats and rowing boats,
overlooked by the red-brick hulk of the Royal
Shakespeare Theatre. The Stratford-on-Avon
canal basin can be seen beyond the entrance
lock below Tramway Bridge, which was built in
1823 to carry the Stratford and Moreton Horse
Tramway from the Bancroft basin to
Moreton-in-Marsh. It is now a footbridge. The
14-arched road bridge was built c1480 by Sir
Hugh Clopton, once Lord Mayor of London,
and was widened in 1814. The surroundings
become quieter as the river gently winds to its
effective head of navigation by The Red House,
although shallow-draught craft may proceed to
just below Alveston Weir.

Stratford-upon-Avon
Warwicks. EC Thur. MD Wed, Fri. All services.
Tourism has been established a very long time
in Stratford, ever since 1789 when the first big
celebrations in William Shakespeare's honour
were organised by the actor David Garrick.
They are now held annually on St George's
Day, *23 April*, which is believed to be
Shakespeare's birthday. An annual Mop Fair
on the *12 October* reminds the visitor that
Stratford was already well-established as a
market town long before Shakespeare's time.
(The first grant for a weekly market was given
by King John in 1196.) Today, Stratford is well
used to the constant flow of charabancs and
tourists, ancient charm vying with the expected
commercialism that usually mars popular
places like this. There are wide streets of
endless low, timbered buildings that house
dignified hotels and antique shops: plenty of
these are also private houses. On the river,
hired punts and rowing boats jostle each other
while people picnic on the open parkland on the
banks. The Royal Shakespeare Theatre,
opened in 1932, is a splendid institution on an
enviable site beside the Avon, but the aesthetic
appeal of its massive 'industrial' style is limited.
It was designed by Elizabeth Scott to replace an
earlier theatre, destroyed by fire in 1926.
Shakespeare Birthplace Trust Stratford-
upon-Avon. (0789 204016). This Trust was
founded in 1847 to look after the five buildings
most closely associated with Shakespeare; four
of these are in Stratford (listed below) and the
other is Mary Arden's cottage at Wilmcote (see
page 178). *There is a standard opening time for
these properties, any variation on this standard is
shown in the individual entries. Open Apr–Oct
09.00–18.00 Mon–Sat, 10.00–18.00 Sun (to
17.00 Oct); Nov–Mar 09.00–16.30 Mon–Sat,
closed Sun.* Admission charge.
Shakespeare's Birthplace Henley Street. An
early 16thC half-timbered building containing
books, manuscripts and exhibits associated
with Shakespeare and rooms furnished in
period style. Next door is the Shakespeare
Centre. *Open Sun afternoons Nov–Mar.*
Hall's Croft Old Town. A Tudor house
complete with period furniture – the home of
Shakespeare's daughter Susanna and her
husband Dr John Hall.
New Place Chapel Street. The foundations of
Shakespeare's last home set in a replica of an
Elizabethan garden.
Anne Hathaway's Cottage Shottery, 1 mile
west of Stratford. Dating from the 15thC this
fine thatched farmhouse was once the home of
Anne Hathaway before she married William
Shakespeare. It has a mature, typically English
garden, and long queues of visitors in the

summer. The cottage was badly damaged by fire in 1969, but has since been completely restored. *Also open Sun afternoons Nov–Mar.*

Holy Trinity Church Attractively situated among trees overlooking the recently restored lock on the River Avon. It is mainly of the 15thC but the spire was rebuilt in 1763. Interesting misericords depict amusing scenes, and fine monuments include one of William Shakespeare who is buried in the chancel. His tomb bears a curse against anyone who dares to disturb it.

Shakespeare Royal Theatre (Box office 0789 292271). The home of the Royal Shakespeare Company, who produce Shakespeare plays to a very high standard *from Apr to Dec every year.*

Clopton Bridge A very fine stone bridge over the Avon, originally built by Sir Hugh Clopton c1480–90 – he later became Lord Mayor of London. The bridge is close to the canal basin. The brick bridge nearby was built in 1823 to carry a horse-drawn tramway connecting Stratford with Shipston-on-Stour. It is now a footbridge.

Information Centre Judith Shakespeare House, 1 High Street, Stratford-on-Avon. (0789 293127). Judith Shakespeare was William's younger daughter. In 1616 she married and moved into this former tavern, once called The Cage. It is a characteristic Elizabethan building of three storeys. Judith Shakespeare is buried in the graveyard of Holy Trinity church in Stratford.

BOATYARDS

There are trip boats and many rowing and motor boats for hire in Stratford-upon-Avon.

Ⓑ **Stratford Marina**, by Clopton Bridge, Stratford-upon-Avon. (0789 69669).

Ⓡ Ⓢ Ⓦ Ⓓ Ⓔ Pump-out, gas, narrowboat hire, day boats, overnight mooring, long-term mooring, winter storage, slipway, groceries, chandlery, books and maps, boat building, boat

sales, engine sales and repairs, toilets.

MOORING

See also Boatyards. There are free overnight moorings at Weir Brake Lock, below Stratford New Lock, by the Recreation Ground opposite the theatre, in the Stratford Canal Basin, and at the Old Bathing Place ¾ mile above Clopton Bridge.

BOAT TRIPS

Lady of Camelot Restaurant and conference boat for charter. Up to 60 people. Ring (0789) 297459 for details.

PUBS

There are numerous restaurants, snack bars, fast-food joints and pubs in Stratford-upon-Avon, many named for the benefit of visitors, such as 'The Pen & Parchment'. Also:

🍺✕ **Black Swan** (known as the Dirty Duck) Waterside. (0789 297312). Theatrical pub with a small terrace. Flowers real ale, bar snacks and restaurant meals *(L & D).*

🍺✕ **Arden Hotel** Waterside, opposite the theatre. (0789 294949). Courage and Ind Coope (Burton) real ale, restaurant meals *(L & D),* garden.

🍺 **Old Tramway Inn** Shipston Road. Davenports real ale in a one-roomed pub with a large garden. Meals at *lunchtime.*

🍺✕ **Shakespeare Hotel** Chapel Street. (0789 294771). Fine old beamed hotel in the town centre. Visit the Froth & Elbow bar for Hook Norton, Davenports, Courage and Bass real ale. Meals *(L & D),* children's room, garden.

🍺 **Slug & Lettuce** Guild Street. (0789 299700). Good choice of expensive real ale, and French cuisine *(L & D).* Garden.

🍺 **Ferry Inn** Alveston. Food, garden.

🍺 **Alveston Manor Hotel** Banbury Road. Food.

Peace and quiet on the Upper Avon. *David Perrott.*

GRAND UNION

Maximum dimensions

Regent's Canal
Length: 72'
Beam: 14' 6"
Headroom: 8' 6"
*Brentford and Paddington to Camp Hill
top lock (Birmingham)*
Length: 72'
Beam: 12' 6"
Headroom: 7' 6"
*Camp Hill top lock to Aston and
Salford Junctions*
Length: 72'
Beam: 7'
Headroom: 7'
Aylesbury and Northampton Arms
Length: 70'
Beam: 7'
Headroom: 7' 6"

Manager

London Area: 071-286 6101
Cowley to Cosgrove: (044 282) 5938
Cosgrove to Foxton, Norton Junction to
Braunston: (0604) 858233
Napton to Camp Hill: (0926) 492192
Camp Hill to Salford Junction: 021-456 2723

Mileage

Thames, BRENTFORD to:
Bull's Bridge: 6
Black Jack's Lock: 16
Watford: 22
Berkhamsted: 33
Bulbourne: 38
Leighton Buzzard: 47½
Fenny Stratford: 55
Cosgrove: 67
Stoke Bruerne: 73
Gayton Junction: 77
Buckby Locks: 89
Braunston: 93½
Napton Junction: 98½
Leamington Spa: 109
Shrewley: 115½
Salford Junction: 137

Locks: 166

Paddington Arm: 13½
No locks

The Grand Union Canal is unique among English canals in being composed of at least eight separate canals. This system links London with Birmingham, Leicester and Nottingham. Up to the 1920s all these canals were owned and operated by quite separate companies: there were five between London and Birmingham alone.

The original – and still the most important – part of the system was the Grand Junction Canal. This was constructed at the turn of the 18thC to provide a short cut between Braunston on the Oxford canal and Brentford, west of London on the Thames. Previously, all London-bound traffic from the Midlands had to follow the winding, narrow Fazeley, Coventry and Oxford canals down to Oxford, there to tranship into lighters to make the 100-mile trip down river to Brentford and London. The new Grand Junction Canal cut this distance by fully 60 miles, and with its 14ft wide locks and numerous branches to important towns rapidly became busy and profitable. The building of wide locks to take 70-ton barges was a brave attempt to persuade neighbouring canal companies – the Oxford, Coventry and the distant Trent and Mersey – to widen their navigations and establish a 70-ton barge standard throughout the waterways of the Midlands. Unfortunately the other companies were deterred by the cost of widening, and to this day those same canals – and many others – can only pass boats 7ft wide. The history of the English canals might have turned out very differently had the Grand Junction's attempt succeeded.

The mere proposal of the building of the Grand Junction Canal was enough to generate and justify plans for other canals linked to it. Before the Grand Junction itself was completed, independent canals were built linking it

in a direct line to Warwick and Birmingham, and a little later a connection was established from the Grand Junction to Market Harborough and Leicester, and thence via the canalised River Soar to the Trent. Unfortunately, part of this line was eventually built with narrow locks, thereby sealing the fate of the Grand Junction's wide canals scheme.

Meanwhile in London in 1812 the Regent's Canal Company was formed to cut a new canal from the Grand Junction's very busy Paddington Arm, round London to Limehouse, where a big dock was planned at the junction with the Thames. This was duly opened in 1820, narrowly escaping conversion at an early stage into a railway, and proved extremely successful. Ten years later a 1½-mile-long canal – the Hertford Union – was built: this remains a useful short cut from Regent's Canal to the River Lee.

These were the canals that made up the spine of southern England's transport system until the advent of the railways. When in this century the Regent's Canal Company acquired the Grand Junction and others, the whole system was integrated as the Grand Union Canal company in 1929. The new company, aided by the Government, in 1932 launched a massive programme of modernisation: widening the 52 locks from Braunston to Birmingham, piling and dredging, etc. But when the grant was all spent, the task was unfinished and broad beam boats never became common on the Grand Union Canal.

The great attempt to break loose from narrowboat carrying had failed, and after this the Grand Union could only begin to decline. Now narrowboat carrying on the canal is finished, although there is still some barge trade at the London end.

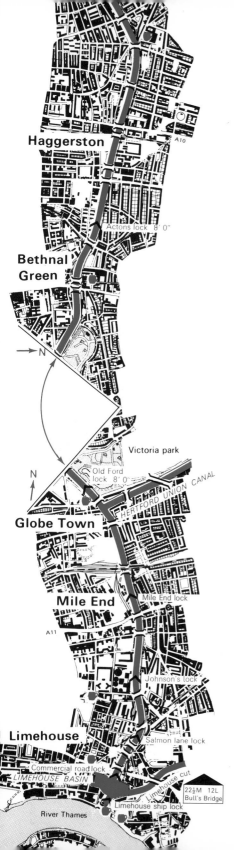

Limehouse

In the Greater London area little specific
information is given that does not relate directly
to the canal; but canalside pubs and restaurants
are included together with some nearby places
to eat and drink. Places and features of interest
can be found in Nicholson's *London Guide*.
The Regent's Canal begins at Limehouse Basin
(previously known as Regent's Canal Dock) in
London's dockland and climbs up round
central London towards Paddington. It is
mostly flanked by the backs of houses and
factories which usually enclose the canal in a
remarkably private and peaceful world of its
own. The towpath can now be followed from
Salmon Lane Lock along the whole length of
the Regent's Canal to West London, and there
are frequent access points. New visitor
moorings have been provided at Camden,
Islington (above City Road), Cowley Lock and
Brentford, near the High Street. The IWA
organise guided towpath walks *Feb–Nov*,
details available on 071-586 2510/2556 (modest
charge). The entrance to the Regent's Canal
and to the River Lee Navigation from the
Thames is through the rebuilt ship lock and
across Limehouse Basin. The Hertford Union
Canal (often known as Duckett's), is a useful
short cut between the Regent's Canal and the
Lee Navigation, running along the attractive
Victoria Park (see page 109).

Navigational note 1
The Limehouse Basin Ship Lock can
accommodate craft 98ft 6in × 26ft 3in with a
9ft draught. It is *open 08.00–17.00* except for a
time around low water. Ring 071-790 3444 or
071-895 9930 to check.
Navigational note 2
As with most inner city canals, there is a risk of
vandalism. Locks on the Regent's Canal are
padlocked – a BW key is required.

Victoria Park Hackney. Beside the canal.
Almost 300 acres of parkland which comes as a
relief after so much townscape. Designed by
James Pennthorne, a protégé of Nash, and laid
out between 1842 and 1845.
Limehouse Basin Limehouse. The terminus of
the Regent's Canal and of the Lee Navigation
where they meet the Thames, the basin used to
be crowded with ships, barges and narrowboats. Once known as the Regent's Canal
Dock, this basin is now the subject of a plan to
develop a marina incorporating housing,
offices, pubs and shops, at a cost of £70 million
over a period of six years.

PUBS AND RESTAURANTS

🍺 **Rosemary Branch** 2 Shepperton Road N1.
Free house with a good selection of real ale.
🍺 **Rose & Crown** 13 Mare Street E8. Handy
pub serving Youngs real ale and food *lunchtime
and evening*.
🍺 **Royal Cricketers** 211 Old Ford Road E2.
Canalside pub with Whitbread and guest real
ales. Meals *lunchtime and evening (not Sun)*.
Garden.
🍺 **Fish & Ring** 141a White Horse Road, off
Ben Johnson Road. Warm and friendly East
End pub dispensing Davenports and Fullers
real ales.
🍺 **Queens Head** 8 Flamborough Street E14.
Youngs real ale and *lunchtime* food.
🍺✕ **Grapes** 76 Narrow Street, Limehouse.
(071-987 4396). Fine riverside pub serving
Taylor Walker and Ind Coope (Burton) real ale.
Snacks and seafood restaurant.
🍺 **Barley Mow** 44 Narrow Street. (071-265
4983). In the original Dockmaster's office, at
the entrance to Limehouse Dock. Taylor
Walker, Tetley's and Youngs real ale in a
splendid new waterside pub. Bar food.

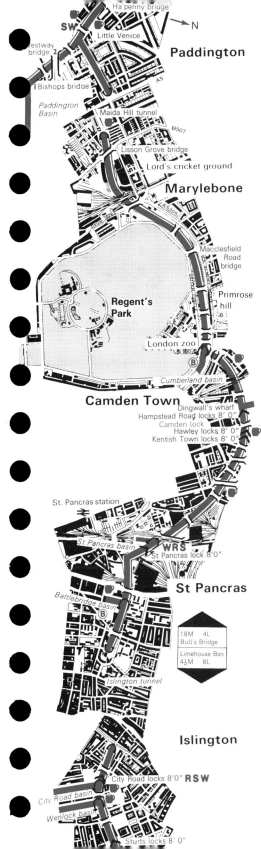

Regent's Park

The canal continues to climb, passing two large
basins before plunging under Islington through
a ½ mile tunnel (forbidden to unpowered
craft), then round the back of St Pancras and
Camden Town passing Battlebridge Basin,
where a Canal Museum Trust has ambitious
improvement plans. Here, at Camden High
Road, the top locks are reached and the long
level begins (27 miles of canal without a lock).
Near the top lock is a castellated youth club;
boatmen should beware of the many young
persons rowing and canoeing nearby, and at
Hampstead Road Locks BW have a Canal
Information Centre in the lock cottage. Soon
the industrial surroundings melt away and,
rounding a right-angled bend, the canal
suddenly enters London Zoo and Regent's Park
– which look splendid from the water. (Do *not*
attempt to tie up and walk into the Zoo without
paying.) The canal continues through a long
wooded cutting, then leaves Regent's Park and
skirts the former Marylebone goods yard – now
a housing estate – beyond which is the short
Maida Hill Tunnel. One emerges into one of
the finest stretches of urban canal in the
country. Tree-lined and flanked by fine
Regency houses, the Regent's Canal ends
gloriously at Little Venice. To the left, under
the new Westway bridge, is the vast
Paddington Basin. To the right is the
Paddington Arm of the former Grand Junction
Canal. The two stop places seen at Little Venice
were used for 'gauging' boats for tolls. There
are good moorings by the Canal Office.

Islington Tunnel 960yds long, the tunnel was
opened in 1816. In 1826 a towing boat was
introduced, which pulled itself to and fro along
a chain laid on the canal bed. This system
remained until the 1930s.
Camden Lock A fascinating craft and canal
centre, with a busy weekend market, around
what was once a timber wharf. The castellated
lock cottage now houses BW Regent's Canal
Information Centre (071-482 0523).
Regent's Park Originally part of Henry VIII's
great hunting forest in the 16thC. In 1811 the
Prince Regent planned to connect the park and
a new palace via the newly built Regent Street
to Carlton House. Although never completed,
the design by John Nash is very impressive: the
park is surrounded by handsome Regency
terraces and gateways. The sanctuary and the
north east corner of the park are excellent
points for watching migrant birds, including
willow warblers, chiffchaff, white throats,
redstarts and redpolls.
London Zoo Regent's Park (071-722 3333).
The canal passes along the edge of the Zoo, one
of the largest in the world. Lord Snowdon's
aviary can be seen from the canal. The Zoo was
originally laid out by Decimus Burton in 1827,
but since then many famous architects have
designed special animal houses. *Closed
Christmas.*
Cumberland Basin A small canal basin by the
Zoo which used to form the junction of the
Regent's Canal Main Line with an arm that led
off round the park to Cumberland Market near
Euston Station. Much of the arm was filled in
during the last war and the Zoo car park now
sits on top of it. Cumberland Basin is now full
of moored boats; there is also a floating
restaurant.
Lord's Cricket Ground St John's Wood Road
NW8. (071-289 1611). The ground of the
MCC, which is also the governing body for
British cricket. Test matches *Jun–Aug.*
Canalside walk From Lisson Grove (at the east
end of Maida Hill Tunnel) to Regent's Park
Zoo, 2 miles of the canal towpath make one of
London's most attractive waterside walks. The
bridges are nicely painted and wooden seats
installed at intervals. With the ducks, the
overhanging trees, the passing boats and
London Zoo on either side, this is a remarkable
stretch of urban canal.
Little Venice A very canal-conscious area
centred on the junction of the Regent's and
Grand Junction canals, famous for its elegant
houses, colourful boats and excellent canalside
views. The island and pool were named after
Robert Browning. The area is sometimes
referred to as Paddington Stop.

BOATYARDS

BW St Pancras Basin Camley Street, NW1. Apply to St Pancras Yacht Club (071-278 2805). R S W Toilet. Clubhouse open to the public *Sat afternoon & evening. Sun lunchtime & Wed evening.*
B **Turner Marinas** 57 Fitzroy Road, NW1. (071-722 9806). In Cumberland Basin. R W Overnight mooring by arrangement, chandlery, books and maps. Moorings in Cumberland Basin, at Lisson Grove and Blomfield Road, Little Venice, where there is pump-out and gas.
London Narrow Boat Assn New Wharf Road, N1. (071-837 9256). W S Temporary moorings by prior arrangement only. Laundry, baths.

BOAT TRIPS

London Waterbus Co. Camden Lock (071-482 2550). A *30 minute* trip from Little Venice through Regent's Park to the Zoo and then continuing on to Camden Lock. *Hourly service both ways in summer, reduced service on winter weekends.*
Jason's Trip Opposite Blomfield Road moorings. (071-286 3428). *1¹/₂ hour* trip in a narrowboat through Regent's Park and the Zoo to Hampstead Road Locks. Commentary on return trip, advisable to book. Also *Lace Plate* restaurant boat available for private hire. Seats 12.
Canal Cruises 250 Camden High Street, NW1. (071-485 6210/4433). *Nb Jenny Wren* makes a *1¹/₂ hour* trip through Regent's Park, the Zoo and Maida Hill Tunnel to Little Venice and back. Advisable to book. Also *My Fair Lady* cruising restaurant makes an *evening dinner cruise Tue to Sat, and lunchtime cruise on Sun.* Must book.

PUBS AND RESTAURANTS

🍺 **Bridge House** Little Venice, next to the BW Canal Office. Charrington and Bass real ale, and bar *lunches.*
🍺 **Warwick Castle** Warwick Place W9. At Little Venice, decorated with old canal prints. Charrington and Bass real ale, and bar *lunches.*
🍺 **Crockers** 24 Aberdeen Place NW8. Close to Maida Hill Tunnel. A monument to Victorian extravagance, this pub was built as part of a hotel, when it was thought the Marylebone railway terminus would be situated here. Sampson and Wards Sheffield real ale.
🍺 **Engineer** 65 Gloucester Avenue NW11. Commemorates Brunel. Charrington and Bass real ale.
🍺 **Lock Tavern** 35 Chalk Farm Road NW1. By Hampstead Road Lock, this is a popular pub. Charrington and Bass real ale.
🍺 **Waterside Inn** 82 York Way N1. Hoskins and other guest real ales in a reconstructed 17thC building on Battlebridge Basin. Hot food and *Sunday lunches.* Expensive.
🍺 **Island Queen** 87 Noel Road N1. Near City Road Locks, this is a busy pub noted for its selection of topical 'puppets' hanging above the bar. *Lunchtime* food, Bass and Charrington real ale.
🍺 **Narrowboat** 119 St Peters Street N1. Canalside pub with a strong canals theme. Food, Bass and Charrington real ale.
✕🍴 **Gallery Boat** Prince Albert Road NW1. (071-485 8137). Converted floating barge at Cumberland Basin. Chinese (Peking-style) restaurant. *Open LD Mon–Sun.*
✕🍴 **The Gourmet Pizza Company** Camden Lock, Chalk Farm Road NW1. (071-485 0360). Well-appointed overlooking the canal, various craft workshops and brightly painted barges. Seating outside in summer. 12 varieties of pizza including Chinese Duck and English breakfast. *Open LD Mon–Sun.*

Grand Union crossing the busy North Circular Road. *Derek Pratt.*

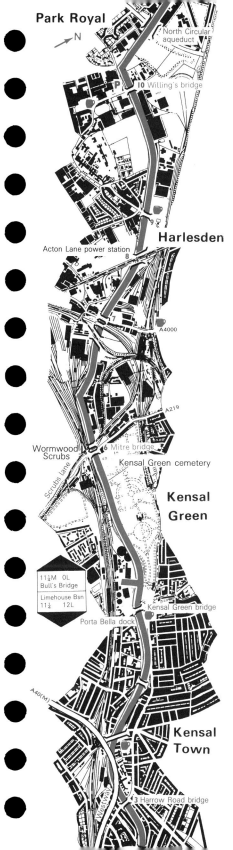

Kensal Green

The Paddington Arm continues west. Starting at a big housing estate, one passes the backs of houses in Harrow Road and then goes along the side of the well-known Kensal Green Cemetery. The huge concrete structure sweeping out over the canal is the elevated Westway Road. The main Western region tracks run just below the canal to the south, and beyond them can be seen the towers of Wormwood Scrubs. Acton Lane Power Station straddles the canal; not far away are the twin townships of Harlesden and Willesden. The canal crosses the North Circular Road on a large aqueduct: a strange contrast between the tranquillity of the canal and the roaring traffic below.

Kensal Green Cemetery North bank of canal. Opened in 1833, the huge cemetery flanks the canal. The monuments are now all romantically overgrown, and scattered among trees. Water gates set in the wall indicate that at one time coffins for burial could be brought up by barge. Leigh Hunt, Thackeray, Macready, Trollope, Wilkie Collins and Blondin are among the famous buried here.
Porta Bella Dock Ladbroke Grove W10. A marina/market/office complex.
St Mary Magdalene Alongside the canal west of Little Venice. Built by Street, 1868–78, the church with its tall Gothic spire is now curiously isolated among modern flats. The richly decorated crypt is very striking.
Wormwood Scrubs South of canal. Expanse of open space with the famous prison on the southern boundary.

PUBS

Plumes Abbey Road. Recently modernised pub serving Whitbread real ale.
Grand Junction Arms Acton Lane NW10. A large pub with good moorings and a children's playground. Youngs real ale and *lunchtime* food *(not Sun)*.
Fisherman's Arms 50 Old Oak Lane NW10. Friendly local serving Ind Coope (Burton) and Benskins real ale.
Narrowboat 346 Ladbroke Grove W10. Attractively refurbished canalside pub with moorings. It has a warm atmosphere and is always busy. Waterside seating. Fullers real ale and *lunchtime food (Mon–Fri)*.
Carlton Ale House 45 Woodfield Road W9. Canalside pub serving real ale.
Paddington Stop Formosa Street. Canalside pub serving *lunches*.

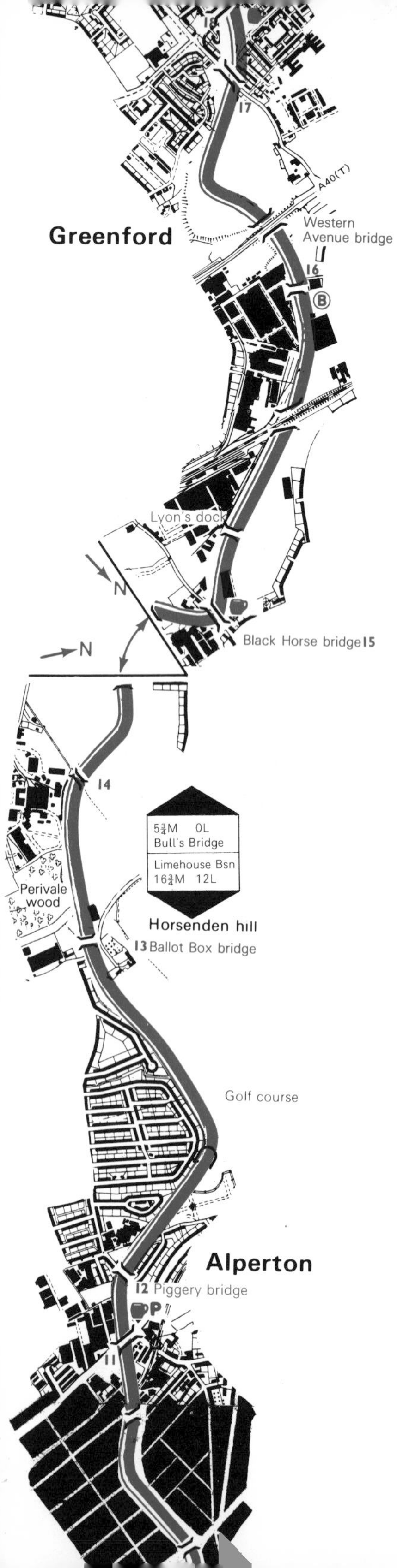

Greenford

The Paddington Arm continues west through Alperton and Greenford. The surroundings are mostly flat, but Horsenden Hill and Perivale Wood provide a long stretch of beautiful hilly parkland; an old timber yard completes the rural scene and Sudbury Park Golf Course adjoins the canal. Soon afterwards the canal turns south into suburban Middlesex.

BOATYARDS
Ⓑ **Highline Yachting** Rowdell Road, Northolt. (081-845 9924). Ⓡ Ⓢ Ⓦ Ⓓ Gas, overnight mooring, long-term mooring, winter storage, toilet. *Closed Mon, Wed, Fri & Sun.*

PUBS
🍺 **Civil Engineer** by bridge 18.
🍺✗ **Black Horse** Black Horse Bridge, Greenford. (081-578 9384). Canalside. Food, garden.
🍺 **Pleasure Boat** Ealing Road, Alperton. Canalside. Food.
🍺 **Ballot Box Inn** Horsenden Lane North. North of bridge 13.

Greenford

Western Avenue bridge

A40(T)

17

16

Ⓑ

Lyon's dock

N

N

Black Horse bridge **15**

14

5¾M 0L
Bull's Bridge
Limehouse Bsn
16¾M 12L

Perivale wood

Horsenden hill

13 Ballot Box bridge

Golf course

Alperton

12 Piggery bridge

P

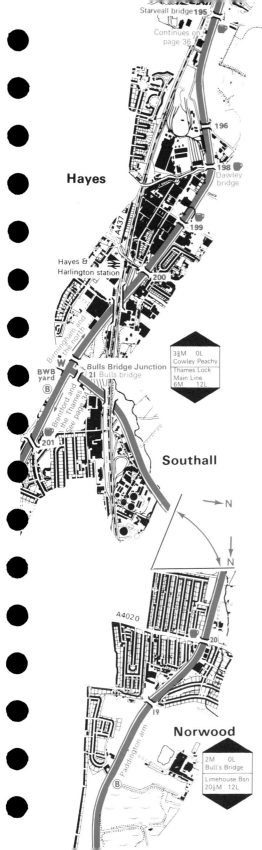

Continues on page 36

Bull's Bridge

Continuing south through the industrial estate, the Paddington Arm soon reaches the junction with the main line of the Grand Union at Bull's Bridge. Here is a large BW yard – formerly the Grand Union Canal Carrying Fleet depot – where maintenance boats are built and repaired. Turning left leads east towards Brentford and the Thames past a colourful collection of houseboats: turning right goes to Birmingham and the north. Along here the canal now enters the indivisible conurbation of Hayes, Harlington, West Drayton and Yiewsley: a good area for shops and pubs.

Hayes & Harlington
Middx. EC Wed. All services. Much-industrialised area, home of such famous brand names as Nestlés, Heinz and EMI.
Southall
Middx. EC Wed. All services. Extensive modern shopping centre.
Martinware Pottery Collection Southall Public Library, Osterley Park Road. (081-574 3412). Representative collection of Martinware, including birds, face mugs and grotesqueries. Of exceptional interest to admirers of 'art nouveau'. *Closed Sun & Mon.*

BOATYARDS

BW Bull's Bridge Depot Bull's Bridge, Hayes Road, Southall. (081-573 2368). ⒹD emergency only.
T & D Murrell Bull's Bridge Junction. (01-848 4485). ⓇⓈ ⓌⒺ Overnight mooring, long-term mooring, boat sales.
Yeading Marina West Quay Village, Glencoe Road, Yeading. ⓇⓈ ⓌⒹ Pump-out, gas, moorings, slipway, engineer, shop, café. A new development opened in 1991.

PUBS

🍺 **Woolpack** Canalside at bridge 198.
🍺 **Foresters Arms** West Drayton. (80yds from bridge 195). Food.
🍺✕ **Blue Anchor** Hayes. (081-573 0714). Canalside, at bridge 199. Food.
🍺 **Grand Junction Arms** Southall. (By bridge 201). Canalside. Food.
🍺 **Hambrough Tavern** Southall. Canalside, at A4020 bridge.

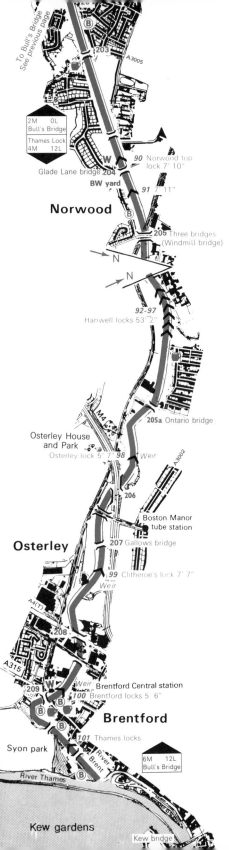

Brentford

This section follows the main line of the Grand Union east from Norwood down to the junction with the Thames at Brentford. At Norwood is a BW maintenance yard; here begins the 11-lock drop to the river, including the Hanwell flight of six locks. It is in parts an interesting and attractive stretch: Osterley and Syon parks are nearby. Brentford is still a busy canal depot and there are several canalside pubs in Norwood. The River Brent joins the canal at the bottom of Hanwell Locks; there is a rare intersection of canal, road and railway at the top of these locks and several of the bridges are of the brick arched type more commonly seen on the rural canals. Near the big M4 embankment is a very attractive cast iron 'roving' bridge, dated 1820. Towards Brentford, the towing path disappears under the roof of a large BW warehouse – an odd experience for a walker. Kew Gardens is just across the Thames. Access for walkers to the towpath is easily gained at the top and bottom (from Green Lane) of Hanwell Locks and at Brentford Locks (from Brentford High Street), but there is no towpath from Brentford Locks to the Thames.

Navigational note 1
Norwood top lock and Hanwell bottom lock are locked at *18.30 (summer)* and *16.30 (winter)* and re-open at *08.00*.
Navigational note 2
The Thames at Brentford is tidal; Teddington Locks are 5 miles upstream. Application to navigate the non-tidal Thames should be made in advance to the National Rivers Authority, 2nd Floor, King's Meadow House, Reading, Berks, RG1 8DQ. (0734 535000). Craft entering the canal from the Thames without the necessary BW licence may complete the formalities at Brentford Depot office at Brentford Locks. No licence is required on the tidal river. Brentford and Thames Locks are controlled by lock keepers and are of course subject to the tide. They operate for two hours either side of high water and the lock keeper can be informed of your imminent arrival on 081-560 1120.

Osterley House Isleworth (081-560 3918). Set in a large park – a superb remodelled mansion with elegant interior decorations by Robert Adam, 1760–80. Gobelins and Beauvais tapestries and fine carpets. Elizabethan stables in large park. *Open 11.00–17.00. Closed Mon.* Access is unfortunately on the south side of the M4, 1½ miles from the canal. But Osterley Park tube station is close to the entrance, which is just north of the A4.
Boston Manor House Boston Manor Road, Brentford, ½ mile north of bridge 208. (081-560 6597). Tudor and Jacobean house with excellent examples of period ceilings. *Open summer afternoons.* Nearest tube station: Boston Manor (¼ mile north of the house).
The National Music Museum High Street, Brentford. (081-560 8108). In the church at the foot of the tall gas holder east of the locks. Exceptional collection of automatic, old and odd musical instruments. Many of them are demonstrated during the *90-minute* guided tour. *Open Sat & Sun afternoons. Closed Nov–Feb.*
Syon House Brentford. (081-560 0881). Entrance 300yds west of Brentford Locks on A315. Seat of the Duke of Northumberland. Noted for its fine Adam interior and period furniture, also its paintings. Its historical associations go back to the 15thC. *Open summer afternoons. Closed Fri & Sat.*
Syon Park Gardening Centre Park Road, Brentford. (081-580 0134). Very wide selection of plants and gardening equipment for sale.
Syon Park Gardens Brentford. (081-560 0881). 55 acres of Capability Brown gardens. In the grounds are the Gardening Centre, Live Butterfly House and Motor Museum. Gardens *closed Xmas Day & Boxing Day.*
Kew Gardens Kew. (081-940 1171). On the south bank of the Thames, opposite Brentford. (Access from south side of the Gardens or from the Thames towpath.) One of the world's great botanic gardens, with thousands of rare outdoor and hothouse plants. Kew Palace, also worth a visit, was built in 1631 in the Dutch

style. *Open daily 10.00–sunset.* The famous glasshouses *open 11.00, closing times vary.*

BOATYARDS

BW Norwood Yard at Norwood top lock. (081-574 1220). R S W.
Ⓑ **T & D Murrell** Adelaide Dock. (081-571 5678). D Gas, winter storage, slipway, crane, boat building, boat and engine sales and repairs, toilet, showers.
Ⓑ **Brent Marine** Brent Wharf, High Street, Brentford. (081-847 1538). W E Gas, overnight mooring, long-term mooring, winter storage, crane, chandlery, boat building, boat storage, engine sales and repairs. Toilet and showers.
Ⓑ **Brentford Dock Marina** (081-568 0287). Tidal access 2¹/₂ hours each side of high water. R S W Gas, overnight mooring, long-term mooring, chandlery, provisions, books and maps, minor boat and engine repairs, boat sales, outboard engine sales, toilet.
BW Brentford Depot Brentford. A busy warehousing depot near the junction of the canal and the Thames. The depot is at Brentford Locks, just off Brentford High Street (bridge 209).

PUBS

🍺 **Old Oak Tree** Southall (at bridge 202). Canalside. Food; grocery and tel nearby.
🍺 **Lamb** Norwood (at bridge 203). Canalside. PO, shops nearby.
🍺 **Fox** Green Lane, Hanwell (at bottom of Hanwell Locks 50yds from canal). Food.
🍺 **Brewery Tap** off Brentford High Street.
🍺 **Northumberland Arms** near Brentford Locks.

Ice and snow at Denham. *Derek Pratt.*

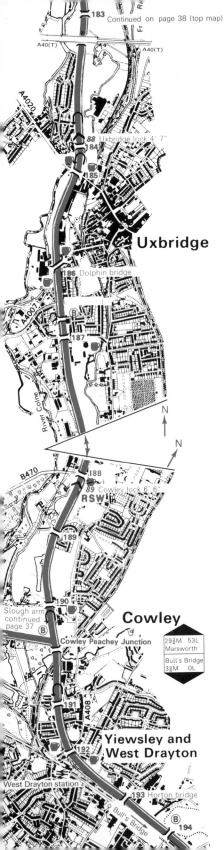

Continued on page 38 (top map)

Cowley Peachey Junction

The canal begins to bend towards the north, passing at bridge 192 a new building erected on the site of Colham Wharf. An incised stone from the wharf has been preserved and built into the new building, and can be seen from the road. At Cowley Peachey Junction, the Slough Arm branches off to the west. Cowley Lock marks the end of the 27-mile pound and the start of the climb up the Colne valley and the Chiltern Hills. Uxbridge, just to the north, signals the limit of the outer-suburban belt that surrounds London. Uxbridge Lock has an attractive setting with its lock cottage, a turnover bridge and a tall modern flour mill standing nearby in grounds that are splendidly landscaped down to the water's edge. The *Paddington Packet Boat* used to run daily from Paddington to Cowley – one of the few passenger boats plying regularly along the Grand Junction Canal. It was pulled by four horses and had precedence over all other boats, so it covered the 15-mile lock-free run in a time that was remarkable at the beginning of the 19thC. A reminder of this boat service survives in the Paddington Packet Boat Inn at Cowley.

Uxbridge
Middx. EC Wed. PO, tel, stores, garage, station, cinema. The Battle of Britain was directed by the late Air Marshal Lord Dowding from the RAF Headquarters in Uxbridge. The town is not otherwise particularly noteworthy.

BOATYARDS
ⓑ **Denham Yacht Station** By bridge 184. (0895 39811). WDE Pump-out, gas, narrowboat hire, overnight mooring, long-term mooring, winter storage, chandlery, books and maps, boat building, boat sales, engine repairs, toilets, club house.
ⓑ **Uxbridge Boat Centre** Uxbridge Wharf, Waterloo Road, Uxbridge. (0895 52019). RSWDE Gas, overnight mooring, long-term mooring, winter storage, slipway, dry dock, crane, DIY facilities, groceries, chandlery, books and maps, boat building, boat and engine repairs, engine sales, toilet. *Closed Mon (also Sun Dec & Jan).*
ⓑ **Highline Yachting** Packet Boat Lane, Cowley Peachey, Uxbridge. (0895 442290). RSWD Pump-out, gas, overnight mooring, long-term mooring, covered wet dock, chandlery, provisions, books and maps, boat building, boat and engine sales and repairs, toilet. *Closed Sun & Mon.*
ⓑ **Stockley Park** Iron Bridge Road, Stockley. New development for 1991. RSWD Pump-out.

BOAT TRIPS
Colne Valley Passenger Boat Services (0895 812130). Trips from the Swan & Bottle.
Pisces, Gemini I & II Owned and operated from Cowley Lock by the London Borough of Hillingdon. Education Department, 265 High Street, Uxbridge, Middlesex. (0895 50111).

PUBS AND RESTAURANTS
🍺 **Crown & Treaty** Oxford Road, Uxbridge, near bridge 185. A very handsome pub dating from 1576, where unsuccessful negotiations were held between King and Parliament during the Civil War. Wethered real ale and *lunchtime food.* Traditional jazz on *Sat eve.*
🍺 **Dolphin** At bridge 186. Friendly local serving Courage real ale and food. Small canalside garden with roses.
🍺 **General Elliot** St John's Road, Uxbridge. At bridge 186. A quiet canalside pub of great character, serving Ind Coope (Burton) and Benskins real ale. Garden.
✕🍺 **Shovel** Cowley Lock. (0895 33121). Restaurant, steak bar and bar, with canal decor. *L & D.*
🍺 **Paddington Packet Boat** Down the road from bridge 190. Fullers real ale and *lunchtime food* in a fine traditional pub. Garden.
🍺✕ **de Burgh Arms** Near bridge 192. (0895 442018). Smart and comfortable pub with a grill bar (*L & D*). Taylor Walker, Benskins and Ind Coope (Burton) real ale.

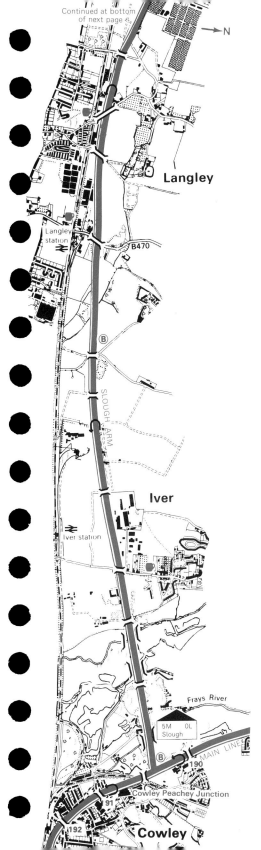

Iver

Striking off to the west from Cowley Peachey Junction, this 5-mile lock-free arm leads in an almost straight line to Slough. Built as late as 1883 (the last canal to be built in Britain except for the Manchester Ship Canal), it sweeps easily over several aqueducts and through a long cutting. West of Iver the water is amazingly clear, and there are often attractive weeds and reeds to be seen growing in the canal in summer.

Iver
Bucks. EC Wed. PO, tel, stores, garage, station.
The church has a Saxon nave with Roman bricks visible in the walls. Norman arches, medieval art and Tudor monuments. The 700-year-old tower owes its great height to the 15thC bell chamber.
Old Slade Nature Reserve 1 mile south of Iver station. Gravel pit taken over by the Berkshire, Buckinghamshire and Oxfordshire Naturalists' Trust and now a wealth of bird and animal life.
Iver Grove Shredding Green, Iver (north of the boatyard). A fine mansion built by Sir John Vanbrugh in 1724. Not open to the public.

BOATYARDS

Ⓑ **Highline Yachting** Mansion Lane, Iver. (0753 651496). Ⓡ Ⓢ Ⓦ Ⓓ Ⓔ Pump-out, gas, narrowboat hire, overnight mooring, long-term mooring, winter storage, slipway, chandlery, provisions, books and maps, boat building, boat and engine sales and repairs, toilet, showers. Also issues a brass plaque to those who navigate the arm; telephone before you start, and be prepared to pay a modest fee. *Closed Mon.*

PUBS

- **Chestnuts** Langley.
- **North Star** by Langley Station.
- **Fox & Pheasant** Thorney Lane, Iver.
- **Swan** High Street, Iver. (0753 655776). Food.
- **Red Lion** Shredding Green, Iver. Food.

Continued on page 39

27M   49L
Marsworth

Cowley Peachy
2¾M   4L

Denham

Denham deep lock 11′ 1″ **87**

182

183

A40(T)

88 Uxbridge lock 4′ 7″

184

continued page 36

Denham

The main line of the canal continues
northwards up to the Colne valley past the
village of Denham and across Harefield Moor, a
stretch of common land of considerable interest
to naturalists. Denham Lock, with a rise of
11ft 1in, is the deepest on the Grand Union.
The large mooring site of the Harefield
Cruising Club is in one of the flooded gravel
pits that are linked to the canal here.

Langley
Bucks. EC Wed. PO, tel, stores, station. A new
town development; but there are unspoiled
woodlands at Langley Park.
Denham
Bucks. EC Wed. PO, tel, stores, station. West of
the canal and of the River Colne, Denham is
split into two parts: the new part is north of the
railway. In the old village is the church set
among the cottages. It contains a Doom
painting of 1460 and some Renaissance effigies
and monuments. Denham Court, which stands
in the Colne meadows, and Denham Place, the
17thC home of the Vansittart family are both
fine examples of English architecture.

PUBS

All these are 1 mile north west of the lock:
🍺 **Falcon** Denham. Snacks.
🍺 **Green Man** Denham.
🍺 **Swan** Denham.

Cowley Peachy
5M   0L

Slough

Slough station

A412

continued
page 37

Grand Union Slough Arm

Slough

The Slough Arm continues westwards under
the A412 to its terminus, passing dull housing
and industrial estates on its way to the terminal
basin.

Slough
*Berks. EC Wed. MD Tue. PO, tel, stores,
garage, station, cinema.* This is the largest town
in Berkshire; it is a new town, undistinguished
architecturally and remembered more for its
very wide range of light industries and its
immortalization in verse by John Betjeman who
wrote (in 1981):
'Come, friendly bombs, and fall on Slough
It isn't fit for humans now
There isn't grass to graze a cow.'
St Mary's Church is, however, interesting for
its stained glass by Kempe and Alfred J.
Wolmark: the church was completed in 1876.
Herschel Park, in the town centre, is also worth
a visit.

PUBS
🍺 **Nags Head** near Slough Basin.
🍺 **Grapes** south of the basin.
🍺 **Rising Sun** further south of the basin.

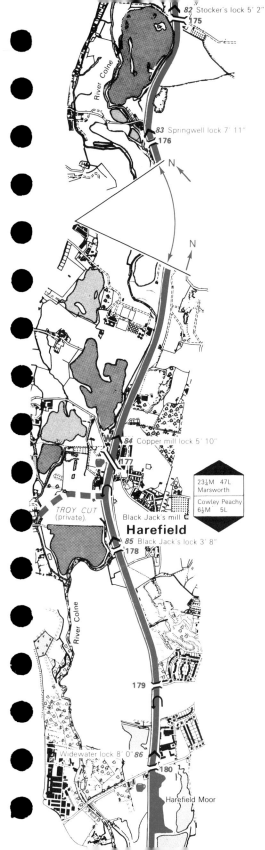

Harefield

Leaving Widewater Lock, the canal continues north up the Colne valley through a landscape of interesting contrasts which contains woods, mills, lakes and a large sewage works. Black Jack's Lock is beautifully framed by a small mill and a tiny timbered cottage used as a restaurant, while Copper Mill Lock is just upstream of an attractive group of canalside buildings. Old chalk quarries adjoin the canal as it turns north east towards Rickmansworth. Meanwhile flooded, worked-out gravel pits cover the floor of this wooded valley. Stockers is yet another lock with an interesting group of old farm buildings close by: they date from the 16thC.

Navigational note
There is a strong cross current between bridge 177 and Copper Mill Lock.

Springwell and Stocker's Locks This stretch is of interest to naturalists: there is a great variety of plants along here, and disused watercress beds are nearby. Orchids have been found growing in the adjacent chalk pits.
Copper Mill An interesting canal settlement. The big mill was once a paper mill, but after the canal was built it turned to making copper sheets for the bottoms of boats. The old cast iron bridge by the pub has now been replaced by a concrete one. South of here is the unnavigable Troy Cut, which leads to the very ancient Troy Mill.
Harefield
Middx. PO, tel, stores. Harefield represents the first escape from the stranglehold of outer London suburbia. The church set at the foot of the hill is almost a small museum: Norman masonry, box pews, 16thC screen, 19thC Gothic gallery, Georgian pulpit, and a huge collection of monuments including brasses, and work by Grinling Gibbons, Rysbrack and Bacon.

PUBS AND RESTAURANTS

Fisheries Inn Canalside at bridge 177. A very fine old pub virtually surrounded by water. Ind Coope (Burton) and Benskins real ale, extensive range of bar meals *lunchtime and evening*, and a nice garden.
Black Jack's Mill Restaurant Harefield. (089 582 3120/2205). In a startlingly pretty situation overlooking Black Jack's Lock. International cuisine *L & D* (no credit cards).
Horse & Barge By bridge 180. Recently refurbished in a tasteful and restrained manner, with a comfortable and spacious lounge and a Victorian conservatory bar. The large canalside garden has colourful flowerbeds and an adventure playground. Ruddles, Websters and Coombe real ale, good food *lunchtime and evening*.

Map labels:
82 Stocker's lock 5' 2"
175
River Colne
83 Springwell lock 7' 11"
176
N
N
84 Copper mill lock 5' 10"
177
TROY CUT (private)
Black Jack's mill
Harefield
85 Black Jack's lock 3' 8"
178
179
River Colne
Widewater lock 8' 0" 86
180
Harefield Moor

23¼M	47L
Marsworth	
Cowley Peachy	
6¼M	5L

Rickmansworth

Continuing north east, the canal reaches Batchworth Lock on the outskirts of Rickmansworth. (There are in fact two locks here, one of them leading up into the River Chess which is navigable for a short distance. Northbound navigators should take the right hand lock to stay on the Grand Union Canal.) Here the River Colne comes in from the east and the Chess from the north west, while the Gade continues to accompany the canal to the north east. Past Rickmansworth is Common Moor, north of this is Croxley and the outskirts of Watford. The canal keeps well away from this town and climbs instead into the superb Cassiobury Park, a long and lovely stretch of wooded parkland. The A404 crosses at Rickmansworth and the A412 at Croxley.

Cassiobury Park The canal flows through the park, once part of the 17thC gardens of the Earls of Essex. The avenue of limes was planted by Moses Cook in 1672 and many of the trees are as old as 300 years. The park stretches for 190 acres and is adjoined by Whippendell Woods. Watford's carnival takes place here every *Whitsun*.

Croxley Green
Herts. PO, tel, stores, garage, station. Despite being swamped by new housing, part of the old village survives around the green, where there are several attractive houses. There is a large medieval barn south of the village.

Rickmansworth
Herts. EC Wed. PO, tel, stores, station, cinema. Very little of the medieval town remains today: the Vicarage in Church Street has late medieval timberwork, but 18thC and 19thC alterations are intermingled. Despite this, there are several other buildings well worth a look: the 17thC Bury and the timber-framed but much restored Priory, both lying near the 19thC Church of St Mary, which lends a wonderful feeling of unity because it is almost entirely the work of one man – Sir Arthur Blomfield. The town centre is north of bridge 173.

Rickmansworth Aquadrome Bury & Batchworth Lakes. The canal flows along the south east edge of the lakes. Facilities for all types of water sport, especially sailing. Picnic areas for onlookers, and swimming in Bury lake. *Open daily.* An aqua show is held *every Whit Mon.*

BOATYARDS

ⓑ **Bridgewater Basin** Cassio Bridge Wharf, Croxley Green, Watford. (0442 863615). ⓦⒹⒺ Gas, overnight mooring, long-term mooring, winter storage, slipway, chandlery, books and maps, boat sales, engine sales and repairs.

BOAT TRIPS

Arcturus Cruises Cassio Wharf, Watford. Part or whole day cruises by narrowboat, for parties of up to 54 passengers. Public trips *Sun afternoon* from lock 77. (Enquiries to 043 871 4528).

PUBS

🍺 **New Halfway House** near Cassio Bridge (169).
🍺 **Batchworth Arms** Near Batchworth Lock. Attractive small pub near the church serving Courage real ale. Garden.
🍺 **White Bear** Near Batchworth Lock. Cottagey pub dispensing Courage real ale and *lunchtime food (Mon–Fri)*.

77 Iron Bridge lock 9′ 4″
167
Jacotts hill
Cassiobury park
168
Cassio Bridge 78
lock 9′ 0″
Ⓑ Watford
169
A412
Croxley Green station

18¾	41L
Marsworth	
Cowley Peachy	
11M	11L

79 Common Moor lock 9′ 5″
170
River Gade
A412
Rickmansworth
River Colne
Lot Mead lock 6′ 3″ 80
Batchworth
81 Batchworth lock 6′ 8″
RSW A404
173
174
Rickmansworth aquadrome
82 Stocker's lock 5′ 2″
175

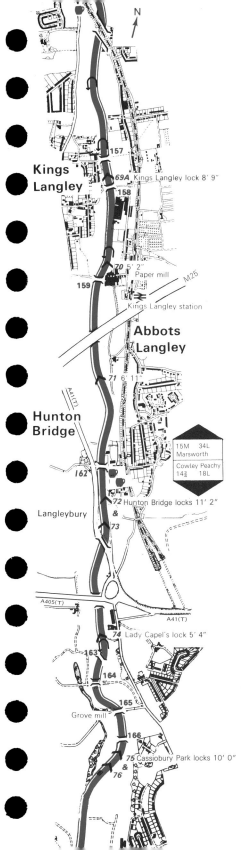

Kings Langley

The canal climbs in a northerly direction
through Cassiobury Park to Grove Mill, a water
mill where the mill stream doubles as a private
canal arm. Just north of the mill is the
deservedly famous ornamental stone bridge
ordered by the Earl of Essex before he would
allow the Grand Junction Canal Company to
cut a navigation through his park. The canal
winds considerably along this valley as it
follows the course of the River Gade. This
results in several wide stretches; do not attempt
to turn in these without ascertaining the depth.
The M25 north orbital road and the A41 cross
the canal as it approaches the lovely village of
Hunton Bridge. A little further north is Kings
Langley.

Kings Langley
Herts. EC Wed. PO, tel, stores, station. Once a
country village but now ravaged by the heavy
motor traffic that thunders through the town.
Its name derives from its royal associations;
there are still the remains of a palace in the
town. The tomb of Edmund de Langley,
brother of the Black Prince, lies in the Norman
Church of All Saints. Sir John Evans, the
famous archaeologist, is also buried here.

Abbots Langley
*Herts. EC Wed. PO, tel, stores, station (shared
with Kings Langley)*. The Church of St
Lawrence has 12thC arcades to the nave and a
14thC south chapel, an octagonal Perpendicular
font and a 14thC wall painting of Saints
Thomas and Lawrence.

Hunton Bridge
Herts. PO, tel, stores. Peaceful canalside village,
with a spired church and the pleasing
Langleybury Park.

PUBS

Lots of pubs west of Kings Langley Lock,
including:
- **Swan** High Street, Kings Langley.
- **Saracens Head** High Street, Kings
Langley.
- **Dog & Partridge** Old Mill Lane, Hunton
Bridge. Benskins real ale and *lunchtime* food
(Mon–Fri) in a fine old village pub.
- **King's Head** Hunton Bridge. A village pub
of great character, with an extensive garden.
Benskins real ale and food *(not Sun)*.

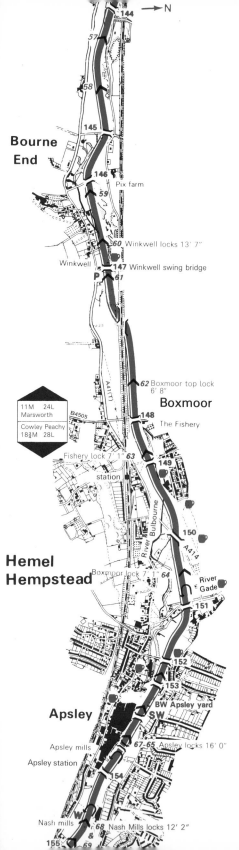

Hemel Hempstead

The canal begins to climb more steeply to the north west, passing several large paper mills in Apsley and the quaint double arch of bridge 154. The River Gade leaves the canal for Hemel Hempstead, a handsome modern town standing back from the canal beyond spacious urban parkland known as Boxmoor. The canal turns further west, accompanied now by the little River Bulbourne. The busy railway line is never far away, interrupting the peace of this very attractive valley. Watercress beds are to be found along here; they owe their existence to the mineral waters from the many chalk springs of the Chilterns which are the source of the River Bulbourne. The nearby A41 is fortunately shielded by trees; its many petrol stations, pubs and shops may be useful to the canal traveller.

Navigational note
A BW key is required to operate Winkwell Swing Bridge.

Hemel Hempstead
Herts. EC Wed. MD Thur, Fri, Sat. PO, tel, stores, garage, station, cinema. A developing, well-planned new town with excellent shops.
Piccotts End Medieval Murals 138 Piccotts End. Remarkable 14thC wall paintings in a hall believed to have been a pilgrims' hospice. Also an Elizabethan painted room.

BOATYARDS

BW Apsley Yard Ebbems Road, Apsley. (0442 56910). Ⓡ Ⓢ Ⓦ

BOAT TRIPS

Reach Out Projects Base Nash Mills, south of bridge 155. (0707 332321). Specialists in boat hire for youth work and the disabled. *Closed in winter.*

PUBS AND RESTAURANTS

Ⓟ✕ **Three Horseshoes** By bridge 147, Winkwell. (0442 862585). A popular inn with a real fire, an over 30s bar and Benskins and Ind Coope (Burton) real ale (the John Bull Bitter is *not* real ale). Meals at *lunchtime (not Sun)*, garden.
Ⓟ **Fishery Inn** Fishery Road, Boxmoor. A large, friendly canalside pub serving Ind Coope (Burton) real ale and meals *lunchtime and evening (not Sun eve)*. Family room, large garden with swings and slides.
Ⓟ **Old Kings Arms** High Street, Hemel Hempstead, in the old town. Historic pub serving Charles Wells real ale. *Lunchtime* food.
Ⓟ **Three Blackbirds** 194 St John's Road, Boxmoor. Ind Coope (Burton) and Benskins real ale in a friendly pub with an emphasis on games. Meals *lunchtime and evening (not Sun)*, family room, garden.
Ⓟ **Steam Coach** St John's Road, Boxmoor. Small friendly pub offering Ind Coope (Burton) and Benskins real ale and food *lunchtime and evening (not Sun)*. Children's room, garden, folk club *on Monday.*
Ⓟ **Heath Park** St John's Road, Boxmoor. Large pub convenient for the shops. Youngers real ale, food *lunchtime and evening (not Sun)*.
Ⓟ **Albion** Durrants Hill Road, Apsley. Benskins real ale in a friendly canalside pub. Meals *lunchtime and evening (Mon–Fri)*, snacks *lunchtime Sat.* Large, pretty garden and family room.
Ⓟ **Fountain** London Road, Apsley. There is live music *Wed and Sun* in this pub, which offers Benskins and Friary Meux real ale. *Lunchtime* food *(Mon–Sat)*, garden.
Ⓟ **White Lion** London Road, Apsley. Quiet, friendly pub with an open fire where you can enjoy Coombe and Websters real ales, and food *lunchtime and evening (not Sun)*. Children welcome.

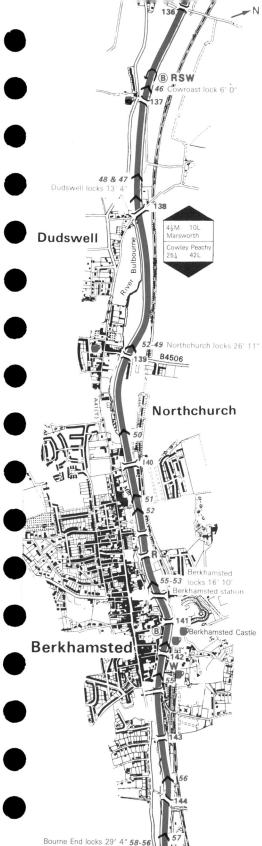

Berkhamsted

The canal now enters Berkhamsted by its back door and steals inconspicuously through the middle of the town, the northern limit of the Grand Union as a barge canal. Leaving Berkhamsted and still climbing up the Chilterns, one passes Northchurch, where a pump draws canal water supplies from a deep borehole in the chalk beds. The summit level is reached at Cowroast Lock which, in the days before the pump was installed at Northchurch, used to be the scene of long lines of boats tied up in the dry summers as the canal engineers struggled to maintain the water supply in the three-mile summit level – which was constantly being drained by the use of locks at either end. (It is perhaps worth noting that every time a boat crosses this summit level it draws off nearly 200,000 gallons of water.) At Cowroast Lock the old toll office still stands.

Ashridge House *Herts*. 3½ miles north of Berkhamsted. (044 284 3491). Built 1808 as a large romantic mansion in the Gothic taste by James Wyatt, the house gives an impression of what his famous Fonthill must have been like; the chapel is particularly splendid. The grounds were laid out by Capability Brown, and altered later by Repton. *Gardens only open, on weekend afternoons.*
Northchurch
Herts. EC Wed. PO, tel, stores. Built round the flint church which contains some Saxon work, and fine 19thC stained glass. In the High Street are several timber-framed houses.
Berkhamsted
Herts. EC Wed. MD Sat. All services. Good-looking large town with buildings of all periods, the A41 running through the middle. The High Street is dominated by the Church of St Peter, which contains work from practically every period, including a restoration by Butterfield of 1871. There are several brasses. Only the ruins of the Norman castle remain, where William I received the offer of the English crown in 1066. The 17thC Sayer almshouses are completely intact. The Common is known as a haven for wild birds including nightjars, woodcocks, grasshopper warblers, redpolls and bramblings.

BOATYARDS

Ⓑ **Cowroast Marina** By Cowroast Lock, Tring. (044 282 3222). Ⓡ Ⓢ Ⓦ Ⓓ Pump-out, gas, narrowboat hire, overnight mooring, long-term mooring, slipway, wet dock, chandlery, books and maps, boat sales, boat and engine repairs.
Ⓑ **Bridgewater Boats** Castle Wharf, Berkhamsted. (0442 863615). Ⓦ Ⓓ Pump-out, gas, narrowboat hire, overnight mooring. Their base has won an environmental award.

PUBS

🍺 **Cow Roast** Cowroast Lock. Large, smart 17thC inn near the marina. Benskins, Taylor Walker and Ind Coope (Burton) real ale and meals *lunchtime and evening (not Sun).* Garden.
🍺 **Crystal Palace** Station Road, Berkhamsted. Panelled pub near the castle remains. Benskins real ale, food *lunchtime and evening (not Sun).*
🍺 **Boat** Gravel path, by bridge 142. Fullers real ale.
🍺 **Brownlow Arms** Ravens Lane, Berkhamsted. Quiet backstreet pub serving Aylesbury real ale. Garden.
🍺 **Rising Sun** George Street, Berkhamsted. Excellent canalside local close to Bridgewater Boats. Benskins real ale, meals *lunchtime and evening (not Sun),* garden.
🍺 **Bull** High Street, Berkhamsted. Pleasant pub with canalside garden. Benskins and Friary Meux real ale and *lunchtime food (not Sun).*

Bulbourne

The canal continues north west through the long wooded cutting that contains the Tring summit level. At the hamlet of Bulbourne are the BW workshops where to this day traditional wooden lockgate-making is carried out by a small team of craftsmen. Just to the west the old Wendover Arm joins the canal, constantly feeding water into the summit level. This arm no longer goes to Wendover, but it is still navigable for small boats as far as Little Tring and the Tringford pumping station. Back at Bulbourne Junction, the first of the Marsworth locks begin to wind down the hill past the reservoirs; at the bottom of the flight there is an interesting double-arched bridge, a sight often repeated between here and Stoke Bruerne 33 miles to the north. This type of bridge was built by the Grand Junction Canal Company in the expectation that the locks would later be paired – a programme that was never completed. 100yds north of the double bridge is Marsworth Junction, dominated by the BW workshops. At the junction the main line bears round to the north east, while the Aylesbury Arm (7ft wide only) starts its fall west through the first eight narrow locks towards Aylesbury.

Marsworth
Bucks. PO, tel, stores, garage. A quiet scattered village centred around the Grand Union Canal and the Aylesbury Arm. The Icknield Way, a Roman road, passes the village. Dunstable Downs rise to the south east, gliders are a common sight and occasionally a hot air balloon may be seen floating along in the sky.

Tringford Pumping Station At the present terminus of Wendover Arm. Built by the Grand Junction Canal Company to pump water up from the three reservoirs just down the hill, and from the 100-acre Wilstone reservoir over to the west. This water, plus the supply from springs in Wendover was – and still is – fed down the arm into the Tring summit level. Originally the pumping station housed big beam engines, but these were replaced in the 20thC by heavy diesels. Now quiet, smooth, electric motors perform this vital task, lifting some four million gallons of water each day. The system was recently overhauled, having been in constant use since 1929.

Tring Reservoirs South of Startops End (bridge 132) and beside Marsworth locks. Four reservoirs with many wildfowl and waterside birds, notably the Black Tern and the Great Crested Grebe. Also abundant marsh and water plants. National nature reserve, managed by the Nature Conservancy, 20 Belgrave Square, London SW1. Public access is permitted along waymarked pathways.

Bulbourne
Herts. Tel. Canalside settlement around the BW workshops which are a well-preserved example of early 19thC canal architecture, with characteristic fanlights. To the north east is the long railway cutting built by Robert Stephenson in 1834–38, an engineering feat of the age.

Aldbury
Herts. PO, tel, stores. A charming village pond and stocks are sheltered below the hillside which rises to the east towards Ashridge. Note the quaint cottages along Stocks Road and to the north east and west of the Church of St John the Baptist, which dates from the 13thC. The monument to the third Duke of Bridgewater (an urn and a Greek Doric column) was erected on the brow of the hill beyond Stocks Road in 1832 to commemorate his pioneering work for the English canals.

Aldbury Common 1½ miles east of bridge 135 past Tring station. Acres of open land which adjoin Berkhamsted Common, Ashridge Park and Ivinghoe Common.

BOATYARDS

BW Bulbourne Workshops Bulbourne. (044 282 2261). Home of the maintenance yard and the lock-gate making team. No services.
BW Tring Yard Marsworth. (044 282 5938).

Map labels

AYLESBURY ARM
See page 46

2 Dixon's gap bridge

Marsworth narrow locks **1-8**

6¼M 16L
Aylesbury

Marsworth
Marsworth Junction
BW Marsworth yard

continued page 47

130

131

Tringford pumping station

Startop's end
W

Tring reservoirs

132 Lower Icknield way bridge
B489

reservoirs

45-39 Marsworth locks
42' 3"

50 ft

WENDOVER ARM

New Mills

Bulbourne Junction
W

Bulbourne

BW Bulbourne workshops

N

B488

133 Upper Icknield way bridge

N

134

TRING SUMMIT LEVEL

2½M 7L
Marsworth

Cowley Peachy
27¼M 45L

135

Tring station

Aldbury

A41(T)

136

PUBS

🍺 **Red Lion** Vicarage Road, Marsworth. A splendid village pub with an open fire, dispensing Aylesbury, Everards and Morrells real ales, along with guest beers. *Evening meals during the summer*, children's room.

🍺 **White Lion** Startops End, Marsworth. Canalside at bridge 132. A large pub serving Marstons and Youngers real ale. Meals *lunchtime and evening (not Sun)*, children's room, garden.

🍺 **Grand Junction Arms** Bulbourne. Canalside at bridge 133. Quiet, attractive pub with a large garden, serving Benskins and Ind Coope (Burton) real ale in a bar with an open fire. Meals *lunchtime and evening (not Mon)*.

🍺 **Queens Head** Marsworth, near bridge 132.

🍺 **Royal Hotel** Station Road, Tring. Hotel with two bars, where Chiltern Beechwood and Abbot real ale can be enjoyed. Food *lunchtime and evening (not Sun)*, children's room, garden, accommodation.

Grand Union Canal on the Tring Summit. *Derek Pratt.*

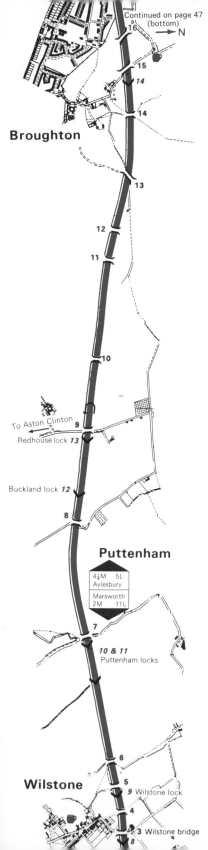

Continued on page 47
(bottom)

16

N

15

14

14

Broughton

13

12

11

10

To Aston Clinton

9

Redhouse lock *13*

Buckland lock *12*

8

Puttenham

4¼M   5L
Aylesbury

Marsworth
2M   11L

7

10 & 11
Puttenham locks

6

Wilstone

5

9 Wilstone lock

4

3 Wilstone bridge
8

Puttenham

The Aylesbury Arm continues to fall to the
west. Totally isolated and remote, it is one of
the most peaceful stretches of canal in the
country, passing through modest farmland with
good views of the Chiltern Hills over to the east
and, in the distance to the west, of tall new
buildings in Aylesbury. The locks are 7ft wide,
and the bridges too are narrow. This canal was
once semi-derelict, but an energetic programme
of dredging and lock repairing restored it to a
good navigable condition.

Wilstone
Herts. PO, tel, stores. Quiet village running
away from the canal to Wilstone reservoir, a
national nature reserve.

PUBS AND RESTAURANTS

Prince of Wales North of bridge 15. White
walled pub with bars on two levels. Aylesbury
real ale.
Bell 1 mile south of bridge 9. (0296
436055). Large rambling old inn with
internationally famous cuisine (*L & D*).
Marstons real ale.
Rising Sun South of bridge 9. A lively and
cheerful roadside pub serving Courage real ale
and *lunchtime* meals.
Buckingham Arms Wilstone.
Half Moon Wilstone. Nicely refurbished
old inn. Aylesbury and Everards real ales,
lunchtime food (*not Sun*). Open fire, garden.

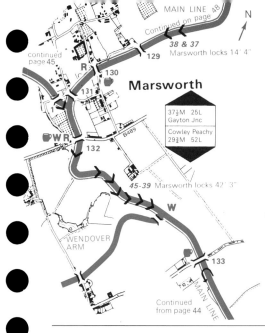

MAIN LINE 48
Continued on page 48

38 & 37
Marsworth locks 14' 4"
129

continued
page 45

R
130

Marsworth

131

1

37¾M 25L
Gayton Jnc
Cowley Peachy
29¾M 52L

W R
132

B489

45-39 Marsworth locks 42' 3"

W

WENDOVER
ARM

133
Continued
from page 44

MAIN LINE

Marsworth

The main line heads north east and continues its descent through Marsworth locks before entering the remote countryside beyond Ivinghoe. There is a useful licensed canal shop, The Ship, by bridge 130.

PUBS

White Lion Startops End, Marsworth. Canalside at bridge 132. A large pub serving Marstons and Youngers real ale. Meals *lunchtime and evening (not Sun)*, children's room, garden.

Red Lion Vicarage Road, Marsworth. A splendid village pub with an open fire, dispensing Aylesbury, Everards and Morrells real ales, along with guest beers. *Evening meals during the summer*, children's room.

Grand Junction Arms Bulbourne. Canalside at bridge 133. Quiet, attractive pub with a large garden, serving Benskins and Ind Coope (Burton) real ale in a bar with an open fire. Meals *lunchtime and evening (not Mon)*.

Aylesbury

The canal now runs under the Aylesbury ring road and drops down through the last two locks into the town; boaters should be aware of the iron girder bridge 18 which is extremely narrow. Aylesbury basin itself is spacious and full of boats, although there is no longer a boatyard as such. However, there are moorings for visitors, and pubs nearby, and all the amenities of the town centre are a mere three-minute walk away.

Aylesbury
Bucks. EC Thur. MD Wed, Sat. PO, tel, stores, garage, station, cinema. A busy market town where the 20thC has not taken over completely; the centre of Aylesbury is made up of a number of attractive squares, and the 13thC church lies hidden in its secluded churchyard a short distance away. There are some interesting Georgian buildings too. 'The King's Head', dating from the 15thC, has outstanding windows, gateway and courtyard, and Oliver Cromwell's chair in the bar.
Buckinghamshire County Museum Church Street, Aylesbury. (0296 88849). Illustrates county archaeology, geology and history, local crafts, costume, natural history. Also small collection of prints and paintings. *Closed Sun.*

PUBS

Bell Hotel Market Square, Aylesbury. A traditional country town pub, serving Wethered real ale and food *lunchtime and evening*.

Kings Head Market Square, Aylesbury. 15thC inn owned by the National Trust, with original timber front and stained-glass windows. Bass and Brakspear real ale, meals *(L & D)*.

Old Millwrights Arms Walton Road, Aylesbury. ¼ mile west of bridge 17. Aylesbury, Chiltern Beechwood and Morrells real ale in a friendly 30s style pub. *Lunchtime* food.

Ship Walton Street, Aylesbury, beside the canal basin. Ind Coope real ale and snacks.

White Swan Walton Street, Aylesbury. Lively 16thC pub serving a good choice of real ale and meals *lunchtime and evening* (booking advised).

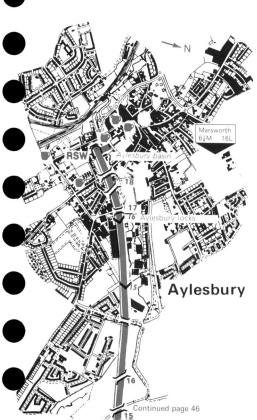

N

Marsworth
6¼M   16L

RSW   Aylesbury basin

18

17
16   Aylesbury locks

Aylesbury

15

16

Continued page 46
15

Ivinghoe

Northwards from Marsworth the canal falls
steadily away from Dunstable Downs and the
Chilterns, leaving the hills as a backdrop to the
west. As the hills give way to open grasslands,
the canal becomes more remote, a quiet, empty
section that terminates in the peace of Grove
Church Lock. Villages are set back from the
canal, only Slapton, with its superb pub, being
under 1 mile away. The main feature of the
section is the locks, carrying the canal down
from the Chilterns toward Leighton Buzzard
and the Ouzel valley; these occur frequently,
often in remote and attractive settings. The
railway and the B488 run parallel to the canal to
the west; there is a station at Cheddington.

Grove
Bucks. An attractive group formed by the
bridge, lock, lock cottage and the tiny church, a
14thC chapel with a later bell turret.
Slapton
Bucks. EC Thur. PO, tel, stores. Compact
residential village; the Perpendicular church
contains several brasses of the 15th and 16thC.
Cheddington
Bucks. EC Thur. PO, tel, stores, garage, station.
1 mile north of bridge 126. A residential area
spread around the station, clearly a commuter
development. The church contains a richly
carved Jacobean pulpit. On the hills south of
the village are the remains of a medieval field
cultivation.
Mentmore House 1½ miles west of Horton
Lock. A Tudor-style stone mansion built in the
1850s by Sir Joseph Paxton for the Rothschild
family. Large plate glass windows, central
heating and fresh air ventilation made the house
advanced for its time, reflecting the ingenuity
of the architect.
Whipsnade White Lion On Dunstable Downs,
visible from the canal from around Slapton and
Cheddington. The lion was cut in 1935 and is
over 480ft long.
Ivinghoe
Bucks. EC Wed. PO, tel, stores, garage. 1 mile
east of bridge 123 or 126. An attractive
although greatly expanded village, which
centres round the large 13th and 14thC church,
notable for its crossing tower and Jacobean
pulpit. The main street, leading west from the
church, contains the old town hall, partly
16thC. ¼ mile south of the village is Pitstone
Green Mill, a post mill scheduled as an ancient
monument.
Iron Age Hill Fort 1 mile north east of
Ivinghoe, on top of Beacon Hill. The triangular
hill fort encloses six acres: within this area
stands a bowl barrow thought to date from the
Bronze Age. There is a tumulus to the south
and another to the east of Beacon Hill.

BOATYARDS

Ⓑ **Grebe Canal Cruises** Pitstone Wharf,
Cheddington. (0296 661920). Ⓡ Ⓢ Ⓦ Ⓓ
Pump-out, gas, narrowboat hire, long-term
mooring, winter storage, slipway, books and
maps, boat sales, boat and engine repairs, gift
shop, toilet. *Closed winter weekends.*
Ⓑ **Sovereign Narrowboats** Pitstone Wharf.
(0296 662047; bookings 0252 615103).
Pump-out, narrowboat hire.

BOAT TRIPS

Grebe Canal Cruises Pitstone Wharf,
Cheddington. (0296 661920). Trips *every
weekend May–Sep, daily in school holidays.* Also
private charter for up to 60 persons.

PUBS

🍺 **Carpenters Arms** Slapton, north east of
bridge 120. Superb thatched pub dispensing
Benskins and Ind Coope (Burton) real ale
straight from the barrel. Open fire, unspoilt
public bar decorated with old carpentry tools.
Excellent food *lunchtime and evening*, garden.
Well worth finding.
🍺 **Duke of Wellington** Cook's Wharf,
Cheddington Road, Pitstone. Large, quiet and
friendly pub. Adnams and Marstons real ale,
meals *lunchtime and evening (not Sun eve).*

Grove

116
29 Church lock 6′ 9″

River Ouzel

Slapton

118

Slapton lock 7′ 1″ 30
120
Slapton wharf

121
31 Horton lock 6′ 9″

Horton wharf

37½M 18L
Gayton Jnc

Marsworth
3¾M   7L

33 & 32
Ivinghoe locks 14′ 3″
122

Cheddington station

Cheddington

B488

Little Seabrook
Ivinghoe bridge 123

Seabrook locks 20′ 4″ 36–34

Great Seabrook

Ivinghoe

125 swing bridge

126
R

Pitstone

Leighton Buzzard

The canal now runs parallel to the River Ouzel
to the east and, leaving the open fields behind,
passes through the joined towns of Linslade
and Leighton Buzzard, effectively acting as a
boundary between them. Leighton Buzzard
station is actually in Linslade. The A418
crosses the canal in the town centre. Leaving
these towns, the canal enters the valley of the
Ouzel and meanders sharply, following the
river. Steep hills rise to the east and west,
thickly wooded to the east. A low towpath
hedge allows fine views of this beautiful valley.
This section contains a good mixture of canal
townscape and landscape. Grove and Leighton
Locks both having attractive and well-kept lock
houses. The railway and the B488 continue to
follow the canal to the west.

Leighton Buzzard
*Beds. EC Thur. PO, tel, stores, station, garage,
cinema, take-away food (near the bridge).* A
picturesque market town with a superlative
church. 17th and 18thC houses and
half-timbered cottages are to be found in the
streets leading to the Market Cross, which has
stood for some 600 years in the centre of the
town. There are also some fine 19thC buildings;
note particularly Barclay's Bank. In North
Street stand the almshouses founded by
Edward Wilkes in 1633 on condition that the
bounds of the parish be beaten every Rogation
Monday. The custom is still maintained, and
on 23 *May* a choir boy stands upon his head in
front of the almshouses while the appropriate
extracts from the donor's will are read.
All Saint's Parish Church Dates from 1288 and
is notable for its 191ft tower and spire and the
15thC wooden roof. It retains its ancient
sanctus bell, 13thC font, misericordes, brasses
and a medieval lectern. The medieval graffiti
are interesting and include a depiction of Simon
and Nellie arguing about whether the
Mothering Sunday Simnel cake should be
boiled or baked.
Linslade
Bucks. PO, tel, stores, garage, station. Linslade
is virtually a residential extension of Leighton
Buzzard. Traces of the old village can just be
found to the north, especially the church, near
the canal, easily recognised by its battlements;
the front and parts of the structure date from
the 12thC. West of the church is a railway
tunnel with an extraordinary neo-Gothic portal
in grey brick, looking delightfully incongruous.
Ascott House 2 miles to the west, along the
A418 from Linslade. (0296 688242). Attractive,
irregular timber-framed house built in 1606,
with extensive additions made in 1874 and
1938. Collection of paintings, French and
Chippendale furniture, oriental porcelain.
Twelve acres of grounds and gardens
containing rare trees. *Opening times are liable to
vary – ring for details.*

BOATYARDS

Ⓑ **The Wyvern Shipping Company**
Rothschild Road, Linslade. (0525 372355).
Ⓡ Ⓢ Ⓦ Ⓓ Ⓔ Pump-out, gas, narrowboat hire,
long-term mooring, dry dock, books and maps,
boat building, engine repairs, toilets.

BOAT TRIPS

Leighton Lady Canal Cruises Ring (0525)
384563 for details.

PUBS

🍺 **Globe Inn** Globe Lane, Linslade. Canalside,
near bridge 111. Food.
🍺 **Bedford Arms** By bridge 114. Websters real
ale and food *lunchtime and evening* in a busy
town pub.
🍺 **Smugglers** Friendly bar with a canalside
terrace right by bridge 114. Marstons and
Youngers real ale.
🍺 **White Horse** Near the railway station,
Linslade. Friendly local serving Aylesbury and
Bass real ale.

Soulbury

The canal meanders along the Ouzel valley to
the north west through beautiful scenery. The
hills rising steeply to the west and the natural
woods to the east make the canal seem like a
river, which is rare on the Grand Union. As the
valley widens, the canal continues its steady fall
towards Bletchley, following the Ouzel closely.
Flat meadows reaching to the west precede the
approach to Bletchley. All the locks, the
Soulbury flight of three, and one at Stoke
Hammond, form an attractive canalscape, the
double-arched bridges showing where the locks
were once doubled. Remains of the
supplementary locks can still be seen at
Soulbury alongside the small pumping station
that returns water back up the flight whenever
necessary. Next to the flight is Vic Roberts'
metalworks, for wrought iron and canal
souvenirs. The railway and the B488 run
closely to the west of the canal.

Stoke Hammond
Bucks. EC Sat. PO, tel, stores, garage. Set above
the canal to the west, the village overlooks the
valley as it spreads untidily along the B488. The
church, weighted down by its squat central
tower, contains a decorative 14thC font.

Soulbury
*Bucks. 1 mile west of the Three Locks. PO, tel,
stores.* The church contains a monument in
white marble by Grinling Gibbons, 1690. To
the south is Liscombe House, a rambling 17thC
brick mansion with a fine Gothic façade of
1774, set in a large landscaped park.

BOATYARDS

Ⓑ **Willowbridge Marina** Stoke Road,
Bletchley. (0908 643242). Ⓡ Ⓢ Ⓦ Ⓟ Ⓓ
Pump-out, gas, overnight mooring, long-term
mooring, winter storage, slipway with gantry
crane, chandlery, provisions (hot pies, stamps),
books and maps, boat and engine sales and
repairs, toilet, showers, laundry, off-licence,
telephone.

PUBS

🍺 **Dolphin** Stoke Hammond. Pleasant pub
with an open fire and piano. Aylesbury real ale
and *lunchtime* food.
🍺✕ **Three Locks** Stoke Hammond. (0525
27393). Ⓦ Ⓡ Lunches, afternoon teas,
Aylesbury and Everards real ales in a very
attractively sited canalside pub. Terrace.

Waterhall

99

Ⓑ

A4146

102

25M   9L
Gayton Jnc
Marsworth
12½M 16L

104

N

Stoke Hammond lock 6' 11" 23

N

**Stoke
Hammond**

P

105   swing bridge
(derelict)

A4146

106

26-24 Soulbury Three locks 20' 3"

R W

Three locks

107

Soulbury

108

109

Childs Way Manor house

82a New bridge

83

Little Woolstone

84

85 P

Great Woolstone

86

87

Woughton on the Green

88

(Information board)

89 90

Milton Keynes
hospital 90B

B 488

Walton Hall

20¼M 8L
Gayton Jnc

Marsworth
17¼M 17L

90C

Groveway
bridge

Bowlers bridge

91

A 421

A 5(T)

92

92A

93

94

22 Fenny Stratford
lock 1'1"

R S W

Fenny Stratford station

95

Bletchley

96

97

Fenny Stratford

98

Water Eaton mill

River Ouzel

Bletchley

The canal runs through open country, but to
the south lie the suburbs of the rapidly
expanding town of Bletchley. There is a canal
shop at Fenny Stratford Lock. Once north of
the town the canal again meanders gently
through villages, still following the course of
the River Ouzel as far as Woolstone. There is
only one lock on this section, but the old arched
accommodation bridges abound. The main
railway leaves the canal south of Bletchley, but
another line, to Bedford, crosses at Fenny
Stratford. There is a station close to the canal
here. Through the whole of the Milton Keynes
area to Wolverton the tow path is excellent –
either gravel or tarmac.

Little Woolstone
Bucks. A tiny hamlet with a pub and a garage.
Great Woolstone is even smaller. Willen Lake
recreation area is best approached from
bridge 83.
Woughton on the Green
Bucks. PO, tel, stores. The village is attractively
scattered round a huge green flanked by the
canal to the west. There are houses of all
periods, mixed in a random but harmonious
manner and presided over by the church built
on a mound to the east.
Simpson
Bucks. PO, tel, stores. A main-road village,
much redeveloped as a suburb of Bletchley, but
still retaining elements of independence. The
church is mainly 14thC; note the wooden roof
and a monument by John Bacon, 1789. Beyond
Woughton Park to the north is Walton Hall,
the Open University.
Bletchley
*Bucks. EC Wed. MD Thur, Sat. PO, tel, stores,
garage, station, cinema.* This formerly
agricultural and lace-making town is now a
large, modern place that has swallowed up its
neighbour, Fenny Stratford. A small part of the
12thC St Mary's Church remains; much
restoration and alteration has been done.
Fenny Stratford
Bucks. PO, tel, stores, garage, station. The town
is now merged into Bletchley. The building of
the red-brick church, 1724–30, was inspired by
Browne Willis, the antiquarian; as a result it is
an early example of Gothic revival. The old
pump house is now a gift shop and cafeteria,
run by handicapped youth.

PUBS
🍺 **Wayfarer Hotel** East of bridge 82a.
Aylesbury real ale in a stylish new hotel on the
shore of Willen Lake. Meals *lunchtime and
evening*.
🍺✕ **Barge** Newport Road, Little Woolstone.
(0908 679596). Smart old pub with a carvery.
Charrington and M & B real ale, garden.
🍺 **Cross Keys** Newport Road, Great
Woolstone. Thatched village pub with a
prize-winning garden, serving Charles Wells
real ale, meals *lunchtime and evening (not Mon &
Tue eve).*
🍺 **Woughton House Hotel** Woughton on the
Green. Aylesbury real ale in a country hotel.
Meals *lunchtime and evening*, garden,
accommodation.
🍺 **Ye Old Swan** Opposite the church,
Woughton on the Green. 17thC tavern with
Dick Turpin associations. Ushers and Wilson's
real ale, *lunchtime* food, garden.
🍺 **Plough** Simpson, by the aqueduct. Charles
Wells real ale is available, and there is a lovely
garden. Snacks and meals.
🍺 **Beacon** Mount Farm Lake, Bond Avenue,
Bletchley. A sports orientated place, with a
nine-hole pitch and putt, football pitches and
facilities for other games. A circular upper
gallery gives views over the lake. Aylesbury,
Everards and Ind Coope (Burton) real ale,
meals *lunchtime and evening*, garden.
🍺 **Red Lion** Fenny Stratford Lock. Garden for
children, camping, groceries. R W
🍺 **Plough** West of bridge 98. Modern pub
serving Benskins and Ind Coope (Burton) real
ale and snacks. Garden.

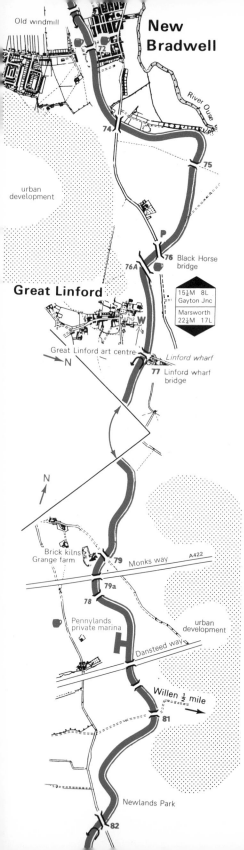

Milton Keynes

Continuing north west, and then at Great Linford turning sharply to the west, the canal runs through attractive, lightly wooded scenery that gradually gives way to hills and follows the Ouse valley, clinging to the south side. Either side, where once were open fields, the new town of Milton Keynes has been built. Willen and Great Linford are well worth visiting. There are no locks, but a variety of bridges. At Great Linford Wharf there is a winding hole that marks the junction with the Newport Pagnell branch, closed many years ago.

New Bradwell
Bucks. PO, tel, stores, Chinese take-away. A Victorian railway town, built on a grid of extreme monotony and regularity. The church, by Street, 1858, is of interest, especially for its Victorian stained glass. The 19thC Bradwell Windmill is now restored. Access from bridge 72 where there are good moorings.

Great Linford
Bucks. PO, tel, stores. Great Linford is magnificent: a traditional village street running away from the canal, with a marvellous group formed by church, manor, farm and almshouses, all in rich golden stone. The 14thC church right alongside the canal contains Georgian box pews and pulpit, and fine 19thC stained glass. The almshouses are 17thC with strong Dutch gables. The manor, symmetrical, dignified and elegant in a totally 18thC way, completes the picture.

Milton Keynes
Bucks. All services and a major shopping centre accessible by bus from bridge 82a. An exciting new town development encompassing Bletchley and the scattered villages to the north. Work on the 22,000-acre area began in the early 1970s and the original population of 40,000 has grown to around 100,000. Strategically placed between Birmingham and the capital, close to the M1 and the main railway line, the Development Corporation has been successful in attracting many companies to the area. The housing schemes are imaginative, and well endowed with green space and trees. Great emphasis is placed on the social and recreational needs of the population and in this respect the new town makes good use of the canal.

Willen
Bucks. 1/2 mile east of bridge 81. PO box, tel. A hamlet wholly dominated by the Wren church, which is well worth a visit. All the interior fittings are original, and the plaster work, pews, organ case and font should be seen. The 170-acre lake is a watersports centre, with sailing, canoeing etc.

PUBS
● **New Inn** Canalside near bridge 72. Friendly, stone built pub with good value food (*L & D*). Charles Wells real ale, garden.
● **Black Horse** Canalside at Black Horse Bridge. A popular pub with a choice of bars and open fires in the winter. Meals *lunchtime and evenings on weekdays*. Aylesbury, Everards and Ind Coope (Burton) real ale, children's room and garden.
● **Eager Poet** Nr Pennylands Marina, bridge 79a, Milton Keynes. Modern pub with facilities for the disabled. Wethered and Brakspear real ale, snacks, garden. Chinese take-away next door. The Eager Poet is a keen Milton (ouch!).

Milton Keynes: a new town that really appreciates its canal. *Derek Pratt.*

Cosgrove

The canal continues westwards past industrial
Wolverton, and then turns north west prior to
crossing the Ouse valley by means of an
embankment and aqueduct. Hills now begin to
dominate the landscape to the west as the canal
follows the course of the River Tove, an
indication of the climb ahead up to Stoke
Bruerne. After Wolverton the canal becomes
more remote, with only Cosgrove exploiting it.
The railway 1 mile to the east provides the only
intrusion. There is plenty of canalscape;
Wolverton Aqueduct, Cosgrove Lock ending
the 11-mile Fenny Stratford Pound, Cosgrove
Bridge and the disused and long abandoned
Buckingham Arm branching away to the west.
(Part is now a nature reserve, and a nature trail
follows the disused canal.) After Cosgrove and
the old junction, the A508 runs parallel to the
West.

Castlethorpe
Bucks. PO, tel, stores. A quiet village, thatched
houses around a green, 1 mile north east of
Castlethorpe Wharf. The main railway running
in a cutting below the village is the only
disturbance. Parts of the church date back to
1200, although the tower was built in 1729.
North of the church is the site of a castle.

Cosgrove
Northants. EC Wed. PO, tel, stores. The village
climbs west away from the canal, its spread
visually terminated by the wooded church. The
best parts are by the canal: a range of
warehouses, a curious pedestrian tunnel under
the canal, and a splendid stone bridge
charmingly decorated in the Gothic taste, built
in 1800. Its style is unique among canal
bridges, and there is no obvious reason for its
solitary splendour. The Georgian house that
dominates the west bank by the lock is
Cosgrove Hall; in 1958 a Roman bathhouse was
discovered in front of the hall.

Wolverton
*Bucks. EC Wed. MD Fri. PO, tel, stores,
garage, station.* Ignore the regularity of New
Wolverton, and continue further west where
the remains of the old village still survive
among the trees. The Norman-style church was
built in 1815, its large size perhaps anticipating
the coming of the railway! By the church is the
rectory with a handsome portal, built in 1729.

Great Ouse Aqueduct
North of Old Wolverton the canal crosses the
Ouse via an iron trunk aqueduct, a square
cast-iron trough carried on stone pillars. Built
in 1811, it replaced a brick structure that
collapsed in 1808. This in turn had replaced
nine locks that enabled the Ouse to be crossed
on the level, a system abandoned because of the
danger of floods.

BOATYARDS

Ⓑ **Cosgrove Marina** The Lock House,
Cosgrove. (0908 562467). Ⓡ Ⓢ Ⓦ Ⓓ Pump-out,
gas, overnight mooring, long-term mooring,
winter storage, chandlery, boat building, boat
sales, engine sales and repairs, toilets, 24hr
mobile breakdown service.
Ⓑ **Wharfside Fitters** Galleon Wharf, Old
Wolverton. (0908 371321). By bridge 68. Ⓦ Ⓓ
Long-term mooring, chandlery, boat fitting.

BOAT TRIPS

Linda Day Cruises Cosgrove Lock. (0908
563377). Cruises from Cosgrove Wharf and
Stoke Bruerne etc, for private parties.

PUBS

🍺 **Navigation** Castlethorpe Wharf, Cosgrove.
Spacious and friendly pub with a large open
fire. Offers Adnams, Hook Norton and Bass
real ale and meals *lunchtime and evening*. There
is a garden, children's room and a canal level
cellar bar during the summer.
🍺 **Barley Mow** Cosgrove, by bridge 65.
Snacks, large garden with swings and a slide,
mooring.
🍺 **Galleon Inn** Old Wolverton. Attractive and
comfortable inn with a balcony overlooking the
garden and canal; many curios decorate the
walls. Ind Coope (Burton) and Wadworths real
ale, meals, garden and children's room.

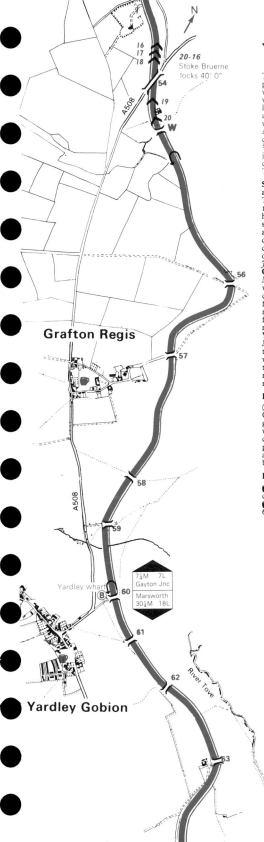

Yardley Gobion

The canal leaves the low hills to the west and passes through open fields to Grafton Regis, where the hills reappear. A quiet, rural stretch, with only the noise of the railway. The villages lie set back to the west, but are easily approached. Accommodation bridges occur with even regularity, mostly old brick arches. After Grafton Regis the River Tove joins the canal and then branches away to the west after ¾ mile; there is a winding hole by this junction. At once the canal starts the seven-lock climb to Stoke Bruerne, via single wide locks. The A508 crosses after the second lock.

Stoke Park Approached via Stoke Bruerne, or along a footpath that leaves the canal at lock 20. The park is then ½ mile west of the canal. Built 1629–35 by Inigo Jones for Sir Francis Crane, head of the Mortlake Tapestry Works, the symmetrical façade with its flanking pavilions and colonnade made Stoke Park House (now demolished) one of the earliest Palladian or classical buildings in England. The exterior only, and the gardens may be visited. *Open Jul–Aug, Sat & Sun only.*

Grafton Regis
Northants. EC Sat. PO, tel, stores. A quiet stone village that runs gently westwards from the canal, it still preserves a strong manorial feeling. The large church, near the canal, is mostly 13th and 14thC, but contains a Norman font. There is also a fine Neo-classical monument by Flaxman, 1808.

Yardley Gobion
Northants. EC Wed. PO, tel, stores. A small thatch and stone village, set on a slope to the west of the canal. The village is cut in half by the A508, which has prompted much redevelopment. The church that overlooks the road was built in 1864.

BOATYARDS

ⓑ **Baxter Boatfitting Services** Yardley Gobion. (0908 542454). Ⓡ Ⓢ Ⓦ Ⓓ Ⓔ Pump-out, gas, overnight mooring, long-term mooring, winter storage, slipway, day hire boat, crane, dry dock, chandlery, provisions and farm produce, books and maps, boat building, boat and engine sales and repairs, toilet, laundry, baths, B & B.

PUBS

🍺 **White Hart** Grafton Regis. On A508 west of canal from bridge 57. Food.
🍺 **Coffee Pot** Yardley Gobion. South of bridge 60. Food.

Map labels (left)

See page 60
MAIN LINE
N
3
47
NORTHAMPTON ARM
2
See page 58
48
RS
Gayton Junction
DW BW Gayton yard
49
A43(T)
50
B
Blisworth
51
P
Blisworth mill
Blisworth
Blisworth hill
Blisworth tunnel
(closed)

3¼M   0L   Gayton Jnc
Marsworth   34¼M   25L

WR
B
BW Waterways museum
53
Stoke Bruerne
15 & 14 Stoke Bruerne locks 16' 0"
16
A508

Stoke Bruerne

Now the hills become more dominant, especially to the west and north west, anticipating Blisworth Tunnel. After the tunnel and the thickly wooded approach cutting, the hills recede to the west, and the canal, becoming wider but shallow at the edges, reaches Gayton Junction through open fields. The villages are very much on top of the canal, partly because of the landscape, and partly because of their importance to the canal; Stoke Bruerne is an ideal canal village. After Stoke Bruerne Top Lock the level remains unchanged for several miles. A deep cutting leads to Blisworth Tunnel, the longest in Britain still open to navigation. The Waterways Museum at Stoke Bruerne makes this altogether an exciting stretch. The A43 crosses in the middle of Blisworth, but Blisworth station is closed.

Blisworth
Northants. PO, tel, stores, garage. A large brown stone village built around the A43, it climbs up steeply from the canal, which passes through in a cutting shortly after leaving the tunnel. The church, mostly 14thC, is just to the east of the canal, but appears to sit astride it. There are houses of all periods, the most striking built of local stone in the 18thC. Blisworth stone was quarried extensively. On the road that runs above the tunnel, marked by the regular grey caps of the air vents, are several elegant stone houses one, now a farm, is handsomely titled in carved lettering, 'Blisworth Stone Works'.

Blisworth Tunnel
At 3057yds long, Blisworth is the longest canal tunnel open to navigation in Britain. No towpath, but the channel is wide enough to allow the passing of two 7ft boats, so keep to the right. *Boats over 7ft beam must give advance notice to the section inspector on (0788) 890666 so that boats can be prevented from entering the tunnel at the opposite end.*
The Grand Junction Canal was completed and opened in 1800 with the exception of this tunnel. The first attempt at excavation failed, and so a tramway was built over Blisworth Hill, linking the two termini. Boats arriving at either end had to be unloaded onto horse-drawn waggons, which were then pulled over the hill, and reloaded on to boats. A second attempt at the tunnel was more successful, and it opened on 25 March 1805. Originally boats were legged through. (Note the leggers' hut at the south end.) 1984 saw the completion of the British Waterways Board's £4.3 million restoration project.

Stoke Bruerne
Northants. EC Sat. PO, tel, stores. Perhaps the best example of a canal village in this country. Built mostly of local Blisworth stone, the houses flank the canal, clearly viewing it as a blessing. To the west the hilly landscape warns of the approaching tunnel under Blisworth Hill. The Perpendicular church with its Norman tower overlooks the village, while the warehouses and cottages along the wharf have become a canal centre, greatly encouraged by the presence of the Waterways Museum. As a canalscape Stoke Bruerne has everything: a pub, locks, boat scales, a double-arched bridge, museum and canal shops and a nearby tunnel.

Waterways Museum Stoke Bruerne. (0604 862229). Housed in a fine old stone warehouse, a unique collection brings to life the rich history of over 200 years of canals. Exhibits include a traditional narrowboat, boat weighing scales, a reconstructed butty boat cabin, steam and diesel engines, and extensive displays of clothing, cabinware, brasses, signs, models, paintings, photographs, and documents. Museum shop selling canal literature, maps, postcards, souvenirs and other ephemera. *Open daily (except Christmas, Boxing Day and winter Mon).* Charge. Pleasure trips to Blisworth Tunnel mouth *during summer* from the museum.

BOATYARDS

BW Gayton Yard Blisworth. (0788 890666).
R S W Overnight mooring, long-term mooring, slipway, toilet.

D Blagrove Wharf Cottage, Stoke Bruerne. (0604 862174). D E Canal carriers, coal sales, B&B.

B **Blisworth Tunnel Boats** Gayton Road, Blisworth. (0604 858868). R S W D E Pump-out (*not Sat, ring in advance*), gas, narrowboat hire, day hire boats, overnight mooring, long-term mooring, wet dock, chandlery, souvenirs, books and maps, boat and engine repairs, boat sales, toilet.

PUBS AND RESTAURANTS

Royal Oak Blisworth. Food, garden for children.

Boat Inn Stoke Bruerne. (0604 862428). Canalside. Food, skittles. Can get very crowded.

Bruerne's Lock Restaurant Stoke Bruerne. Classic English fare (*L & D*). Reservation is advised (0604 863654).

Braunston Bottom Lock. *David Perrott.*

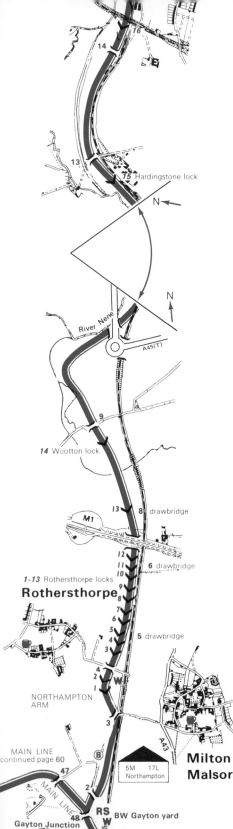

Milton Malsor

At Gayton Junction the Northampton Arm of
the Grand Union branches away to the north
east. It falls steeply through 5 miles of open
country to Northampton where it connects with
the navigable River Nene and thus with
Peterborough, the Fens and ultimately the
Wash. There are no villages on the canal, and
the main feature of interest is the flight of 17
locks down to Northampton. Most of the long
flight is visible from the top, as is Northampton
in the distance. Several traditional drawbridges
cross the canal, which look very pretty but are
hard work to operate. Only the M1 bridge, a
long concrete tunnel, interferes with the
unchanged feeling of the arm. A guide sheet is
obtainable from the box at Gayton Junction,
and those who navigate the arm can obtain a
plaque and certificate from J. Faulkner,
Hillside View, 10 The Jetty, Creaton,
Northampton.

Rothersthorpe
Northants. EC Sat. PO, tel, stores. A
comfortable mixture of brick and stone built
round a large square. The church contains a
Tudor pulpit. To the west of the village is a
large circular dovecot with 900 nesting places.
Milton Malsor
Northants. PO, tel, stores. Attractive,
meandering brick stone village, spreading east
towards the 14thC church. Around the church
are several elegant stone houses of the 17th and
18thC, making an exploration on foot worth
while. New houses have been well incorporated
with the old.

BOATYARDS

Ⓑ **Alvechurch Boat Centre** Gayton Marina,
Blisworth. (0604 858685). On the
Northampton Arm, 400yds from Gayton
Junction. [R][S][W][D] Pump-out, gas,
narrowboat hire, overnight mooring, long-term
mooring, winter storage, boat sales and repairs,
toilets, gift shop. BW and River Nene licences.
Telephone.

PUBS

🍺 **Chequers** North Street, Rothersthorpe.
There is an open fire on chilly days in this
village pub which serves Manns real ale and
snacks.
🍺 **Greyhound** Towcester Road, Milton
Malsor. A fine village pub in 17thC cottages,
once occupied by workers from the brewery
next door (now closed). There is an open fire in
the bar, where Manns real ale and *lunchtime*
food can be enjoyed. Garden.
🍺 **Compass** Green Street, Milton Malsor.
Small 18thC village local dispensing Manns real
ale. Snacks (*not Sun*) and garden.

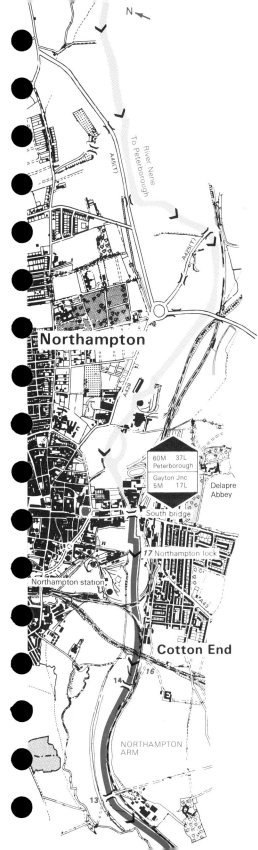

Northampton

Continuing north east and then swinging east after Hunsbury Hill, the canal leaves the open country behind as it approaches Northampton. Housing estates fringing the canal soon appear. The entry into the town passes factories, disused wharves and railway junctions before reaching Cotton End Wharf. Anyone considering stopping in Northampton is advised to pass through the bottom lock and into the Nene Navigation, where surroundings are more inviting. A brass plaque and certificate are available for a modest fee to those who make the journey to Northampton. Apply to J. Faulkner, 10 The Jetty, Creaton, Northampton.

Navigational note
The River Nene is a fully navigable river from Northampton down to the Wash. At Peterborough, which is 60 miles and 37 locks away, the river becomes tidal. The river is covered in great detail in the *Nicholson/Ordnance Survey Guide to the Broads and Fens.*

Northampton
Northants. EC Thur. MD Wed, Sat. PO, tel, stores, garage, station, cinema, theatre. The centre of the town was destroyed by fire in 1675, and so little remains of Northampton's famous history. Today it is a centre of the shoe industry. Only an archway of the 12thC castle remains, one of the best-known Norman castles. Thomas à Becket was tried here in 1164. There are several churches of interest, including a rare round Norman one of c1110. The richly decorated Town Hall was built during the 19thC in the Gothic style.
Abington Museum Abington Park. Period rooms, toys, bygones, Northampton lace, ceramics, natural history exhibited in a manor castle. *Closed Sun in winter.*
Central Museum and Art Gallery Guildhall Road. Archaeology, antiquities, paintings, furniture and the finest collection of historical footwear in Europe, including Queen Victoria's wedding shoes and ballet shoes of Nijinsky.
Delapre Abbey London Road (A50). ½ mile south of canal. A former Cluniac nunnery, founded in 1145, the Abbey underwent major alterations in the 16th and 17thC. *Open Thur & Sat afternoons.* South of the Abbey park is Eleanor Cross, one of three surviving crosses set up by Edward I in 1290 to mark the last resting places of Queen Eleanor on her way to burial in Westminster Abbey from Harby in Leicestershire where she had died.
Battle of Northampton 10 July 1460 ½ mile south of Northampton Lock, between Delapre Abbey and Hunsbury Hill. A significant battle in the Wars of the Roses in which the Lancastrian King Henry was defeated by Edward of York. Beaumont, Shrewsbury, Egremont and Buckingham were slain and many bodies floated in the River Nene.

PUBS AND RESTAURANTS
Plough Bridge Street, Northampton. (0604 230554). A plush Victorian hotel offering Wilson's real ale in the comfortable lounge. *Lunchtime* bar meals, restaurant *(closed Fri–Sun)* and carvery *(D and Sun L).*
Bull & Butcher Bridge Street, Northampton. Sturdy local pub dispensing Manns and Wilson's real ale and *lunchtime* bar snacks *(not Sun).* Accommodation.
King William IV Commercial Street, off Bridge Street, Northampton. A truly exceptional range of real ales in this pub, owned by CAMRA. *Lunchtime* bar meals.
Saddlers Arms Bridge Street, Northampton. 18thC listed building with a wood panelled bar, a cosy snug and a large lounge. Davenports real ale is there to enjoy, along with *lunchtime* bar meals *(not Sun).* Accommodation.
W & R Shipman The Drapery (northerly confirmation of Bridge Street), Northampton. Old and long established wine bar just off the Market Square, with many unique and interesting features. Wines, spirits and Sam Smith's real ale in half pints only. *Lunchtime* snacks. *Closed Sun.*

Gayton Junction

Continuing north west after Gayton Junction, the canal enters a relatively empty stretch of agricultural land, open fields falling away to the north and steep hills to the south through which the railway cuts its way parallel to the canal. At Banbury Lane Bridge there is an attractive group of buildings – once the Anchor pub and wharf. As it approaches Bugbrooke, the only village on this stretch, it begins to meander as the hills become more dominant. There are no locks, but a large number of old brick arched bridges provide some interest. The canal is accompanied by the A5 and M1, both in the distance, while the B4525 crosses at Bugbrooke.

Bugbrooke
Northants. EC Sat. PO, tel, stores, garage.
Although much rebuilding has taken place in the north, there are still fine 18thC houses to the south and a pretty Baptist church of 1808. The parish church is set by itself in parkland and is mainly 14thC incorporating a 12thC chapel. A well proportioned building of golden stone, it was sensitively restored in 1921. Look for the plaque in the belltower, which warns, in rhyme, against improperly dressed bellringers. One of the great pleasures of this manorial village is the well marked footpaths and bridleways.

Gayton
Northants. PO, tel, stores. Set on a hill to the west of the canal junction, the village seems to be composed of large, handsome stone houses, ranging in style from the 16thC to the 19thC; trees among the houses increase the rural grandeur. The large church with its ornamented tower maintains the unity of the village.

PUBS AND RESTAURANTS

Old Wharf Inn Cornhill Lane, Bugbrooke. (0604 832585). By bridge 36. A new pub serving Ind Coope (Burton) and Tetley's real ale, and bar meals *lunchtime & evenings.* À la carte restaurant (booking advisable), large garden and ample moorings.
Bakers Arms High Street, Bugbrooke. Garden.
Five Bells 14 Church Lane, Bugbrooke. Very fine old pub opposite the church serving *lunchtime* food (*not Sun*) and Manns real ale. The garden is shaded by willows and the tables are well spaced. Swings, a climbing frame and pet rabbits will amuse the children. The stocks in front of the pub recall less tolerant times.
Eykn Arms Gayton.
Queen Victoria Inn Gayton. (0604 858438). Restaurant, reductions for children.

(map labels)

N

B4525

34

35

36

P

Bugbrooke

38

40

41

Bugbrooke Downs

Lower farm

42

43 Banbury Lane bridge

44

45

Gayton

46

47

Gayton Junction

continued page 58

12½M 7L
Norton Jnc

Marsworth
37½M 25L

48

RSW

Northampton arm

BW Gayton yard

49

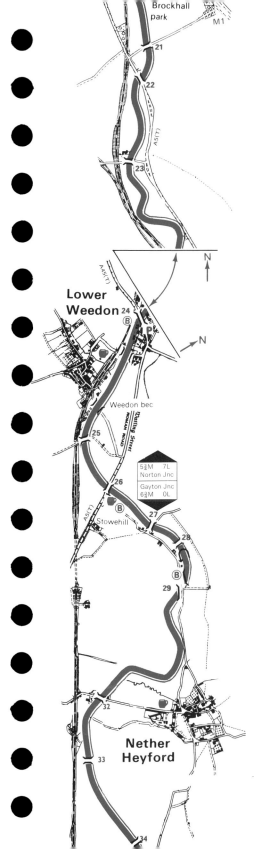

Weedon

The canal begins to meander sharply because of
the hills encroaching to the west; at the same
time the landscape becomes more dramatic as
the valley steepens on both sides of the canal.
Weedon is passed on a long embankment that
dominates the village, and then a quiet open
stretch follows which gives way to the
landscaped woods of Brockhall Park. The canal
avoids most villages, passing directly only
through Weedon, where there is much of
interest: aqueducts over a road and the River
Nene, an embankment, the old wharf (private)
and the elegant barracks. There are good
moorings above the church. Several transport
routes merge now to produce a strange picture
of three totally different means of transport
running parallel: the old Roman road, Watling
Street (A5), keeping as straight a course as
possible through the hills; the canal, its junior
by 1800 years, now looking more outdated than
the Roman road; the London–Midland railway
line and the 20thC motorway complete the set
of contrasts. Of all the thousands of travellers
passing through this area every hour, it must
surely be those who travel on the canal who
enjoy it the most as they compare the canal's
dignity and quiet progress to the noise and rush
of the roads and the railway.

Weedon
Northants. EC Thur. PO, tel, stores, garage.
The canal passes much of Weedon via an
embankment, and so the village seems to be set
in a valley. Sandwiched curiously between
railway and canal embankments is the Victorian
church with a Norman tower. Upper Weedon
runs west from the canal, a long L-shaped
street flanked by fine houses of all periods. To
the north are the remains of Weedon barracks,
begun in 1803; at one time very extensive,
including a Royal Pavilion to be used by George
III in case of invasion, the barracks were built
here because it was the furthest point from any
coast! Many buildings survive, although the
canal arm cut to serve the barracks was closed
when the railway was electrified.

Nether Heyford
Northants. PO, tel, stores. A small residential
village dwarfed by pylons on all sides. The
canal skirts the village. A large Roman building
was discovered to the east of the village in 1699.

BOATYARDS

Ⓑ **Concoform Marine** The Boatyard, High
Street, Weedon. (0327 40739). W P D
Pump-out, gas, narrowboat hire, overnight
mooring, long-term mooring, slipway. *Closed
Sun & Mon in summer, and winter weekends.*
Ⓑ **Waterways Services** High Horse Wharf,
Heyford Lane, Weedon. (0327 42300).
R S W D Pump-out, gas, long-term mooring,
boat building, boat sales, engine sales and
repairs, toilets.
Ⓑ **Stowe Hill Marine** Stowe Hill Wharf,
Weedon. (0327 41365). R S W D Gas,
overnight mooring, long-term mooring, winter
storage, slipway, groceries, chandlery, books
and maps, boat building, boat sales, engine
sales and repairs, toilets, gifts, BW licences.

BOAT TRIPS

Saucy Sue 47 seat boat available for party hire.
Details from Waterways Services, Weedon.
(0327 42300).

PUBS AND RESTAURANTS

🍺 **New Inn** Weedon, near bridge 24.
🍺✕ **Crossroads Hotel** Weedon. (0327 40354).
Real ale, children welcome. Restaurant.
🍺 **Narrowboat** Weedon. Charles Wells ales. A
popular venue.
🍺 **Globe** Weedon. Near bridge 24.

Norton Junction

Continuing north west the canal follows a valley whose course is closely shared with the M1, A5 and the main railway. Despite all these, there is a quiet, wooded stretch past Brockhall Park. Now the landscape opens out and the M1 and the railway take over. Whilton and Buckby Locks climb up to Norton Junction, accompanied by attractive terraces of red-brick cottages – in one of these, by lock 8, there is a canal craft shop. By lock 9 are the remains of Long Buckby Wharf. All the locks have side ponds, now disused, and ivy leafed toadflax grows in the lockwalls. The system for pumping water back up the flight has been restored, using an electric pump. Above Buckby Locks is Norton Junction, where the Leicester section branches off to the north (this is covered in the *Nicholson/Ordnance Survey Guide to the Waterways 2: Central*). The main line continues west towards Braunston.

Buckby Wharf
Northants. PO box, tel, stores.
Whilton
Northants. PO, tel, stores. 1 mile east of the canal at the end of a road that goes nowhere. Whilton is quiet and unchanged, especially at the east end. There are several fine stone houses, including a pretty Georgian rectory.
Brockhall
Northants. PO box. A large, lightly wooded landscaped park climbs gently east away from the canal. In the centre a manorial brown stone village and church are still intact and remote despite the M1 roaring through the west end of the park. The Hall is Tudor in part, with fine 18thC interiors; large trees screen it from the motorway.

BOATYARDS

Ⓑ **Whilton Marina** Whilton Locks. (0327 842577). Ⓢ Ⓦ Ⓟ Ⓓ Ⓔ Gas, overnight mooring, winter storage, slipway, dry dock, groceries, chandlery, books and maps, boat sales, engine sales and repairs, toilets, showers.
Ⓑ **Weltonfield Narrowboats** Weltonfield Farm, by bridge 2 on the Leicester section. (0327 842282). Ⓡ Ⓢ Ⓦ (*not Sat*) Ⓓ Ⓔ Pump-out, gas, narrowboat hire, overnight mooring, long-term mooring, dry dock, boat lift, chandlery, books and maps, boat building, boat sales, engine sales and repairs, toilets.

PUBS AND RESTAURANTS

🍺✕ **Stag's Head** Watford Gap. (0327 703621). A canalside pub and restaurant (*L & D*) serving Adnams real ale.
🍺 **New Inn** Canalside, at Buckby Top Lock. Cosy alcoved free house, serving Marstons and Wilson's real ale and *lunchtime* food. Next door is Ginger's Canal stores, for provisions and souvenirs.
🍺 **The Locks** By bridge 15. Large modern pub serving Charles Wells real ale and meals *lunchtime and evening*. Family room.

Map labels

Continued in
Waterways Guide Book 2

N

Watford Gap
service area

B4036

Leicester section

5

P

4

A5(T)

M1

3

Weltonfield farm

Ⓑ

2

4¼M   6L
Braunston Turn
Gayton Jnc
12½M   7L

Norton Junction
MAIN LINE 9 10
To Birmingham
Buckby locks 45' 0" 11-7
1

W W R

Watling Street

11 Watling
Street
bridge

Motorway M1

12

8

13

Long Buckby
wharf

9

10

14

Whilton locks 18' 0" 13 & 12

12

15

Ⓑ

Whilton

16

A5(T)

18

Brockhall park

19

M1

line

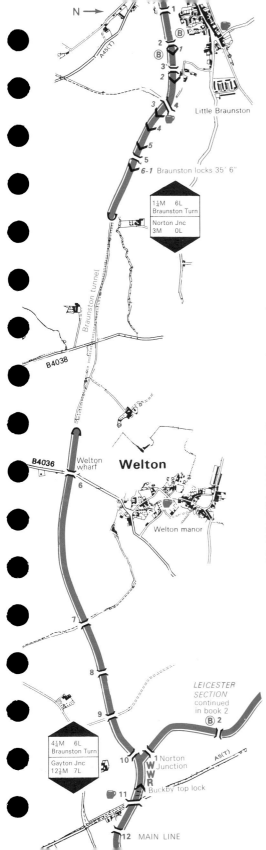

Welton

From Norton Junction to Braunston the canal turns westward through hills and wooded country. At first there are good views to the north and north east, with the embankment carrying the Leicester line branching away to the north. The canal then runs into a wooded cutting which leads to Braunston Tunnel. Before Welton Wharf, the feeder from the Daventry reservoir, built 1804, is reached; the Welton feeder enters by bridge 6 and the Drayton feeder enters the canal at the east end of Braunston Tunnel. A similar cutting follows the tunnel, and then the landscape opens out although the hills stay present on either side. The flight of six wide locks takes the canal down towards Braunston, a big canal centre. A canal shop by Braunston Bottom Lock stocks fresh fruit and veg, milk, bread, crafts and chandlery.

Braunston Tunnel Opened in 1796, to bore through the Northamptonshire heights, the tunnel is 2042yds long. Its construction was hindered by quicksands, and a mistake in direction has given it a slight 'S' bend.
Two boats of 7ft beam can pass in this tunnel, but wide beam boats must get permission from BW on (0788) 890666 to arrange a passage.
Welton
Northants. PO, tel, stores. The village climbs up the side of a steep, winding hill, which makes it compact and attractive, especially round the church.

BOATYARDS

ⓑ **Weltonfield Narrowboats** Weltonfield Farm, by bridge 2 on the Leicester Section. (0327 842282). Ⓡ Ⓢ Ⓦ *(not Sat)* Ⓓ Ⓔ Pump-out, gas, narrowboat hire, overnight mooring, dry dock, boat lift, chandlery, books and maps, boat building, boat sales and repairs, toilet.

PUBS

🍺 **Admiral Nelson** By lock 3, Little Braunston. Dating from 1730 and originally a farmhouse, this building still retains much of its traditional charm. Warmed by a log fire in winter, there is home cooked food *lunchtime and evening every day*. Breakfast, morning coffee and afternoon teas are also available during the summer. Good choice of real ale, and Northamptonshire skittles for amusement. Canalside garden.
🍺 **White Horse** High Street, Welton. A sloping pub with skittles downstairs. Wilson's real ale, meals *lunchtime and evening*, garden.
🍺 **New Inn** Canalside, at Buckby Top Lock. Cosy alcoved free house, serving Marstons and Wilson's real ale, and *lunchtime* food. Next door is Ginger's Canal Stores, for provisions and souvenirs.

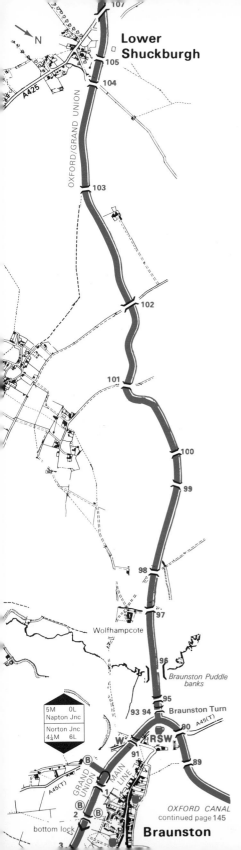

Braunston

Long rows of moored craft, including many narrowboats, flank the canal at Braunston and there is a fine selection of old buildings. A large marina with many beautifully restored buildings situated on an arm to the south meets most boating needs; note also the iron side-bridge and the 18thC dry dock. The arm in fact was part of the old route of the Oxford Canal before it was shortened by building a large embankment (Braunston Puddle Banks) across the Leam valley to Braunston Turn. The entrance to this arm was thus the original Braunston Junction. Leaving Braunston, the canal runs south west towards Napton Junction. This stretch of the Oxford Canal was used jointly by the Grand Junction Company, and as a result the Oxford charged excessive toll rates in an attempt to get even with their rival, whose more direct route to London had attracted most of the traffic. Flowing through open country with a background of hills to the south, the canal is curiously quiet and empty after the activity around Braunston. The land is agricultural, with few houses in sight. There are no locks, no villages and few bridges, making this a very pleasant rural stretch of canal, although the state of the towpath, nonexistent in many places, will be a great disappointment to walkers. The A425 crosses through Lower Shuckburgh.

Lower Shuckburgh
Warwicks. PO box. A tiny village along the main road. The church, built 1864, is attractive in a Victorian way, with great use of contrasting brickwork inside. The farm, west of bridge 104, sells eggs.
Braunston
Northants. PO, tel, stores. Set up on a hill to the north of the canal, so that the spire of Braunston church dominates the valley for miles around. The village is really a long main street, with houses of all periods that give the feeling of a spacious market town. The village is a very well known canal centre, and as such is no less significant today than when the Oxford and Grand Junction Canals were first connected here.

BOATYARDS

Ⓑ **Braunston Marina** The Wharf, Braunston. (0788 891373). Under the fine bridge dated 1834. Ⓡ Ⓢ Ⓦ Ⓓ Gas, pump-out, overnight mooring, long-term mooring, winter storage, dry dock, wet dock, chandlery, boat building, engineering – all services. Toilets.
Ⓑ **Braunston Boats** Bottom Lock, Braunston. (0788 891079). Ⓦ Ⓓ Pump-out, gas, narrowboat hire, long-term mooring.
Ⓑ **Union Canal Carriers** Canalside, Braunston. (0788 890784). Ⓢ Ⓓ Pump-out, gas, narrowboat hire, overnight mooring by arrangement, long-term mooring, books and maps, boat building, boat sales, engine sales and repairs. 24hr breakdown service (ring 812156 *evenings*).

PUBS AND RESTAURANTS

Ⓧ **Boatman** Braunston. (0788 891313). Once the Rose & Castle, now a comfortable and friendly modern hotel/restaurant/pub. Ushers and Wilson's real ale, bar meals (vast helpings) and candlelit dinners. Children's room, canalside garden with swings and overnight moorings for patrons.
Old Plough High Street, Braunston. Imposing 17thC pub of great character, serving Ind Coope (Burton) and Ansells real ale, and food *lunchtime and evening*. Family room, garden.
Wheatsheaf The Green, Braunston. A locals' pub with a striking red bar, dispensing Wilson's real ale and food *lunchtime and evening*. Garden.

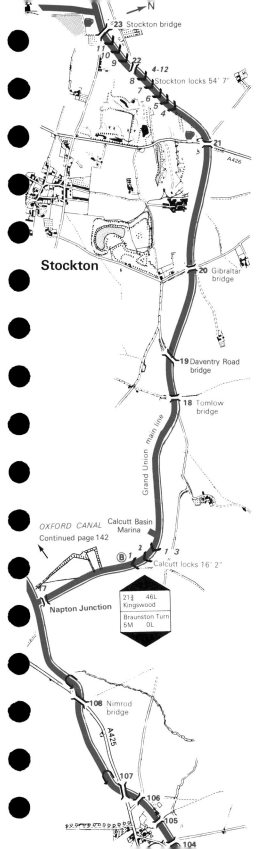

Napton Junction

Continuing west from Lower Shuckburgh, the canal flows through wide open fields to Napton Junction, where the Oxford Canal continues to the south and the Grand Union branches north towards Birmingham. The empty landscape rolls on, broken by Calcutt Locks, towards Stockton where there is a sudden change. Hills come close to the canal, broken by the quarries and thick woods along the south bank. The quarries produce Blue Lias, a local stone, and cement. This industrial belt contrasts with the open landscape that precedes and follows it. Stockton Locks continue the fall towards Warwick. The B4100 crosses before Stockton locks.

Stockton
Warwicks. EC Sat. PO, tel, stores, garage.
Stockton is a largely Victorian village in an area dominated by the smoking chimneys of the cement works to the west. The church is built of Blue Lias, quarried near Stockton Locks.

BOATYARDS
Ⓑ **Calcutt Boats** Calcutt Top Lock, Stockton, Rugby. (092 681 3757). Ⓡ Ⓢ Ⓦ Ⓓ Pump-out, gas, narrowboat hire, overnight mooring, long-term mooring, winter storage, slipway, crane, dry dock, groceries, chandlery, books and maps, boat building, boat sales, engine sales and repairs, breakdown service.

PUBS AND RESTAURANTS
🍺 **Blue Lias** Canalside, at bridge 23. Modernised with a bare brick and wood interior. Meals *lunchtime and evening*. Flowers real ale and garden.
🍺 **Boat** Canalside at bridge 21. A pleasant old pub with a collection of dolls and plates. Bass real ale, food *lunchtime and evening*, garden.
🍺✕ **Barley Mow** School Street, Stockton. (0926 812713). Modernised pub with a restaurant (*L & D*). Courage real ale.
🍺 **Crown** High Street, Stockton. A refurbished village pub, with settees in the lounge. Ansells, Hook Norton and Theakstons real ale.

Long Itchington

Continuing west, the canal leaves the industry around Stockton and runs through open arable land flanked on both sides by hills. The pleasant emptiness is broken by the locks that occur steadily through this section, continuing the fall to Warwick. Of interest are the top two locks at Bascote, which form a staircase. The A423 crosses at Long Itchington, a village with a large number of pubs, including two on the canal.

Long Itchington
Warwicks. PO, tel, stores, garage. A large housing estate flanks the busy A423; the village proper lies to the north west, and is very attractive. Apart from several pubs there are houses of the 17th and 18thC, and a largely 13thC church whose spire was blown down in a gale in 1762. There are impressive poplars around the village pond. St Wulfstan, who later became Archbishop of Worcester, was born here in 1012.

BOATYARDS
Ⓑ **Warwickshire Fly Boat Company** Shop Lock Cottage, Stockton. (092 681 2093). By the Kayes Arm. Ⓢ Ⓦ Ⓓ Pump-out, gas, skippered 12-berth narrowboats, overnight mooring, long-term mooring, winter storage, slipway, crane, dry dock, groceries, chandlery, books and maps, boat building, boat sales, engine sales and repairs, toilets, showers, laundry.

PUBS AND RESTAURANTS
Cuttle Canalside at bridge 25. One bar locals' pub, serving Bass and M & B real ale and *lunchtime* food. Garden.
Two Boats Inn Canalside at bridge 25. Unusual pub where the lounge resembles a log cabin. Flowers real ale and meals *lunchtime and evening*. Garden.
Green Man Long Itchington, past the church. A fine traditional country pub with a very low ceiling in the corridor. Davenports real ale, family room.
Harvesters Church Road, Long Itchington. (0926 812698). Popular pub and restaurant (*L & D*). Hook Norton and Ruddles real ale.
Jolly Fisherman Long Itchington. Large pub overlooking the village green and pond. Ansells real ale, wide range of food *lunchtime and evening*, garden. Interesting period records on the juke box. Queen Elizabeth I stayed in the black-and-white-timbered building opposite.

Royal
Leamington Spa

After Fosse Locks the canal continues west
through attractive and isolated country to
Radford Semele, where there is a fine wooded
cutting. Emerging, the canal joins the A425 and
then carves its private course straight through
Leamington. Midway through the town the
canal enters a deep cutting that hides it from
the adjacent main road and railway. The A425
accompanies the canal through Leamington.
There are good moorings and shops by
bridge 40.

Royal Leamington Spa
*Warwicks. EC Mon/Thur. PO, tel, stores, by
bridge 40, garage, station, cinema.* During the
19thC the population of Leamington increased
rapidly, due to the late 18th and 19thC fashion
for spas generally. As a result the town is
largely mid-Victorian, and a number of
Victorian churches and hotels dominate the
town, several designed by J. Cundall, a local
architect of some note who also built the brick
and stone town hall. The long rows of villas,
elegant houses in their own grounds spreading
out from the centre, all express the Victorian
love of exotic styles – Gothic, Classical,
Jacobean, Renaissance, French and Greek are
all mixed here with bold abandon. Since the
Victorian era, however, much industrialisation
has taken place.
Art Gallery & Museum
Avenue Road. British,
Dutch and Flemish paintings of the 16th and
17thC. Also a collection of modern art, pottery
and porcelain through the ages and a specialist
series of 18thC English drinking glasses.
Victorian costume and objects. *Open Mon–Sat
and Sun afternoons.*
All Saints' Church
Bath Street. Begun in 1843
to the design of J. C. Jackson, the church is of
Gothic style, not always correct in detail. The
north transept has a rose window patterned on
Rouen Cathedral; the west window is by
Kempe.
Jephson Gardens
Alongside Newbold Terrace,
north of bridge 40. Beautiful ornamental
gardens named after Dr Jephson (1798–1878),
the local practitioner who was largely
responsible for the spa's high medical
reputation.
Radford Semele
Warwicks. EC Thur. PO, tel, stores, garage. A
main road suburb of Leamington, Radford
Semele takes no notice of the canal that runs
below the village, alongside the River Leam
and the closed railway line to Rugby. Among
the bungalows are some fine large houses,
including Radford Hall, a reconstructed
Jacobean building. The Victorian church is set
curiously by itself, seemingly in the middle of a
field.
Offchurch
Warwicks. PO, tel, stores, garage. A scattered
residential village reflecting the proximity of
Leamington. It takes its name from Offa, the
Saxon King of Mercia, reputedly buried near
here. The church, with its tall grey stone tower,
contains some Norman work. To the west lies
Offchurch Bury, whose park runs almost to the
canal. Originally this was a 17thC house, but it
has since been entirely rebuilt. The façade is
now early 19thC Gothic.

PUBS
● **Emscote Tavern** Canalside at bridge 46.
● **Royal Exchange** Tachbrook Road,
Leamington Spa. 100yds north of bridge 41.
● **Queens Head** Canalside at bridge 40.
● **George** High Street, Leamington Spa. ¼
mile north of bridge 40.
● **Stags Head** Offchurch. Popular thatched
pub with garden, snacks.
● **White Lion Inn** Southam Road, Radford
Semele. Smart village pub, once a coaching inn,
built in 1622. Garden.

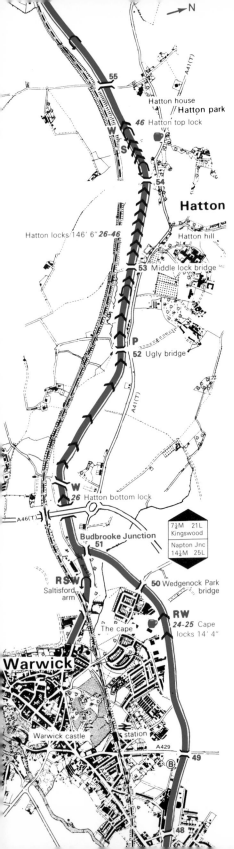

Warwick

After leaving Leamington the canal swings
north west under the A425 and then crosses the
railway and the River Avon on aqueducts.
Warwick is best approached from bridge 49, as
the canal skirts round the town to the north.
After climbing the two Cape Locks, it swings
south to Budbrooke Junction, where the old
Warwick and Napton Canal joined the
Warwick and Birmingham. Turn to the west,
pass under two large road bridges, and then the
first of the 21 locks of the Hatton flight appears,
with the distinctive paddle gear and gates
stretching up the hill ahead, a daunting sight
for even the toughest boatman. Consolation is
offered by the fine view of the spires of
Warwick as you climb the flight. On reaching
the top, the canal turns to the west, passing the
wooded hills that conceal Hatton village and
Hatton Park. The A41 follows the canal to the
north, the railway to the south; there is a station
at Hatton.

Hatton
Warwicks. This heavily wooded village is
scattered around the top of the Hatton Locks.
The church, set by itself, is partly
Perpendicular, partly Victorian. North of
Hatton, and seemingly inseparable from it, is
Haseley, also surrounded by woods; its small
church is pretty and relatively unrestored, still
retaining its box pews. Parts of it date from the
13thC.
Warwick
Warwicks. EC Thur. MD Wed, Sat. All services.
An historic town which still contains many
medieval buildings.
Church of St Mary's Of Norman origin, it
contains a large 12thC crypt. Unfortunately
much of the building was burnt down in 1694
and only the 14thC chancel and the Beauchamp
chapel were left. The most striking feature of
the rebuilt church is its pseudo-Gothic tower.
Warwick County Museum Market Place.
Mainly local natural history, geology,
archaeology and the history of Warwickshire.
Includes the Sheldon tapestry map of
Warwickshire which dates from 1588. *Closed
Fri and Sun morning.*
Doll Museum Oken's House, Castle Street.
Closed Sun morning.
Court House Jury Street. The present
building, which dates from 1725, was built on
the site of a 16thC civic building. The ball room
is decorated in Regency style.
Lord Leycester Hospital High Street. The
hospital was founded by the Earl of Leycester
in 1571 in the buildings of the guilds. It is now
a hospital for retired or disabled servicemen.
Warwick Castle Castle Hill. The exterior is a
famous example of a 14thC fortification. Inside
are pictures by Rubens, Van Dyck and
Velazquez. The castle overlooks pleasant
grounds laid out by Capability Brown. *Open
daily (except one week Feb for cleaning).*

BOATYARDS

Ⓑ **Kate Boats Warwick** The Boatyard, Nelson
Lane, Warwick. (0926 492968). Ⓢ Ⓦ Ⓓ
Pump-out, gas, narrowboat hire, overnight
mooring, long-term mooring, winter storage,
groceries, chandlery, books and maps, boat
building, boat sales, engine repairs, toilets.

PUBS AND RESTAURANTS

Waterman Hatton. Upmarket
food-orientated pub, serving meals *lunchtime
and evening every day.*
Dun Cow Saltisford. ¼ mile east of bridge
51.
Cape of Good Hope Cape Locks, Warwick.
Canalside. Food.
Lord Leycester Hotel Jury Street,
Warwick. (0926 491481). Restaurant.
Westgate Arms Bowling Green Street,
Warwick.
Gold Cup Castle Street, Warwick. Snacks
and meals.

Looking down Hatton Locks towards Warwick. Note the distinctive caps on the ground paddle mechanism. *Derek Pratt.*

Kingswood

The canal now enters the wooded cutting that
precedes Shrewley Tunnel. After the tunnel
the hills surround the canal on all sides as it
travels through steep wooded folds. A tall
embankment carries it to Rowington, and then
this gives way to wooded meadows that
continue to Kingswood and the junction with
the Stratford-on-Avon Canal. There are no
locks, a relief after the exhausting Hatton
flight; instead the curious tunnel and the
junction provide canal interest. The villages on
this stretch tend to be scattered and shapeless,
but there are plenty of facilities near at hand,
and Packwood House is worth a visit. The
railway continues to flank the canal to the west,
occasionally interrupting the peaceful
landscape: there is a station at Lapworth
(Kingswood). The B4439 follows the canal to
the east. The Stratford-on-Avon Canal is
covered on pages 171 to 180.

Kingswood
Warwicks. PO, tel, stores, garage, station. The
village is scattered over a wide area from the
Grand Union Canal to the Stratford-on-Avon
Canal. The centre is 1 mile to the west, around
the ambitious 15thC church, and the area
immediately around the canal is residential, its
character determined by the railway station.
The main feature of interest is the canal
junction with the Stratford-on-Avon Canal and
resulting basin. Note particularly the iron
turnover bridge by the lock at the junction,
which is split to allow the towing rope to pass
through without being unhitched from the
horse. Such bridges are a feature of the
Stratford-on-Avon Canal.

Wroxall
Warwicks. 1 1/2 miles north east of Rowington.
Little remains of the Benedictine abbey
founded in c1135; the 14thC nave and 17thC
tower of its church, and fragments of the
buildings around the cloisters survive. The
mansion, a gloomy Victorian pile set in wooded
parkland, replaced a Tudor house bought by
Sir Christopher Wren for his son in 1713.

Rowington
Warwicks. PO, tel, stores. A residential village
of Tudor-style houses, handsome but
suburban. Hidden among them are occasional
17thC and 18thC buildings, while near the
canal the 13thC church retains some
furnishings and a fine peal of bells.

Shrewley
Warwicks. PO, tel, stores, garage. Runs in an
untidy line along a minor road crossing the
north end of the tunnel. Most of the village is
recent ribbon development – useful as a source
of supplies.

Shrewley Tunnel 433yds long, the tunnel was
opened in 1799 with the completion of the
Warwick and Birmingham Canal. It is
remarkable for the very clearly defined path
over the top of the hill that a towing horse
would use while its boat was 'legged' through
the tunnel. This horsepath in fact goes through
its own miniature tunnel for 40yds and emerges
at the north west end above and beside the
canal tunnel.
*This tunnel allows two 7ft boats to pass: keep to the
right.*

PUBS

Navigation Canalside at Kingswood. A comfortable pub with a real fire. M & B and Bass real ale, and snacks at *lunchtime (Mon–Fri)*. Garden.

Tom o'the Wood Finwood Road, Rowington. Fine 16thC beamed canalside pub serving Flowers and Samuel Whitbread real ale, snacks and meals *lunchtime and evening*. Garden, family room. It is named after one of the three windmills which used to exist in the village.

The Case is Altered Just off Five Ways, Haseley. A 45-minute walk from bridge 62, but worth it. Pass Rowington Hall then north east past South Lawn, to find set amidst beautiful countryside this completely unspoilt pub, with an open fire in the bar. The real ale, Ansells and Flowers, is drawn straight from the barrel using barrel handpumps.

Cock Horse Old Warwick Road, Rowington. Flowers real ale in a basic pub with an open fire. Outside seating.

Durham Ox Shrewley. M & B real ale in a large modernised pub. Snacks, garden.

About to ascend Knowle Locks. Only one gate need be opened for narrow craft. *Derek Pratt*.

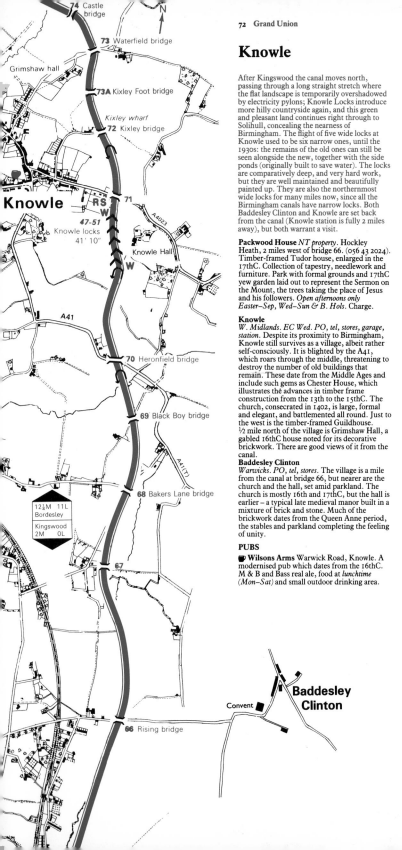

Knowle

After Kingswood the canal moves north, passing through a long straight stretch where the flat landscape is temporarily overshadowed by electricity pylons; Knowle Locks introduce more hilly countryside again, and this green and pleasant land continues right through to Solihull, concealing the nearness of Birmingham. The flight of five wide locks at Knowle used to be six narrow ones, until the 1930s: the remains of the old ones can still be seen alongside the new, together with the side ponds (originally built to save water). The locks are comparatively deep, and very hard work, but they are well maintained and beautifully painted up. They are also the northernmost wide locks for many miles now, since all the Birmingham canals have narrow locks. Both Baddesley Clinton and Knowle are set back from the canal (Knowle station is fully 2 miles away), but both warrant a visit.

Packwood House *NT property.* Hockley Heath, 2 miles west of bridge 66. (056 43 2024). Timber-framed Tudor house, enlarged in the 17thC. Collection of tapestry, needlework and furniture. Park with formal grounds and 17thC yew garden laid out to represent the Sermon on the Mount, the trees taking the place of Jesus and his followers. *Open afternoons only Easter–Sep, Wed–Sun & B. Hols.* Charge.

Knowle
W. Midlands. EC Wed. PO, tel, stores, garage, station. Despite its proximity to Birmingham, Knowle still survives as a village, albeit rather self-consciously. It is blighted by the A41, which roars through the middle, threatening to destroy the number of old buildings that remain. These date from the Middle Ages and include such gems as Chester House, which illustrates the advances in timber frame construction from the 13th to the 15thC. The church, consecrated in 1402, is large, formal and elegant, and battlemented all round. Just to the west is the timber-framed Guildhouse. ½ mile north of the village is Grimshaw Hall, a gabled 16thC house noted for its decorative brickwork. There are good views of it from the canal.

Baddesley Clinton
Warwicks. PO, tel, stores. The village is a mile from the canal at bridge 66, but nearer are the church and the hall, set amid parkland. The church is mostly 16th and 17thC, but the hall is earlier – a typical late medieval manor built in a mixture of brick and stone. Much of the brickwork dates from the Queen Anne period, the stables and parkland completing the feeling of unity.

PUBS

🍺 **Wilsons Arms** Warwick Road, Knowle. A modernised pub which dates from the 16thC. M & B and Bass real ale, food at *lunchtime (Mon–Sat)* and small outdoor drinking area.

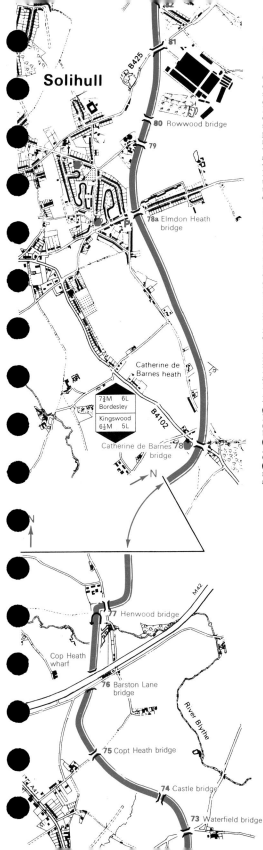

Solihull

Continuing north west through wooded country, the canal crosses the River Blyth on a small aqueduct and enters the long wooded cutting that carries it all the way to Olton Bridge. This attractive screen conceals the expanding suburban areas. The presence of suburbia means that supplies are available in plenty, but the embankment makes access rather difficult. Catherine de Barnes is the last village easily approached. There are no locks, and the bridges tend to be high above the water. Traffic noise and the presence of Birmingham city airport, 2 miles to the north, tend to disturb the illusion of peace created by the cutting. The B4102 and the B425 cross the canal, while the A41 bisects Solihull.

Solihull
W. Midlands. EC Wed. PO, tel, stores, garage, cinema, station. A modern commuter development, with fine public buildings. What used to be the town centre, dominated by the tall spire of the parish church, is now a shopping area. The church, built of red sandstone, is almost all 14thC. The interior contains work of all periods: 17thC pulpit and communion rail, 19thC stained glass.
Elmdon Heath
W. Midlands. EC Thur. PO, tel, stores, garage. Suburb of Solihull. The athletic navigator in need of supplies can climb up the embankment by bridge 79 and find all he needs – but the return journey can be difficult if laden.
Catherine de Barnes
W. Midlands. Tel, stores, garage. A higgledy-piggledy village in an area of isolation hospitals, far from the romanticism implied by the name. However, a convenient supply centre with easy access from the canal before the bulk of Birmingham.

PUBS

◗ **Greville Arms** Damson Lane, Elmdon Heath. M & B real ale and *lunchtime* food (*Mon–Fri*) in an unremarkable pub with a bowling green.
◗ **Red House** Hermitage Road, Solihull. M & B real ale and *lunchtime* food (*Mon–Fri*). Garden.
◗ **Boat Inn** Catherine de Barnes. A choice of real ale and Westons real cider in a pub which also has *lunchtime* food. Garden.

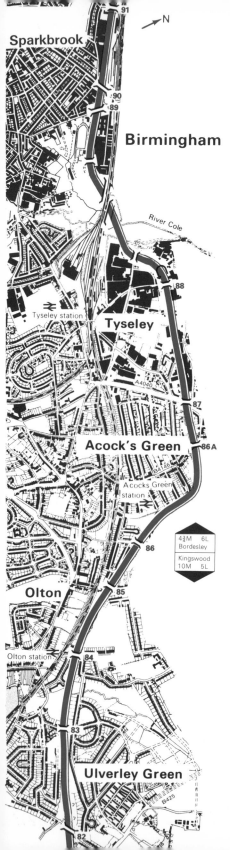

Tyseley

Continuing north west into Birmingham, the wooded cutting ends abruptly at Olton Bridge. From this point on, housing estates and disused wharves accompany the canal. The boatman should be wary of rubbish in the canal as he approaches the city. Factories flank the canal, and presently these give way to a short stretch of open wasteland to which Tyseley Goods Yard forms a suitable backdrop. Then the factories take over again, and access to and from the canal becomes increasingly difficult. Camp Hill Locks and all the succeeding locks are narrow: only boats of 7ft beam or less can pass. After passing through subterranean vaults formed by the criss-crossing of railway viaducts, Camp Hill Bottom Lock and Bordesley Junction are reached.

Tyseley Goods Yard ¼ mile south west of bridge 88. Here the Standard Gauge Steam Trust has a large depot for maintaining, storing and running private steam railway engines. *Open to visitors weekends Apr–Oct* (there is usually at least one locomotive in steam every *Sunday* and on two big open days every *summer*).

Birmingham

The Birmingham and Warwick Junction Canal runs north from Bordesley Junction to join the Birmingham & Fazeley and Tame Valley canals at Salford Junction. It was opened in 1844 to by-pass the heavily-locked stretches of the B & F at Ashted and Aston. The 2¾-mile cut runs through industrial surrounds. The five very tidy Garrison Locks carry the canal down to the Erdington level, where there is a stop lock (left open). The area of the junction itself is completely covered by elevated motorways, which join here in a huge multi-level interchange; this provides an awe-inspiring contrast between the old and the new forms of transport. Beyond Bordesley Junction the canal continues towards the Birmingham Canal Main Line, passing Digbeth Basin, and a very fine collection of old wharf buildings climbing the six Ashted Locks and 13 Farmer's Bridge Locks to join the Birmingham & Fazeley Canal at Farmer's Bridge Junction.

Navigational note 1
There is a risk of vandalism here; moor only at recognised sites in the city, such as Gas Street, Cambrian Wharf or boatyards (by arrangement).

Navigational note 2
Garrison and Camp Hill Top Locks are both kept locked. You will need your BW key to open them.

Deykins Ave bridge
Perry Barr bottom Lock
Witton Turnover bridge

| 5M | 13L |
| Rushall Jnc |
| Fazeley Junc |
| 11¾M | 14L |

Tame Valley Canal
see book 2

Birmingham & Fazeley canal

urban development

Salford Junction

Cuckoo bridge

64

Nechells shallow lock 6"

Aston

Birmingham and Warwick Junction Canal

Birmingham & Fazeley Canal

105

11 Aston locks 70'0"

108

107

| 1¾M | 11L |
| Salford Jnc |
| Farmer's Br |
| 1¾M | 13L |

Aston Junction

06

6 Ashted locks 35'1"   5 Garrison locks 34'5" **59-63**

Ashted tunnel

Digbeth branch

105

Barkers bridge

Snow Hill bridge

04

13 Farmers Bridge locks 81'0"

Digbeth Basin

103
102
101
100
99

Birmingham canal see book 2

Bordesley Junction

Cambrian wharf

New Street station

| 1¾M | 6L |
| Aston Jnc |
| Kingswood |
| 14¾M | 11L |

Bordesley

94

Camp Hill locks **52-57** 41' 8"

Farmers Bridge Junction

Gas Street basin **RSW**

93

92

91A

BW Sampson road depot

88

Worcester & Birmingham Canal See book 1

87

86

Grand Union canal
continued from previous page

91

Birmingham
*W. Midlands. EC Wed. MD Thur. PO, tel,
stores, garage, station, cinema, theatre, university.*
It is strange to think that the medieval town
that centred round the parish church and the
moated manor originally stood on the site of the
present Smithfield market. The Bull Ring, a
modern shopping centre, used to be the village
green. Industrial and commercial development
continued with such speed during the 19thC
that Birmingham began to be considered as the
trade centre of the Midlands. The town is
famous for such men as John Baskerville,
William Murdoch, Joseph Priestley, Matthew
Boulton and James Watt.
Farmer's Bridge A canalside development at
Cambrian Wharf in which four skyscrapers, a
new canal pub and a restored 18thC street
complete with gaslights are grouped beside a
canal basin.
Saltley Reservoir Joins the Saltley Canal below
Garrison Locks. A rare wildlife haven in the
city.
Tourist Information Centre 2 City Arcade,
Birmingham. (021-643 2514).

BOATYARDS

Ⓑ **Brummagem Boats** Sherborne Street
Wharf, Oozell's Street Loop west of Farmer's
Bridge Junction. (021-455 6163/0691).

Ⓡ Ⓢ Ⓦ Ⓓ Pump-out, gas, narrowboat hire, day
boat hire, overnight mooring, winter storage,
wet dock, books and maps, boat building, boat
sales, toilet.

BOAT TRIPS

Evening trips for private parties of up to 48
people. Details from 021-455 6163.

PUBS

🍺 **The Queens Head** Garrison Top Lock.
Banks's real ale and food in a pub engulfed by
factories and railways.
🍺 **Australian Bar** Bromsgrove Street, ½ mile
south east of Gas Street Basin. Lunchtime
snacks.
🍺 **White Lion** Horse Fair, ½ mile south east of
Gas Street Basin.
🍺 **St Paul's Tavern** Ludgate Hill, in the
jewellery quarter. Near Farmer's Bridge
Locks.
🍺 **Long Boat** Farmer's Bridge Top Lock,
Kingston Row, Birmingham 1. Canalside.
Food.
🍺 **Prince of Wales** Cambridge Street. Past the
Long Boat, turn left and the pub is on the right.
🍺 **Crown** Broad Street, 200yds west of Gas
Street Basin. Out back is the old Butler's
Brewery, used before he became part of
Mitchells and Butler in 1898.

Farmer's Bridge Locks, Birmingham. *Derek Pratt.*

KENNET & AVON

Maximum dimensions

Reading to Bath, junction with River Avon
Length: 72'   or   70'
Beam: at 7'   at 13' 9"
Headroom: 6' 6"
Bath to Hanham Lock
Length: 75'
Beam: 16'
Headroom: 8' 9"

Manager

(0380) 722859

Navigational note

Although the Kennet & Avon Canal is now open throughout its entire length, limited water supply to sections of the navigation is resulting in restricted use of some lock flights. Those particularly affected are Crofton and the Caen Hill flight at Devizes where it is likely that a booking system will be in operation. On some occasions restricted use of locks on the Widcombe flight at Bath and at Wootton Rivers may be enforced. For details contact The Manager.

Mileage

READING to
Aldermaston Wharf: 10
Tile Mill Lock: 8
Aldermaston Wharf: 10
Newbury Lock: 18½
Kintbury: 24½
Hungerford: 27½
Crofton Top Lock: 35
Pewsey Wharf: 41½
Devizes Top Lock: 53½
Bradford-on-Avon: 65½
Dundas Aqueduct: 70
Bath, junction with River Avon: 75¼
HANHAM Lock (start of tidal section): 86½
Bristol Docks: 93
AVONMOUTH entrance to Severn
Estuary: 100¾

Locks: 105

The Kennet & Avon Canal is one of the most splendid lengths of artificial waterway in Britain, a fitting memorial to the canal age as a whole. It is a broad canal, cutting across southern England from Reading to Bristol. Its generous dimensions and handsome architecture blend well with the rolling downs and open plains that it passes through, and are a good reminder of the instinctive feeling for scale that characterised most 18th and early 19thC civil engineering.

The canal was built in three sections. The first two were river navigations, the Kennet from Reading to Newbury, and the Avon from Bath to Bristol, both being canalised. Among early 18thC river navigations the Kennet was one of the most ambitious, owing to the steep fall of the river. Between Reading and Newbury 18 locks were necessary in as many miles, as the difference in level was 138ft. John Hore was the engineer for the Kennet Navigation, which was built between 1718 and 1723 and included 11 miles of new cut. Subsequently Hore was in charge of the Bristol Avon Navigation, carried out between 1725 and 1727. These river navigations were interesting in many ways, often because of the varied nature of the country they passed through. The steep-sided Avon Gorge meant that a fast-flowing river had to be brought under control. Elsewhere the engineering was unusual: for example the turf-sided locks on the Kennet, now being replaced with brick structures.

For the third stage, a canal from Newbury to Bath was authorised in 1794. Rennie was appointed engineer, and after a long struggle the canal was opened in 1810, completing a through route from London to Bristol. The canal is 57 miles long, and included 79 broad locks, a summit level at Savernake 474ft above sea level and one short tunnel, also at Savernake. Rennie was both engineer and architect, anticipating the role played by Brunel in the creation of the Great Western Railway; in some ways his architecture is the more noteworthy aspect of his work. The architectural quality of the whole canal is exceptional, from the straightforward stone bridges to the magnificent Neo-classical aqueducts at Avoncliffe and Limpley Stoke. Rennie's engineering, however, left something to be desired; the summit level was too short, and so pumping stations had to be installed at Crofton and Claverton to maintain the water level and feed the locks; in other places the canal bed was built over porous rock, and so leaked constantly, necessitating further regular pumping.

Nevertheless the canal as a whole was a striking achievement. West of Devizes the canal descends Caen Hill in a straight flight of 16 locks. In total 29 locks are navigated within two miles of Devizes. The many swing bridges were designed to run on ball bearings, one of the first applications of the principle. The bold entry of the canal into Bath, a sweeping descent round the south of the city, is a firm expression of the belief that major engineering works should contribute to the landscape, whether urban or rural, instead of imposing themselves upon it as often happens nowadays.

Later the Kennet & Avon Canal Company took over the two river navigations, thus gaining control of the whole through route. However traffic was never as heavy as the promoters had expected, and so the canal declined steadily throughout the 19thC. It suffered from early railway competition as the Great Western Railway duplicated its route, and was eventually bought by that railway company. Maintenance standards slipped, and this, combined with a rapidly declining traffic, meant that navigation was difficult in places by the end of the 1914–18 war. The last regular traffic left the canal in the 1930s, but still it remained open, and the last through passage was made in 1951 by n.b. *Queen*, with the West Country artist P. Ballance on board. Subsequently the canal was closed, and for a long time its future was in jeopardy. However, great interest in the canal had resulted in the formation of a Canal Association shortly after the 1939–45 war, to fight for restoration. In 1962 the Kennet & Avon Canal Trust was formed out of the Association, and practical steps towards restoration were under way. Using volunteers to raise funds from all sources, and with steadily increasing inputs from BW, the Trust have catalysed the reopening of the entire navigation as a through route from Reading to Bristol. This achievement was commemorated on 8th August 1990, with HM The Queen navigating through Lock 43, at the summit of the Caen Hill flight, which now bears her name. However, this must be seen as very much a beginning and not an end. Water supplies to the long pounds and the summit level have still to be secured by a combination of back pumping on several lock flights and the sealing of the remaining areas of porous canal bed. This will require substantial capital expenditure by BW and the Trust, while the waterway will always incur considerable ongoing running costs. Basic facilities such as water and pump-outs are still few and far between and will only appear in response to demand.

Natural history

This canal forms a unique series of freshwater habitats which vary along its length according to depth of water, aspect, height of the banks and the time of year.

The stonework of bridges, locks and aqueducts provides additional habitats for shallow-rooting plants. The three ferns, hartstongue, wall-rue and black spleenwort, are of special interest. Where the lock walls are capped with limestone, lime-loving plants such as fairy flax and quaking-grass are found.

For much of its length the canal is bordered on one or both banks by trees, including several species of willow, and bushes, predominantly hawthorn. A detailed survey in 1972 showed that plants along the towpath vary little, growing in profusion along its length. There are many kinds of grasses; other frequent species are white deadnettle, hogweed, meadow cranesbill, ground ivy and fine specimens of the ratstail plantain. Apart from the marsh marigold, the yellow iris and the greater pond sedge, there are few flowers at the water's edge and on

the canal bank until after mid-summer when purple loosestrife, the three-petalled arrowhead and flowering rush, together with the clusters of small creamy-white flowers of meadowsweet and pink-tinged angelica, contrast with the tall reed-grass and reedmace (often mistakenly called 'bulrush'). Rooting just in the water, the most common plant is the branched bur-reed. It has a profusion of leaves but the green, spherical, prickly-looking flowers are often sparse. Large tufts of tussock sedge, clumps of water dock and short stretches of common reed, having all the leaves on the tall stems turning to face away from the wind, can be found at the water's edge. Of all the marginal plants, perhaps the most handsome is the flowering rush, which is commonest near Bath. Deeper water supports such plants as yellow water-lily, water crowfoot and several pondweeds that root in the mud but hold their leaves and flowers above the water surface. A few plants are entirely submerged, the commonest being hornwort, which grows in long bushy, brittle tassels.

In the summer and autumn much of the water surface is covered with small floating plants that are moved by the wind. There are species of duckweed and a water fern, azolla, accidentally introduced from North America, which turns the canal red in autumn. The weed is only killed by a hard frost, when it sinks to the bottom and decays.

A botanist has recorded 190 different species of plants associated with the presence of the canal along a four-mile stretch near Melksham. The different plant zones make not only for numerical and visual diversity but also for the diversity of animals dependent on them. Mute swans, coots and moorhens nest and take refuge in the dense vegetation at the water's edge, water voles feed on it and use rushes and grass to line their nests. These are four of the canal's largest animals but they, like all wildlife, are part of the food chains that depend on the oxygen in the water and the light that filters into it. Amongst the tangle of submerged green plants and their roots lives a host of small animals, many visible only under a microscope. Some of the water snails, the large swan mussels (8in long), freshwater shrimps and flatworms feed on decaying plant matter, while others such as water beetles, water spiders, water boatmen, dragonfly nymphs and the strange water stick insects, represent the hunting predators, actively seeking out their quarry, which is often much larger than themselves. Many of these freshwater creatures are found only in the comparatively still water of canals and ponds, for they would be swept away in the streams and rivers. They provide food for water shrews, fish, frogs and, occasionally, grass snakes, which can be seen on sunny days curled up on the towpath or swimming across the canal in a few regular haunts.

The shy little grebe, with its trilling call, has spread from Wilton Water and now nests, on platforms made by willow branches dipping into the water, as far west as Devizes. Kingfishers have returned to the localities they frequented prior to the severe winters of the early 1960s and single herons are regular fishermen along the canal, though their diet also includes frogs, etc. The abundance of newly-emerged insects attracts many small birds to the canal. In spring, the bushes are sometimes full of chiffchaffs and willow warblers, eagerly feeding after their long flight from their winter quarters. Later, sedge and reed warblers arrive, take up their territories along the canal, sometimes singing all day and night, and build their nests in rushes and reeds. Swallows and house martins leave their nesting sites in the villages on summer evenings to feed over the canal, skimming low to pick up insects off the surface of the water. In late summer brambles growing on the banks are in flower, attracting butterflies to feed on them. The commonest are meadow brown, speckled wood, small tortoiseshell, peacock, brimstone and the quaintly named gatekeeper. In autumn, pied wagtails converge on the canal pounds near Devizes at dusk to roost in the rushes. By December they number around 300.

The canal offers a wealth of interest and for students of all ages it can serve as an open-air natural history laboratory. If restoration work succeeds in producing the healthy ecological balance that has emerged near Bath, then naturalists, anglers and all other users will benefit.

The Kennet & Avon Canal Trust, The Wharf, Couch Lane, Devizes, Wilts. Tel: (0380) 721279.

Now restored throughout, the Kennet & Avon Canal is proving a valuable recreational asset for all. *David Perrott.*

Reading

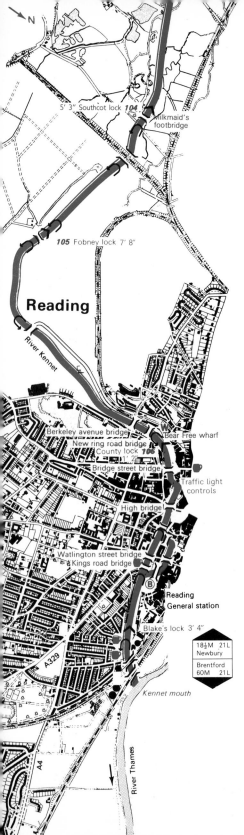

The River Kennet leaves the Thames east of
Reading. The mouth of the river is marked by
gasometers and the main railway, which runs
parallel to the south bank of the Thames. The
Kennet leads south west towards the centre of
Reading, passing Blake's Lock, the only lock
maintained by the Thames Conservancy that is
not actually on the Thames. A variety of
sensitive new developments complement the
river's passage through this section of the town.
The Kennet through Reading is narrow,
shallow and fast-flowing, being a river
navigation; also there are several sharp blind
bends in the town so great care in navigation is
needed. Keep a sharp lookout for other boats
and remember to allow for the flow of the river.
The river cuts across the middle of the town,
and so access to all facilities is easy. Rows of
riverside cottages and a surprising variety of
bridges decorate the Kennet in Reading, High
Bridge being the most central access point. The
Kennet passes over a weir with County Lock
adjoining. The weirs are a feature of river
navigation that should be treated with respect,
as the current they create can often affect the
course of a boat, especially when making a slow
approach to a lock. The river gradually leaves
the town, passing through Fobney Meadow to
Fobney Lock.

Navigational note
The Kennet & Avon Canal locks require
windlasses of an intermediate gauge – 1⅛in
instead of the normal 1in or 1¼in.

Reading
Berks. EC Mon, Wed. MD Mon. All services.
The town lies at the extremity of the Berkshire
Downs and the Chiltern Hills, where the
Thames becomes a major river. It is the
Victorian architecture that makes this town
interesting, as the university buildings are not
to everyone's taste. Canal walkers in Reading
will find there is no towing path in the centre of
town; however west of Reading the whole canal
is a public right of way. (Because of the risk of
vandalism only recognised mooring sites should
be used.)
Blakes Lock Museum Entry from the premises
of Reading Marina. (0734 55911, ex 2199).
Housed in a handsome pumping station built in
the 1870s, the museum depicts all aspects of
navigation in and around Reading. There are
also reconstructions of a printer's workshop, a
bakery and a barber's shop, and displays of
local industry. *Open 10.00–17.00 Wed–Fri,
14.00–17.00 Sat & Sun. Closed Mon & Tue.*
Free. Temporary mooring for visitors.
Abbey Ruins Fragmentary remains of this
12thC abbey built by Henry I lie on the edge of
Forbury Park. The 13thC gatehouse, altered by
Scott in 1869, still stands.
The Gaol Forbury Road. Designed by Scott
and Moffat in 1842–44 in the Scottish Baronial
style. Oscar Wilde wrote his *Ballad of Reading
Gaol* while imprisoned here.
Museum of English Rural Life White Knights
Park. A fascinating collection of relics of old
English agriculture, and a small display of
painted canal ware with a set of tools used for
making narrowboats. *Closed Sun, Mon,
B. Hols.*
Museum & Art Gallery Friar Street. Has an
exceptional natural history and local
archaeology collection. Also prehistoric
collection. *Open weekdays.*
Tourist Information Centre Central Library,
Belgrave Street, Reading. (0734 55911).

BOATYARDS

Ⓑ **Reading Marine Co.** Gasworks Road,
Reading. (0734 573917 or 509123). Ⓡ Ⓦ Ⓓ
Pump-out, gas, boat hire, slipway, boat and
engine repairs, mooring, chandlery, toilets.

BOAT TRIPS

Kennet Cruises 69ft trip boat *Lancing* for
charter and public trips. Also one narrowboat
for hire. For details ring (0734) 871115.

PUBS AND RESTAURANTS

Horn St Mary's Butts, Reading. North of Bridge Street Bridge. Courage real ale, food.

Fisherman's Cottage Kennetside, Reading. A pretty 18thC canalside pub, west of Blake's Lock, serving Fullers real ale. Food, beer garden. Children welcome.

Jolly Anglers Kennetside, Reading. East of Blake's Lock. There is a quaint façade to this pub which marks the last refreshment point before the Thames. Courage real ale, pub food, garden, children welcome.

Lynhurst Arms Queen's Road, Reading. South of Watlington Street Bridge. Whitbread real ale, food.

Wharf Wine Press King's Bridge, Reading. A modern canalside wine bar and restaurant.

Kennet Arms East of Berkeley Avenue Bridge. Courage real ale pub serving bar snacks.

County Lock and Weir, Reading. There are several blind corners downstream. *Derek Pratt.*

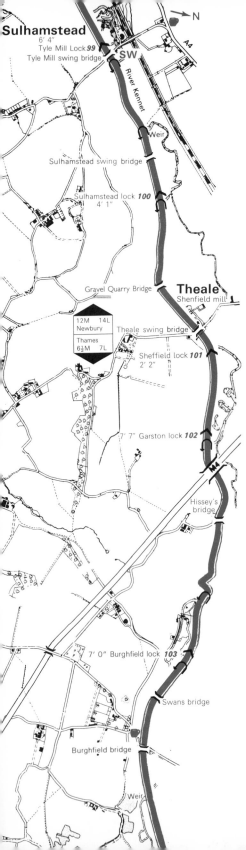

Theale

Continuing west, the canal passes Burghfield
Bridge, a handsome stone arch. The Kennet
winds through water-meadows, the straight
stretches marking the canal sections. The M4
motorway and the railway inevitably affect the
peace and quiet of this stretch, although the
country to the south of the Kennet improves
steadily as it progresses westwards. Berkshire is
well-known as orchard country. At Theale
there is the first of the swing bridges that occur
along the Kennet & Avon. Fortunately, since
the completion of the M4, this bridge has
reverted to carrying relatively infrequent road
vehicles, so the passage of a boat no longer
causes a major traffic hold-up. Opening the
bridge is hard work, but there are instructions
to help you. Make sure that you close the traffic
barriers first of all and open them behind you.
Theale village is ½ mile north of the bridge.
After Theale, the Kennet flows steadily
through wooded fields towards Sulhamstead
and reaches Tyle Mill after a pleasant tree-lined
straight cut. The nature reserves of Cumber
Lake to the north and Woolwich Green Lake to
the south can be reached by a short walk from
Sulhamstead Lock. Originally gravel pits
excavated since 1960, the lakes offer an
undisturbed habitat for all forms of wildlife.
The moorings at Tyle Mill and at Burghfield
are administered by BW. Ring (0380) 722859.

Navigational note
Garston Lock has a slight bend in it. Two 'long'
narrowboats can have difficulty fitting in
side-by-side.

Sulhamstead
Berks. A scattered village ¼ mile south east of
Tyle Mill, but with no real centre. There are
several large houses standing in their own
grounds; the most impressive is Folly Farm,
built by Lutyens in 1906 in a William and Mary
style. In 1912 Lutyens extended the house, this
time using a Tudor style. The mixture of the
two periods is most successful. The house is
private.
Theale
*Berks. EC Wed. PO, tel, stores, garage, bank,
chemist, station.* ¾ mile north west of Sheffield
Lock. Although largely a Reading suburb,
Theale has been given a new lease of life by the
opening of the bypass and the M4 motorway.
The main street is now quiet and relatively
traffic-free, and the Georgian terraces can be
enjoyed. The large church with its tall tower is
interesting. It was designed by E. W. Garbett
and built 1820–32 in a style based entirely on
Salisbury Cathedral. Theale station is half-way
between the town and Theale swing bridge.

PUBS AND RESTAURANTS

🍺 **Falcon** High Street, Theale. An 18thC pub
serving Courage real ale. Bar food and garden.
🍺 **Railway** Theale, next to the station. The
pub nearest the canal in this village. Halls real
ale, bar food and garden.
🍺 **Lamb at Theale** Courage real ale and bar
food.
🍺 **Red Lion** Theale. Halls real ale and bar
food.
🍺 **Crown Inn** Theale. Wethered's real ale.
Food (*not Sun*).
🍺✕ **Cunning Man** Burghfield Bridge. A family
pub with large canalside garden. Courage real
ale. Food, including burger bar and ice-cream
parlour. Restaurant serving vegetarian food.
✕ **Mulligan's Fish and Chips Restaurant and
Oyster Bar** Bath Road, Sulhamstead. Half mile
north of Tyle Mill.

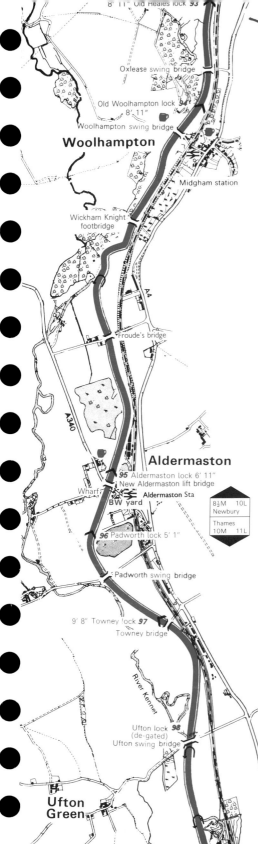

Woolhampton

Leaving Tyle Mill the canal continues south west, constantly joining and leaving the River Kennet. Swing bridges are very common, often carrying busy roads. The A4 runs parallel for many miles, but always keeps its distance; the Great Western Railway also runs parallel but much closer.

Woolhampton
Berks. PO, tel, stores, garage, station. A village on the A4 that owes its existence to the days of mail coaches on the old Bath road. There is a good mixture of buildings in the main street, several pubs and hotels. Up on the hill to the north of the village are the Victorian church, the Georgian buildings of Woolhampton Park and Douai Abbey and School, the latter a fine group of 19thC buildings with more recent additions.

Aldermaston
Berks. PO, tel, stores. Attractively placed at the foot of a wooded hill, 1½ miles to the south of Aldermaston Wharf (along a minor road), the village is particularly fine. Mellow brick houses of all periods face each other across the sloping main street, which has survived the inroads of traffic. At the top of the street is the pebble-dashed church, and Aldermaston Court, a private house containing magnificent 17thC woodwork.

Aldermaston Wharf
Berks. PO, tel, stores, station. A small canalside settlement bisected by the busy A340. The old swing bridge has been replaced with a hydraulic lift bridge, push-button operated with the aid of a BW key. It cost the local council £250,000 to build.

Ufton Green
Berks. A lush, peaceful hamlet built round a small triangular green. All that remains of the church is one flint wall, standing proudly in the middle of a field, and capped with a marvellous mantle of ivy.

BOATYARDS

BW Padworth Yard near Aldermaston Wharf. (0734 712277). Information about the canal, and moorings on the navigable sections. Special K & A-sized windlasses for sale.

PUBS AND RESTAURANTS

Row Barge Station Road, Woolhampton. This canalside pub offers both restaurant and bar food, catering for vegetarians (*no food Tue eve*). Real ales include John Smith's Yorkshire, Courage Directors and Best Bitter as well as Blackthorn Cider. Children welcomed, garden. Music *alternate Tuesdays*.

Falmouth Arms Woolhampton. Eldridge Pope real ale and bar food.

Angel Inn Woolhampton. An imposing ivy-clad building in the centre of the village. The pub serves a variety of guest beers along with Wethered real ale. There is a wide range of food, including vegetarian, served in both the bar and restaurant, including Sunday lunch. Garden, children welcome, B&B.

Butt Inn Aldermaston Wharf. Wethered and Flowers real ales. Food. Children welcome. Garden.

Hind's Head Aldermaston. An imposing building which faces up the main street. Formerly The Congreve Arms, until it changed hands following the devastation of a great fire. The Hind's Head once brewed its own beer, selling at 2d a pint; now Wethered real ale is served from the bar. The pub also offers good food in both bar and restaurant, catering for both vegetarians and curry fans. Garden, children welcome, B&B.

Text appearing on the map:

8' 11" Old Heales lock 93

Oxlease swing bridge

Old Woolhampton lock 94
8' 11"
Woolhampton swing bridge

Woolhampton

Midgham station

Wickham Knight footbridge

A4

Froude's bridge

A340

Aldermaston

95 Aldermaston lock 6' 11"
New Aldermaston lift bridge
Wharf
BW yard   Aldermaston Sta

8½M   10L
Newbury
Thames
10M   11L

96 Padworth lock 5' 1"

Padworth swing bridge

9' 8" Towney lock 97
Towney bridge

River Kennet

Ufton lock 98
(de-gated)
Ufton swing bridge

A4

Ufton Green

Thatcham

The canal leaves Midgham Park to the north and continues due west through water-meadows, the woods and hills receding to the south. At Colthrop a large industrial estate appears unexpectedly beside the canal; much of it consists of paper mills. Thatcham station is conveniently beside the canal; an hotel is nearby. The village itself is a mile to the north west. The canal now flows very straight through isolated water-meadows under a railway bridge to Bull's Lock. This section of canal probably best serves to illustrate the wide variety of works jointly undertaken by a Consortium made up of County and District Councils, Manpower Services job creation programmes, British Waterways and the Kennet & Avon Canal Trust, who have been at the forefront of fund raising for 25 years. For example, Old Heale's Lock to the east and Bull's Lock to the west have both been rebuilt with Consortium labour, while Widmead Lock has been re-constructed to a very high standard by outside contractors at a cost in excess of £250,000. The many swing bridges have either been totally rebuilt or, in some cases, replaced by a high level structure: Colthrop Bridge being privately funded. Old Monkey Marsh Lock, the last remaining example of a turf-sided lock, has been listed as an ancient monument by English Heritage. It is now restored with wooden piling to two feet above low water level, turf-lined banks sloping to the top of the lock, together with a timber framework to delineate the actual lock chamber when full. Elsewhere along the canal generous funding, be it from British Waterways, District and County Councils or the Kennet & Avon Canal Trust itself, has achieved a series of impressive examples of renewal and improvement which together have rescued this navigation, reopened in August 1990 by HM The Queen.

Thatcham
Berks. EC Wed. All services. The main square of this rapidly expanding village, now almost a suburb of Newbury, is all but dominated by sprawling housing development. Set back from the A4, it manages to retain some peace which carries over into the nearby cluster of older buildings grouped at the east end of the pretty Victorian church and churchyard.

PUBS AND RESTAURANTS
Crickets High Street, Thatcham. Ushers real ale and bar food.
White Hart High Street, Thatcham. A choice of real ales including Courage and John Smith. Good food served in both the bar and restaurant.
Old Chequers Thatcham. Comfortable old pub serving Halls real ale. English and continental cuisine in the restaurant. Bar food, garden, children welcome.
Kings Head Thatcham. Courage real ale. Bar food. B&B.

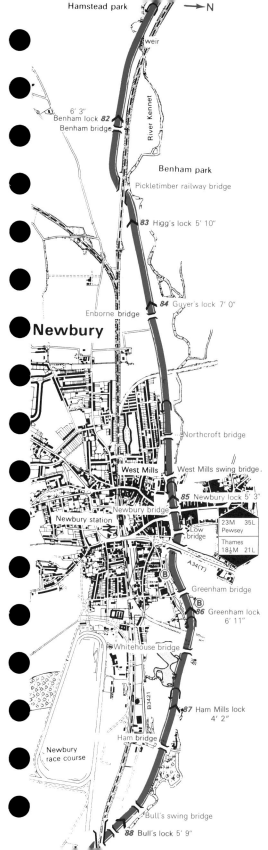

Newbury

The navigation enters Newbury under a handsome new road bridge. Just beside this bridge is Newbury Wharf, where there is a stone building used by the K & A Canal Trust as an information centre and museum, and old warehouses, which have been ingeniously converted into bus station buildings. This large wharf used to be the terminus of the Kennet Navigation from Reading, before the Kennet & Avon Canal Company extended it to link up with the Avon at Bath. West of the wharf the channel gets narrower and faster until it reaches a splendid stone balustraded bridge. Just beyond is Newbury Lock, where there is a mooring site. The river cuts right through the town, and the town makes the most of it. West of the lock is the delightful, quiet West Mills area, where rows of terraced houses face the navigation. West of Newbury, the navigation again passes through extensive water-meadows before the wooded hills of Hamstead Park close in from the south.

Navigational note
The lower sill at Bull's Lock is shallow. Take care through bottom gates.

Newbury
Berks. EC Wed. MD Tue. All services. Newbury developed in the Middle Ages as a cloth town of considerable wealth, its stature indicated by the size of the church. Although the cloth trade has long vanished, the town has managed to retain much of its period charm. It is a busy shopping centre, and the shop fronts in the main streets have buried many 17th and 18thC houses. Elsewhere in the town the 18thC is well in evidence, especially in the West Mills area. There are fine almshouses, and a pretty, ornamental stone bridge over the navigation. There are also signs of the agricultural importance of Newbury: the 19thC Italianate Corn Exchange, for example.
St Nicholas Church West Mills. Borders the canal on the south bank. A large Perpendicular church, built c1500 at the height of Newbury's prosperity as a wool town. Its 17thC pulpit is most unusual.
St Nicholas School Enborne Road. By Butterfield, 1859.
Borough Museum Wharf Road. Originally built in 1626 as a cloth-weaving workshop to give employment to the poor, this is one of the most interesting buildings in Newbury. Adjoining is the corn store, once on the edge of the Kennet Wharf. The museum collection illustrates the prehistoric and Saxon history of the region, as well as the medieval and modern. Also a natural history section with an excellent display of moths and butterflies. Models illustrate the Battle of Newbury. *Closed Sun. EC Wed.*
Round Barrow Cemetery Wash Common, near the site of the 1st Battle of Newbury in 1643. Memorial stones to the victims surmount the two smaller mounds.
Newbury Fair Northcroft Lane, Northcroft. Leave canal at Kennet Bridge. Annual Michaelmas fair held since 1215. *Thur following 11 Oct.*
1st Battle of Newbury, 20 Sep 1643 Site of Wash Farm off A343. 1¾ miles south of Guyer's Lock. The Royalists were defeated by the Parliamentarians in one of the bloodiest onslaughts of the Civil War. Guyer's and Higg's Locks are named after troop commanders in the battle.
2nd Battle of Newbury, 28 Oct 1644 Donnington Castle, Donnington. 1½ miles north of Newbury Lock off the A34. The Royalists were in possession of Donnington Castle when the Parliamentarians attacked. Charles' army withdrew to Oxford, but a week later they returned and relieved the castle. There is a reconstruction model of the battle in Newbury Museum.

BOATYARDS

Ⓑ **Newbury Boat Co.** Greenham Lock Cottage, Newbury. (0635 42884). Ⓡ Ⓢ Ⓦ Ⓓ Pump-out, gas, overnight mooring, long-term mooring, winter storage, books and maps, slipway, crane, boat and engine repairs, toilet.

BOAT TRIPS

Kennet Horse Boat Co. 32 West Mills, Newbury, Berks. (0635 44154). Horse-drawn and motor barge. Mostly private charter. *Easter–end Sep.* Public trips on the motor barge *Sun, B. Hols, some weekdays Aug*, and also on the horse-drawn boat – ring for details. Must book.

PUBS AND RESTAURANTS

There are many pubs and restaurants in Newbury, the following are simply those closest to the canal.

Old Waggon & Horses 100yds east of Newbury Bridge. This comfortable pub has a pleasant terrace overlooking the river. Courage real ale, food served in both the bar and restaurant.

Bricklayers Arms 200yds south of Newbury Bridge. Courage real ale. Bar food (*not Sun*).

Catherine Wheel Cheap Street, south of Westmills Bridge. A small, town pub offering Courage and John Smith real ales. Bar snacks. Garden, children welcome.

Berni Inn Riverside, Newbury, just east of Whitehouse Bridge.

Public trip boat at West Mills, Newbury, Kennet & Avon Canal. *Derek Pratt.*

Kintbury

Passing the beautiful woods of Hamstead Park, the canal reaches Hamstead, Copse, Drewett's and Kintbury Locks. Wooded rolling hills flank the canal to the south as it climbs up the locks towards Kintbury, making this a particularly attractive stretch. The canal enters the village beside the railway, and the Dundas Arms, which overlooks the lock. The centre of Kintbury is up on the hill to the south of the lock. Leaving the wharf, the canal follows the railway, passing the Victorian Gothic vicarage, and then continues westwards through pleasing open countryside.

Navigational note
Allow for river current when winding.

Kintbury
Berks. PO, tel, stores, station. A quiet village with attractive buildings by the canal, including a watermill and canalside pub. The church is originally 13thC, but was restored in 1859; the railway lends excitement, and noise, to the situation.
Hamstead Park A very fine park bordered by the canal. There used to be a castle here and several interesting buildings adjoin the church on the side of the hill. There is an old watermill by the lock. The hamlet of Hamstead Marshall lies to the south, 1½ miles from Hamstead Lock.

PUBS AND RESTAURANTS

🍺 **Blue Ball** Kintbury. 500yds south of Kintbury Bridge. John Smith and Courage real ales. Bar food *lunchtimes only*. Children welcome in garden. Pool table.
🍺 **Prince of Wales** Kintbury. 300yds south-east of Kintbury Bridge. Ushers beers. Bar food and *Sunday lunch*. Children welcome; garden with play area.
🍺✕ **Dundas Arms** Kintbury. The River Kennet and the canal flow on either side of this pub, which was named after the Lord Dundas who opened the canal in 1810. Real ales include Adnams, Morlands and Thomas Hardy County Bitter. The restaurant has an interesting French menu and a good wine cellar. Children welcome; garden; B&B.
🍺 **Crossways Inn** Inkpen Road, Kintbury. Bass, Marston and Arkells real ales. Bistro and bar snacks. Children welcome; garden; pool table.
🍺✕ **White Hart** Hamstead Marshall. 1 mile south of Hamstead Lock. Real ales include John Smith, Badger Best and Aldridge Pope. Restaurant (*closed all day Sunday*).
🍺✕ **Red House** Marsh Benham. ¼ mile north-east of Hamstead Lock. Pub in a thatched estate village near Benham Park. Brakspear, Flowers and Boddingtons real ales. Restaurant with a good menu. Garden; children welcome. B&B.

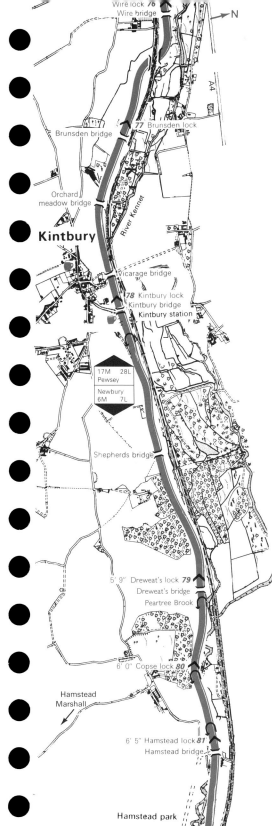

Map (left side)

→N

Hungerford

A4

Hungerford Church
swing bridge

A419

8'0"

74 Hungerford lock

Hungerford wharf

Hungerford bridge

A338

RSW

Hungerford station

Station Road
foot bridge

A338

14M	24L
Pewsey	
Newbury	
9M	11L

River Kennet

A4

75 Dunmill lock 5'8"

Dunmill lock bridge

Mill

Hungerford Park

76 Wire lock 6'10"

Wire lock bridge

Avington Manor

Brunsden lock *77*
4'11"

Brunsden lock bridge

Avington

Orchard Meadow bridge

Barton Court

Vicarage bridge

Kintbury

78 Kintbury lock 5'9"

Kintbury bridge

Kintbury station

River Kennet

Hungerford

The canal continues westwards through open
countryside. The railway and the River Kennet
are constantly present, the canal leaving the
river bed for the last time west of Kintbury.
Locks 77 and 76 carry the canal past Avington,
with its Norman church visible among the
trees. Pretty woods accompany the canal to the
south as it approaches Hungerford, while to the
north river and canal run side by side through
water-meadows, separated only by a narrow
ridge carrying the towpath. As the diminutive
River Kennet accompanies the canal past
Dunmill lock, the towpath turns over to the
south bank. From the bridge there is a good
view of Denford Mill. As the canal enters
Hungerford, the Kennet swings away to the
north, feeding the trout farm that lies between
canal and river. Gardens flank the canal as it
comes into the centre of the town. Access to
Hungerford is easy by the town bridge, which
leads directly to the handsome main street.

Hungerford
*Berks. EC Thur. PO, tel, stores, garage, bank,
station.* Hungerford is built along the A338,
which runs through the town southwards from
the junction with the A4. The pleasant 18th and
19thC buildings are set back from the road,
giving the spacious feeling of a traditional
market town. None of the buildings are
remarkable, but many are individually pretty.
Note the decorative ironwork of the house by
the canal bridge. The manor was given to John
of Gaunt in 1366, and any monarch passing
through the town is given a red rose, the
Lancastrian emblem, as a token rent.
Hocktide Ceremonies On the *second Tuesday
after Easter*, 99 commoners (those living within
the original borough who have the rights of the
common and the fishing) are called to the Town
Hall by the blowing of a horn. Two Tuttimen
are appointed, who have to visit the houses of
the commoners to collect a 'head penny' from
the men and a kiss from the women: they give
oranges in return. All new commoners are then
shod by having a nail driven into their shoes.
This ceremony dates from the medieval period.
Avington
Berks. The village is best approached along the
track that runs east from lock 76, although the
more adventurous can go directly across the
water-meadows, crossing the Kennet on a small
footbridge. The little church is still wholly
Norman, and contains a variety of original
work; the chancel arch, the corbels and the font
are particularly interesting.

BOAT TRIPS
Kennet & Avon Canal Trust *1½-hour* trips to
Dunmill Lock from Hungerford on *Rose of
Hungerford* on weekends and B. Hol afternoons.
Also longer *4-hour* trip to Froxfield. Available
for private charter, up to 50 persons. Details
from (0488) 683006.

PUBS AND RESTAURANTS
John of Gaunt Hungerford. 16thC pub
north of the canal, serving Morlands real ale.
Bar menu including take away food. Pleasant
dining room; garden; B&B; children welcome.
Three Swans Hotel Hungerford. Resort
hotel. South of canal.
The Bear Charnham St. North of canal.
Resort hotel with 13thC restaurant serving
cordon bleu menu.
The Plume Hungerford. South of canal.
Courage real ale. Bar food and garden.
The Sun Charnham St. North of canal.
Morlands real ale. Bar food; garden; children
welcome; pool table.
The Toad & Trout Charnham St. North
of canal. Bistro serving Bass and Ushers real
ale. Children welcome.
The Lamb Charnham St. North of canal.
Courage beers, bar food; garden with play area;
B&B.
Railway Tavern 200yds south of Station
Road footbridge. Ushers real ale. Bar food.
Garden; children welcome. Pool table, darts.

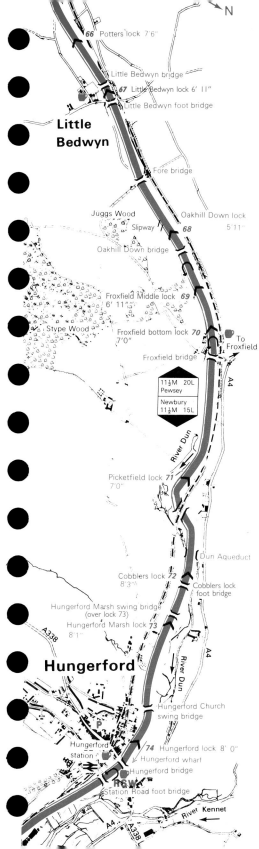

Froxfield

Leaving Hungerford, the canal passes the old wharf. An original stone warehouse survives, but much of the wharf area has now been built on. West of the wooded 19thC church, the canal suddenly enters an open landscape. Water-meadows and pastureland, rich in buttercups, flank the waterway, which seems to be more river than canal. The railway is in a cutting to the south, and the quiet browsing cattle give a feeling of 18thC rural serenity. The canal is then carried on to an embankment as the wooded hills reappear on both banks, crossing the River Dun on a small brick aqueduct. The railway crosses the canal west of the aqueduct, and now hugs the north bank for several miles. The roar of the frequent diesel expresses to and from the West Country is the only interruption in the natural peace and solitude of the canal. Froxfield lies to the north, flanking the A4; the best access is from the new bridge. This was rebuilt in 1972 during a road improvement scheme using traditional methods and materials, even to the correct colour of brick. Three locks carry the canal past Froxfield, and then the spire of Little Bedwyn Church comes into view, half-hidden by trees on the north bank. The village is cut in half by the canal and the railway. In the centre the lock continues the climb towards the summit.

Navigational note
Hungerford Marsh Swing Bridge is over Hungerford Marsh lock. Boats over 30ft long (approx.) will have to swing it clear before using the lock.

Little Bedwyn
Wilts. PO, tel. Divided by the canal, the village falls into two distinct parts. North is the estate village, pretty 19thC terraces of patterned brick running eastwards to the church, half-hidden among ancient yew trees. To the south is the older farming village, handsome 18thC buildings climbing the hill away from the canal. The PO is to be found within The Harrow public house.

Froxfield
Wilts. Tel. The village is ranged along the A4, which has obviously affected its development. The main feature of the village is the Somerset Hospital, a range of almshouses founded by the Duchess of Somerset in 1694, extended in 1775 and again in 1813. Facing onto the road, the hospital is built round a courtyard, which is entered by a Gothic-style gateway, part of the 1813 extension.

Littlecote 1½ miles north of Froxfield. (0488 84000). A Tudor building of the 16thC. Littlecote is the most important brick mansion in Wiltshire. The formal front overlooks the gardens that run down to the Kennet. Inside, the Great Hall, the armoury and Long Gallery are particularly notable. Now extensively developed as a tourist attraction, 'The Land of Littlecote' offers a full day's entertainment for the whole family. *Open 10.00–18.00 daily Apr–Sep.*

PUBS
● ✕ **Harrow** Little Bedwyn. In the southern half of the village, serving Pedigree, Hook Norton and guest beer. Bar food and restaurant (*no food Mon eve*). Vegetarians catered for. Garden; children welcome. Games night *Mon.*
● **Watermeadow Inn** Froxfield. On A4. ¼ mile north of the new bridge. Ushers ales, food, B&B, garden.

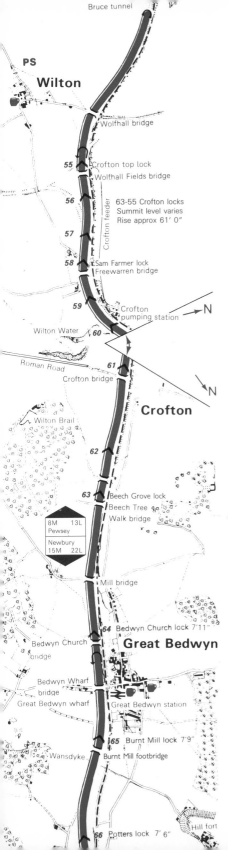

Crofton

Leaving Little Bedwyn, the canal continues
through a rolling landscape towards its summit,
closely accompanied by the railway. To the
north is a hill fort, overlooking ridges that
break up the farmland. The canal stays on the
south side of the valley, a shallow side-cutting
carrying it into Great Bedwyn. The village is
ranged over the hillside to the north of the
canal, newer houses spilling downwards
towards the canal and railway station. The
canal leaves the village past the church, and
enters a wooded stretch that takes it up towards
Crofton. The hills encroach more sharply as the
summit draws nearer. Crofton appears as the
canal starts a wide swing to the north west. The
engine house stands on a rise above the canal,
its blunt, iron-bound chimney making its
purpose unmistakable. To the south lies the
long expanse of Wilton Water, a natural lake
from which the Crofton pumps draw their
supplies. After Crofton the country opens out
for a while as the flight of locks continue the
final climb to the summit. Then, as the land
rises steeply on both banks, it prepares itself for
the short Bruce Tunnel. A wooded cutting
leads towards the tunnel, taking the canal
through the fringes of the Old Savernake
Forest. To the north are the extensive
parklands of Tottenham House, and Savernake
Forest itself. The towpath climbs over the top
of the tunnel.

Wilton
Wilts. Tel. A compact village at the southern
end of Wilton Water, with a pretty duck pond
in the centre.
Crofton
Wilts. The scattered village is dominated by the
brick pumping house with its separate
chimney. It houses two 19thC steam engines,
one built in 1812 by Boulton and Watt, the
oldest working beam engine in the world, the
other in 1845 by Harveys of Hayle, Cornwall.
Both have been restored to working order, and
are steamed on several weekends in the year.
The pumping house and the engines are open
for viewing *every summer Sun*. For details of
'steaming' weekends, ring (0672) 63498.
Wilton Windmill 1 mile south of the canal,
along footpath at lock 60.
Great Bedwyn
Wilts. PO, tel, stores, garage, station. The main
street climbs gently away from the canal and
the railway. It is wide, with generous grass
verges; attractive houses of all periods line the
street. At the top is the pub. The large church,
with its well-balanced crossing tower, is mostly
12th and 13thC; inside are some interesting
monuments. The road running westwards to
the church passes the Bedwyn Stone Museum,
an amazing establishment.
Bedwyn Stone Museum A collection of stone
work of all types, showing the work of seven
generations of stone masons. There are statues,
tombstones, casts, even the fossilised footprint
of a dinosaur. *Open daily.*

BOAT TRIPS
Kennet & Avon Canal Trust n.b. *Jubilee*. 44
passenger trip boat operating from Crofton
Pumping Station to Great Bedwyn. Ring (0488)
82760 for details.

PUBS
🍺 **Swan Inn** Wilton. ½ mile south of lock 61,
on road running beside Wilton Water, serving
Whitbread ales.
🍺 **Three Tuns** Great Bedwyn. Bar food and
Whitbread ales.
🍺 **Cross Keys** Great Bedwyn. Offers food,
B&B and real ale from the Wiltshire Brewery.

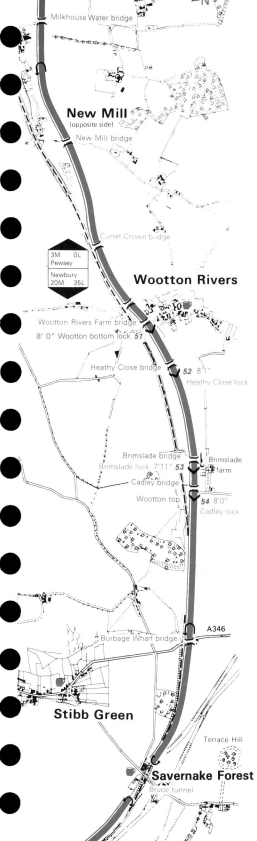

Wootton Rivers

The canal emerges from the western portal of
Bruce Tunnel into a deep cutting. Woods line
both banks, hiding the railway, which is now
on the south bank having crossed over the
tunnel. The towpath passes under the railway
and descends steeply to the canal. The cutting
continues westwards to the high brick bridge
that carries the A346, and then the landscape
opens out: the rolling hills still follow the canal,
but recede slightly. Immediately after the
bridge is Burbage Wharf; several of the original
brick canal buildings still stand, attractively
converted to domestic use, and a restored
wooden wharf crane hangs beside the water.
Pasture and arable land flank the canal on its
course to the first of the four Wootton Locks.
This flight ends the short summit, and starts
the long descent towards Bath. By the first lock
there is a pretty cottage and garden, while the
second is in the middle of Brimslade Farm,
whose attractive tile-hung buildings date from
the 17thC. The last two locks take the canal to
Wootton Rivers; the houses stretch northwards
away from the canal, which is overlooked by
the church. As the country undulates, the canal
maintains its level, moving alternately from low
cutting to low embankment. Woods break up
the hills, giving fine views to the south. New
Mill is a small hamlet south of the canal where
there is still evidence of a small wharf. At the
end of this section the railway moves away to
the south to pass through Pewsey, leaving the
canal in peace at last.

New Mill
Wilts. Tel. A pretty hamlet scattered below the
canal. The mill that gave it its name is now a
house, with a fine garden.

Wootton Rivers
Wilts. Tel. A particularly pretty village
composed almost entirely of timber-framed
thatched houses, climbing gently up the hill
away from the canal. Even the walls by the
canal are thatched. All the houses are attractive,
including the large manor by the canal. The
little church with its wooden bell turret is set
among trees; it was extensively rebuilt in the
19thC. The church has a most unusual clock,
its face having letters in place of numbers.
Inside, its mechanism is equally eccentric,
being assembled from a bizarre collection of
cast-off agricultural implements.

Bruce Tunnel
Named in honour of Thomas
Bruce, Earl of Ailesbury. 502yds with chains on
the walls, with which to pull boats through.

Savernake Forest
Wilts. A small village grew up in the 19thC
around the hotel and the two railway stations,
to cater for an early holiday trade. Today the
stations have vanished, but the hotel, a fine
example of Victorian railway architecture, still
thrives on the hill above Bruce Tunnel. Timber
from the forest was used to restore the
handsome crane at Burbage Wharf.

BOAT TRIPS
Sarah Davey Office: (0703) 266200. Boat:
(0672) 811075.

PUBS AND RESTAURANTS
Royal Oak Wootton Rivers. A very
attractive pub in the main street, serving
Wadworth's real ale and the local Stitchcombe
wines. Bar food. B&B.
Savernake Forest Hotel Savernake
Forest. Mole's, Marstons and other guest real
ales. Restaurant, buttery and bar food. The
hotel has fishing rights on the canal.
Three Horseshoes Stibb Green. ¾ mile
south west of the above hotel. Wadworth's real
ale and food.

Pewsey

This 15-mile-long pound continues westwards towards Devizes through rolling hills. To the north, hills descend to the water's edge, and to the south the land opens out, giving fine views over the Vale of Pewsey. The canal crosses this landscape with a mixture of cutting and embankment, passing through woods from time to time. The railway lies to the south, and is now out of sight. The canal turns towards Pewsey, but still passes well outside the town, which fills the Vale to the south. Pewsey Wharf is ½ mile from the town centre, and so has developed as a separate canalside settlement, with a pub, cottages, and warehouse buildings. The canal leaves Pewsey in a low wooded cutting, swinging back to its usual westerly course. The woods continue past Stowell Park, whose landscaped grounds extend to the north. The house, built early in the 19thC, can be seen clearly from the canal. A miniature suspension bridge, the only surviving example of its kind, carries a private footpath from the park across the canal. A straight stretch leads to the first cottages of Wilcot; the rest of the village is to the south. The steep bare mound of Picked Hill dominates the canal as it passes Wilcot and enters the wooded Wide Water. In 1793 this stretch was owned by Lady Susannah Wroughton who objected to the canal cutting through her land. She was appeased by £500, the building of an elaborately decorated bridge (dated 1808 and attributed to Rennie) and the landscaping of the marshy area around it. This area is now a haven for wildlife. The canal skirts Picked Hill, giving a good view of the field terracing that is a relic of Celtic and medieval cultivation. The equally dominant Woodborough Hill now fills the north bank, while to the south open country leads to the village of Woodborough.

Wilcot
Wilts. Tel. A pretty village scattered round the green; there are several thatched houses, and a converted village school with a prominent bell. Parts of the church date from the 12thC, but it was mostly rebuilt in 1876 after a fire.
Pewsey
Wilts. EC Wed. PO, tel, stores, garage, bank, station (but very few trains stop). The little town is set compactly in the Vale of Pewsey. At its centre, overlooking the young River Avon is a fine statue of King Alfred, erected in 1911. From this all the roads radiate. There is the usual mixture of buildings; but while many are attractive, none is noteworthy. The church is mostly 13th and 15thC, but parts of the nave are late Norman: the altar rails were made from timbers of the *San Josef* captured by Nelson in 1797.
Pewsey White Horse 1½ miles south of the town. Dating from the 18thC, the horse was re-cut in 1937, by members of the Pewsey Fire Brigade, to celebrate the coronation of George VI. It is 66ft long.

BOAT TRIPS

Ⓑ *Tom Pudding* A 12-seater operated from Pewsey Wharf by the K & A Canal Trust. Ring (0380) 71279 for details.

PUBS

🍺 **Golden Swan** Wilcot. A one-handed ghost is said to haunt this pub, which stands beyond the green at the far end of the village. Wadworth's real ale, food, B&B.
🍺 **French Horn** Pewsey. Canalside, on the A345 by the wharf. A friendly pub serving Wadworth's real ale. Interesting menu, including vegetarian dishes. Garden, children welcome.
🍺 **Royal Oak** Pewsey. In the town centre. Wadworth's real ale and food (including vegetarian and vegan dishes).
🍺 **Phoenix** Pewsey. In the town centre. Food, B&B.
🍺 **Coopers Arms** Pewsey. Websters, Ushers and Ruddles real ales. Bar billiards is played here.
🍺 **Greyhound** Pewsey. Lively, welcoming Courage pub. Food. B&B.
🍺 **The Crown** Pewsey. Ushers, Whitbread and Wadworth's real ale. Bar snacks (*not Sun*).

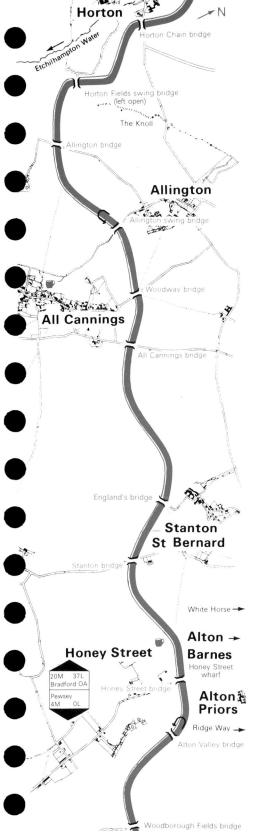

Honey Street

Leaving Woodborough Hill behind, the long
pound continues westwards towards Devizes.
To the south the land falls away, while to the
north the tower of Alton Priors Church comes
into view. Beyond the village can be seen the
white horse, cut into the hill in 1812, a copy of
the one at Cherhill. The canal passes Honey
Street Wharf, where there is a canalside pub.
The canal now begins to meander through the
open countryside, roughly following a contour
line to maintain its level. Its progress is marked
by a succession of shallow cuttings and low
embankments. Several villages are near the
canal, all visible and easily accessible from the
many bridges, but none actually approach the
waterside. Their interests lie rather in the rich
agricultural lands that flank the canal. Leaving
Allington the canal curves round the Knoll, a
major feature of the landscape to the north.

Allington
Wilts. Tel. A small agricultural village scattered
round a Victorian church. East of the village is
All Cannings Cross, a large Iron Age
settlement.
All Cannings
Wilts. PO, tel, stores. An attractive village built
round a square, with houses of all periods. To
the south there is a large green, overlooked by
the church with its tall central tower. Although
the church is mostly 14thC, its most interesting
feature is the ornamental High Victorian
chancel, added in 1867.
Stanton St Bernard
Wilts. PO, tel, stores. Built in a curve of the
hills, the village has one main street, flanked by
pretty gardens. The best building is the 19thC
manor, which incorporates relics of an earlier
house. The battlemented church is Victorian.
Honey Street
Wilts. A traditional canalside village
incorporating some new development.
Alton Barnes
Wilts. Tel, stores, garage. The village runs along
the road northwards from Honey Street. The
best part is clustered round the church. Fine
farm buildings and an 18thC rectory are
half-hidden among the trees. The church is
essentially Anglo-Saxon, but has been heavily
restored; everything is in miniature, the tiny
gallery, pulpit, and pews emphasising the
compact scale of the whole building.
Alton Priors
Wilts. Tel. Approached along a footpath from
Alton Barnes churchyard, the isolated church is
the best feature of this scattered hamlet. This
pretty Perpendicular building with its wide,
well-lit nave contains a most interesting
monument: a big box tomb is surmounted with
a large engraved Dutch brass plate, dated 1590,
rich in extravagant symbolism. To the east of
the village the Ridgeway runs southwards
towards Salisbury; this Bronze Age drover's
road swings north east along the downs for 50
miles, finally joining the Thames valley at
Streatley. The path is not clearly defined here,
but 5 miles to the north, by the A4 crossing, it
becomes a wide unmistakable track, which
continues unbroken to the Thames.

PUBS

🍺 **Kings Arms** All Cannings. ¼ mile south of
Woodway Bridge. A very comfortable and
charming village pub, serving Wadworth's real
ale, and food *lunchtime and evenings*. Garden.
🍺 **Barge Inn** Honey Street. An imposing
canalside pub which was once a slaughterhouse,
a bakehouse, a brewery and a grocers. Courage
real ale, food *lunchtime and evenings (not Tue)*.
Ⓦ®. Rowing boat hire.

Sir Hugh Stockwell
lock
A361
44
BW centre
Devizes yard bridge
N

45 8'2" The Cave lock
46 8' 2" A P Herbert lock
A342
Prison bridge
47 8' 2" Manifold lock 8'2"
48 8'
Dunkirk
49 Maton lock 8' 2"
12M   37L
Bradford OA
Devizes Town bridge
Pewsey
50 Kennet lock 8' 2"
12M   OL
Devizes wharf
Devizes Castle
R
Devizes
Cemetery Road bridge
Park Road bridge
Roundway
London Road bridge
A361
Brickham bridge
Coates bridge
Clay farm
Laywood bridge
A361
Bishops
Cannings
Horton bridge
Bishops Cannings
swing bridge
Horton
Horton Chain
bridge

Devizes

Leaving Horton, the long pound continues westwards towards Devizes. Following the contour of the land, it swings in a wide arc towards Bishops Cannings. The rolling hills climb fairly steeply to the north, while the pastureland falls away to the south. After a low cutting, the tower of Bishops Cannings church comes into view, half-hidden by trees: a footpath from the swing bridge is the quickest way to the village. At Horton Bridge, where there is a convenient canalside pub, the canal enters another short cutting. The landscape opens out again, to allow a view of the handsome Victorian barracks outside Devizes. The canal passes the barrack buildings, which are partly hidden by trees, and then enters the long wooded cutting that carries it through Devizes. Houses appear, their gardens overlooking the cutting, and the traffic noise on the busy A361 marks the return to civilisation. Several very elegant large stone bridges (many listed as ancient monuments) span the cutting. Access to the town is easy at all the bridges. At Cemetery Road Bridge the towpath turns over to the north bank for a short stretch, returning to the south at the next bridge. Between these two bridges is Devizes Wharf, where the K & A Canal Trust have a museum and shop in a converted warehouse. Beyond the wharf, the long pound ends at the first lock of the famous Caen Hill flight, preceded by the generous stone bridge with its separate towpath archway. Locks now come at regular intervals, preparing the canal for the dramatic descent down Caen Hill.

Devizes
Wilts. EC Wed. MD Thur, Sat. PO, tel, stores, garage, bank, cinema. Despite the effects of traffic, Devizes still retains the atmosphere of an old country market town. Originally the town grew up around the castle, but as this lost its significance the large marketplace became the focal point. Handsome 18thC buildings now command the square, while the market cross records the sad story of Ruth Pierce. Elsewhere there are timbered buildings from the 16thC. The two fine churches, one built for the castle and the other for the parish, tend to dominate the town, and hold it well together. Only the mount and related earthworks survive of the original Norman castle; the present building is an extravagant Victorian folly. The town's own brewery, Wadworth's in Northgate Street, fills the air with the aroma of malt and hops.
St John's Church Built by Bishop Roger of Sarum, who was also responsible for the castle, this 12thC church with its massive crossing tower is still largely original. There are 15thC and 19thC additions, but they do not affect the Norman feeling of the whole.
St Mary's Church Dating from the same time as St John's, this church was more extensively rebuilt in the 15thC; plenty of Norman work still survives, however.
Wiltshire Archaeological and Natural History Museum Long Street. (0380 727369). The collections include finds from the Neolithic, Bronze and Iron Age sites in Wiltshire, the most famous being the Stourhead collection of relics excavated from burial mounds on Salisbury Plain. There are also Roman exhibits. Open Mon–Sat.
The Wharf Devizes. (0380 721279). Kennet & Avon Canal Trust Central Offices, canal shop, theatre and exhibition.
Canal Forge Lower Wharf, Northgate Street, Devizes. (0308 721759). A working forge and exhibition. Open Mon–Fri and Sat morning.
Tourist Information Centre Market Place, Devizes. (0308 729408). Open Easter–Sep.
Battle of Roundway Down, 13 July 1643 Devizes was held by a Royalist army that had already tested the Roundhead forces, who were tired, dispirited and short of supplies after their defeat at Lansdown Hill, near Bath. A Royalist cavalry charge took the Roundheads by surprise, and most of the confused and battle-weary Roundheads were killed or captured. The battlefield, off the A361 north east of Devizes, is still largely intact, and can easily be explored on foot. Mock battles are re-enacted here.

Devizes to Westminster Canoe Race The toughest and longest canoe race in the world takes place *every Easter*. The course, from Park Road Bridge, Devizes, to County Hall Steps, Westminster, includes 54 miles of the Kennet & Avon, and 71 miles of the Thames, the last 17 of which are tidal. There are 77 locks. The race grew from a background of local rivalry in Pewsey and Devizes to find the quickest way to the sea by boat; in 1948 the target was 100 hours. In 1950 the first regular annual race over the course took place; three years later the junior class was introduced. The number of entries increases every year, and is now well above 300. Anyone may enter for the race, but they would have difficulty in beating the highly-trained army and navy teams from Britain and Europe.

Bishops Cannings
Wilts. PO, tel, stores. Apart from one or two old cottages, the main feature of this village is the very grand church. This cruciform building, with its central tower and spire, is almost entirely Early English in style; its magnificence is unexpected in so small a village. Traces of the earlier Norman building survive. Inside is a 17thC penitential seat, surmounted by a giant hand painted on the wall with suitable inscriptions about sin and death.

BOAT TRIPS

Kenavon Venture Operates from The Bridge Inn, Horton. Telephone (0380) 86273 for details.

PUBS
There are many good pubs and inns in Devizes. The following are simply those closest to the canal.

🍺 **Black Horse** By lock 48, on the Caen Hill flight. Well placed to refresh those exhausted by the locks. Wadworth's real ale, and food *lunchtime and evening (after 19.30 and not Sun evening)*. Canalside garden.

🍺 **Artichoke** Bath Road, 100yds north-west of Devizes Town Bridge. Known locally as the Vegetable, it is not far from Wadworth's Brewery, and serves their beers, delivered by a dray and horses. Bar food *daily*, garden and live music on *Sun evening*.

🍺 **Royal Oak** New Park Street, south of Devizes Wharf. A 16thC coaching inn, serving Ushers real ale, which makes a change from the excellent Wadworth's ales, so readily available hereabouts. *Lunchtime* food, discos *Thur, Fri and Sat evenings*.

🍺 **Old Crown** New Park Street, south of Devizes Wharf. Wadworth's traditional ale, delivered by horse and dray. Food *lunchtime and evening*.

🍺 **Bridge Inn** At Horton Bridge. The trip boat *Kenavon Venture* operates from this welcoming pub. You can also hire rowing boats. Wadworth's real ale, and *evening* bar snacks. Garden.

🍺 **Crown Inn** Bishops Cannings. A friendly village local, serving locally brewed Wadworth's beer. Extensive range of food served *lunchtime and evening*. Garden.

Caen Hill Locks, Devizes, now restored after many years of dereliction. *Derek Pratt*.

Caen Hill

Leaving Devizes, the canal continues westwards. Ahead the landscape falls away, giving advance warning of the steep descent at Caen Hill. Locks occur at regular intervals west of Devizes, each separated by a long, wide pound. These were designed to hold sufficient water while permitting the locks to be close together to follow the slope. The towpath is in very good condition; apart from the attraction to visitors of the Caen Hill flight, the whole area is obviously used for recreation by the people of Devizes. To the south the busy A361 accompanies the canal down the hill, but it is out of sight for most of the way. At lock 44 the major flight starts; wide lock follows wide lock down the hill, each with an enormous side pound. The scale of the whole flight is most impressive. At lock 29 the Caen Hill flight ends, but the locks continue the descent, now separated once again by longer pounds. The canal passes under the B3101 road bridge, and then at lock 22 reaches the end of the long fall – 29 locks in 2 miles. At Lower Foxhangers Bridge the towpath turns over to the north bank. Water-meadows accompany the canal to the south, with views of the hills that rise in the distance. The canal turns past Sells Green in a low cutting that hides most of the village, and then strides along the valley. The hills to the south climb steeply up to the village of Seend, and to the north flat pastureland stretches away. After two swing bridges the canal reaches the first of the five Seend Locks; this is the best point for access to the village. By the third lock there is a pub, and a lane leading to Seend Cleeve village.

Seend Cleeve
Wilts. Tel. An agricultural village built on the steep slopes of the hills that overlook the canal. Some new development has merged well with the existing houses.
Seend
Wilts. PO, tel, stores, garage. Although the main road cuts the village in half, Seend is still attractive. Elegant 18thC houses flank the road, and conceal the lane that leads to the battlemented Perpendicular church.
Sells Green
Wilts. Tel, garage. A scattered main road village, the houses doing their best to hide from the traffic behind decorative gardens.

BOATYARDS
BW Centre (0380 722859).

PUBS
Brewery Inn 200yds south of lock 19. Once a brewery, now a friendly village local serving Websters and Ruddles real ale. Meals *lunchtime and evening*, garden, children's room.
Barge Seend Cleeve, by lock 19. Wadworth's real ale in a tastefully decorated pub which was once the home of the Wiltshire Giant (8ft 4in). Excellent food *lunchtime and evening*; fine canalside garden. Children welcome; post box.
Bell Inn ½ mile from lock 21. Pub with a collection of canal memorabilia in an old brewhouse. Wadworth's real ale and Taunton real cider. Food *lunchtime*, garden, children welcome.
Three Magpies 200yds south of Sells Green Bridge. Wadworth's real ale and Taunton real cider in a comfortable inn. Meals *lunchtime and evening*, garden, children's room.

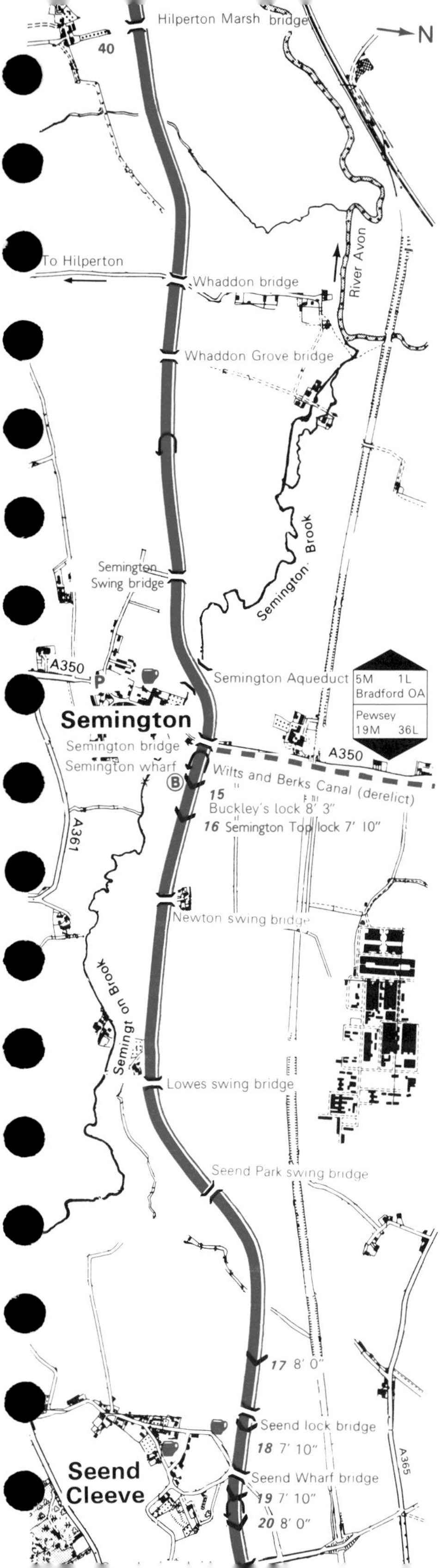

Map labels (left side):

40

Hilperton Marsh bridge

→ N

To Hilperton

Whaddon bridge

River Avon

Whaddon Grove bridge

Semington
Swing bridge

Semington Brook

A350

Semington Aqueduct

5M	1L
Bradford OA	
Pewsey	
19M	36L

Semington

Semington bridge

A350

Semington wharf

Ⓑ

Wilts and Berks Canal (derelict)

A361

15 Buckley's lock 8' 3"

16 Semington Top lock 7' 10"

Newton swing bridge

Semington Brook

Lowes swing bridge

Seend Park swing bridge

17 8' 0"

A365

Seend lock bridge

18 7' 10"

Seend Wharf bridge

19 7' 10"

20 8' 0"

Seend Cleeve

Semington

Leaving Seend Locks behind, the canal continues its western course, maintaining a fairly straight line through open country. The steep hills around Seend are left behind, giving way to rolling farmland extending into the distance on both banks. This is a quiet and secluded stretch with no villages beside the canal; however, farms occur regularly along the bank, each generally with its own swing accommodation bridge. In the distance to the north the embankment of the disused railway follows the course of the canal. The two Semington Locks continue the descent towards Bath with an attractive lock house by lock 15. Just beyond the lock the canal is crossed by the A350; this is the best access point for Semington. A close examination of the north bank just before the bridge will reveal a bricked-up side bridge; this marks the site of the junction with the long abandoned Wiltshire & Berkshire Canal, which used to go to Abingdon. Beyond the bridge the canal curves round past Semington on an embankment, crossing the Semington Brook on a small stone aqueduct. A long straight stretch now leads towards Hilperton, while to the south the hills return to follow the canal. To the north the River Avon draws gradually nearer, and the two waterways begin to share the same valley.

Semington

Wilts. PO, tel, stores, garage. Despite the main road, Semington is a pretty village. Large handsome houses with fine gardens run beside the road. Several date from the 18thC. The little stone church, crowned with a bellcote, is at the end of a lane to the east of the village. The old village school is beside the church, built in the same style.

The Wiltshire & Berkshire Canal

Opened in 1810, the canal wound in a meandering course for 51 miles between Semington on the Kennet & Avon and Abingdon on the River Thames. A branch was opened in 1819 from Swindon to connect with Latton on the Thames & Severn Canal. Although the carriage of Somerset coal was the inspiration for the canal, its eventual role was agricultural. Profits were never high, partly because the wandering line of the canal and its 45 locks made travel very slow, and so it suffered early from railway competition. By the 1870s, moves were afoot to close the canal, and despite various efforts to give it a new lease of life, the situation had become hopeless by the turn of the century. Traffic finally stopped in 1906, and the canal was formally abandoned in 1914. Little remains of it now, but its course can be traced with difficulty.

BOATYARDS

Ⓑ **Tranquil Boats** Lock House, Semington. (0380 870654). Electric day boat, dry dock, slipway, DIY. B&B.

PUBS

🍺 **Somerset Arms** ¼ mile south of Semington Bridge. Ushers and Founders real ale and Bulmers real cider in a 400-year-old pub. Meals *lunchtime and evening* and garden.

Avoncliff aqueduct

→ N

Westwood

Avoncliff station

Avoncliff

Becky Addy Wood

Westwood Manor

Belcombe
Court

Bradford swing bridge

B3109

10M   6L
Bath

Pewsey
24M   37L

Quarry

Bradford lock bridge

Tithe Barn

Frome road wharf

Underwoods bridge

14 Bradford

Bradford

10' 3" wharf ℞ station

**Bradford on
Avon**

Widbrook bridge

A363

Marina

Great Bradford Wood

Ladydown
bridge

River Avon

Biss Aqueduct

River Biss

Staverton

Ladydown aqueduct

Balls
bridge

Marina

Parsons bridge

Wyke House

Ⓑ

Ⓑ

B3106

Hilperton
wharf

Hilperton bridge

**Hilperton
Marsh**

Hilperton Marsh
bridge

B3105

Hilperton

Bradford on Avon

Continuing its westerly course, the canal passes
through open pastureland: the wide Avon
valley, which the canal now follows, begins
gradually to narrow as the hills encroach to the
north and the south. The canal curves round
below Hilperton; although the main village is a
mile to the south, there is a convenient pub,
post office and stores by the road bridge and
wharf where a large new marina has been built.
West of Hilperton, the canal passes the grounds
of Wyke House, whose Jacobean-style towers
stand among the trees; then the land to the
north falls away as the canal returns to its
original course on a sweeping curve. Canal and
river now converge as the canal swings on a
huge embankment towards the Avon, crossing
the railway and the River Biss on two stone
aqueducts. The classical arch over the river is
particularly handsome; it is necessary to walk
down the side of the embankment in order to
see it properly. The view northwards across the
Avon valley is very fine. For a while river and
canal run side by side, the river down in the
valley, the canal high above in a side cutting,
shielded by trees, and then they part again to
make their separate entries into Bradford. The
canal stays high above the town, which fills the
steep-sided valley, while the river cuts the town
in two. Bradford basin appears suddenly,
followed by the lock, and then the canal turns
to pass to the south of the town. It rejoins the
course of the river, and now the two run closely
together all the way to Bath. West of Bradford
the canal passes through beautiful woods on the
steep southern slope of the valley. From this
point there are fine views of the town, spread
out beyond the Tithe Barn, which is right
beside the canal. Cyclists appear on the
towpath, since this is part of the Wiltshire
Cycleway route. The Avon rushes along the
valley and beyond it the railway appears and
disappears among the trees on the far side,
while high above the canal pursues its more
sedate course towards Bath. The thick woods
often give the canal user a feeling of total
seclusion. The elegant stone arches of the
Avoncliff Aqueduct carry the canal high above
the fast flowing river and the railway. A canal
shop, and a separate canal bookshop make this
a worthwhile stop. The canal then turns west
again to continue its wooded course. The
towpath crosses back to the south side by the
aqueduct.

Avoncliff
Wilts. Station. A hamlet clustered in the woods
beside the canal. Originally it was a centre of
weaving, and many traces of the old industry
can be seen: weavers' cottages, and the old mills
on the Avon, which falls noisily over a weir at
this point. The hamlet is dominated by
Rennie's aqueduct, built in 1804 to take the
canal across the valley to the north side. A
classical stone structure, the aqueduct suffered
from casual repair work and patching in brick
when owned by the GWR.
Bradford on Avon
*Wilts. EC Wed. PO, tel, stores, garage, bank,
station.* Set in the steeply wooded Avon valley,
Bradford is one of the beauty spots of
Wiltshire, and one of the highlights of the
canal. Rather like a miniature Bath, the town is
composed of fine stone terraces rising sharply
away from the river, which cuts through the
centre of the town. Until the 19thC it was a
prosperous centre for weaving, but a depression
killed the industry and drove most of the
workers away. Bradford is rich in architectural
treasures from the Saxon period to the 19thC,
while the abundance of fine 18thC houses make
an exploration of the town a positive pleasure.
The centre is very compact, and so the walk
down the hill from the canal wharf lays most of
it open to inspection, including the town
bridge, Holy Trinity Church, the Victorian
town hall, and the fine Gothic revival factory
that dominates the riverside. There is also a
swimming pool near the canal.
Bradford Wharf The canal wharf is particularly
attractive. There is a small dock with some of
the original buildings still standing, plenty of
mooring space, and an old canal pub beside the
lock.

Town Bridge The nine-arched bridge is unusual in having a chapel in the middle, one of the few still surviving in Britain. Parts of the bridge, including the chapel, are medieval, but much dates from a 17thC rebuilding. During the 17th and 18thC the chapel fell out of use, and was turned into a small prison, serving as the town lock up.

Holy Trinity Church Basically a 12thC building with additions dating over the next three centuries. Inside are some medieval wall paintings, and fine 18thC monuments.

Saxon Church of St Lawrence Founded in 705, this tiny church was enlarged in the 10thC. Since then it has survived essentially unchanged, having been at various times a school, a cottage and a slaughterhouse. The true origins and purpose of the building were only rediscovered in the 19thC, and so it remains one of the best-preserved Saxon churches in England.

Great Tithe Barn Standing below the canal embankment, this great stone building is one of the finest tithe barns in England. It was built in the 14thC by the Abbess of Shaftesbury. Its great length (168ft) is broken by two porches, with massive doors that open to reveal the beamed roof. Maintained by the Department of the Environment the barn now contains a collection of old agricultural implements, and is *open to the public at all reasonable times.*

Westwood Manor 1 mile south west of Bradford. This 15thC stone manor house contains much original Jacobean plaster and woodwork, although much was lost when the manor became a farm in the 18thC. Skilful restoration by the National Trust has returned the manor to its former glory. *Open: Wed afternoons Apr–Sep.*

Staverton
Wilts. Tel, stores. The village lies north of the canal, spreading down to the banks of the Avon, where there is a small Nestlé factory. A small isolated part of the Avon is navigable here, and is used by a few pleasure boats. In the village are terraces of weavers' cottages, a sign of what was once the staple trade of the area.

Hilperton
Wilts. PO, tel, stores, garage. A scattered village that stretches away from the settlement by the canal wharf. Wyke House stands to the west of the village. This very ornate Jacobean mansion

was in fact built in 1865, a replica of the original house. House *not open to the public.*

BOATYARDS

Ⓑ **Hilperton Marina** Hilperton Wharf, Hammond Way, Trowbridge. (0225 765243). Ⓡ Ⓢ Ⓦ Ⓓ Pump-out, gas, slipway, overnight mooring, long-term mooring, chandlery, books and maps, boat and engine sales and repairs, toilets, BW licences.

Ⓑ **Wessex Narrowboats** Wessex Wharf, Hilperton Marina, Trowbridge. (0225 769847). Narrowboat hire, day hire craft, books and maps, boat building, engine repairs, shop, double wet dock.

BOAT TRIPS

Patricia II An electric replica of an Edwardian launch available for private charter; 12 seats for picnic trips from Hilperton Wharf. Gibsons Boat Services, 9 Boreham Road, Warminster. (0985 212094).

Narrowboat Ladywood operated by the K & A Canal Trust. Pleasure and charter trips from Bradford Wharf. (022 16 6135).

PUBS

🍺 **Cross Guns** Fine 17thC inn by south side of Avoncliff Aqueduct, with an exciting choice of real ales. Riverside garden, meals *lunchtime and evening.*

🍺 **Canal Tavern** Bradford Wharf. Basic locals pub with strong K & A Trust connections which allows children into the bar. Wadworth's real ale and Bulmers real cider, snacks *lunchtime (not Sun)* and garden.

🍺 **Barge Inn** Bradford Wharf. Comfortable one bar pub. Ushers and Founders real ale and Bulmers real cider, *lunchtime* food, garden and accommodation.

🍺 **Beehive** Widbrook Bridge, Bradford on Avon. Popular stone built pub dispensing Ushers real ale and Bulmers real cider. Meals *lunchtime and evening (not Sun eve)*, garden.

🍺 **Old Bear** Staverton, 1/3 mile north west of Hilperton Bridge. 300-year-old inn serving Bass, Marstons and Wadworths real ale along with *lunchtime* food. Garden.

🍺 **Kings Arms** 100yds south of Hilperton Wharf. A renovated pub with a 6ft 5in tall ghost, offering Ushers and Websters real ale and food *lunchtime and evening (not Sun eve)*. Garden.

Avoncliff Aqueduct, where the Kennet & Avon crosses over the Bristol Avon. *David Perrott.*

Claverton

Leaving the Avoncliff Aqueduct, the canal
continues westwards through the woods above
the River Avon. The valley gets steeper and
narrower as it approaches Bath and thick woods
cover both sides as the river and canal run side
by side. The canal passes Limpley Stoke,
scattered over the southern valley side. The
country opens out slightly, to allow views
across the valley as the canal approaches the
Dundas Aqueduct, perhaps the best known
feature of the Kennet & Avon. Emerging from
the woods, the canal turns suddenly onto the
aqueduct, which carries it across the Avon
valley and the railway to the south side. At the
southern end of the aqueduct is a small wharf
and basin, with an old crane standing over the
water. Here was the junction with the
Somersetshire Coal Canal, which, until its
closure in 1904, ran south from the Kennet &
Avon Canal towards Paulton. Beyond the basin
the towpath turns over to the north bank,
where it remains until Bath is reached. The
canal enters another thickly wooded stretch, a
side cutting taking it towards Claverton. The
woods soon give way to allow fine views to the
north, across rolling country and the railway
and River Avon in the valley below. Claverton
flanks the canal, but it is hidden by the folds of
the land to the south. Access is easy, and both
the village and Claverton Manor are worth a
visit. Claverton Ram, a water-powered pump
which lifts water up from the Avon to feed the
canal has been restored by the Kennet & Avon
Canal Trust, with help from engineering
students from Bath University. The more open
country continues, allowing views across the
valley to Warleigh Manor, now a college, and to
Bathford church. The canal follows the
contours of the land as it turns towards Bath,
maintaining the level of the 9-mile pound that
runs from Bradford to Bath Top Lock.

Claverton
Somerset. Tel. Although devoid of all facilities,
Claverton is well worth a visit. It is a manorial
village of stone houses, surrounding the 17thC
farm, and in early days clearly dependent upon
Claverton Manor. The main road misses the
village, increasing the peace and seclusion.
Claverton Manor The American Museum in
Britain. The manor was built in 1820 by Sir
Jeffry Wyatville in the Greek revival style. It
now houses a museum of American decorative
arts from the late 17th to the mid 19thC. *Open:
Apr–Oct, Tue–Sun afternoons.*
Claverton Pump The waterwheel pump at
Claverton is the only one of its kind on British
canals. Designed by John Rennie, the pump
was built to feed the 9-mile Bradford–Bath
pound, and started operating in 1813. The two
undershot breast wheels, each 15ft in diameter
and 11ft wide, then powered the pumping
machinery until a major breakdown in 1952
prompted its closure, and replacement by a
temporary diesel pump. The original
machinery has now been restored, and
'pumping weekends' are organised – details
(0272) 515954. New electric pumps now do the
day-to-day work, raising water from the Avon
47ft below.
Dundas Aqueduct
Built in 1804, this three-arch classical stone
aqueduct is justifiably one of the most well-
known features of the canal, and stands as a
fitting monument to the architectural and
engineering skill of John Rennie. It is necessary
to leave the canal and walk down into the valley
below to appreciate the beauty of the aqueduct,
and see it in the context of the narrow Avon
valley into which it fits so well.
Somersetshire Coal Canal Opened in 1805,
this narrow canal was sponsored by the
Somerset Coal owners, who wanted a more
efficient means of moving their coal to Bath,
Bristol and the rest of England. Originally
surveyed by Rennie in 1793, the canal was to
run from Limpley Stoke to Paulton, with a
branch to Radstock. There were steep gradients
to overcome at Midford and Combe Hay, and
these plagued the canal throughout its life. The
Radstock Arm was never completed and
tramroads were built over the difficult
stretches. The canal was never profitable, and

was sold to the Somerset & Dorset Railway in
1871. The main line was completed
throughout, but not before some remarkable
solutions to the problems of the Combe Hay
gradient had been tried out. First there was
Robert Weldon's caisson lock; a watertight
caisson, large enough to hold a narrowboat and
crew, was pulled up and down an 88ft-deep
water-filled cistern by means of a rack and
pinion. This terrifying device was soon
replaced by an inclined plane, which in turn
was replaced by a conventional flight of locks.
Once open, the canal carried a large tonnage of
coal throughout the 19thC: it served 30 colleries
more directly than the railway. However, by
the end of the century the inevitable
competition was taking away the traffic, which
finally stopped in 1898. The canal was officially
abandoned in 1904. The first ¼ mile has now
been restored and is used by a boatyard, and for
moorings. A stop lock at the entrance restricts
its use to craft of 7ft beam only.

Limpley Stoke
Avon. PO, tel, stores. Built on the side of the
valley overlooking the river, Limpley Stoke is a
quiet village, a residential outpost of Bath. The
little church includes work of all periods, from
Norman to the 20thC: inside is a collection of
carved coffin lids.

Freshford
Somerset. PO, tel, garage. Although not on the
canal, Freshford is well worth the ½-mile walk
south from Limpley Stoke. It is a particularly
attractive village, set on the side of the steep hill

that flanks the confluence of the rivers Avon
and Frome. At the top of the hill is the church,
and terraces of handsome stone houses fall away
in both directions, filling the valley below, and
crowding the narrow streets. At the bottom of
the hill is the river, crossed by the medieval
bridge.

BOATYARDS

ⓑ **Bath & Dundas Canal Co.** (Anglo Welsh)
The Boatyard, Monkton Combe. (0225
722292). At the end of the Somersetshire Coal
Canal, where boats up to 62ft can turn, BUT do
not bring your boat in without first walking
along the main road to the office to check if
space is available. ⟨S⟩⟨W⟩⟨D⟩ Pump-out, gas,
narrowboat hire, day hire craft, long-term
mooring, slipway, dry dock, books and maps,
boat sales, ices, drinks.

PUBS

▶ **Viaduct Hotel** Monkton Combe. Moor west
of Dundas Aqueduct, the pub is 400yds south
on the A36. Courage real ale, food *lunchtime and
evening.* Garden, children welcome.
▶ **Hop Pole** Limpley Stoke. Moor at Limpley
Stoke Bridge, walk down to railway bridge and
turn left to find this popular oak-panelled pub.
Courage real ale, meals *lunchtime and evening,*
children's room, garden.
▶ **The Inn** Freshford. An attractive pub
overlooking the river. Ushers real ale and bar
food. Garden, children welcome.

Cleveland House, standing over the canal in Sydney Gardens, Bath. *Derek Pratt.*

Bath

Following the course of the River Avon, the canal turns west towards Bath, leaving behind Bathford church on the opposite side of the valley. Groups of houses appear more frequently scattered among the trees of the Avon valley; these form the outposts of Bath, whose suburbs are now visible to the west. The canal passes through Bathampton, on a low embankment above the school and church, and then continues on a straight course, closely flanked by the railway, which is in a cutting below. On the south bank there are gardens running down to the water, which accompany the canal into Bath. The entry into Bath is magnificent. The canal sweeps round the south of the city, cut into the side of the hill, and so there are extensive views across Bath. From this point it is possible to pick out many of the features of the city, and the Georgian terraces can be seen spread out over the far side of the valley. As the buildings fill the valley, canal and River Avon part, to make their separate entries into Bath. The first Georgian buildings flank the canal as it reaches Sydney Gardens. A short tunnel with a fine Adamesque portal takes the canal under a road, and then it passes two pretty cast iron bridges, both dated 1800. A cutting carries the canal through this attractive part of Bath, and so the houses seem to hang over the water. Another ornamental tunnel actually carries houses over the canal, among them Cleveland House, the old canal company's headquarters. The towpath turns over briefly to the south side, returning to the north at the next bridge. The cutting then ends, once more allowing magnificent views over the city before the canal reaches lock 13, the top lock of the Widcombe flight. This flight of six locks takes the canal down to join the Avon. Locks 8 and 9 were merged together as part of a road-building scheme, making one new lock with a fall of over 19ft. The canal joins the Avon immediately beyond Bath Lower Lock (number 7) in the middle of the industrial quarter of Bath. The railway station is opposite the junction of canal and river, and factories and warehouses flank the Avon as it leaves Bath. The fine Georgian city surrounds the unnavigable Avon to the east. The junction is the best point of access for Bath as a whole. A long belt of industry accompanies the river out of Bath but access to the towpath is always easy. There are several footbridges across the river, some of them private, and a disused railway crosses twice as the river meanders in long, gentle curves. As the industry gradually falls away, the river divides; the right fork leads to Weston Lock, the left to a weir, as the river continues its fall to the sea.

Navigational note
Restrictions on the Widcombe flight should be checked with BW. Ring the office at Devizes on (0380) 722859.

Navigating the Bristol Avon
Pleasure boats should always give way to barges, and should let them use the locks first. In general, downstream traffic has right of way, especially through bridges. All the locks are accompanied by weirs, and so boatmen should take great care to turn into the lock cuts, and avoid the weir channel. Remember that a river always has a current, and is liable to changes in speed and level of flow. When mooring, allow enough slack on lines. Do not moor in lock cuts or near weirs. All pleasure boats should moor up at night, and show a white light. With the exception of Hanham, the locks are not manned. Remember that boats should always be held by ropes while the locks are being operated, for there is a strong flow in these large locks.

Bath
Avon. EC Thur, MD Wed. All services. Bath was first developed by the Romans as a spa town and resort because of its natural warm springs. They started a trend of bathing and 'taking the waters' which survives today. There are extensive Roman remains to be seen in the city, not least the baths themselves. The city

Map labels

Widcombe flight

7 Bath lower lock 9′ 3″
Bath deep lock 19′ 5″

10 Wash House lock 8′ 6″
11 Abbey View lock 9′ 0″
12 Pulteney lock 9′ 5″
13 Bath top lock 9′ 0″

6 Weston lock 9′ 3″

Weir
W

Weston cut

Dolphin bridge

A431

A4

River Avon

Royal Victoria Park

11M 6L Hanham
Bradford OA 10M 6L

Crescent Gardens

Churchill road bridge

Bath

Abbey
Bath station
Dolmead bridge

Baptist Chapel bridge
Bath Deep lock
10′
11 Horse Shoe bridge
12 13

Henrietta Park

A4

Sydney Gardens foot bridge
Sydney Wharf bridge
Cleveland House tunnel
Sydney Gardens (No. 2 tunnel)

A36(T)

River Avon

Folly Foot bridge

Bathampton Down

Candy's bridge

Golf Course

Bathampton
P D
Bathampton bridge
R

A36

River Avon
B
Holcombe swing bridge

grew further during the medieval period, when it was a centre of the wool trade; the fine abbey dates from this time. But the true splendour of Bath is the 18thC development, when the city grew as a resort and watering place that was frequented by all levels of English society, from Royalty downwards. Despite heavy bombing in the 1939–45 war, Bath is still a magnificent memorial to the 18thC and Neo-classicism generally. The terraces that adorn the steep northern slope of the Avon valley contain some of the best Georgian architecture in Britain. Much of the city was designed by John Wood the Younger, who was responsible for the great sweeping Royal Crescent. Other architects include Thomas Baldwin, who built the Guildhall, 1766–75, and the Pump Room, 1789–99, and Robert Adam, whose Pulteney Bridge carries terraces of shops across the Avon. Plagued by traffic, Bath is best seen on foot, for its glories and riches are far too numerous to list. Visitors should not fail to try the waters, which gush continuously from a fountain outside the Pump Room.

Bath Abbey Set in an attractive piazza, the abbey is a pleasingly uniform Perpendicular building, founded in 1499. Twin towers crown the west front, decorated with carved angels ascending and descending ladders. Inside, the abbey is justly famous for its fan vaulting, which covers the whole roof of the building but is not all of the same date. Inside also is a wealth of memorials of all periods, an interesting indication of the vast range of people who, over the ages, have come to die at Bath.

Holburne of Menstrie Museum Great Pulteney Street, Bath. (0225 466669). Housed in an 18thC Palladian building that was designed as part of the Sydney pleasure gardens, it contains collections of silver, ceramics and 18thC paintings and furniture. *Open daily mid Feb–mid Dec (closed Mon Feb–Easter).*

Museum of Costume Assembly Rooms. (0225 461111). Display of fashion from the 17thC to the present day; one of the largest collections of costume in the world. *Open daily.*

Bath Roman Museum Abbey Churchyard, Bath. (0225 461111). The great bath buildings with their dependent temple were the centre of Roman Bath. Much of these survive, incorporated into the 18thC Pump Room. The museum, attached to the bath buildings, contains finds excavated from the site. *Open daily all year.*

1 Royal Crescent A typical mid-18thC house, complete with original furniture and fittings. *Open Mar–Oct weekdays and Sun afternoons.*

Victoria Art Gallery Bridge Street, Bath. (0225 248144). Collection of 18thC and modern paintings, prints and ceramics. Visiting exhibitions. *Open Mon–Sat.*

Tourist Information Centre Abbey Churchyard, Bath. (0225 462831).

Bathampton
Avon. PO, tel, stores, garage. The centre of the village surrounds the canal and is still compact and undeveloped, but new housing around the village has turned it into a suburb of Bath. The church is mostly 19thC.

BOATYARDS
Ⓑ **T. J. & K. Knill** By Holcombe Swing Bridge, Bathampton. (0225 66634). W̅ Pump-out, long-term mooring, books and maps, refreshments.

BOAT TRIPS
John Rennie A restaurant boat available for private charter and offering public trips on *Thur, Fri & Sat evenings.* Details from (0225) 447276.
K & A Canal Trust Weekend trips from Widcombe Top Lock. Details (0225) 62313.
K & A Horse Drawn Boat Co. 1½ hour trips from Bathampton to Claverton. Ring (022 16) 5152.

PUBS AND RESTAURANTS
Bath is well-endowed with distinguished restaurants, lively wine bars and excellent real ale pubs. The following is a selection of real ale pubs nearest to the canal.
🍺 **Dolphin** On the Western Cut. Flowers real ale. Pub food (*not Tue or Sun evenings*). Garden. Children welcome.
🍺 **Golden Fleece** 1–3 Avon Buildings, Lower Bristol Road. One bar local 50yds south of the river, serving an exciting selection of real ales. John Smith, Courage ales, Exmoor Ale plus guest beer. Bar food, catering for vegetarians *lunchtimes only* (*not Sun*).
🍺 **Windsor Castle** Upper Bristol Road. Bass and Worthington real ales. Bar food (*not Sun*). Children's room. Barbecue, live music, bar games.
🍺 **New Esthall** Upper Bristol Road, opposite large children's play park. Marstons and Border real ale. Food (*not Sun evening*), vegetarians catered for. Bar games, garden.
🍺 **Hop Pole** Upper Bristol Road. Ushers and Butcombe ales. Food *lunchtimes only.* Barbecue *in summer.* Vegetarian food. Bar games. Live music *last Sat in month.*
🍺 **Golden Fleece** 150yds down footpath from lock 11. Newly refurbished pub serving Flowers and Whitbread real ales. Bar food (*not Mon evenings*). Barbecues *at weekends during summer.*
🍺 **Ram** 150yds south of lock 8. Friendly local catering for jazz enthusiasts. Ruddles and Ushers real ales. Bulmers cider. Bar food *lunchtime, weekdays only.*
🍺 **Ring o'Bells** 100yds south of lock 8. Ruddles and Websters real ales. Bar food. Live music *Sun evening.*
🍺 **White Hart** South of lock 8. Spacious lounge and basic public bar where you can enjoy Flowers, Pedigree and West Country real ales. Bar food *Mon–Sat lunchtimes, Mon–Fri evenings.* Live music *Wed, Fri, Sat, Sun.* B&B.
🍺 **Royal Oak** 100yds down footpath from lock 11. Comfortable pub serving Gibbs Mew real ale. Bar food. Live music *Tuesdays and first Sunday in month.*
✕🍺 **Bathampton Mill** 400yds north of Bathampton Bridge. A Beefeater restaurant serving Flowers real ale and meals. Garden.
🍺 **George Inn** Bathampton Bridge. Family pub with a canalside garden serving Courage real ale and bar meals. Family garden.

Entrance to the Kennet & Avon Canal at Bath. *Derek Pratt.*

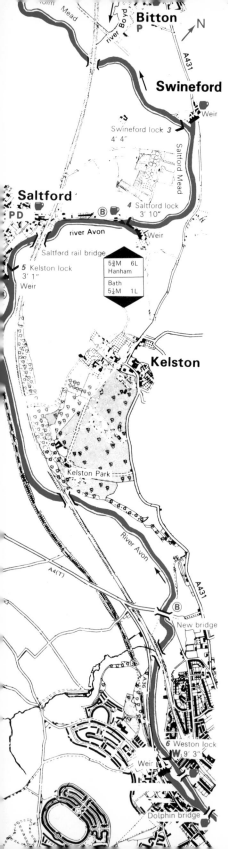

Saltford

The River Avon at last leaves behind the
industries of Bath, and enters a wooded stretch.
The railway closely follows the south bank,
vanishing at one point into a tunnel. As the
river continues its wide, wandering course
westwards, the valley opens out, and rolling
hills and pastureland flank both banks. A
disused rail bridge is followed by the elegant
single stone arch of New Bridge, carrying the
A4. At this point the towpath crosses to the
south bank, although, as on all river
navigations, its position is never well-defined.
After New Bridge there is a small boatyard, and
a line of moored craft along the north bank.
The river passes Kelston Park in a series of
gentle bends, against a background of wooded
hills to the north. The disused railway crosses
the Avon for the fourth time, an indication of
the river's winding course. The river
straightens as it approaches Kelston Lock,
where the stream again divides. Navigators
should take the right fork to the lock, and avoid
the weir on the left. Saltford can be seen among
the trees on the south bank. Mooring is possible
by the lock, and this is the best access point for
boaters visiting the town. The towpath
continues along the north bank, as the river
curves towards Saltford Lock. At one time
there was a horse and passenger ferry near the
lock that allowed the towpath to cross to the
south bank. By Saltford Lock is Saltford
Sailing Club where there is a riverside pub. At
Saltford the lock is on the left. The river then
turns past Saltford Mead towards Swineford,
passing a large factory on the low-lying land to
the south. At Swineford the river again divides,
the left fork leading to the particularly
attractive lock, which is set against a
background of trees and old mill buildings.

Swineford
Avon. PO, tel, stores. Although bisected by the
A431, the settlement by the river is still
attractive; old mill buildings overlook the long
weir.
Saltford
Avon. EC Wed. PO, tel, stores, garage.
Although Saltford has been developed as a
large-scale dormitory suburb, the older parts by
the river are still pretty and secluded.
Saltford Manor Situated by the church, the
manor is one of the oldest inhabited houses in
England. Much of the building is still original
Norman work, but it is hidden behind a 17thC
façade.

BOATYARDS

ⓑ **Bristol Boats** by Saltford Lock, Mead Lane,
Saltford. (0225 2032). Boat building, boat sales
and repairs, inboard and outboard engine sales
and repairs, slipway, chandlery, gas. *Closed
Sun in winter*.
ⓑ **Saltford Marina** The Shallows,
Saltford. (0225 2226). Ⓡ Ⓦ Ⓓ Overnight
mooring, engine repairs, slipway, crane.
Restaurant and bar.
ⓑ **Bath Marina** Newbridge, Bath.
Ⓡ Ⓦ Ⓓ Ⓢ Pump-out, engine repairs, overnight
mooring. Restaurant and bar.

PUBS

Swan near Swineford Lock. 200-year-old
stone built cottage pub, dispensing Courage
real ale. Good pub food served in the bar and
restaurant. Garden, children welcome.
White Hart Bitton. Courage real ale. Varied
menu including vegetarian dishes. Garden,
children welcome.
Jolly Sailor By Saltford Lock. A delightful
pub dating back to 1727. An original painting
of the lock and its activity hangs above the
fire-place, whose surround is scarred with
holes, where newly promoted skippers thrust a
red-hot poker into the oak lintel before buying
a florin's worth of ale for those assembled.
Courage, John Smith and Butcombe Bitter.
Gazebo restaurant; barbecues at *weekends
during the summer*. Children welcome.
Bird in Hand Saltford. A beautifully kept
village local which offers Courage and
Wadworths real ales. Taunton cider. Good bar
food (*not Sun or Mon evening*). Large garden
and pleasant terrace. Children welcome.

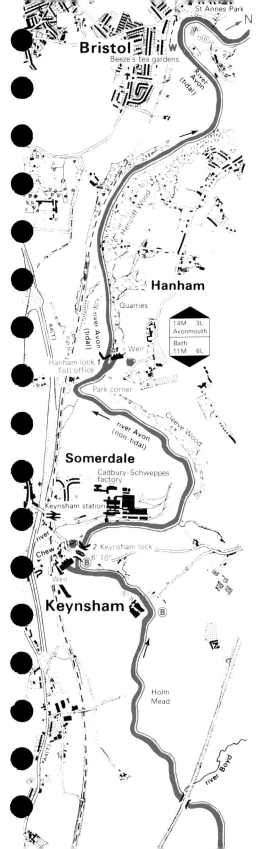

Keynsham

As the river passes Bitton it reaches another
disused railway bridge. Low-lying pasture and
arable land continue to flank the river in its
meandering course towards Keynsham. After
passing a vast brick and stone factory complex,
dated 1881, which dominates the south bank,
the river starts a long horseshoe bend that leads
to Keynsham. The river divides, the right fork
leading to the lock. Keynsham lies well to the
south of the river, but is easily accessible.
There is a small settlement round the lock,
rather over-awed by the industry that
surrounds it. As the valley narrows, steep
wooded hills return to follow the north bank of
the river as it twists and turns. After a
particularly sharp bend, the southern hills
approach as well, and Hanham Lock appears.
Again the river divides, the left fork leading to
the lock. This is lock 1, the last lock between
Reading and Bristol, the end of BW's
jurisdiction, and the beginning of the Port of
Bristol Authority area. Note that the River
Avon is tidal west of Hanham Lock. There is a
small hamlet on the north bank, overlooking
the weir, and two pubs, side by side. From here
the River Avon continues through a steeply
wooded valley to Bristol; a canal takes boats
through Bristol harbour and then the
navigation rejoins the river which flows down to
join the Severn estuary at Avonmouth, having
passed the Clifton Suspension Bridge and the
Avon gorge.

Navigational note
Do not navigate in tidal waters without charts,
tide-tables, anchor etc. Ensure your craft is
suitable. Seek expert advice if in any doubt (the
lock keepers are extremely helpful).

Keynsham
Avon. All services. Keynsham has grown
steadily along the Bristol road, and so is now a
vast shapeless suburb. However, the centre still
retains a feeling of independence, and has many
traces of Keynsham's past. An Augustinian
abbey was founded here in 1170, and there are a
few surviving remains in Abbey Park.
Elsewhere in the main street are a few 17th and
18thC houses, but bungalows and modern
shops predominate. The main feature of
interest is the large church. Originally 13thC,
the interior is now attractively Victorian, after
the restoration of 1861. The ornamental west
tower was built in 1734, after the earlier tower
was blown down in a storm. There is a fine
16thC monument to Sir Henry Bridges.
Bitton
Avon. PO, tel, stores, garage. Although a
main-road village, Bitton's heart survives intact
south of the road. Here is a fine group formed
by the church, the grange, and the 18thC
vicarage, all built around the churchyard. The
church is very splendid; it has a long Saxon
nave with Norman details, a 14thC chancel,
and a magnificently decorative late 14thC
tower. On the main road is an attractive early
19thC Wesleyan chapel.

BOATYARDS

BW Hanham Lock Toll office. (0272 862550).
K & A windlasses.
Ⓑ **Port Avon Marina** Bitton Road, Keynsham.
(0272 861626). Ⓡ Ⓢ Ⓦ Ⓓ Ⓔ Gas, overnight
mooring, winter storage, slipway, chandlery,
books and maps, boat sales, engine sales and
repairs, toilets, showers.
Ⓑ **Jondeblin Marine** Broadmead Lane,
Keynsham. (0272 866066). Ⓡ Ⓢ Ⓦ Ⓓ
Pump-out, overnight mooring, winter storage,
crane, chandlery, repairs, toilets.

PUBS AND RESTAURANTS

Old Lock and Weir Hanham. Riverside, overlooking the lock. Once used as a boatyard, this pub retains the simplicity of the old cottages which it occupies. Whitewashed walls and flagged floors contribute to the atmosphere. Ruddles, Smiles, Pedigree and Ushers real ales. Bar food and barbecue. Pleasant riverside garden.

Chequers Hanham, riverside. A sharp contrast to its neighbouring pub although under the same ownership, the Chequers offers refreshment in very plush surroundings. Courage, Pedigree and Ushers real ales and Taunton cider. Bar food and carvery. Riverside garden, children welcome. R W.

Lock Keeper Keynsham Lock. (0272 862383). Unpredictable flood waters forced many a crew to stay the night at the Lock Keeper. Now serving Courage real ale and bar food. Garden. Children welcome.

The River Lee Navigation at Hertford. *Derek Pratt.*

LEE & STORT

Maximum dimensions

Limehouse Basin to Old Ford
Length: 87'
Beam: 19'
Headroom: 8'
Old Ford to Enfield Lock
Length: 85'
Beam: 18'
Headroom: 6' 9"
Enfield Lock to Hertford
Length: 85'
Beam: 15' 9"
Headroom: 6' 9"
River Stort
Length: 85'
Beam: 13' 3"
Headroom: 5' 9"

Manager
(0992) 764626

Mileage

River Lee

LIMEHOUSE BASIN TO
Old Ford Locks: 2¾
Lea Bridge: 4¾
Pickett's Lock: 10
Enfield Lock: 13
Waltham Abbey: 14
Broxbourne: 18½
FEILDE'S WEIR (junction with River Stort): 20½
St Margaret's: 22½
Ware Bridge: 25
HERTFORD, head of navigation, 27¾

Locks: 19

River Stort

FEILDE'S WEIR (junction with River Lee) to
Roydon station: 1½
Burnt Mill: 4½
Harlow Lock: 6¾
Sawbridgeworth: 8¾
BISHOP'S STORTFORD, head of navigation: 13¾

Locks: 15

Parts of the River Lee (often known as 'Lea': the spelling is optional) were used as navigations in Roman times, and much of the river was navigable before the reign of Elizabeth I. The first major attempt to speed up traffic by means of an artificial cut was made under the powers of an Act of 1571. In the same year an early pound lock was built at Waltham Abbey, using two sets of mitred gates, a principle that then became a standard feature of lock design. In the 17thC the Lee was established as a source of water supply for London, a role it still fulfils. The navigation was steadily improved throughout the 18th and 19thC, under the direction of various well-known engineers. During and immediately after the 1914–18 war enlargements were carried out to allow 130-ton boats to reach Enfield, and 100-ton boats to Ware and Hertford. In the 1930s further canalisation was carried out and more recently locks have been mechanised and duplicated. Timber has always been the main support of the Lee navigation, a trade that still survives today.

The River Stort has never been a very significant navigation commercially, and has not in fact carried any traffic for some years. The navigation as such dates back over 200 years, and has been owned by a series of individuals and companies, including Sir George Duckett; but it would have prospered far more if the ill-fated scheme to build a canal from Bishop's Stortford to Cambridge and the Fenland waterways had ever succeeded.

Lee Valley Park
In making the Lee Valley a regional park (the first area in Britain to be so designated) the Authority has realised the need of a rapidly increasing population for an expanse of open space where this new-found leisure can be both utilised and enjoyed. An amazing factor of the park is its sheer size; it runs from Eastway (A106) in the south to Ware in the north.

The Authority caters for all types: young, old, beginners, experts, teams and individuals. Outdoor and indoor sports, social centres, cultural activities and play centres have all been built.

This ambitious scheme has not been, of course, without its difficulties; there was serious danger of flooding, which has since been alleviated by the construction of drainage channels; massive areas of soil have had to be moved from one area to another; and natural vegetation has largely disappeared except for the woodlands north of Waltham Abbey. As one of the chief aims of the Authority is to make the Park visually pleasing, trees and other vegetation have been planted (especially in areas where pylons march conspicuously across the landscape), and buildings of historical interest within the park, many of which are mentioned in the text, have been preserved.

For more information and a brief guide, the address of the Lee Valley Park Authority is Middleton House, Bulls Cross, Enfield, Middx. (0992 717711).

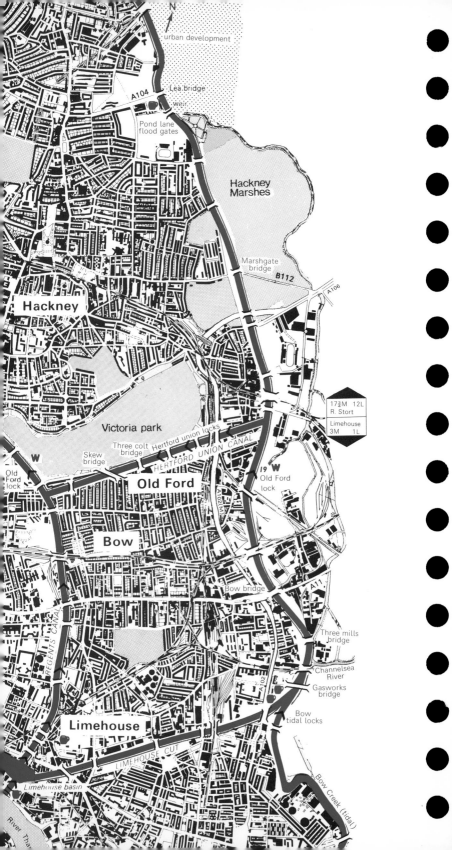

N

urban development

Lea bridge
A104
weir

Pond lane
flood gates

Hackney
Marshes

Marshgate
bridge
B112

A106

Hackney

17¾M   12L
R. Stort
Limehouse
3M   1L

Victoria park

Three colt   Hertford union locks
Skew   bridge
bridge   HERTFORD UNION CANAL

W

19 W
Old Ford
lock

Old
Ford
lock

Old Ford

A102(M)

Bow

Bow bridge   A11

Three mills
bridge

REGENTS CANAL

Channelsea
River

Gasworks
bridge

A102

Bow
tidal locks

Limehouse

LIMEHOUSE CUT

Bow Creek (tidal)

Limehouse basin

River Thames

Bow

The River Lee is navigable from London up to
Hertford. The River Stort, which joins the Lee
at Feilde's Weir, is canalised as far as Bishop's
Stortford. Entrance to the river navigation can
be made from three places:
  From the Regent's Canal via the Hertford
  Union Canal (recommended).
  From the Thames via Limehouse Basin.
  From the Thames direct up Bow Creek, and
  through Bow Locks.

The Hertford Union Canal is a short (1¼ miles)
canal built in 1830 by Sir George Duckett
(hence it is often referred to as 'Duckett's') as a
useful junction between the Regent's Canal and
the Lee Navigation. It is straight, has three
locks, and borders the attractive Victoria Park
for most of the way. The western entrance to
Duckett's is difficult to find, and very easy to
pass without noticing. It is just below Old Ford
Locks and looks just like any of the private
dock entrances that are common on the London
canals. The route up into the River Lee from
the Thames is through the new ship lock into
Limehouse Basin (1½ miles below Tower
Bridge), then east through the new short cut
and along the Limehouse Cut to Bow Locks
and Old Ford. The other entrance to the Lee
Navigation is by way of Bow Creek, whose
mouth is 5 miles down the Thames from the
Limehouse Basin entrance. Bow Creek is a tidal
river – it is in fact the mouth of the River Lee.
It is very twisting, 2 miles long and only
navigable around high tide. The Three Mills at
Bow still remain from the 18thC, although they
were modified some years later. Nearby is the
Abbey Mills Pumping House of Gothic-
Byzantine style designed in 1868 by Bazalgette,
who was also responsible for the Thames
embankments. Hackney Marsh on the east
bank of the canal is a footballer's delight: there
are many pitches here by the Eastway Sports
Centre.

Navigational note 1
The Limehouse Basin Ship Lock can
accommodate craft 98ft 6in × 26ft 3in with a
9ft draught. It is open *08.00–17.00* except for a
time around low water. Ring 071-790 3444 or
071-895 9930 to check.
Navigational note 2
Bow Locks are open from four hours before
high water until two hours after high water
Mon–Sat, and from two hours before high
water until two hours after high water on *Sun*.
Ring 071-987 5661 to check.
Navigational note 3
Old Ford, Tottenham, Pickett's and Ponders
End locks can be operated yourself if there is no
lock-keeper (BW key needed at Tottenham).
Stonebridge can only be operated by the
lock-keeper *08.30–18.30 Mon–Fri,
08.30–12.30 weekends*.

PUBS
🍺 **Rising Sun** St Leonard Street, E14.
🍺 **Queen Victoria** St Leonard Street, E14.
Both the above near Bow Locks, west of Three
Mills Bridge.
🍺 **Ship Aground** Lea Bridge Road (A104),
E14. Canalside. Food.
🍺 **Prince of Wales** Lea Bridge, E14.
Canalside. Food.
🍺 **Barley Mow** 44 Narrow Street, E14.
(071-265 4983). In the original Dockmaster's
office, at the entrance to Limehouse Dock.
Taylor Walker, Tetley and Youngs real ale in a
splendid new waterside pub. Bar food.

**THE RESERVOIRS OF
THE LEE VALLEY**

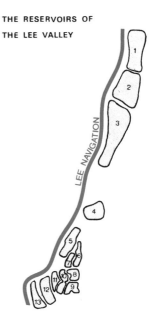

1 King George's reservoir (fishing)
2 King George's reservoir (fishing and
  sailing)
3 William Girling reservoir (fishing at
  selected spots only. Nature reserve)
4 Banbury reservoir (fishing and sailing)
  Banbury Sailing Centre (081-531 1129).
  Courses to all RYA standards
5 Lockwood reservoir (fishing and nature
  reserve)
6 High Maynard reservoir (fishing and
  nature reserve)
7 Low Maynard reservoir (nature reserve)
8 Fishing and nature reserve
9 Fishing
10 Nature reserve
11 Nature reserve
12 Warwick east reservoir (fishing and nature
  reserve)
13 Warwick west reservoir (fishing and nature
  reserve)

Tottenham

The river now begins to follow the wider
sweeping course that is typical of this
navigation. The Walthamstow reservoirs close
in from the east, blocking off the river with
their high embankments bordering the
navigation, while the river begins to adopt the
bleak, stark appearance that characterises it for
miles ahead. Racing 'fours' and 'eights'
emanate from the occasional rowing club, but
riverside life is sparse for the next 15 miles and
there is little to see. Flotsam is, happily, not as
common as in the Bow area, but there are
plenty of timber yards on the river and here and
there a massive baulk of wood lurks just on the
surface of the water. It is inadvisable to venture
up any of the side creeks feeding into the river;
they are usually heavily silted up. At
Walthamstow, ¼ mile north east of the Lee
Valley Marina, is the old Copper Mill built
c1800 to process the copper that was brought
from the port of London along the Lee.

Walthamstow Reservoirs Alongside the east
bank of the navigation: an important part of
London's water supply, controlled by Thames
Water. Access is allowed only for bird-watching
or fishing by permits obtained from Thames
Water (081-808 1527). There is a variety of land
and water birds, including great crested grebes
and yellow wagtails, as well as two thriving,
long-established heronries on islands in
reservoirs 1 and 5. The stock of fish in the
reservoirs is being steadily increased and the
reservoirs where fishing is permitted may vary
each year; details can be obtained from TW.

BOATYARDS
Ⓑ **Lee Valley Marina** Springfield Marina,
Springhill, Clapton. (081-806 1717).
Ⓡ Ⓢ Ⓦ Ⓓ Ⓔ Pump-out, gas, overnight
mooring, long-term mooring, winter storage,
slipway, boat lift (36ft), toilet, showers.

BOAT TRIPS
Pride of Lee Public trips at weekends, and
private charter for up to 52 persons. Ring
081-806 1717 for details.

PUBS
🍺✕ **Cook's Ferry Inn** Edmonton. Canalside.
Food.
🍺✕ **Ferry Boat Inn** Tottenham Locks,
Tottenham. Food.
🍺 **Robin Hood** High Hill Ferry, Upper
Clapton. Food.
🍺 **Anchor & Hope** High Hill Ferry, Upper
Clapton. Food.

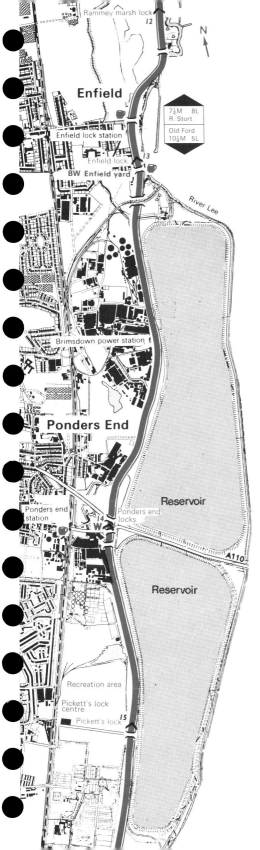

Enfield

Straight as a die for over a mile, the river passes
Pickett's Lock, where the Regional Park
Authority has built a large covered leisure and
sports centre, as well as a golf course. The King
George & William Girling reservoirs
accompany the navigation (fishing on these
reservoirs is restricted to clubs); so do vast
power lines, which stride along as purposefully
as the river. Ponders End Locks provide canal
interest in this rather bleak area, with a handy
wine merchant situated in a converted
warehouse on Columbia Wharf, close by.
Enfield Lock signals the end of nearly 4 miles of
reservoirs and north of here the landscape
opens out. Near Enfield Lock there are plenty
of shops and pubs and also the Royal Small
Arms factory. This very large establishment
used to be extremely busy, especially during
the last war, but no manufacturing takes place
here now, only servicing and testing of
weapons. The famous Lee-Enfield rifle was
made here.

Enfield
Middx. All services. Interesting features in this
town include the Church of St Andrew in the
market place; the chancel window is 13thC.
Gentlemen's Row, which probably dates from
the early 18thC, is completely preserved from
numbers 9 to 23. (Charles Lamb stayed at no.
17 in 1827.)
Pickett's Lock Centre Edmonton (081-803
4756). All sorts of sports activities, including
squash, yoga, swimming, golf and many others.
Sauna, solarium. *Open daily.*
Chingford
Essex. All services. Uninteresting town except
for All Saints Church, which is medieval. To
the north of the town, which is east of the river
along the A110, is a pole obelisk on a 300ft hill
1½ miles from Ponders End Locks. It was
erected in 1825 as a North mark for Greenwich
Observatory. 1 mile east of the obelisk is Queen
Elizabeth I's hunting lodge – a timber-framed,
three-storeyed building from where the hunting
could be viewed, now housing a local museum.
The 10 square miles of Epping Forest lie to the
north east of Chingford: the forest is
remarkable for the large number of hornbeams
and a diminishing herd of deer.

BOATYARDS

BW Enfield Yard Ordnance Road, Enfield
Lock. (0992 764626). No services.

PUBS

🍺 **Greyhound** Enfield Lock. Canalside. Food.
🍺 **Royal Small Arms** Enfield Lock. Canalside.
Food, snooker table.
🍺 **Railway** Ponders End station.
🍺 **Granville** Northampton Road, Ponders
End. Not far from the lock.

Waltham Abbey

Rammey Marsh Lock is the first of five locks in this section. Waltham Abbey is a fine old town where the ancient abbey, an architectural gem, looks down unperturbed on the traffic that flounders round it. The intermittent glinting of glasshouses around shows that this is a market gardening area. North of here the navigation runs into a massive water parkland with sailing clubs on the worked out gravel pits.

Cheshunt
Herts. EC Thur. PO, tel, stores, station, cinema.
The Church of St Mary's was built in 1418–48 by the then rector of Cheshunt and is an example of the Perpendicular style. Of Cheshunt House not much remains: only one wing of a courtyard house. There is a carnival every *Jul.*
Waltham Cross
Herts. EC Thur. PO, tel, stores, station, cinema.
The Eleanor Cross, 1 mile west along the A121, is one of the 12 crosses (of which only three survive) erected by Edward I to commemorate the resting places of his dead queen, Eleanor of Castile, on her last journey from Leicestershire where she died, to Westminster Abbey. The Cross was built in 1291, but was greatly restored in Ketton stone in the 19thC.
Waltham Abbey
Essex. EC Thur. PO, tel, stores, station, cinema.
The history of the town goes back to before the Norman Conquest when King Harold chose it for development as a centre of learning and religious instruction. Local museum in Sun Street.
Abbey Church Founded in 1030 as a collegiate church of secular canons. In 1184 it was nominated a mitred abbey and was soon one of the most prosperous and important in the country. Today's building is largely 19thC, but the Norman nave and aisles still stand. The south chapel is 14thC and the west tower, 16thC. The Jesse window at the east end is a fine example of Burne-Jones, 1861. Within the abbey grounds and just outside to the north are several interesting archaeological remains.

PUBS
🍺 **Red Cow** next to Cheshunt station.
🍺 **Angel** Sun Street, Waltham Abbey.
🍺 **Old English Gentleman** Waltham Town Lock. Canalside. Food.

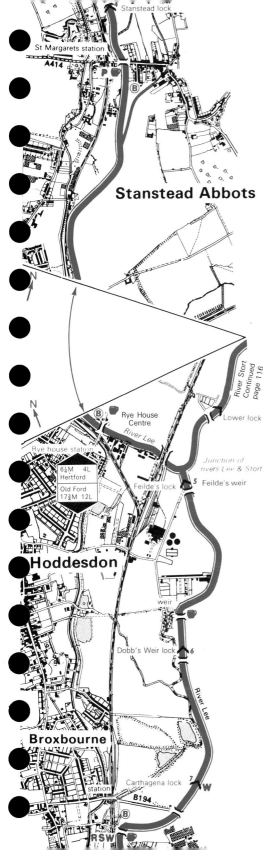

Broxbourne

At Broxbourne can be seen the first of many
holiday chalets and houseboats. Sailing and
rowing boats can be hired by the hour; this
attractive area becomes busy on a summer
weekend, with fishermen becoming more
numerous. At Feilde's Weir the beautiful River
Stort flows in from the north east and the Lee
bears round to the north west, past Rye House
and the Rye House Centre (nature reserve,
speedway, greyhound and go-kart racing) to
Stanstead Abbots, an attractive old town with
all useful facilities. Already one feels that the
character of the river is changing dramatically –
it is smaller, shallower and in every way more
attractive than further south, and the pylons,
which have relentlessly dogged the river since
the outskirts of London, at last recede. Boaters
should be extremely careful when ascending the
Stanstead Lock: the top paddles are, unusually,
on the *gates*: the unexpected rush of water into
the lock chamber can cause great harm to the
unwary, as can the swing bridge *over* the lock,
which should be swung out of the way.

Stanstead Abbots
Herts. EC Thur. PO, tel, stores, garage, station.
A picturesque village with the Church of St
James, interesting particularly because of its
15thC open timber south porch and 16thC
brick north chancel chapel. Stanstead Bury
nearby was originally a 15thC manor house at
the west end of the village and dates from 1752.
Rye House Plot During the reign of Charles II,
Rye House (the building, not the village) was
owned by Rumbold, an ex-officer of the
Parliamentarian army. It was here that he and a
group of other discontented conspirators
decided to ambush the King and his son James,
heir to the throne. The plot failed miserably
because the royal party passed by sooner than
expected, and many of the traitors were put to
death. The Rye House itself is no more, but the
nearby gatehouse, which is scheduled as an
ancient monument, has been restored by the
LVRPA as a feature of a picnic area.
Hoddesdon
*Herts. EC Thur. MD Wed. PO, tel, stores,
station.* St Monica's Priory was the manor house
of Marmaduke Rawdon from 1622. A clock
tower stands in the centre of the town from
where the two main streets of Hoddesdon
begin. A fair is held in *Jun*.
Broxbourne
Herts. EC Wed. PO, tel, stores, station. The
church is entirely 15thC and 16thC. In the
High Street there are several timber-framed
17thC Georgian brick houses. Broxbourne Lido
is a beautiful indoor heated pool, by the river
(*0992 442841, open daily*).

BOATYARDS
Ⓑ **Stanstead Abbots Marina** South Street,
Stanstead Abbots. (0920 870499). Ⓡ Ⓢ Ⓦ
Pump-out, overnight mooring, long-term
mooring, winter storage, crane, boat building,
engine sales and repairs, toilets, showers.
Ⓑ **Broxbourne Boat Centre** Old Nazeing
Road, Broxbourne. (0992 462085). Ⓡ Ⓢ Ⓦ Ⓓ
Pump-out, narrowboat hire, day hire craft,
overnight mooring, toilets, gifts.

BOAT TRIPS
Lady of Lee Valley 85-seater available for
functions. Ring (0992) 462085.

PUBS
🍺 **Jolly Fisherman** Stanstead Abbots.
Canalside. Food.
🍺✕ **Rye House** Hoddesdon. (0992 465151).
Trumans real ale, food.
🍺 **Fish & Eels** Dobbs Weir, Broxbourne.
Canalside. Food.
🍺 **Crown Inn** Old Nazeing Road, Broxbourne.
Canalside. Food, garden.

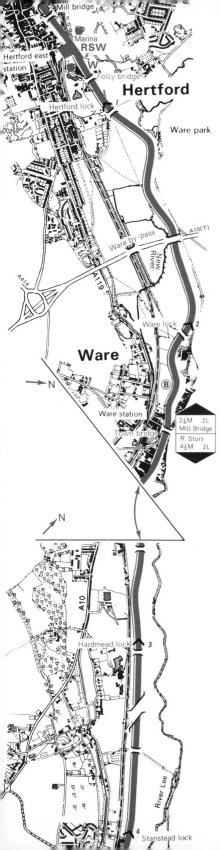

Hertford

Leaving Stanstead Lock, the navigation runs dead straight for 1½ miles north west, flanked by beautiful green, uncluttered water-meadows contained by the nearby wooded hills. A lovely old branch railway line once ran from Stanstead Abbots to Buntingford – it now forms part of the Amwell Walkway to Easneye Woods. The river turns west into Ware, the 'granary of London', where the river bisects this fine old town. There are some remarkable 18thC summer houses along the riverfront and Ware Lock is surrounded by beautifully maintained flower beds. Above this lock, the river wanders along one side of the valley, with water-meadows on one side and wooded parkland on the other. The river enters Hertford via a deep lock, then passes a marina used for pleasure-boat moorings. A weir in the centre of the town prevents further progress, but craft may wind beyond Mill Bridge, overlooked by a fine wooden warehouse.

Hertford
Herts. EC Thur. MD Mon. PO, tel, stores, garage, stations. A large and mostly attractive county town with a long history. Two of its medieval parish churches still stand, and other buildings in the town bear witness to the Middle Ages. A new relief road through the town has destroyed many interesting and attractive houses; but it has ensured the survival of the compact old town centre, which is now a delightful place to stroll around in. In the 9thC the area was invaded with great regularity by the Danes; they were eventually seen off by King Alfred the Great. Dane End, 3½ miles north of Hertford, marks the northern limit of their incursions into this region.
The Castle Built in 1100, the castle belonged to the Cecil family since Prince Charles, son of James I, sold it. King John of France and David Bruce of Scotland were both imprisoned here; and it was here that Bolingbroke drew up charges against Richard II that led to Richard's dethronement in 1399. A few medieval structures remain, including a 12thC curtain wall. The lawns and trees which extend to the river make an attractive setting. The 15thC gatehouse was extensively altered about 1800. Those houses in Water Lane numbered 4 to 16 are thought to have been outhouses of the castle. Several buildings in Castle Street itself are noteworthy, and also those in Fore Street, including Shire Hall, built by James Adam (brother of Robert) in the 18thC. The castle now belongs to the Council and contains the Tourist Information Centre.
Hertford Museum 18 Bull Plain, Hertford. (0992 582686). Local archaeology, history, geology and natural history. *Open Tue–Sat.*
Ware
Herts. EC Thur. MD Tue. PO, tel, stores, garage, station, cinema. There is much evidence of a former medieval town here, while other buildings with their projecting upper storeys show the importance of through-traffic during the coaching days.
Ware Priory Priory Street. Built from the remains of a Franciscan friary founded by Thomas Wake, Lord of the Manor in 1338.
St Mary's Church Church Street. Its battlemented clock tower is surmounted by a spire. There is a fascinating story connected with the oak railings enclosing the children's corner.
New River
Opposite Ware Park is the intake from the River Lee of the New River, which continues 24 miles south, terminating at Stoke Newington. It was a great feat of engineering designed by Sir Hugh Myddelton in the 17thC to bring a fresh water supply from Amwell Springs, which have since run dry, to north London to replace the polluted supply obtained from the Thames. Work started on this remarkable plan in 1609 and the original 44-mile course, including several large wooden aqueducts, was completed within four years. As Amwell Springs had ceased to flow by the end of the 19thC, most of the water in the New River is now drawn from the River Lee. A monument, overhung by weeping willows and a

yew tree, commemorating Myddelton's great achievement, can be seen on an island at the foot of the slope below Great Amwell church, ¼ mile west of the iron footbridge half way between Hardmead and Stanstead Locks.

BOATYARDS

ⓑ **Lea Valley Narrowboat Co.** Lock-keeper's Cottage, Stanstead Lock, Amwell Lane, Stanstead Abbots. (0920 870068). D E Pump-out, gas, long-term mooring, chandlery, books and maps, boat sales.

BOAT TRIPS

Jonas Fosbrooke Widebeam boat available for private hire. 60 persons. Ring (0920) 870068.

PUBS

Woolpack Near Mill Bridge, Hertford. Food.

Salisbury Arms Hotel Fore Street, Hertford. (0992 583091). Food.
White Hart Hotel Salisbury Square, Hertford. (0992 583605). Food.
Old Barge 2 The Folly, Hertford. (0992 581871). A riverside pub with an excellent range of food offered in a separate dining area (*not Sun evening*). Vegetarian food, children's portions, reasonably priced wine. Waterside patio.
Bottles Old Cross, Hertford. Wine bar, food.
Bell & Crown 29 Cowbridge, Hertford. ¼ mile west of end of navigation.
White Horse Castle Street, Hertford. ¼ mile west of end of navigation.
Spread Eagle Amwell End, Ware.
Punch House High Street, Ware.
Saracen's Head Ware. Canalside. Food.

Springtime at Feilde's Weir lock, near Broxbourne. *Derek Pratt.*

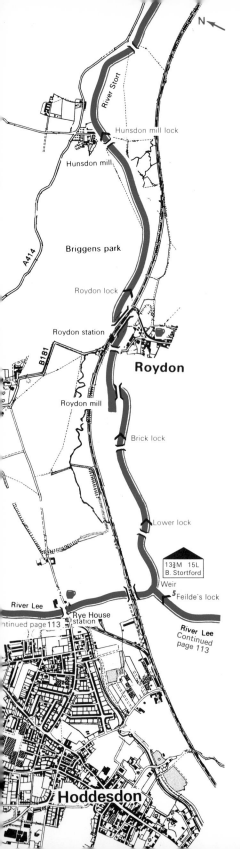

Roydon

The River Stort joins the Lee at Feilde's Weir.
It is instantly different from the Lee: narrow,
winding, totally rural along almost its entire
length, and very beautiful. There is no longer
any commercial traffic on the river, which with
its winding course, shallow draught and slightly
narrow locks (about 13ft wide), became
financially uncompetitive long ago. Water mills
are seen at many of these locks: the attendant
clapboarded buildings are a handsome feature
of this navigation. Low bridges are also
common, and when the river is swollen by
excessive rainwater, the headroom under the
bridges is even further reduced.
Starting at Feilde's Weir, the Stort follows a
line of hills past Lower Lock and Brick Lock to
Roydon. Roydon Mill is now the centre of a
large caravan site, and contains a useful
grocery. (Southbound boats should turn left
under the bridge before the mill.) Roydon
village itself stretches up a hill away from the
river, which is crossed by the railway on an
extremely low bridge (about 6ft headroom) and
followed by Roydon Lock. East of Roydon the
river flows through quiet water-meadows, with
Briggens Park up to the left to Hunsdon Mill
and Lock – an enchanting spot.

Roydon
Essex. EC Wed. PO, tel, stores, station. Roydon
Mill is the headquarters of a large residential
and holiday caravan site. The pleasantness of
the village itself is enhanced by the bold
modern housing estate on the waterfront. The
church is small but attractive and dates from
the 13thC. Note the shield of Sir George
Jackson, later Duckett (a former owner of the
Stort Navigation) on the lock cottage.

PUBS
 New Inn Roydon. Food.
 White Hart Roydon. Food.
 Crusader Roydon.
 White Horse Roydon.

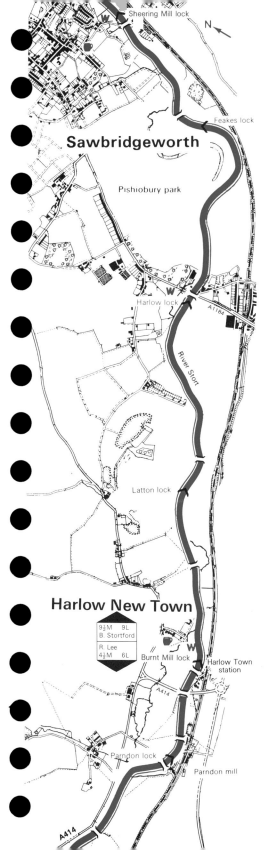

Sawbridgeworth

Leaving Eastwick to the north, the navigation passes the attractive Little Parndon Mill, then Burnt Mill; perhaps the name explains its absence. South of the railway lies Harlow New Town; it does not intrude on the navigation. Winding on north eastwards up the valley, one comes to Harlow Mill. There are usually skiffs for hire at the lock. Walkers should note that the towpath changes side at this point – do not be deceived by the path continuing up the west bank. Passing under the A11, the river continues to wind tortuously through water-meadows past Pishiobury Park. Sheering Mill Lock, with its lock cottage, is a good point from which to enter the very attractive town of Sawbridgeworth. A little further north is Sawbridgeworth Lock and Mill.

Sawbridgeworth
Herts. EC Thur/Sat. PO, tel, stores, garage, station. An attractive town with houses from the 16th to the 19thC, including many white clapboarded ones. The large 14th and 15thC church is rich in monuments and brasses, and has a collection of 18thC gravestones of great elegance. The town is well shielded from the A11, but makes the most of the Stort; the group of clapboarded mill buildings are particularly pretty. There is an impressive array of maltings near the river.
Hyde Hall East of the Stort, 1 mile from town centre. Built in 1806 by Sir Jeffrey Wyatville in Tudor style, the mansion stands in a wooded park of 300 acres.
Pishiobury Castellated mansion rebuilt in 1782 by James Wyatt from earlier Tudor house. Still retains some Tudor and Jacobean work inside. Park and lake by Capability Brown. Now a school.
Harlow
Essex. EC Wed. MD Tue, Fri, Sat. PO, tel, stores, garage, station, cinema. Harlow Old Town, which contains several 18thC houses, a Norman chapel at Harlowbury and the site of a Romano–Celtic temple has been swallowed up by Harlow New Town, set up in 1947 as a balanced area for London's overspilling population. Frederick Gibberd master-minded the plan, and the New Town is now well known as an important breakthrough in town planning.
Harlow Town Pets' Corner Harlow Park. Animals roaming free in the park. Also aquarium, vivarium and aviaries. *Open daily, school holidays and week-ends; afternoons during term-time.*
Parndon Mill at Parndon Lock, Harlow. (0279 415063). A fine tall wooden watermill now housing offices.

PUBS

🍺 **King William IV** Fairgreen, Sawbridgeworth, ¼ mile west of Sheering Mill Lock.
🍺 **Old Bell** Sawbridgeworth. Good food.
🍺✕ **Churchgate Manor Hotel** Churchgate Street, Harlow. (0279 20246). Food, reductions for children.
🍺✕ **Dusty Miller** ¼ mile north of Burnt Mill Lock. (0279 24180). Food.

Bishop's Stortford

Leaving Sawbridgeworth and its riverside
malthouses, the river passes a very low railway
bridge and wanders round to Tednambury
Lock. Just to the north of this an arm leads off
to Little Hallingbury Mill in its attractive
setting at the bottom of a hill. Walbury Camp is
half a mile upstream beside Spellbrook Lock,
but there is little about the camp to interest the
layman. Twyford House, Mill and Lock form a
very attractive group in the water-meadows that
flank the river; then a final sweep of the river
past trees and fields brings the outskirts of
Bishop's Stortford. A petrol station adjoins the
towpath before the river reaches the town
centre. The navigation almost reaches the
middle of the town, but navigators are not
advised to proceed further than the car park,
where the river divides: there are only a few
inches of water beyond this junction, and most
boats tend immediately to get stuck.

Bishop's Stortford
*Herts. EC Wed. MD Thur. PO, tel, stores,
garage, station.* A thriving market town that has
retained much of its old world atmosphere.
Many of the inns are centuries old. St Michael's
Church has a Norman font, which survives
from an earlier church built on the same site.
Rhodes Memorial Museum South Road,
Bishop's Stortford. (0279 51746). Contains a
collection illustrating Cecil Rhodes' life,
particularly in relation to his activities in
Rhodesia. The old vicarage where Rhodes was
born contains descriptive maps, pictures and
documents devoted to him.
Waytemore Castle Bridge Street. Only the
foundations of the rectangular keep remain,
and what used to be the bailey is now the
pleasure gardens.
Thorley
Herts. The church retains its Norman south
doorway and a west tower from the 15thC.
However, extensive restoration was done in
1854 by Vulliamy. Thorley Hall nearby is a
15thC farmhouse which was modernised in the
18thC.
Little Hallingbury
Essex. PO, tel, stores. The church has a Norman
doorway made with Roman bricks. The south
porch is of timber. Note the pretty
timber-framed house behind the little pond
near the church.

PUBS AND RESTAURANTS

- **Three Tuns** London Road, Bishop's
Stortford. Near the station.
- **Cock** Bishop's Stortford.
- **Star** Bishop's Stortford.
- **Old Bull's Head** London Road, Bishop's
Stortford. Food.
- **Tanners Arms** Station Road, Bishop's
Stortford. Canalside. Food.

MONMOUTHSHIRE & BRECON

Maximum dimensions

Length: 50'
Beam: 8'
Headroom: 6'
Draft: 2'

Manager
(0873) 830328

Mileage
PONTYPOOL to
Goytre Wharf: 6
Llanfoist: 11½
Gilwern: 14½
Llangattock Bridge: 18
Talybont: 26½
BRECON: 33¼

Locks: 6

In 1792 the Act of Authorisation for the Monmouthshire Canal was passed. This gave permission for a canal to be cut from the estuary of the River Usk at Newport to Pontnewyndd, north of Pontypool. In addition to this 11-mile main line, there was to be an 11-mile branch from Malpas to Crumlin. The canal was designed to connect with a large network of tramways that were to be built to serve the iron ore, limestone and coal mines of the area. Thomas Dadford was appointed engineer, and the canal was opened in 1796, with many of the tramways still to be built.

The close relationship between canal and tramway from the start of the scheme was a feature of South Wales. The promoters of the canal saw these embryo railways as a means of increasing their revenue, without suspecting that they were encouraging the development of a means of transport that later was to cause the downfall of the canals.

When the Act for the Brecknock & Abergavenny Canal was passed in 1793, it was conceived in very similar terms to its southerly neighbour. The canal was planned to connect Brecon with the River Usk at Caerleon, to serve as a link between the various tramways and the Usk Navigation. The directors of the Monmouthshire Canal persuaded the promoters of this rival venture to alter their plans to include a junction with their own canal, whose construction was well under way by this date. And so the Brecknock & Abergavenny Canal, with Thomas Dadford again as engineer, was cut from Brecon to Pontymoile Basin, where it joined the Monmouthshire Canal. Construction was begun in 1797. It progressed slowly because the company's first priority was the building of the tramways, a more immediate source of revenue. The canal was only to be built when all the tramways were in operation, to serve as a keystone for the whole system. After the usual delays caused by shortage of money, the Brecknock & Abergavenny Canal was opened throughout in 1812.

For a while the two canals were profitable, because the iron and coal cargoes justified the use of both canal and tramway. However, the greater speed and efficiency of the railways soon became apparent, and by the 1850s there were many schemes to give up the canals and rely entirely on the rail system. Some were put forward by the canal companies, in order to protect their interests as best they could. In 1865 the Monmouthshire and the Brecknock & Abergavenny Canal Companies amalgamated, becoming the Monmouthshire & Brecon Canal Company; but already it was too late for the merger to be effective. Revenues were dropping fast as the railway tentacles reached through the South Wales coalfields. Later the whole system was bought by the Great Western Railway, and by the turn of the century only a few boats were still using the canal. Bit by bit the original Monmouthshire Canal was closed, but the Brecon line was kept open as a water channel. In 1962 the network was formally 'abandoned', and parts were filled in.

However, with the development of the Brecon Beacons National Park, the amenity potential of the Brecon line was realised. In 1964 the slow task of restoration was begun by BWB, with the help of Brecon and Monmouth County Councils. The locks were restored, and soon boats were once more able to cruise from Pontymoile to Talybont. In 1970 the low fixed bridge at Talybont was replaced with a new lifting bridge, and once again navigation was open all along the old Brecknock & Abergavenny Canal. The Monmouthshire line from Pontymoile to the Usk at Newport may never be reopened in its entirety, for stretches have vanished completely; but parts have been restored as far south as Cwmbran, where it is proving a valuable asset to the developing new town.

Natural history

A diversity of interesting and colourful wild plants and animals can be seen along the Monmouthshire & Brecon Canal. For much of its length the canal is tree-lined, mostly by alders, which can be recognised by their smooth, roundish leaves with jagged edges and their clusters of little cones. Interspersed with the alders, or in small copses nearby, is a variety of other trees such as oak, ash and sycamore. Between Llanfoist and Govilon fine beech trees clothe the hillside and reach down to the canal, and in spring wild cherries are conspicuously beautiful in blossom between Llangynidr and Crickhowell.

The smaller aquatic plants grow best in less shady places. Rooted in the mud at the bottom of the canal, and completely submerged in water, are the true aquatics like the feathery-leaved water milfoil and Canadian pondweed. The latter, a North American plant, spread rapidly after its introduction into this country halfway through the last century. Other water plants to be seen include bur-reeds, with long ribbon-shaped leaves floating on the surface, and water plantains with oval leaves thrust above the water and tiny pink or white three-petalled flowers.

Bordering the canal grow many gaily coloured marsh plants, in bloom from July until autumn. Especially conspicuous are the tall 'codlins and cream', with rose flowers, and hemp agrimony with fluffy heads of pink flowers. The sweetly scented, feathery clusters of cream meadowsweet contrast effectively with the lovely blue of water forget-me-not. Marsh woundwort with its lilac flowers is frequent and here and there along the banks the blue trumpets of skullcap can be seen.

The animal life is also rich and varied, although it has lately suffered considerably from predation by wild mink. The kingfisher with its scintillating blue-green plumage is always an exciting sight. Fortunately it is now fairly frequent again along the canal. Another bird which comes to fish is the tall grey heron, which flaps away on slow wingbeats when disturbed. The largest bird likely to be encountered is the mute swan; a family party including four or five cygnets may often be seen near Brecon. Moorhens can be observed at several spots, either swimming along in their inimitable jerky style or walking about on the banks in search of food. Where the canal overlooks the River Usk as at Llanhamlach or crosses it via Brynich Aqueduct, the dipper – a dark, tubby, thrush-sized bird with a white front – may be seen bobbing up and down on stones in the river. Although its main habitat is the fast-flowing river, it may forsake this for the canal on occasions and be seen on the towpath. In summer, from bramble thickets and hedgerows along the towpath issue the songs of whitethroats and garden warblers. Many small birds such as tree creepers, nuthatches and tits feed in the overhanging trees, and in winter the alders are sometimes thronged with twittering parties of siskins, searching the cones for seeds.

Of the wealth of smaller animal life along the canal, the dragonflies are perhaps the most noticeable, as they patrol to and fro over their particular stretch of water. Occasionally the female dragonflies may be seen dipping their long abdomens into the water at intervals to lay eggs on the submerged water plants. Pond skaters are the numerous small dark insects with long legs that dart away over the surface of the water at your approach. On marsh plants like the fragrant water mint, beautiful beetles with a greenish metallic lustre may be found. During May and June, orange-tip butterflies are on the wing along the banks, where the females (with grey, not orange-tipped wings) lay eggs on milkmaid plants, on which their caterpillars feed. Later in summer, speckled wood butterflies may also be seen flying or basking in sunny glades.

Brecon Beacons National Park

The Park covers 519 square miles of mountain and hill country, embracing parts of the old counties of Herefordshire, Monmouthshire, Breconshire and Carmarthenshire. Apart from a great variety of fine scenery, the Park also includes three nature reserves, a forest reserve, opportunities for fishing, caving, pony trekking, sailing and boating, and several towns of interest to tourists, notably Brecon, Crickhowell, Talgarth and Hay-on-Wye; in addition Abergavenny, Llandovery and Llandeilo are just outside the Park boundary.

Virtually all the canal is within the Park – a factor that greatly strengthened the case for its restoration and reopening. The canal is an excellent introduction to the Park, crossing it roughly from south-east to north-west; in several places there are foot and bridle paths leading away into the mountains from the towpath. Various main roads cross the Park, and so access by car is easy, but the whole area is best explored on foot. A good place to start any exploration is the Mountain Centre, 1000ft up on Mynydd Illtud, above the village of Libanus, 4 miles south west of Brecon. There are rest and refreshment rooms, car parks and picnic sites overlooking the Brecon Beacons, and the wardens at the Centre give lectures to visitors and youth groups on the Park and the use of the countryside.

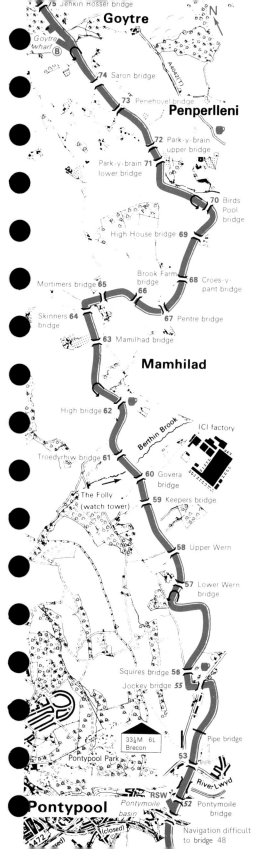

Pontypool

Before the closure of the Newport section, the old Monmouthshire & Brecon Canal used to run from Brecon to the estuary of the River Usk at Newport, and thus to the sea. After a quarter of a century of decay, the upper section, from Pontypool to Brecon, was restored and reopened to craft in 1970. The limit of navigation is at the pleasantly landscaped Pontymoile Basin, although craft may pass through the bridge to moor by the playing fields. The town centre is about one mile to the north west, through the lovely Pontypool park. After a few canalside gardens, all traces of the town are left behind, and the canal starts its meandering contour course towards Brecon. The character of this canal is quickly apparent; it twists and turns, clinging to the hillside on the west, while to the east wide views open up across the rolling pastures and woods of the Usk valley. The winding course, and the frequent stone bridges make the canal interesting, for every bend offers a different view of the steep hills to the west and the valley to the east, while the canal itself remains entirely quiet, rural and isolated. Navigators should look out for the cast iron mile posts, which survive irregularly along the length of the canal. There are no villages by the canal in this section, but services and pubs are never more than a short walk away, at Pontymoile, at Mamhilad and at Penperlleni. Provisions are available at Ty-bach, west of bridge 62. Main roads also keep their distance, although they are generally clearly visible in the valley below the canal. After passing the long tunnel-like Saron bridge (no. 74), the seclusion is interrupted by long lines of moored boats, which are the prelude to Goytre Wharf. Old lime kilns can be seen by the wharf, indicating the agricultural nature of the canal in its heyday. The wooded hills sweep down to the wharf, giving it a most attractive setting.

Penperlleni
Gwent. PO, tel, stores, garage. Main road village useful for supplies.
Mamhilad
Gwent. Tel. A little hillside hamlet scattered round the church. Overshadowed by massive yew trees, the pleasantly over-grown churchyard has fine views across the valley.
Pontypool
Gwent. EC Thur. MD Wed, Fri, Sat. Pontypool has been an industrial town since Roman times, concentrating on the production of iron. This reached a peak in the 18th and 19thC, but has declined in recent times. In 1720 tinplate was produced here for the first time in Britain, and in the 19thC the town was a centre for japanning – the coating of objects with an extract of oils from coal, so producing a black varnish similar to Japanese lacquer. Coal mining has also been important. Despite this industrial heritage, Pontypool has always remained a farming centre, and so the hard industrial elements are softened by the traditions of a rural market town. The steep walls of the Lwyd valley have also limited the growth of the town, and made the centre very self-contained.
Pontypool Park Originally the seat of the Hanburys, the famous iron and steel family, this Georgian mansion is now a school. The park is open to the public. The magnificent wrought iron entrance gates at Pontymoile (by bridge 53) were given to John Hanbury by Sarah Churchill, Duchess of Marlborough.
Torfaen Museum Trust Canal museum in the old toll cottage. Details from Park Buildings, Pontypool. (0495 752043). *Open afternoons.*

BOATYARDS

Ⓑ **Red Line Boats** Goytre Wharf, Pontypool, Gwent. (0873 880516). Ⓡ Ⓢ Ⓦ Pump-out, gas, narrowboat hire, day hire craft, overnight mooring opposite, long-term mooring, winter storage, slipway, chandlery, books and maps, boat sales, engine sales and repairs, toilets, showers, café.

PUBS

Goytre Arms Penperlleni. ¼ mile east of
bridge 72. Food, garden, real ale, children
welcome.
Horseshoe Inn Goetre Fawr. ¼ mile north
of bridge 65.
Star Mamhilad. 200yds east of bridge 62.
Food, real ale, children welcome.

Horse & Jockey Pontymoile, on A472.
100yds east of bridge 55.
Bell Inn High Street, Pontypool.
Forge Hammer High Street, Pontypool.
Open Hearth Sebastopol. Canalside,
between bridges 48 and 49, south of
Pontymoile Basin. Food, garden, children
welcome.

Gentle exercise along the 'Mon & Brec'. *Derek Pratt.*

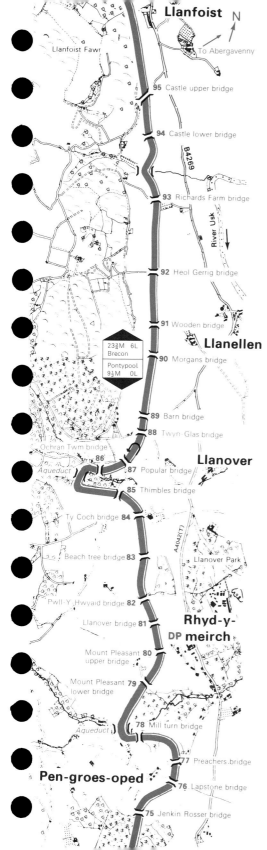

Abergavenny

Beyond Goytre Wharf, the canal continues its meandering course northwards, passing through a thick wooded cutting before returning to the pattern set in the previous section: steep wooded hills to the west, the wide valley rolling away to the east. The canal clings to its contour line high on the side of the hills, at times making horseshoe bends to avoid any change in level. At the apex of each such bend, there is generally a small stone aqueduct taking the canal over a stream that tumbles noisily down towards the valley. In several places these streams serve as feeders for the canal, half their water joining the canal, half passing beneath an aqueduct. 200yds west of bridge 76, in Pen-groes-oped, there is a good general store, a post box and a telephone. After the first horseshoe bend, set among thick woods, the canal passes Llanover Park to the east; the house is out of sight, shielded by trees, but the village can be seen nestling in the hillside. The next bend is much wider; looking back, the course of the canal along the side of the hill can be clearly seen. After the bend there is a long straight for over a mile, which carries the canal through the trees above Llanellen. The River Usk is coming nearer all the time, and its course into Abergavenny is visible below. To the west the hills are now very steep, rising sharply to over 1800ft, at times almost vertically away from the canal. From its elevated position there is an excellent view of Abergavenny, laid out like a model in the valley below, nearly a mile from the canal. In the 19thC the hills to the west were heavily mined and quarried, and many tramways constructed to carry the coal, iron ore and limestone down to the canal to be loaded into boats. There are sometimes still traces of these tramways; often their course into the hills can be followed from the canal bridges. A good example leaves the canal at Llanfoist, by the boathouse. The loading wharves, cut into the steep hillside, can also be seen in many places along the canal.

Abergavenny
Gwent. EC Thur. MD Tue. All services.
Abergavenny lies beside the fast flowing River Usk, surrounded on all sides by mountains and hills; the Sugar Loaf, Blorenge and the Skirrids overlook the town, a dramatic natural wall ranging up to 2000ft. Abergavenny enjoys this magnificent setting, living up to its reputation as the gateway to Wales. Primarily a market town, it contains the traditional mixture of buildings of all periods and styles, from the Tudor houses in the main street to the red stone of the 19thC Gothic town hall.
Abergavenny Castle The mound of the castle dominates the town. Built in the 11thC, the castle was the scene in 1177 of a treacherous massacre of several notable Welsh leaders; invited to the castle to dine by William de Braose, they were put to death with no warning. In this violent way William made sure of his control over the surrounding lands. Parts of walls, towers and a gateway survive. Ruins and grounds *open daily*.
St Mary's Church Originally the chapel of the Benedictine priory, the church was extensively rebuilt in the 14thC, after the destruction of the priory. It contains fine wooden 14thC choir stalls, a wooden figure of Jesse, and rich monuments in the Herbert chapel.
Abergavenny and District Museum Situated in the castle precincts, the museum contains items of local interest, Roman coins, tools and examples of local crafts. *Open daily.*
Sugar Loaf A conspicuous landmark 2 miles north west of Abergavenny, so named because of its shape. 2130 acres, including the 1955ft summit, are owned by the National Trust.
Rural Crafts Museum Llanvapley. 4 miles east of Abergavenny, on B4233. 500 tools, rural and farm equipment and implements, domestic bygones. *Open Sun afternoons.*
Llanellen
Gwent. PO, tel, stores. Although modern housing has greatly extended Llanellen into a suburb of Abergavenny, it is still an attractive village, especially by the three-arch stone bridge over the Usk. The 19thC church is pleasantly set among woods.

Llanover

Gwent. PO, tel, garage. The famous bell Big Ben in Westminster was named after the politician Benjamin Hall (Lord Llanover), who was responsible for the construction of the tower whilst Chief Commissioner of Works. He also initiated the tramway from Buckland House Wharf to Rhymney Ironworks, east of Talybont reservoir. The estate village is particularly elegant; stone cottages and terraces all built in the same style, pleasingly laid out with generous grass verges and trees.

BOAT TRIPS

Owain Glyndwr 46-seater water bus operated by B & M Charters and based at bridge 76 near Goytre. (0291 690201). Licensed bar.

PUBS

Many pubs and restaurants in Abergavenny.

Llanfoist Wharf. *David Perrott.*

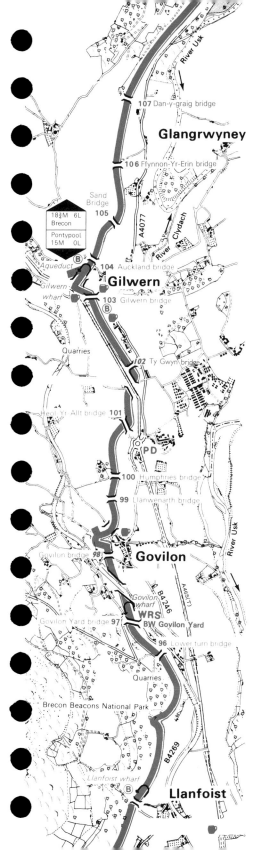

107 Dan-y-graig bridge

Glangrwyney

106 Ffynnon-Yr-Erin bridge

Sand
Bridge
105

18¾M 6L
Brecon

Pontypool
15M 0L

A4077

River Clydach

Aqueduct
104 Auckland bridge

Gilwern

*Gilwern
wharf*
103 Gilwern bridge

Quarries

102 Ty Gwyn bridge

Heol Yr Allt bridge 101

PD

100 Humphries bridge

99 Llanwenarth bridge

River Usk

Govilon bridge 98

Govilon

*Govilon
wharf*
WRS
B4246
Govilon Yard bridge 97
BW Govilon Yard

96 Lower turn bridge

Quarries

Brecon Beacons National Park

A465(T)

B4269

Llanfoist wharf

Llanfoist

Govilon

The canal continues to follow its contour course
northwards, cut into the steep, rocky sides of
the hill. With Abergavenny spread out in the
valley below, and the wooded slopes climbing
up from the water, it is a very dramatic stretch.
Llanfoist comes into view, partly hidden by the
trees. The old wharf buildings, originally built
for the tramway that ran up into the hills from
the canal, are now a boatyard and hire cruiser
base. The boatyard bridge is the best place to
leave the canal on foot for Abergavenny.
Leaving Llanfoist, the canal continues through
the wooded side-cutting. As the course of the
long-abandoned railway swings in to join the
canal, the towpath changes sides to the west,
where it remains until Govilon. The village is
huddled beneath the canal; the wharf buildings
are now used by Govilon Boat Club, who
restored them. The BW section office is also
here. A butcher's shop by bridge 98 sells milk
and eggs. After the big skewed rail bridge (now
disused) the canal makes another horseshoe
bend, crossing a stream on an aqueduct. As it
approaches Gilwern, the presence of the Heads
of the Valley road becomes more obvious, close
to the eastern bank. The canal passes above
Gilwern, which spreads down the hill to the
east, and then turns sharply before Gilwern
Wharf. This area has now been landscaped, and
it is worth stopping the boat to inspect the
information board between bridges 104 and
105, opposite the lime kilns, which illustrates
how the area looked before 1850, when it
served the Clydach Ironworks, situated up the
gorge. The road and the hills swing away to the
west, leaving the canal to pass through a thickly
wooded stretch in comparative quiet; however,
the tumbling waters of the River Usk are never
far away.

Gilwern
Gwent. PO, tel, stores. The village is built along
one main street, which falls steeply away from
the canal; there are fine views of the country
running down to the River Usk, ½ mile to the
east.
Govilon
Gwent. PO, tel, stores, garage. The canal passes
above the village, and little can be seen from the
water. Beside the aqueduct are steps leading
down to Govilon. The village is spread out
along the road, now quiet after the opening of
the new road to the east. It was at one time a
small industrial centre, with iron works and
lime-kilns, but these have long since vanished.
Llanfoist
Gwent. PO, tel, stores, golf course. The
boatyard, housed in the old stone wharf
buildings, has given the little village a new lease
of life. There is a good walk from the boathouse
into the mountains, following the course of the
old tramway.

BOATYARDS
Ⓑ **Castle Narrowboats** Church Road Wharf,
Gilwern. (0873 830001). Ⓦ Pump-out,
narrowboat hire, day boat hire.
Ⓑ **Road House Holiday Hire Narrowboats**
Main Road, Gilwern. (0873 830240).
Pump-out, gas, narrowboat hire.
BW Govilon Yard (0873 830328). ⓇⓈⓌ
Slipway by arrangement, toilets.
Ⓑ **Beacon Park Boats** The Boatyard,
Llanfoist. (0873 78277, bookings 0222 484677).
Narrowboat hire.

BOAT TRIPS
Omega is a 40-seater electric boat available for
charter from Gilwern. Ring (0873) 830001.

PUBS
🍺 **Beaufort Arms** Gilwern. Food. B&B.
🍺 **Bridgend** Gilwern. Canalside at bridge 103.
A welcoming pub offering a good choice of real
ales, food and a garden. Children welcome.
🍺 **Corn Exchange** Gilwern. Food, garden, real
ale, children welcome.
🍺 **Navigation** Gilwern. Canalside at bridge
103. Fine picture of a navvy and his tools on the
sign. Food, garden, children welcome.
🍺 **Bridge End** Govilon, below the aqueduct.
Food, real ale, garden, children welcome.
🍺 **Bridge Inn** Llanfoist.
🍺 **Llanfoist Inn** Llanfoist. Food, garden,
children welcome.

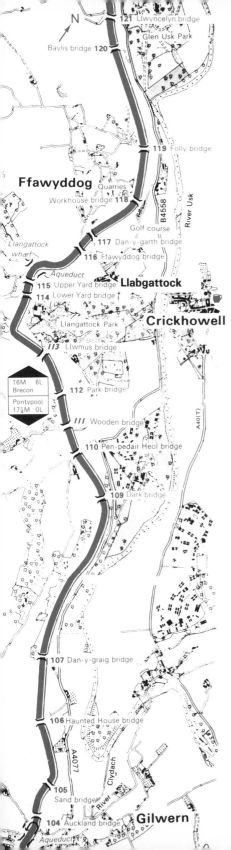

Crickhowell

Continuing north west, the canal clings to its contour on the side of the hill, which separates it from the River Usk for a while. As the canal passes the old army camp laid out in parkland to the east, the hills become less dramatic. The approach to Llangattock is through flatter country, but trees still surround the canal, hiding the extensive parkland that falls away to the east. Llangattock is set below the canal, best approached from bridges 114 and 115; beyond it lies Crickhowell, the fine houses rising out of the valley over the river. Llangattock Wharf is just beyond bridge 115: now a busy mooring site overlooked by the old stone wharf buildings, which include a range of limekilns. This is a good base for exploring the Brecon Beacons; there are opportunities for caving in the surrounding hills, and horses can be hired in Crickhowell for trekking. Leaving Llangattock, the canal crosses a small aqueduct, and is then quickly back among the hills, whose steep wooded slopes fall sharply to the water's edge. As the River Usk and the canal close together again, there are fine views to the east across the valley. One of the best is across the golf course, which comes right up to the towpath. A short straight then takes the canal to Glen Usk Park, through woods that get progressively thicker.

Llangattock
Powys. PO, tel, stores. This little village, just down the lane from bridge 116, was once famous for its weaving and its lime-kilns. It also has a 12thC church, founded in the 6thC. With a handsome square tower, it is well worth a visit. The hills behind the village are riddled with limestone caves and quarries. One cave, Agen Allwedd, has 11 miles of underground passages, the entrance is in the Craig-y-Cilau Nature Reserve, but exploration should only be undertaken by experienced and properly equipped cavers. Permits for rock climbing, and for specimen collecting, must also be obtained from: Nature Conservancy, Plas Gogerddan, Aberystwyth, Dyfed.

Crickhowell
Powys. EC Wed. MD Thur. PO, tel, stores, garage, bank. The road down through Llangattock leads to the 13-arch medieval stone bridge over the Usk, the imposing entry to Crickhowell. This fine market town, once a centre for the production of Welsh flannel, is spread over the northern slopes of the Usk valley. The town is compact and elegant, with terraces of 18th and 19thC houses, and some handsome inns. In the centre are the scant remains of the Norman castle. Once controlling a large area, the castle was destroyed during the 15thC, and only the motte and bailey, parts of the curtain wall and a small tower survive. The 14thC parish church contains interesting stained glass. Crickhowell has long been a famous holiday centre, a role it still enjoys today. Apart from hill walking, there are opportunities for fishing and pony trekking.

PUBS
● **Horse Shoe** Llangattock. 200yds from bridge 114 or 115. Food, garden, real ale, children welcome.
● **Bridgend Inn** Crickhowell. Well worth the one mile walk from either bridge 114 or 116 to this fine old inn overlooking the medieval bridge. Bass, Worthington and Hancocks real ale, food, riverside garden. Good collections of jugs and chamber pots, and a cosy fire in cold weather.
●✕ **Bear Hotel** Crickhowell. (0873 810408). Food. B&B.
● **Six Bells** Mill Street, Crickhowell. Davenports real ale, food, garden.

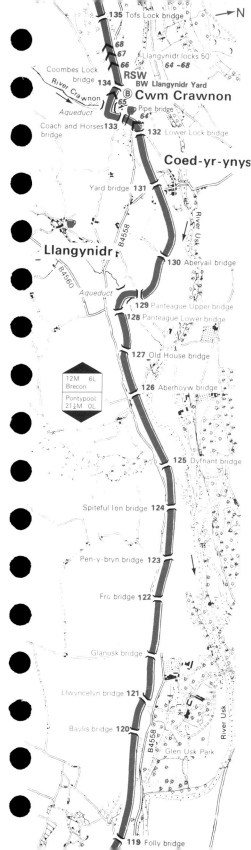

Llangynidr

Leaving the wooded Glen Usk Park behind, the canal continues its north-westerly course along the Usk valley. Among the trees to the east can be seen the Italianate towers of Gliffaes. As the canal approaches Llangynidr, it begins to meander more, leaving the hills and woods behind; river-like, it wanders through open rolling pastureland beside the Usk, passing to the south of the village. Bridge 129 is the best access point for Llangynidr. The small settlement by bridge 131 includes a shop, telephone, tennis courts, and a garage. As this is left behind, the canal reaches the first lock of the Llangynidr flight of five; this, the first lock on the navigable section of the canal, ends the 23-mile-long pound; the short climb to the summit at Brecon starts here. Leaving Cwm Crawnon, where there is a pub and restaurant, the canal turns sharply over an aqueduct and reaches the second lock. On the old wharf beyond the lock is a toll house, now used by BW and a sanitary station. Hire craft operate from here. Thick woods now flank the canal as the steep hills return on both sides. The Usk valley has narrowed, and so canal and river flow close together through the hills; the canal is still high above the river. In the middle of the woods are the final three locks of the flight, following closely upon each other. The surrounding woods and hills make this one of the most beautiful settings on the canal system. Each lock is fitted with two ladders, so you can motor straight in, when ascending. After a disastrous breach in March 1975, the canal between Llangynidr and Llanfoist was de-watered for years while repairs were made.

Navigational note
Llangynidr locks should be left empty with bottom gates open.

Cwm Crawnon
Powys. Clustered round the canal as it climbs the Llangynidr locks, this hamlet is famous for the Coach & Horses pub, with its French cuisine.
Tretower Court and Castle 2½ miles north west of Crickhowell on A479. Ruins of a late 14thC fortified manor house, which was built to replace a Norman castle whose remains still exist nearby. The ruined cylindrical keep is unusual.
Llangynidr
Powys. PO, tel, stores (open every day). Spread out over a plateau, this farming village is scattered round the pretty 19thC church. The grandest house in the village is the old rectory, whose grounds run almost to the canal bank.

BOATYARDS

BW Llangynidr Yard By bridge 134. R S W.

PUBS

Coach & Horses Cwm Crawnon, Llangynidr. Canalside at bridge 133. Food, garden, Ushers real ale, children welcome.
Red Lion Llangynidr. (0874 730223). Food. B&B. Local trout and salmon served in 16thC surroundings. *Closed Mon & Tue lunchtimes and Mon dinner*.

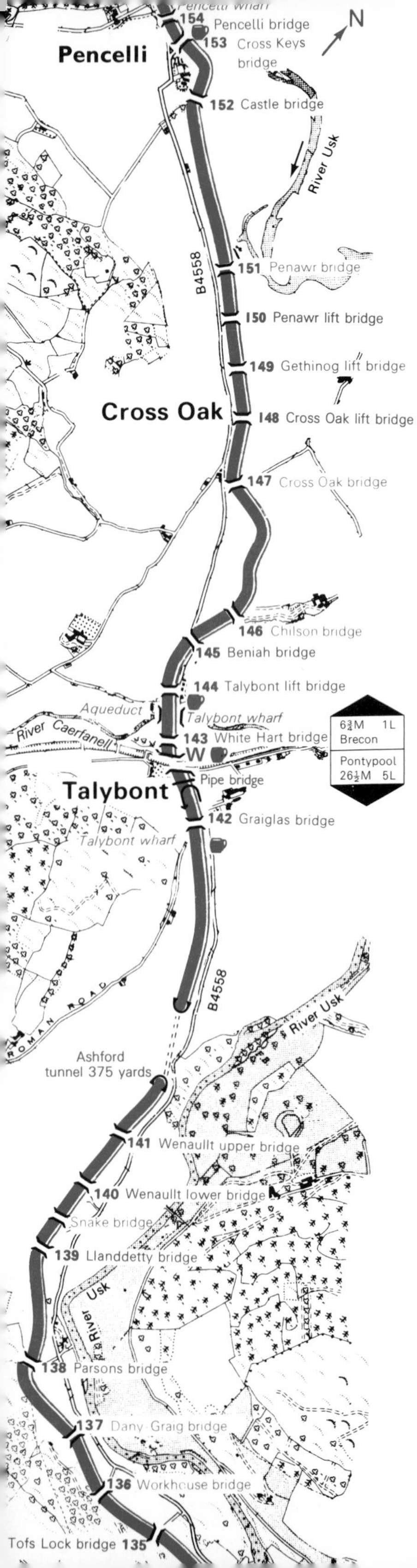

Map labels (north to south):

Pencelli

Pencelli wharf
154
153   Cross Keys bridge
152   Castle bridge

River Usk

B4558

151   Penawr bridge

150   Penawr lift bridge

149   Gethinog lift bridge

Cross Oak

148   Cross Oak lift bridge

147   Cross Oak bridge

146   Chilson bridge

145   Beniah bridge

144   Talybont lift bridge

Aqueduct

Talybont wharf

River Caerfanell

143   White Hart bridge

W

Pipe bridge

Talybont

Talybont wharf

142   Graiglas bridge

| 6¾M   1L |
| Brecon |
| Pontypool 26½M   5L |

B4558

River Usk

ROMAN ROAD

Ashford tunnel 375 yards

141   Wenaullt upper bridge

140   Wenaullt lower bridge

Snake bridge

139   Llanddetty bridge

River Usk

138   Parsons bridge

137   Dany Graig bridge

136   Workhouse bridge

Tofs Lock bridge 135

Talybont

Leaving the Llangynidr locks behind, the canal continues through thick woods passing the three cottages by bridge 135, once a workhouse. The narrow Usk valley pushes the two waterways close together, although the canal stays high above the river. The thick wooded walls of the valley fall steeply on both sides. The minor road that has accompanied the canal all along the valley is still much in evidence, although traffic is luckily very light. The valley starts to open out, and as the hills recede, rolling pastureland flanks the canal as it enters the slight cutting that precedes the short Ashford Tunnel. The tunnel, 375yds long, seems particularly small as it has no portals to speak of; a round hole disappears into the side of a low hill, looking more like a large culvert than a tunnel. The towpath goes over the top, following the line of the tunnel and the B4558. Leaving the tunnel behind, the canal goes straight to Talybont through a low cutting. Passing an old wharf where there is a pub on the road beside the canal, bridge 142, and the disused rail bridge, the canal goes through the village on an embankment, crossing the fast flowing Caerfanell river on an aqueduct. From bridge 142 the remains of a Roman road run to the hill fort above the village. The wharf was used by the Bryn-Oer tramway, which brought limestone down from the quarry above. Lime kilns are much in evidence by the canal. Its course can still be followed. Talybont stretches along the road below the canal, seemingly a typical canal village. At the end of the village is a lift bridge. It is electrically operated and instructions are clearly posted. Leaving the village, the canal enters a different landscape. Pasturelands still roll steeply away to the west, but to the east there are wide flat lands; the canal is carried on a low embankment which continues irregularly for the next 3 miles. Three newly built conventional lift bridges cross the canal. These are sometimes fixed in the open position to stop livestock crossing the canal; navigators should always leave them as they find them. A very wide towpath accompanies the canal along this stretch, while on the west side the steep wooded slopes conceal the minor road. A sharp bend takes the canal into the village of Pencelli; the mound of the old castle dominates the village and the canal. There is a slipway just beyond bridge 154.

Pencelli
Powys. This little village was at one time the head of a medieval lordship: but the only indication of this today is the castle mound.
Talybont
Powys. PO, tel, stores (right by the canal), garage. When the railway and canal were both operating commercially, Talybont must have been a busy village. Today it is a quiet holiday centre with facilities for fishing, pony trekking and hill walking, although there is still a busy livestock market. The large wharf overlooks the village, which is clustered round the Caerfanell Aqueduct. The river falls rapidly from Talybont reservoir in the hills to the south, to join the Usk.
Llangorse Lake 3½ miles north of Talybont is the largest natural lake in South Wales, 502 acres given over to pleasure and recreation. Boating, yachting, water sports, fishing, pony trekking, caravan parks and camping sites are all available among spectacular scenery. Wildlife is abundant, and the goosander is a frequent visitor. The legendary town of Mara is supposed to lie submerged in the lake, and in fact a crannog, or lake dwelling set on stilts, has been found near the lake's outlet.

PUBS
● **Royal Oak** Pencelli. Canalside at bridge 154. Food, garden, children welcome.
● **Star Inn** Talybont. Canalside by the aqueduct. Food, garden, real ale, children welcome.
● **White Hart** Talybont. Canalside at bridge 143. Fine traditional pub with an open fire offering Bass and Felinfoel real ale. Food, children welcome.
● **Travellers' Rest** Talybont. Canalside at bridge 142. Food, garden, children welcome.

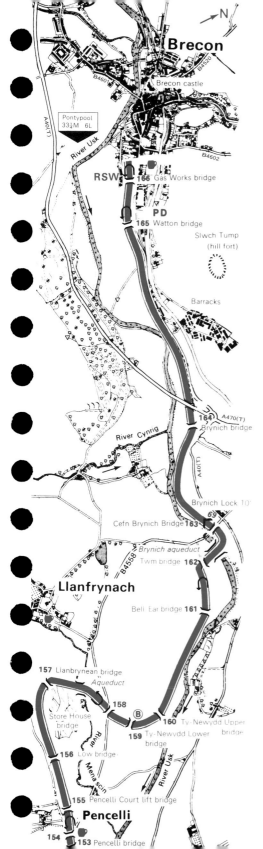

Brecon

Leaving Pencelli, the canal starts on a long
horseshoe bend that carries it through flat
wooded country towards the crossing of the
Usk. After the last lift bridge, a low
embankment carries the canal across marshy
ground towards Llanfrynach, but it never goes
near the village. The best access point is the
B4558 bridge. Before this bridge, a small
aqueduct takes the canal over the Nant
Menascin; this aqueduct was rebuilt while the
canal was closed and so is narrower than the
rest. Beyond the aqueduct there is an old mill,
now converted to a private house, with a
covered loading bay over a small disused arm.
A trip boat operates from here. The canal
completes the long curve back, well above the
fast flowing Usk. Llanhamlach lies across the
river. In addition to its 13thC church, the area
is rich in prehistoric remains. The Usk now
stays in sight all the way to Brecon, apart from
one small interruption. Bridge 162 takes the
towpath to the west bank, where it remains to
the terminus, and then the canal turns sharply
on to the Brynich aqueduct. This four-arched
stone structure takes the canal across the Usk to
the east side of the valley. To the west can be
seen the old bridge that takes the B4558 across
the river. Immediately beyond the aqueduct is
the last lock. Restored in 1970, the lock has a
particularly pretty cottage and garden beside it.
There is a shop and telephone on the A40. The
canal now goes straight to Brecon, passing
through a tunnel-like bridge under the A470.
The final mile of the route is high on the
hillside, overlooking the Usk all the way.
Although all of the canal is very clean, the
stretch into Brecon is remarkably clear and free
of weed. The canal follows the road to the
outskirts of the town, passing the barracks, and
then swings slightly to the west, along the backs
of the houses. The entry into Brecon is
attractive, with many pretty houses and
gardens flanking the canal. Originally the canal
went almost to the town centre, turning sharply
into a right-angled basin, but now it stops
short, just beyond bridge 166. The course of
the canal to the old terminus can still be traced,
although it has vanished beneath a car park and
a builder's yard. A big brick warehouse, dated
1892, marks the old head of the navigation.

Brecon
*Powys. EC Wed. MD Fri. PO, tel, stores,
garage, bank, cinema, swimming pool.* Built at
the confluence of the Usk and Honddu rivers,
Brecon has long been the administrative centre
and market town for the Breconshire uplands.
It dates back to the Roman period, and
although little remains, the narrow streets that
surround the castle give an idea of medieval
Brecon. Today the town is famous as a touring
centre, its cathedral and generous 18thC
architecture making it seem more English than
Welsh. The Usk waterfront is especially
attractive, dominated by the old stone bridge.
Sarah Siddons and her brother Charles Kemble
lived in the High Street.
Brecon Cathedral Originally the Priory
Church of St John, founded by Bernard
Newmarch, it was given cathedral status in
1923. Most of the building is 13thC, although
the nave is a century later. There is some fine
glass, and side chapels dedicated to various
medieval trade guilds.
Brecon Castle Most of the remains of the
11thC castle now stand in the grounds of the
Brecon Hotel, and permission to view must be
obtained from the hotel. A large motte and
bailey, parts of the walls and two towers
survive. The destruction of the castle during
the Civil War was hastened by the inhabitants
of Brecon, who did not want either side to
occupy it.
Brecknock Museum Glamorgan Street,
Brecon. (0874 4121). The collections include
local history, natural history and a large
archaeology section, from pre-Roman to
medieval times. The prize exhibit is a dug-out
canoe found in Llangorse Lake. *Open Mon–Sat
10.00–17.00 (closed Sun).* Free.
**Museum of the South Wales Borderers and
the Monmouthshire Regiment** The Barracks,
Brecon. (0874 3111). History of two famous
regiments over 280 years. *Open Mon–Sat*

*Apr–Sep (closed Sun); Mon–Fri Oct–Mar
(closed Sat & Sun).*
Tourist Information Centre Watton Mount,
Brecon. (0874 4437). *Closed winter.*
Llanfrynach
Powys. An attractive village built in a square
round the pretty church. Nearby is the site of a
Roman bath house. The white painted pub
dates from the 13thC.

BOATYARDS

®**Cambrian Cruisers** Ty Newydd, Pencelli,
Brecon. (0874 86315). Narrowboat hire.

PUBS

Many pubs and restaurants in Brecon,
including:
🍺 **Wellington** Bulwark, Brecon.
🍺 **Boars Head** Watergate, Brecon. Real ales,
garden, *lunchtime* food.
🍺 **Gremlin** The Watton, Brecon.
🍺 **Old Ford** Llanhamlach. On A40. ½ mile
east of bridge 160. Food.
🍺 **White Swan** Llanfrynach, ¾ mile from
bridges 158 or 157. Food, garden, real ale,
children welcome.
🍺 **Blue Boar Inn** 100yds north of bridge 166.
Real ale, food.

The beautifully sited Llangynidr locks. *Derek Pratt.*

OXFORD

Maximum dimensions

Length: 70'
Beam: 6' 10"
Headroom: 6' 6" to Napton, then
6' to Hawkesbury

Manager
(0926) 812882

Mileage

OXFORD (River Thames) to
Duke's Cut: 3
Thrupp: 7½
Lower Heyford: 14¾
Aynho Wharf: 20¼
Banbury: 27
Cropredy: 31½
Fenny Compton Wharf: 37¾
Napton Bottom Lock: 48
NAPTON JUNCTION (Grand Union
Canal): 49¼
BRAUNSTON TURN (Grand Union Canal):
54¼
Hillmorton Bottom Lock: 61¾
Rugby Wharf Arm: 64½
Stretton Stop: 69¾
HAWKESBURY JUNCTION (Coventry
Canal): 77

Locks: 43

This was one of the earliest and for many years one of the most important canals in southern England. It was authorised in 1769, when the Coventry Canal was in the offing, and was intended to fetch coal southwards from the Warwickshire coalfield to Banbury and Oxford, at the same time giving access to the River Thames. James Brindley was appointed engineer; he built a winding contour canal 91 miles long that soon began to look thoroughly out-dated and inefficient for the carriage of goods. Brindley died in 1772, and was replaced by Samuel Simcock; he completed the line from Longford, where a junction was made with the Coventry Canal, to Banbury in 1778. After a long pause, the canal was finally brought into Oxford in 1790, and thereafter through-traffic flowed constantly along this important new trade route.

In 1800, however, the Grand Junction Canal opened (excepting the tunnel at Blisworth) from London to Braunston, and the Warwick & Napton and Warwick & Birmingham canals completed the new short route from London to Birmingham. This had the natural – and intended – effect of drawing traffic off the Oxford Canal, especially south of Napton Junction; but the Oxford company protected itself very effectively against this powerful opposition by charging outrageously high rates for their 5½-mile stretch between Braunston and Napton, which had become part of the new London–Birmingham through route. Thus the Oxford maintained its revenue and very high dividends for many years to come.

By the late 1820s, however, the Oxford Canal had become conspicuously out of date with its extravagant winding course; and under the threat of various schemes for big new canals which, if built, would render the Oxford Canal almost redundant, the company decided to modernise the northern part of their navigation. Tremendous engineering works were therefore carried out that completely changed the face of the canal north of Braunston. Aqueducts, massive embankments and deep cuttings were built, carrying the canal in great sweeps through the countryside and cutting almost 14 miles off the original 36 miles between Braunston Junction and the Coventry Canal. Much of the old main line suddenly became a series of loops and branches leading nowhere and crossed by elegant new towpath bridges inscribed 'Horseley Ironworks 1828'. Now most of these old loops are abandoned and weeded up, although their twisting course can still be easily traced.

This very expensive programme was well worth while. Although toll rates, and thus revenue, began to fall because of keen competition from the railways, dividends were kept at a high level for years; indeed a respectable profit was still shown right through to the 20th century. Now, there is no trade on the canal – but this beautiful waterway has become one of the most popular canals in Britain for pleasure cruising, fishing and walking.

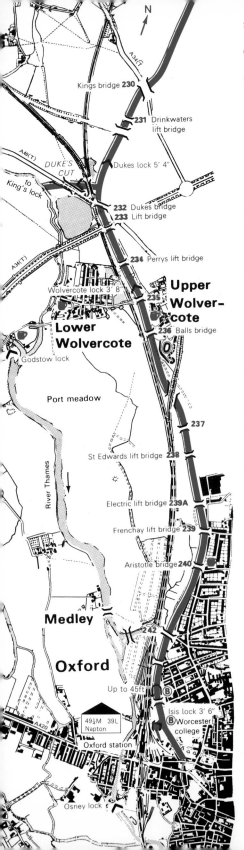

Oxford

The Oxford Canal can be reached from the
Thames in two places; one, via Duke's Cut, is
convenient but by-passes Oxford altogether;
the other, via a backwater under the north end
of Oxford station to the canal at Isis Lock, is
more enjoyable. A railway swing bridge here
was once a notorious obstruction, but this is
now left open. Past this bridge, boats continue
for 50yds along the backwater and should then
join the canal by turning sharp left into Isis
Lock. The canal continues southwards for ¼
mile past Worcester College to its terminus near
Nuffield College. Isis Lock, with its pretty iron
turnover bridge, is wooded and secluded,
despite its nearness to the centre of Oxford.
The canal goes northwards, flanked by houses
to the east whose gardens run down to the
water. This is an attractive stretch of urban
canal. After passing several wharves the houses
give way to industry, while Port Meadow lies to
the west. At bridge 240 there is a PO, stores
and off-licence, also swings for children. The
first Oxford Canal lift bridge appears followed
by an electric lift bridge, opened by push
button controls during working hours, and left
open at other times. Beyond the railway bridge
is Wolvercote, where the canal starts the long
climb up to the Midlands. After a series of main
road bridges, carrying the A40 and the A34,
Duke's Cut branches off to the west to join a
backwater of the Thames, and the canal moves
into open country, leaving Oxford behind.
Those joining the River Thames from the canal
should obtain a copy of the *Nicholson/Ordnance
Survey Guide to the River Thames* and obtain a
licence from the National Rivers Authority,
2nd Floor, King's Meadow House, Reading,
Berks RG1 8DQ. (0734 535000).

Wolvercote
Oxon. PO, tel, stores, garage. Oxford spreads
north along the Woodstock and Banbury roads,
making Wolvercote inseparable from the city.
There is little of interest, although it is useful as
a supply centre, and there are swings for
children. The concrete footbridge that crosses
the canal and railway in one span is impressive.
Oxford
*Oxon. EC Thur, MD Wed. PO, tel, stores,
garage, station, cinemas, theatres, university.*
Oxford was founded in the 10thC and has been
a university town since the 13thC. Its 39
colleges can be visited, but those noted here
have been selected as particularly
representative of their periods.
Merton College dates from 1264 and is one of
the earliest collegiate foundations that is almost
unrestored. Typical of the Perpendicular and
Decorative periods. The Grove buildings are by
Butterfield.
New College Founded by William of
Wykeham, Bishop of Winchester, in 1379. The
Perpendicular chapel was greatly restored by
Sir George Gilbert Scott in the 19thC.
Keble College Built by Butterfield in 1870
entirely in the Victorian Gothic style.
Sheldonian Theatre Broad Street. Built by Sir
Christopher Wren in the 17thC under the
auspices of Gilbert Sheldon, Archbishop of
Canterbury, who disapproved of the annual
performances of plays in St Mary's Church.
University degrees are awarded here. It has an
attractive ceiling by Robert Streeter.
Ashmolean Museum Beaumont Street.
Outstanding collection of Near Eastern and
European archaeology, the Farrer collection of
17th and 18thC silver, a display of early coins
and some drawings of Michelangelo and
Raphael. *Open weekdays and Sun afternoons.*
Christ Church Gallery Christ Church. Built by
Powell and Moya in 1967, it contains drawings
by Michelangelo, Veronese and Tintoretto, and
14th–18thC paintings, mainly Italian. *Open
afternoons.*
Museum of Modern Art Pembroke Street.
Gives unusual art exhibitions – anything from
environment to architecture graphics and
photography. *Open Tue–Sat and Sun
afternoons.*

University Museum Parks Road. A high Victorian Gothic building by Deane and Woodward. Natural history, including the head and claw of a dodo. *Open weekdays.*

Christ Church Meadows Approach from St Aldate's. A path leads down to the Thames, where the rowing eights are to be seen.

University Botanic Garden High Street. Oldest botanic garden in Britain, founded by Henry Danvers, Earl of Danby. In the 17thC the garden was intended for the culture of medicinal plants, but today it fosters extensive collections of rare plants for research and teaching. The gateway is by Inigo Jones.

Tourist Information Centre St Aldate's. (0865 48707).

BOATYARDS

Ⓑ **Orchard Cruisers** Castle Mill Boatyard, Cardigan Street, Oxford. (0865 54043). Ⓡ Ⓢ Ⓦ Ⓓ Pump-out, gas, narrowboat hire, overnight mooring, long-term mooring, winter storage, dry dock, chandlery, boat building, boat and engine sales and repairs, toilets, gift shop.

Ⓑ **College Cruisers** Combe Road Wharf, Oxford. (0865 54343). Ⓡ Ⓦ Ⓓ Ⓔ Pump-out, gas, narrowboat hire, day hire craft, overnight mooring, long-term mooring, winter storage, books and maps, boat building, boat sales, engine sales and repairs, toilets. 24hr breakdown service (*evenings* ring 0491 34155).

PUBS

There are many fine pubs, restaurants, wine bars and snack places in Oxford.

🍺 **Red Lion** Wolvercote.

🍺 **White Hart** Wolvercote.

🍺 **Plough** Upper Wolvercote. Snacks, garden.

🍺✕ **Trout Inn** on the Thames, near Godstow Lock (10 mins walk from canal bridge 235). Dates from 12thC. *Meals served daily* (0865 54485).

🍺 **Gardeners Arms** Plantation Road, Oxford. Children's room. ¼ mile east of bridge 242.

🍺 **Fountain** Cardigan Street, Oxford. 200yds east of bridge 242. Has antique juke-box and 'Aunt Sally' skittle game. It is worth the 1-mile walk from the terminus to visit.

🍺 **Turf Tavern** St Helen's Passage, New College Lane, Oxford. Hidden away. Excellent Stilton washed down with Hook Norton real ale.

Oxford from the air. *Aerofilms.*

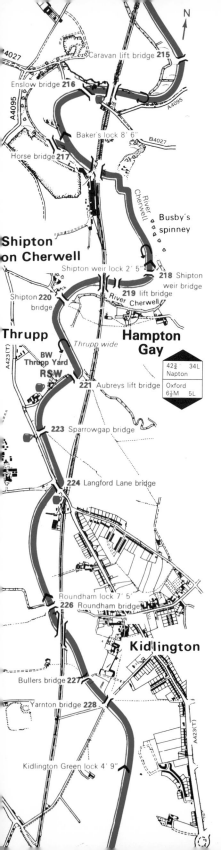

Kidlington

Continuing northwards the canal runs through lightly wooded fields and meadows to Kidlington, which is hidden from the canal by a low cutting. Keeping Kidlington in the distance, it then swings north east to join the Cherwell valley at Thrupp. From Thrupp the canal closely follows the Cherwell and adopts the meandering characteristics of a contour canal. Much of the canal is tree-lined, while its shallow banks and close relationship with the villages make it seem very river-like. At Shipton Weir Lock, whose 1ft rise is made up by its great width, the Cherwell and the canal merge and share a common course for the next mile (this stretch can be hazardous in times of flood). The tall chimney at the quarry and cement works on Bunker Hill dominate the valley for several miles. The Cherwell swings away west under an elegant iron bridge before Baker's Lock, but soon returns to run parallel to the canal. Wooded hills now determine the course of the canal, which passes plenty of villages and places of interest. Only Thrupp yard and the moored maintenance boats, the bridges and the occasional locks give away the fact that this is a canal. The railway follows the canal: the A423 crosses by Thrupp and the A4095 by Bunker Hill. A delightful stretch of rural canal.

Hampton Gay
Oxon. A deserted village. The church stands by itself, overlooking the River Cherwell, it can only be approached on foot, its seclusion and peace rather disturbed by the railway that almost runs through the churchyard. To the east, half-hidden by trees, are the romantic ruins of the manor: gaunt broken stone walls, windows open to the sky. The whole is well worth exploration, but is difficult to approach owing to the presence of the River Cherwell. Leave the canal at bridge 220 and walk east.

Shipton on Cherwell
Oxon. PO box. A magnificent situation: the wooded church overlooks the bridge and the canal, which curls round the foot of the church yard. Behind, the grey stone manor and farm look out over rolling fields to the west. The well-concealed A423 does not intrude. Shipton Bridge, ¼ mile to the east of the village, was the scene of a railway disaster on Christmas Eve 1874. Nine carriages fell from the Bridge on to the frozen canal below and 34 people were killed.

Blenheim Palace *Oxon.* 3 miles west of Shipton, at Woodstock. The English Versailles, built by Sir John Vanbrugh in 1722. Seat of the Dukes of Marlborough and birthplace of Sir Winston Churchill, who is buried in the nearby village of Bladon. Grounds restyled by Capability Brown include a large lake: altogether a superb setting. Fine furniture, paintings, tapestries. *Open daily Mar–Oct.*

Thrupp
Oxon. PO box, tel. A fine canal village, terrace houses running along beside the towpath, with a pub at one end and a BW yard at the other. The quality of the village makes it an unusual survival of early canal prosperity.

Kidlington
Oxon. PO, tel, stores, garage, cinema. The canal skirts round Kidlington, an extended suburb of Oxford. Parts of an older village survive to the north around the tall-spired church, including Sir William Morton's 17thC gabled almshouses. Nearby is the Oxford Air Training School, one of only 20 such places in the world training airline pilots. The town is most easily reached from bridge 228.

BOATYARDS
Ⓑ **BW Thrupp Yard** Kidlington. (0865 2222).
Ⓡ Ⓢ Ⓦ Moorings, toilets.

PUBS
🍺 **Rock of Gibraltar** Canalside, at bridge 216.

Food, garden with children's amusements. PO box.
🍺 **Boat** Thrupp. Canalside. Food.
🍺 **Jolly Boatman** Thrupp, by bridge 223. Canalside. Food.
🍺 **Wise Alderman** Kidlington. Canalside, by bridge 224. Lunchtime food.

Isis Lock, with its pretty iron turnover bridge. *David Perrott.*

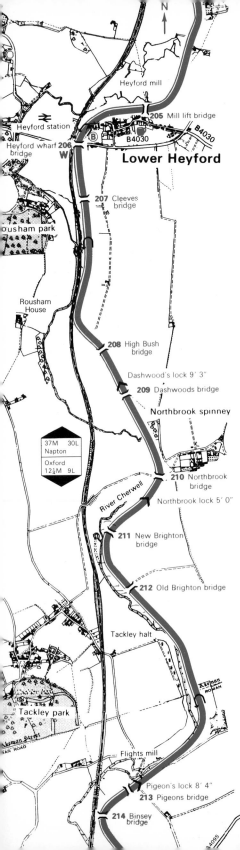

Lower Heyford

The canal continues to follow the Cherwell, winding its way through wooded undulating scenery. The canal does not intrude at all, in fact it is so well landscaped as to be often invisible from the hills on either side. At first the woods are thick, the overhanging trees forming a tunnel through which the canal passes, bounded by old stone walls. Pigeon's Lock marks the centre of the woods, which gradually diminish to reveal rolling farmland to the east and the water-meadows of the Cherwell to the west. The canal passes over the route of Akeman Street, and then the trees and the isolation return to conceal the canal from the grounds of Rousham House. As it reaches Lower Heyford the landscape opens out. The locks continue the rise towards Claydon. Kirtlington and Tackley are set up on ridges away from the canal, but Lower Heyford actually reaches its banks. Here the wharf with its clapboarded warehouses and old crane is now a hire boat base. The railway follows the canal very closely: Heyford station is very convenient. The B4030 crosses here.

Lower Heyford
Oxon. PO, tel, stores, station. Built among woods along the south bank of the Cherwell, and hence the canal. The church, with fine stained glass, overlooks the canal from a slight hill that conceals many of the cottages in a village where motor cars still seem intruders. To the north is a fine and very ancient water mill, screened by a line of willow trees that lead up to an unusual iron lift bridge, believed to be the only iron drawbridge in England.

Rousham House Steeple Aston. A lively picture of fighting during the Civil War is conjured up by the shooting holes made in the doors, which are preserved from the time when a Royalist garrison used the house. It dates from 1635, and was enlarged and its gardens landscaped in 1730 by William Kent. *Open Wed, Sun & B. Hol afternoons, Apr–Sep. Gardens open daily.*

Northbrook Bridge The stone canal bridge adjoins a much earlier packhorse bridge that crosses the Cherwell to the east. Although stylistically different, the marriage is very striking, as both are the same rich golden colour; and the setting in Northbrook Spinney is delightful.

Tackley
Oxon. 1 mile north west of Pigeons Lock across the Cherwell. (Access from the canal is by the footpath and a bridge leading from Pigeons Lock. It is a pleasant walk.) A residential stone village, spreading down towards the canal to include Nethercott where there is a small station, Tackley Halt. The church, set on a hill to the south, contains fine monuments.

Kirtlington
Oxon. 1 mile east of Pigeons Lock. *PO, tel, stores, garage.* Stone village laid out around a green. To the east is Akeman Street, a Roman road that flanks the wooded grounds of Kirtlington Park.

BOATYARDS
ⓑ **Oxfordshire Narrowboats** Canal Wharf, Lower Heyford. (0869 40348). Ⓡ Ⓦ Ⓓ Pump-out (*Mon–Fri*), narrowboat hire, overnight mooring, long-term mooring, dry dock, chandlery, books and maps, boat building, boat sales, engine repairs, boat hoist, gifts.
ⓑ **Boat Maintenance Services** Canal Wharf, Lower Heyford. (0860 577480, *evenings* 086 75 3885). 24hr breakdown service and engine sales and repairs.

PUBS
🍺 **Red Lion** Steeple Aston. Follow the path north from bridge 205. Food.
🍺 **Bell** 21 Market Square, Lower Heyford. Food, bar billiards. Picturesque 16thC inn.
🍺 **Dashwood Arms** Kirtlington. Food.
🍺 **Gardiner Arms** Tackley. Food.
🍺 **Kings Arms** Tackley. Food.
🍺✕ **Oxford Arms** Kirtlington. (0869 50208). Food (hot dinners).

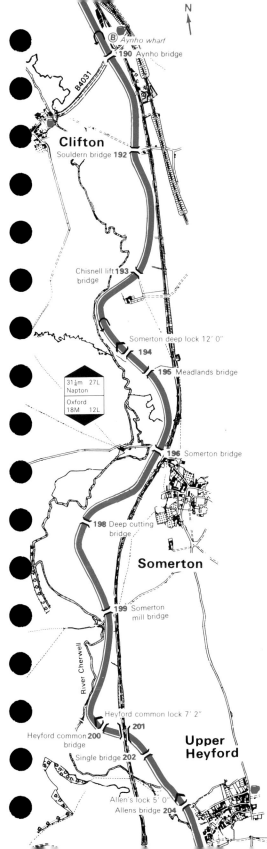

Somerton

Continuing north along the Cherwell valley, the
canal wanders through water-meadows, the
high towpath hedge often obscuring the fine
views across the valley. As it curves towards
Somerton the canal enters a short cutting and
then moves out into open pastureland.
Somerton climbs up the hillside to the east,
altogether a very attractive situation.
Throughout this stretch the canal is isolated in
the middle of the landscape, the locks are
generally remote, and set among trees, a
pattern only broken at Heyford Common Lock.
However, the open country continues after
Somerton Deep Lock, and the canal pursues a
straighter course towards Banbury. After
Somerton two railways run side by side to the
east of the canal, before joining at Aynho.

Aynho
Nothants, EC Tue. PO (mornings only), tel. The
village is 1 mile east of Aynho Wharf, but
must be seen. A self-contained village square
sheltered from the road, very unchanged, very
complete in rich stone. New houses have
been carefully blended with the old. Note the
peach trees that have been trained along the
walls of many of the cottages. On the other
side of the road is the formal classical façade of
Aynho Park, a 17thC mansion rebuilt by Sir
John Soane in the late 18thC. The house is
large but restrained, and does not look out of
place in a village street. Fine paintings,
furniture and Ventian glass. *Open Wed & Thur
afternoons May-Sep.* The church beside the
house was classicised at the same time: the
strange façade added to the nave wall makes it
a charming folly.

Clifton
Oxon. PO, tel. Small village overlooking the
canal, more convenient for supplies than
Aynho as it is nearer, but not as interesting in
itself.

Somerton
Oxon. Tel. A straggling grey stone village
winding up the hill to the east of the canal.
On the highest point is the church with its
decorated tower: there are good 16thC tombs
inside. In all the villages along the Cherwell
valley the churches are placed on mounds or
higher ground, overlooking the valley.

Upper Heyford
Oxon. PO, tel. A main street of thatched
stone cottages falls steeply to the canal, with
views across the valley to Steeple Aston. The
general store is charmingly placed in the old
Nonconformist chapel. The huge USAF
Heyford airfield to the east, makes its
presence felt. F-111's fly from here.

BOATYARDS

Ⓑ **Anglo Welsh Narrowboats** Aynho Wharf,
Banbury. (0869 38483). Ⓡ Ⓢ Ⓦ Ⓓ Pump-out,
narrowboat hire, gas, wet dock, engine repairs,
overnight mooring, toilets, provisions, canal
shop. *Facilities available Mon–Fri.*

PUBS

🍺 **Great Western Arms** Aynho Wharf. The
interior of this fine pub is devoted to
memorabilia of the GWR. Hook Norton real ale
and good food (*not Sun*). Deservedly popular.
🍺✕ **Cartwright Arms Hotel** Aynho. (0869
810656). Food.
🍺 **Duke of Cumberland's Head** Clifton. Food.
🍺 **Barley Mow** Upper Heyford. Food.

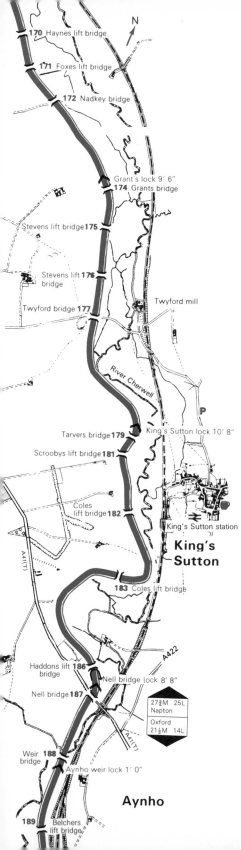

King's Sutton

The canal continues through wooded open
country with a background of hills to the east.
The Cherwell crosses the canal at Aynho Weir
Lock before continuing parallel to it and
forming a large loop lined by trees as it
approaches King's Sutton. Then the tall spire
of the church comes into view. Locks continue
the rise to Banbury: the very narrow Nell
Bridge, where the A41 crosses the canal, is one
of the oldest, having survived the various
road-widening schemes. The railway follows
the canal to the east. This pleasant rural stretch
of the canal along the Cherwell valley is well
punctuated by the characteristic wooden lift
bridges: luckily most of these are nowadays left
open (raised).

King's Sutton
Northants. PO, tel, stores, garage, station. An
attractive village of narrow streets that wander
in every direction. The centre is round a green,
at the top of a hill, where rows of thatched
cottages, two pubs and the church stand in
quiet harmony. The church is superb:
beautifully proportioned with a tall, slender
spire. The River Cherwell makes access to this
village difficult from the canal; the only
practicable access is by walking south east for
1½ miles from bridge 177.

Adderbury
Oxon. On the A41, west of bridge 177.
Thatched cottages, an old yew tree and a
graceful lychgate provide a fitting background
to the Decorated and Perpendicular-style
church, which is one of the finest in the
country. Its 600-year-old spire is one of the
well-known three that stand in line across the
landscape in full view of the Oxford road.

PUBS
- **Bell** The Square, King's Sutton. Food.
- **Butcher's Arms** King's Sutton. Food.
- **Three Tuns** King's Sutton. Food.
- **White Horse** King's Sutton. Food.

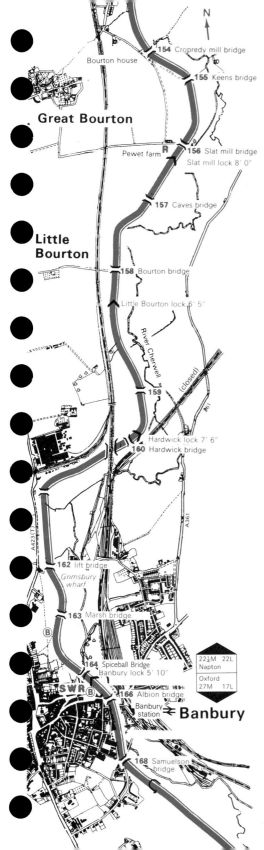

Banbury

Continuing north west along the Cherwell valley the canal enters Banbury through housing estates and an industrial area. North of Banbury the factories continue but gradually give way on the east to open fields. Your nose may tell you there is a General Foods Company factory west of bridge 162. To the west a main road follows the canal, accompanied by power lines and disused railways. Hardwick Lock marks the end of Banbury and the resumption of the more typical Oxford countryside. The canal swings north east and hills rise on the west. Locks continue the steady rise throughout this stretch; north of here all the locks feature double bottom gates, which make for lighter work. The railway follows the canal but crosses to the west after Banbury. The A422 crosses at Banbury.

Little Bourton
Oxon. ½ mile west of bridge 158. PO box, tel, garage. Quiet residential village to the west of the beautifully kept Little Bourton Lock and cottage. Stores in Great Bourton. 1 mile north.

Banbury
Oxon. EC Tue. MD Thur, Sat. PO, tel, stores, garage, cinema, station. The view of Banbury from the canal is not really fair to the town; it is far more attractive than the dismal industry and housing estates imply. Originally a wool town, the castle was pulled down by Cromwell's forces in 1646 and no trace remains. The ancient cross of nursery rhyme fame in the town centre was pulled down in 1602, and the present cross is a 19thC replica. The church was built in 1793 by S. P. Cockrell. The original bake house, which produced the spiced Banbury cakes, was demolished in 1968.

Tourist Information Centre & Museum
8 Horsefair, Banbury. (0295 259855).

Chacombe Priory Chacombe. 2½ miles north east of Banbury, off B4036. The house dates mainly from 1600, although there is a 13thC chapel with fine early stained glass. Picture gallery, furniture and silver. *Open Sun and B. Hols Apr, May, Sep. Sat and Sun afternoons Jun, Aug.*

Broughton Castle Broughton. 3 miles south west of Banbury, on B4035. Mainly moated Tudor castle with fine period fireplaces, ceilings and panelling. Collection of Civil War relics. *Open Wed, Sun, B. Hols afternoons Apr–Sep.*

Sulgrave Manor Sulgrave. 8 miles north east of Banbury. Small Elizabethan manor house completed in 1560 by Lawrence, direct ancestor of George Washington. The design of the American flag is reputed to come from the arms, consisting of three stars and two stripes, which are found in the main doorway. Contemporary furniture, portraits and personal possessions of George Washington. The Great Kitchen contains a range of impressive antique equipment. *Open daily (except Wed).*

BOATYARDS

Ⓑ **Morse Marine** Factory Street, Banbury. (0295 261221). Ⓡ Ⓦ Ⓔ Gas, long-term mooring, dry dock, chandlery, books and maps, boat building, boat sales, engine sales and repairs. 24hr breakdown service.

Ⓑ **Sovereign Narrowboats** Banbury Canal Centre, Compton Road, Banbury. (0295 275657). Ⓡ Ⓢ Ⓦ Ⓓ Ⓔ Pump-out, gas, narrowboat hire, long-term mooring, winter storage, dry dock, chandlery, books and maps, engine repairs, toilets. *This base is planned to open late 1991.*

PUBS

🍺 **Bell Inn** Great Bourton. 1¼ miles west of bridge 153.
🍺 **Swan Inn** Great Bourton.
🍺 **Ye Olde Reindeer Inn** Parson Street, Banbury. Dates from 1570.
🍺 **Wine Vaults** Parson Street, Banbury. 300 years old.
🍺 **Wheatsheaf** George Street, Banbury.
🍺 **Coach & Horses** Butchers' Row, Banbury.
🍺 **Plough** Little Bourton. Food.
🍺 **Bear** Market Place, Banbury. Food.

Cropredy

Continuing north along the Cherwell valley the canal enters Cropredy, whose stone cottages and wharf have been visible for some time. The village flanks the canal on the west bank, and all services are beside Cropredy Bridge. After the village the high towpath hedge conceals the open fields beyond, although there are views across the valley to the west. Milk, eggs and sometimes vegetables can be bought at Forge Farm. Around here the old ridge and furrow field patterns are very pronounced. Claydon comes into sight – here five locks take the canal to the summit level. Light woods border the canal, which is both shallow and very narrow in places. Near the second lock the remains of old stabling for boat horses can be seen; after the locks the canal twists and turns, swinging north west towards Fenny Compton. Hills and trees close in, preparing for the cutting that marks the course of the old tunnel. The feeder from Boddington reservoir, 2½ miles to the east, enters the canal through the towpath bridge 142. The railway, which moved to the west after Cropredy, reappears beside the canal. Bridge 141 is the last that the north-bound traveller sees of the very attractive wooden lift bridges that are such a well known feature of this canal. Much of the towpath is impassable on this section.

Claydon

Oxon. PO, tel, stores. Set in a rolling open landscape to the west of the canal. Claydon is an old-fashioned brown-stone village; in spite of some new development it preserves a quiet unpretentious charm. The curiously irregular Church of St James the Great provides a focal point – parts of it date from before the 12thC and the tower, which has a saddle back roof, contains a clock. There is no face, but the hour is chimed. Opposite is the pub. Clattercote Priory, just to the south, still remains.

The Granary Museum Claydon. Andrew Fox's fascinating museum of local relics continues to grow and never fails to entrance visitors. Children love to handle the objects, and his recreation of a 19thC cottage kitchen is remarkably atmospheric. Admission is free, but there is a well-stocked gift shop which invites spending.

Cropredy

Oxon. PO, tel, stores, garage. Quiet village of wandering streets of old brick houses. There is no real centre, but the whole village is very close to the canal, especially the garage and stores. The stately sandstone church contains fine woodwork; the slow swing of the clock pendulum in the belfry seems to echo the sleepy nature of the village, which only bursts into life during the annual Folk Festival, now Europe's largest. It is held on the second weekend in August, ticket details on (0869) 37142. It all began in 1979, when 'Fairport Convention' held their farewell concert here.

Battle of Cropredy 29 June 1644. Cromwell's forces under Waller attacked Cropredy Bridge in an attempt to open a way to Oxford. Despite greatly inferior numbers the Royalist cavalry managed to scatter Waller's army and capture his artillery, thus protecting Oxford. A plaque on the river bridge recalls the battle.

BOATYARDS

Ⓑ **Cropredy Wharf** Cropredy. (029 575 215). Tea and coffee in the Barn Tea Rooms, gifts and crafts in the Stable. Children's play area. Also Ⓦ Ⓓ Ⓔ Pump-out, gas, long-term mooring, winter storage, overnight mooring, books and maps, boat and engine repairs. Provisions at The Bridge Stores, an excellent general store and off-licence close by.

PUBS

🍺 **Brasenose Inn** Cropredy. Flagstone floors and low ceilings in the bar. Bass and M & B Springfield real ales, and Westons draught cider. Garden, food (*not Sun*).

🍺 **Red Lion** Cropredy (near bridge 152). 15thC pub serving Manns real ale. Dining room and bar food (*not winter Sun*).

🍺 **Sunrising** Claydon. Handsome village pub with cosy bar and fine fireplace. Hook Norton real ale, food, garden.

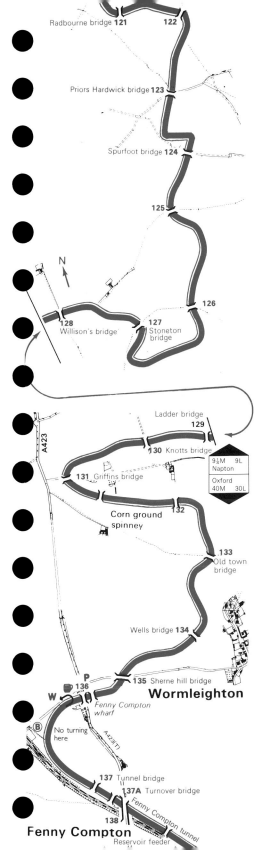

Fenny Compton

The canal continues along the Fenny Compton
'tunnel', a steep, thickly wooded cutting which
ends as it swings in a wide loop eastwards
towards Fenny Compton Wharf. The hills
retreat for a while, although their influence is
still present in the extravagantly indirect course
taken by the canal: Brindley seems to have had
a horror of straight lines. The long winding
route involves a large number of brick arch
accommodation bridges and many are now
un-numbered – it is easy to become
disorientated here. The canal first runs west
before doubling back on itself and running east
to Stoneton Manor, where a steep ridge causes
it to resume a north-westerly direction towards
Napton. Fenny Compton and Wormleighton
are both about a mile from the canal; Priors
Hardwick is nearer, across the fields, but has no
supplies. The railway disappears to the west
after Fenny Compton Wharf; the A423 crosses
twice by Fenny Compton. Much of the towpath
is non-existent – where it has not eroded away it
is completely overgrown with brambles,
hawthorn, great willow-herb and meadowsweet.

Priors Hardwick
Warwicks. East of bridge 124. PO, tel.
Approachable from the canal by a footpath (all
gates along the way must be left closed). A
small, partly deserted village much of which
was pulled down by Cistercian monks in the
14thC. The squat stone church is partly 13thC
while the little cottage opposite the former
school looks as if it were straight out of a
picture book.
Wormleighton
Warwicks. Tel. A manorial village that still
retains a feeling of privacy. Its 13thC brown
stone church contains a Perpendicular screen
and Jacobean woodwork. Further up the road
from the canal (leave at bridge 135) is the early
16thC brick manor house that must once have
been very impressive. South of the house is a
grand stone gatehouse dated 1613. A row of
Victorian mock-Tudor cottages completes the
village, which is well worth a visit for its feeling
of unity and self-reliance.
Fenny Compton
Warwicks. PO, tel, stores, garage. 1 mile west of
the wharf. A scattered brown stone village,
whose attractiveness is rather marred by a large
housing estate near the canal. The church is
partly 14thC and partly Victorian, with a
curious offset tower; alongside is a fine brick
rectory of 1707. Most of the village follows the
road, which forms a central square containing
the most interesting buildings and shops. All
the houses are graced by well-laid out gardens.
Fenny Compton Tunnel is no more, having
been converted into a cutting in 1868.

BOATYARDS

Ⓑ **Cowroast Limited** Fenny Marina, Fenny
Compton. (029 577 461). Ⓡ Ⓢ Ⓦ Ⓓ Pump-out,
gas, overnight mooring, long-term mooring,
slipway, dry dock, chandlery, boat building,
boat sales, repairs, toilets, grocery shop, books
and maps. *Please, no winding (turning) here.*

PUBS

🍺 **Butchers Arms** Priors Hardwick.
🍺✕ **George & Dragon** Fenny Compton
Wharf. (029 577 332). Canalside. Food. Ⓦ
Exotic birds in garden.
🍺 **Merrie Lion** Fenny Compton.

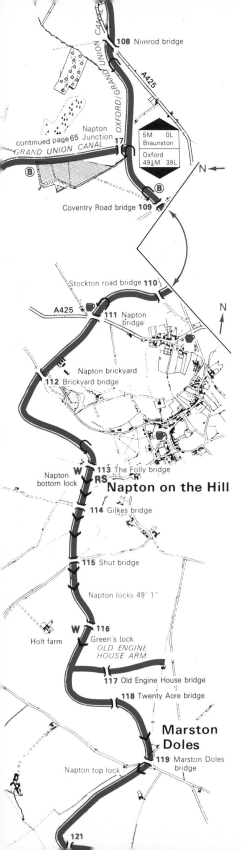

Napton

The canal continues northwards through
rolling open farmland, the view to the west
concealed by the towpath hedge. At Marston
Doles the country opens out and the windmill
on top of Napton Hill comes into view. Here
the summit level ends and the canal starts the
fall towards the junction that continues through
this heavily locked section. The arm to the east,
now used for private moorings, leads to the site
of the former pump house. The canal swings to
the west of Napton Hill, passing Brickyard
Bridge and then turns east to meet the Grand
Union at the junction. Marston Doles is a
typical canal settlement, but Napton is set to
the east on the side of the hill. This is a very
quiet section, although the A425 crosses below
Napton. There are moorings available at
Napton Bottom Lock, and a canal shop for
provisions in the lock house.

Napton-on-the-Hill
Warwicks. PO, tel, stores, garage. Rising to over
400ft, Napton Hill dominates the immediate
landscape. The village is scattered all over the
hill, climbing steeply up the sides. The shops
and pubs are at the bottom, however, and so
only those wishing to enjoy the view or visit the
13thC church need climb to the top. Near the
church is the restored windmill alone on the
hilltop. The canal wanders round the base of
the hill, by-passing the village except for the
wharf alongside Brickyard Bridge.
Napton Nickelodeon of Mechanical Music
High Street, Napton, opposite the Crown. (092
681 2183). A superb collection of music
machines, including a barrel organ, a
mechanical violin and a Wurlitzer Photo
Player. Also a Compton Cinema Organ to
accompany silent films. *Parties of 12 to 65
persons are given presentations by prior booking.
Individuals can book for the last Sat evening of
each month (not Jul or Aug). Individuals may also
book for Theatre Organ Concerts which are usually
held on the last Sun of each month.*
Holt Farm Between Marston Doles and
Napton by Green's Lock. (092 681 2225). Farm
shop, souvenirs, off-licence and moorings *open
daily until 19.30.*
Marston Doles
Warwicks. Tel. Tiny settlement that owes its
existence to the canal. Towing horses used to be
stabled here. To the north, at the end of an
arm, are the remains of the pumping house that
used to pump water up to the summit from the
bottom of the Napton flight.

BOATYARDS

Ⓑ **Calcutt Boats** Calcutt Top Lock (on the
Grand Union), Southam. (092 681 3757).
Ⓡ Ⓢ Ⓦ Ⓓ Pump-out, gas, slipway, narrowboat
hire and building, repairs, long-term mooring,
winter storage, crane, dry dock, chandlery,
toilets and provisions.
Ⓑ **Napton Narrowboats** Napton Marina,
Stockton. (092 681 3644). Ⓡ Ⓢ Ⓦ Ⓓ Pump-out,
gas, narrowboat hire, overnight mooring,
long-term mooring, winter storage, slipway,
crane, groceries, chandlery, books and maps,
boat building, boat sales, wet dock, engine sales
and repairs, toilets, gifts.

PUBS

🍺✕ **Kings Head Inn** 200yds south of bridge
109. (092 681 2202). Ind Coope (Burton) real
ale, food, games room, garden.
🍺✕ **Napton Bridge Inn** Napton. Canalside at
bridge 111. (092 681 2466). A justly famous
pub serving Davenports real ale and food at the
bar or in the restaurant. Large garden with
swings.
🍺 **Crown** Napton. ½ mile east of bridge 113,
with PO and stores nearby. An excellent village
local with an airy lounge and a lively public bar.
Manns real ale, food *lunchtime and evening,*
cheese skittles, garden and games room. A large
horse chestnut tree provides a shady drinking
area on the green.
🍺 **Hollybush** Priors Marston. 1½ miles east of
bridge 119. Fine 15thC inn serving Marstons
real ale along with guest beers. Garden, food.
Priors Marston stores (0327 60900) will deliver
to your boat.

Cruising on the Oxford Canal. *Derek Pratt.*

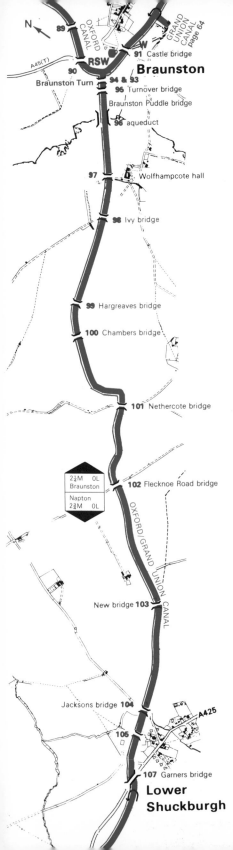

Braunston

Leaving Napton, the canal runs north east towards Braunston Turn. This stretch of the Oxford Canal was used jointly by the Grand Junction Company, and as a result the Oxford charged excessive toll rates in an attempt to get even with their rival, whose more direct route to London had attracted most of the traffic. Flowing through open country with a background of hills to the south, the canal is quiet and empty after the activity around Napton. The land is agricultural, with few houses in sight: the surviving medieval ridge and furrow field system on the south bank reveals the age of the landscape. Note how the canal cuts across the system at right angles. There are no locks, no villages and few bridges: a very pleasant rural stretch of canal. The A425 crosses through Lower Shuckburgh and the A45 in Braunston. The Oxford Canal bears off to the north at Braunston Turn: the Grand Union goes off to the south east at this point, passing through the canal centre of Braunston. Boaters will find everything they are likely to need here. There are good temporary moorings either side of bridge 91.

Lower Shuckburgh
Warwick. PO box. A tiny village along the main road. The church, built 1864, is attractive in a Victorian way, with great use of contrasting brickwork inside. The farm, west of bridge 104, sells eggs.

BOATYARDS
Ⓑ **Braunston Boats** Just beyond Braunston Marina on the Grand Union. (0788 891079). Ⓦ Ⓓ Pump-out, gas, narrowboat hire, long-term mooring.

The Boat Shop Crafts and gifts on board a boat moored at Braunston Bottom Lock. (0788 891310).

PUBS AND RESTAURANTS
Boatman Braunston. (0788 890313). Once the Rose & Castle, now a comfortable and friendly modern hotel/restaurant/pub. Ruddles and Websters real ale, bar meals (vast helpings) and candlelit dinners. Children's room, canalside garden with swings, good overnight mooring for patrons.
Old Plough High Street, Braunston. Imposing 17thC pub of great character, serving Ind Coope (Burton) and Ansells real ale, and food *lunchtime and evening*. Family room, garden.
Wheatsheaf The Green, Braunston. A locals' pub with a striking red bar, dispensing Wilson's real ale and food *lunchtime and evening*. Garden.

Willoughby

North west from Braunston the canal runs
through wide open country, backed by bare
hills to the east. At bridge 87 the medieval ridge
and furrow patterns are in evidence. Skirting
round Barby Hill, the canal swings north east
towards Hillmorton and Rugby. The railway
and the A45 run to the west of the canal, and
the M45 crosses after Barby Hill.

Willoughby
*Warwicks. PO, tel, stores, garage (and transport
café).* Mellow red brick village to which new
buildings have been unobtrusively added. The
small church is dominated by a fine 18thC
rectory.

PUBS
Rose Inn Willoughby.

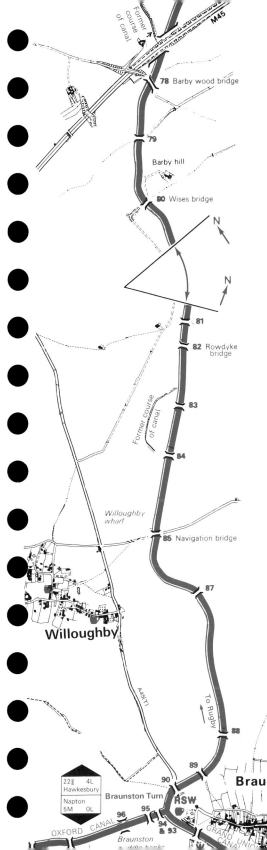

Hillmorton

After turning north east for 2 miles, the canal swings in a wide arc round Rugby. To the east the radio masts dominate the landscape. The canal descends Hillmorton Locks, three paired narrow locks (not often found), which fill and empty very quickly, are well maintained and a pleasure to use, and passes the attractively sited BW maintenance yard. There is an excellent all purpose grocer's shop at bridge 71. The railway accompanies the canal through Hillmorton and the A428 crosses south of the town. The little brick footbridge at the bottom locks is a delight to the eye.

Hillmorton
Warwicks. PO, tel, stores, garage. Its church dates from c1300, but there have been additions as late as the 18thC. There is an interesting medieval cross in the centre of the village, but the independence this implies has long since been swallowed up by Rugby.

BOATYARDS
B **Clifton Cruisers** Clifton Wharf, Vicarage Hill, Clifton on Dunsmore, Rugby. (0788 543570). R W D Pump-out, gas, narrowboat hire, long-term mooring, groceries, chandlery, books and maps, boat building, engine repairs, off-licence, gifts.
BW Hillmorton Yard (0788 561386). R S W Dry dock.

PUBS
Stag & Pheasant School Street, Hillmorton. A good welcoming local offering Ansells real ale and snacks.
Old Royal Oak Crick Road, Hillmorton. A handsome canalside pub at bridge 73. Sam Smith's and Youngers real ale, food *lunchtime and evening.* Family room, garden.

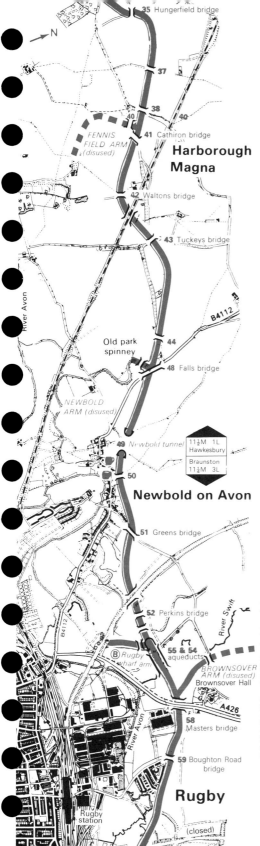

Rugby

Continuing the swing round Rugby, the canal enters a side cut embankment whose tall towpath hedge hides the town from view. There are shops to the south of bridge 59 and a picnic area below bridge 58. The River Avon is crossed by an aqueduct, and the Rugby Arm branches to the west; there is a boatyard on the arm. A short open stretch and then another deep cutting take the canal to Newbold, where the short tunnel and thickly wooded cutting lead the canal into open countryside. The iron bridges over the various arms reveal the course of the old canal. The B4112 accompanies it through Newbold.

Harborough Magna
Warwicks. PO, tel, stores. Quiet red brick village 1 mile to the north of the canal from bridges 43 or 48. The 14thC church has many Victorian additions, including an interesting stained glass window.

Newbold-on-Avon
Warwicks. PO, tel, stores, garage, fish and chips, launderette. A pleasant village with an interesting 15thC church and attractive cottages. At the wharf near the tunnel mouth are two pubs right next door to each other: why not try both?

Newbold Tunnel This 250yd-long tunnel was built during the shortening of the Oxford Canal in the 1820s. The old route was at right angles to the new, and the old tunnel mouth can be seen from the south by Newbold Church. The new tunnel was cut wide enough to allow for a towpath on both sides, a luxury at that date.

Rugby
Warwicks. EC Wed, MD Mon, Fri, Sat. PO, tel, stores, garage, station, theatre, cinema, leisure centre. A settlement for 2000 years, which has grown in turn as an agricultural centre, market town (since 1255), seat of learning and railway centre. More recently the heavy electrical industry has become established here. St Andrew's parish church dates from the 14thC, but in 1879 Butterfield added a nave and a tower, making it probably the only church in England to have a double peal of bells. Butterfield's work is also much in evidence in Rugby School, which gave its name to Rugby Football. A plaque commemorating the birth of the game in 1823 can be seen in the grounds. Nearby in St Matthew's Street are the James Gilbert Museum of Rugby Football and the Tourist Information Centre at Rugby Library, where the Exhibition Gallery and Museum have regular displays. The Leisure Centre is noted for its Zoom Tubes, which catapult swimmers into the water at breathtaking speed. There is a pedestrianised shopping centre and an open market with a Town Crier. The Monday livestock market is one of the largest in the area.
Information boards and town maps will be found near bridges 30, 50 and 66.

BOATYARDS
Ⓑ **Willow Wren Hire Cruisers** Rugby Wharf, off Consul Road, Leicester Road, Rugby. (0788 562183). Ⓡ Ⓢ Ⓦ Ⓓ Pump-out, gas, narrowboat hire, overnight mooring, long-term mooring, wet dock, books and maps. *Closed Sun and Mon.*

PUBS
🍺 **Old Lion** Harborough Magna, on the B4112 north of Falls Bridge. One lounge for the younger set, another, with beams and rough brick for the mature drinker. Ansells real ale, meals *lunchtime and evening*, garden.
🍺 **Boat** Newbold Wharf. At one end of this long pub there are cosy alcoves and an open fire. Davenports real ale and Westons real cider, meals *lunchtime and evening*, garden.
🍺 **Barley Mow** Newbold Wharf. M & B real ale and *lunchtime* food in this pub which has two small bars, a games room and large garden.

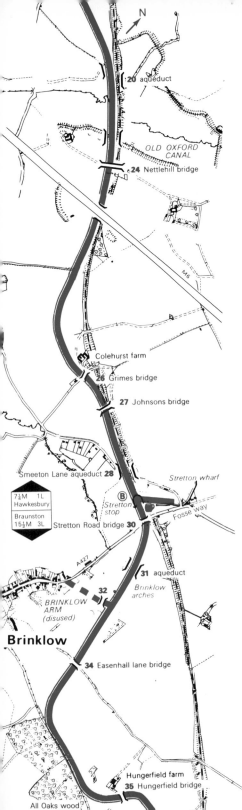

Brinklow

Continuing north west, the canal runs through
fine farming land and passes All Oaks Wood,
where good moorings have been provided. By
Brinklow the canal passes over an
embankment, which was originally an
aqueduct, but the arches have long been filled
in. Brinklow Arm, to the west, is unnavigable.
The long embankment continues through
Stretton Stop, where there is a boatyard and a
pottery, and past Stretton Arm, used for
mooring. Open, rolling fields follow, and then
the canal enters a deep cutting spanned by the
new motorway. The M6 cuts through this
stretch, and has greatly altered the landscape.
The elegant iron bridges that occur periodically
mark the course of the old Oxford Canal, prior
to the 1829 shortening. The railway follows the
canal to the east. The A4114 crosses through
Brinklow.

Brinklow

Warwicks. PO, tel, stores, garage. A spacious
pre-industrial village built along a wide main
street, the A4114. The church is alongside the
earthworks that mark the site of the castle built
to defend the Fosse Way, and is unusual in
having a distinctly sloping floor.

BOATYARDS

Ⓑ **Rose Narrowboats** Brinklow Marina,
Stretton Stop. (0788 832449). R S W P D E
Pump-out, gas, narrowboat hire, day hire craft,
overnight mooring, long-term mooring,
slipway, groceries, chandlery, books and maps,
boat building, boat sales, engine sales and
repairs, gifts, art gallery, pottery next door.

PUBS AND RESTAURANTS

Railway Canalside at Stretton Stop.
Davenports and Marstons real ale in an open
plan lounge. *Lunchtime* food: your children may
accompany you.
White Lion Broad Street, Brinklow. There
is a plush lounge and an old-fashioned public
bar in this village local. M & B real ale, snacks,
garden.
Bull's Head Brinklow. (0788 832355).
Large Family Diner pub and restaurant (*L &
D*). Flowers real ale.
Raven Broad Street, Brinklow, at the top of
the village. Comfortable lounge, bar billiards
and a wide range of food, both *lunchtime and
evening*. Lots of livestock in the garden.

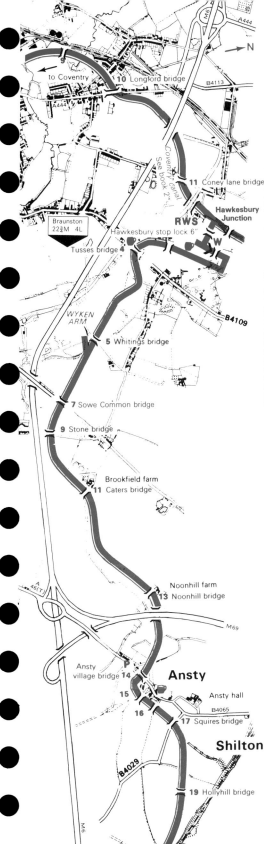

Hawkesbury Junction

Continuing north west, the canal leaves the
cutting and crosses a long embankment, which
is shared by the railway. The open landscape
continues to Ansty, although the motorway is
never far away. After the village the first signs
of Coventry appear, with views of pylons and
housing estates. The new Wyken Colliery Arm
leaves to the west: it was built to replace the old
one eaten up by the motorway which comes
alongside the canal at this point. Sharp bends
then lead to the stop lock before Hawkesbury
Junction, the end of the Oxford Canal where it
joins the Coventry. The last stretch of the
Oxford is characterised by the 1820s
shortenings; the straight cuttings and
embankments obviously date from this period,
while the cast iron bridges mark the old route.
The railway turns away before Ansty.

Ansty
Warwicks. Tel. Tiny village that grew up along
the canal, now disturbed by the motorway. To the
north are the church and Hall together, the
Hall is mostly 18thC. This area has been
much altered by motorway construction.
Shilton
Warwicks. ½ mile north of bridge 17. *PO, tel,*
stores, garage. Main road village left bewildered
by the railway and the A46.

PUBS

🍺 **Greyhound** Canalside at Hawkesbury
Junction. An interesting pub serving Bass real
ale and snacks. Canal shop next door.
🍺 **Elephant & Castle** Canalside at bridge 4.
🍺 **Crown** Ansty. Tiny snug, tiled floor in the
lounge, low ceilings and real fires in both
rooms. M & B real ale and meals *lunchtime and*
evening.
🍺 **Crown** Church Road, Shilton. Traditional
locals' bar with bench seats and a plain lounge.
Ansells real ale.

The Llanthony Lift Bridge at Gloucester Docks. *Derek Pratt.*

GLOUCESTER & SHARPNESS RIVER SEVERN

GLOUCESTER & SHARPNESS CANAL

Maximum dimensions

Length: 190'
Beam: 29'
Headroom: unlimited

Mileage

SHARPNESS Lock to
Purton: 1½
Saul Junction: 8
GLOUCESTER Lock: 15 ¾

Locks: 2

Manager

(0452) 25524

RIVER SEVERN

Maximum dimensions

Gloucester to Worcester
Length: 135'
Beam: 22'
Headroom: 23' 6"
Worcester to Stourport
Length: 89'
Beam: 18' 11"
Headroom: 20'

Mileage

GLOUCESTER Lock to
Ashleworth: 5
Haw Bridge: 8¼
TEWKESBURY Junction with River Avon:
13
Upton upon Severn: 19
DIGLIS Junction with Worcester &
Birmingham Canal: 29
Holt Fleet: 36
STOURPORT Junction with Staffs & Worcs
Canal: 42

Locks: 5

The River Severn has always been one of the principal navigations in England. Its great length has made it an important trade artery since the medieval period. With its tributary, the Avon, it cuts deep into the heart of England, linking the iron and coal fields with the Bristol Channel and the British coastal trade. By using the Severn, boats of a considerable size could sail into the Midlands, and into Wales as far as Welshpool. However the navigation, especially above Worcester, was always difficult, owing to currents, shoals, and the demands of water supply for milling etc.

As boats increased in size, and the cargoes became heavier, the navigational problems increased. The larger boats in common use in the 18thC could rarely sail higher than Bewdley, and so by the end of the century this inland port was beginning to lose its significance. At the same time the sandbanks and shifting shoals in the Gloucester area were seriously affecting the trade on the river as a whole. In order for the

river to survive as a viable trade route, it became necessary for drastic improvements to be made. Various Acts were passed to ensure the maintenance of the towing path, although the Severn maintained its tradition of using gangs of men to bow-haul boats until well into the 19thC. In 1803 over 150 men were still employed in what Telford called 'this barbarous and expensive slave-like office' on the section between Bewdley and Coalbrookdale.

The demands of increasing navigation, and the spread of canals in the West Midlands (the Staffordshire & Worcestershire Canal linking the Severn with Birmingham and the rest of the network was opened in 1772) led to the passing of an Act in 1793 that authorised a canal to be built from Berkeley Pill to Gloucester. Work began on Gloucester Docks in 1794, and over the next few years 5½ miles of canal were cut. Shortage of money then caused work to be stopped, and so the canal remained useless and incomplete. In 1817 Telford was commissioned by the government to report on the feasibility of the canal, with particular reference to the maintenance of navigation on the Severn. He reported in favour of continuing and completing the canal, but recommended that it should run to Sharpness instead of to Berkeley. The government then put up the money for the canal, mainly to relieve acute problems of unemployment, and after considerable delays the Gloucester & Sharpness Canal was opened throughout in 1827.

Some of the structural problems were caused by the decision to build the canal to ship standard. (At the time of opening, this was the broadest, deepest canal in the world.) But although it greatly increased the cost, this farsighted decision has ensured that the canal remains in use, and even today Gloucester and Sharpness docks are commercial ports.

Once the canal was in use, considerable dredging works and improvements became necessary to maintain the navigation of the upper Severn to Worcester and Stourport. This work, carried out extensively since the formation of the Severn Commission in 1842, included the building of locks and weirs, and the canalisation of parts of the river. The links with the Midlands canal network helped the Severn to flourish, and railway competition increased rather than decreased the traffic both in the docks and on the ship canal. In 1874 Sharpness docks were enlarged and modernised, to handle ships of up to 1000 tons. The same year the Gloucester & Berkeley Canal Company leased the Worcester & Birmingham Canal, to maintain their hold on the trade routes to the Midlands. By 1888 the Severn had a minimum depth of over 6ft, and in most places the depth was 8 to 9ft. Trade continued to thrive, and the recession in the 1920s was soon overcome by the rapidly growing oil traffic, which became the mainstay of the river. Although commercial traffic has declined there are, now and again, signs of a revival.

Natural history

Spring is a good time to visit the River Severn, when the river banks are speckled white with cow parsley and the riverside alders and willows are bearing their catkin flowers, providing valuable nectar and pollen for early moths and bees. In March and April millions of young eels come up-river with the high spring tides after a three-year, 3000-mile journey from their breeding grounds in the western Atlantic. The elvers are followed by twaite shad, a sea fish which migrates into fresh water to spawn, and these provide sport for anglers as the fish try to ascend the weirs at Tewkesbury and Gloucester. Other migrants from the sea include 3ft-long sea lampreys and 9-in river lampreys (which are both parasitic, sucking the blood from other fish), sea trout and salmon. Spring is also the time to listen for nightingales, which sometimes sing in the riverside woodlands, and to watch the caddis flies, may flies and stone flies which have newly emerged from their aquatic larvae and now dance across the surface of the water until they have mated, laid their eggs or fallen prey to some surface-feeding fish such as bleak or dace. Other fish found in the Severn include bottom-feeders such as bream, carp, roach, gudgeon, loach and occasionally barbel (which was introduced about 15 years ago), as well as carnivores such as pike, perch and eel.

It is perhaps in August that the river banks look best, with colourful clumps of yellow tansy, purple loosestrife and great willowherb with drooping heads of pink flowers. The recently introduced Himalayan balsam with its handsome pink and white flowers now grows in large clumps at Mythe Bridge near Tewkesbury, Sandhurst near Gloucester and near Gloucester Docks. In marshy areas, riverside pools and withy beds the reedmace grows with brown club-like heads, the common reed with 6ft-high stems and plumed flowerheads, and the greater and lesser pond sedges, which bear separate spikes of male (upper) and female flowers. These areas are the home of the sedge, reed and marsh warbler, although the last-named is rare nowadays.

Very few other birds nest along the Severn, although sand martins and kingfishers sometimes excavate nesting holes where the banks are steep, moorhen and mallard are found in the riverside bushes and two heron colonies are known to inhabit tall trees a little way inland from the tidal part of the river below Gloucester. The best place to look for water birds is undoubtedly the area between Frampton and Slimbridge where the extensive mud flats and sand banks exposed at low tide provide an attractive resting place for spring and autumn passage migrants. This area is especially good for winter visitors such as shoveller, pintail, wigeon, teal, lapwing, golden plover, ringed plover, dunlin, curlew, redshank and turnstone, and holds a roosting colony of about 20,000 common gulls. Two species of geese also come to feed on the riverside pastures in winter: up to 5000 whitefronted geese from Siberia and 100 pink-footed geese from Greenland.

For the most part, the mammals of our rivers are secretive and nocturnal but water vole holes are a common sight in the river banks and the observant walker can sometimes recognise the tracks or other signs of our rare native otter or the accidentally introduced North American mink, a beautifully sleek black animal a little larger than a stoat, which originally escaped from fur farms but is now breeding in the wild along all parts of the Severn which run through Gloucestershire.

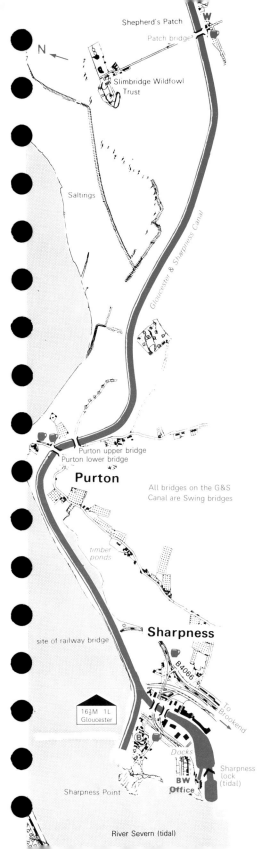

Sharpness

The Gloucester & Sharpness Ship Canal, which was built to bypass the dangerous winding stretch of the tidal River Severn between these two places, has its southern terminus at Sharpness, where there are docks and a large lock up from the Severn. The Gloucester & Sharpness Canal is nowadays the only navigable route between the Severn estuary and the Severn Navigation above Gloucester, so all boats heading upstream must pass through Sharpness Lock and Docks. It should be noted that the entrance to the lock dries out completely at low water, so boats heading in from the estuary should time their arrival for 3 hours before high water, notifying Sharpness in advance. The best time to arrive at the lock is about 2½ hours before high water when locking down, and about 1 hour before high water when locking up. (The lock is normally operated 2½ hours before to 1 hour after high water.) BW maintain free visitor moorings in the docks, which are available for 48 hours. It is important to give prior notice of one's intentions to BW at Dursley on (0453) 811644 ex 21 or 36 (or VHF channel 14). Boatmen wishing to proceed down the Severn estuary from Sharpness are advised not to do so without a pilot. It is important to keep to the marked channel, and the tide runs extremely fast. Immediately above the lock are Sharpness Docks, which handle ships from all over Europe. The docks are a very busy area and an important source of revenue to BW's Freight Services Division. Pleasure boats are encouraged to move on quickly through the two swing bridges out of the docks and onto the ship canal itself. Just north of the two swing bridges is an arm off to the west: this leads to a tidal basin which is now, unfortunately, disused. However the length of the arm leading to it is used for permanent and temporary pleasure craft moorings, and there is a small boatyard at the end of it. It is a fascinating place to walk round and see the tidal Severn flowing strongly at the foot of the stone walls. Across the river is the tree-lined west bank of the river, only ½ a mile across at this point. A railway line runs along the bottom of the hills. However the old 22-arched railway bridge that used to cross the river just north of here has been completely demolished, and only the merest traces of some of the stone piers can be seen at low water. The bridge was badly damaged one foggy night in November 1959, when a vessel collided with it; the bridge then stood with a hole in the middle until it was demolished and the iron girders sold to – of all places – Chile, where they now form a road-carrying viaduct. Along the main line of the canal, the circular stone structure is all that remains of the railway's swing bridge over the canal. A mile from Sharpness Docks, the canal is lined with trees on each side – an uncharacteristically river-like stretch that is belied by the occasional glimpse of the Severn flowing alongside. Old timber ponds open off the canal to the right. Timber was stored afloat here 'in the round'. Then a curve leads to the little village of Purton and its two swing bridges. There is only one bridge keeper and he spends most of his time at the upper swing bridge (0453 811384). The navigation snakes through the village, passing the big new waterworks before settling down to a steady course of wide, straight reaches. It traverses a quiet, green and predictably flat landscape that is well studded with trees and always bounded to the north by saltings and the mud-flats of the Severn estuary – which is here much wider than at Sharpness. At Patch Bridge (0453 890324) there are two pubs; this is the best access point to the Slimbridge Wildfowl Trust. (*See over*). There is a water point by the bridge.

Navigational note 1
As this is a commercial waterway, moor only at recognised sites: Old Arm, Sharpness; Patch Bridge; Fretherne Bridge; Sellars Bridge; Bakers Quay; Gloucester Docks.

Navigational note 2
The mechanical swing bridges are manned *08.00–18.45 (16.30 winter), lunch break 13.00–13.30*, and are guarded by traffic lights. Proceed only on the green.

Navigational note 3
Bridges and locks operate a listening watch on marine band radio channel 74. It is not necessary to contact each bridge or lock unless you are delayed, or have an emergency.

Shepherd's Patch
Glos. This little settlement existed long before the canal: it used to be where the shepherds watched over their flocks grazing the Severn estuary. There are two pubs here, a gift shop, café and youth hostel.
Slimbridge Wildfowl Trust Conveniently situated just ½ mile north west of the canal at Patch Bridge, the Trust is well worth visiting. It is close to the River Severn and apart from containing the largest collection of captive wildfowl (160 kinds) in the world, the Trust's grounds and adjacent water-meadows attract many thousands of migrant birds – white fronted geese, Bewick's swans and all kinds of ducks and waders. Visitors are free to walk all round the Trust's grounds and study the inhabitants, which are fascinating for their variety, quantity and behaviour. The Trust also incorporates an important research establishment that studies all biological aspects of wildfowl, with special reference to ecological trends – it also plays an important role in the defence of the various species from extinction and can already be credited with the rescue of several important species. *Open throughout the year except on Christmas Day.*
Purton
Glos. PO, tel, stores. A tiny village of lean, modest houses. It derives an unusual charm from being bisected by the Ship Canal. The canal is not particularly wide here, and to have a large German coaster quietly throbbing past the cowering post office seems an incredible distortion of scale. The village has, surprisingly, two pubs – one is on the canal bank, the other is 100yds away on an enviable site beside the Severn estuary. There used to be a ford for cattle across the river nearby – the herdsman had to judge the time to cross the treacherous river to within a few minutes. Just outside Purton, a huge waterworks has been built for the city of Bristol, where up to 24 million gallons of water can be drawn daily from the Ship Canal, purified and pumped through a new 4ft pipe-line down to Bristol for drinking purposes. Small reservoirs have been constructed on the other side of the canal: these will provide a temporary feed if and when a recording device beside the canal nearer Gloucester indicates that the water is too heavily polluted to draw on.
Sharpness
Glos. Tel, bank (Mon, Thu & Fri only). Stores & garage distant. Sharpness exists only for its docks with their tall cranes, old and new

warehouses and ever-changing display of foreign ships. It has a strange atmosphere and an interesting situation beside the River Severn. The Severn is wide here, and wild: the tidal range at Sharpness is believed to be the second biggest in the world and the current is very swift, especially when accompanied by the very high winds that often race up the estuary from the sea. Across the water is the hilly Forest of Dean, with a main railway line running almost along the shore. It is only half a mile away, but it could as well be another country, so remote does it seem. In terms of population, Sharpness is very strung out; here and there is a row of terraced cottages, inhabited mainly by dock workers. Along the lockside – the focus of the docks – are the buildings housing the offices of various shipping firms, HM Customs & Excise and BW. The annual tonnage handled here is now approaching the million mark, with cargoes consisting mainly of animal feedstuffs, grain, fertilisers, timber and scrap metal, coming from Ireland, Europe, Russia and Scandinavia. Finnish wooden telegraph poles are also imported at Sharpness. Ships handled here displace up to 5000 tons (the limiting dimensions of the entrance lock are 55ft beam by 21ft 6in draught). An interesting development at Sharpness is the recent conversion of the old Merchant Navy training camp (on the hill by Sharpness Marine) into an outdoor leisure activity centre for the youth of land-locked Birmingham.

BOATYARDS

ⓑ **Sharpness Marine** Floating Yacht Services Store, The Old Dock, Sharpness, Glos. (0453 811476). Ⓦ Ⓟ Ⓓ Gas, overnight mooring, long-term mooring, chandlery, books and maps, boat building, toilets.
BW Sharpness Office beside Sharpness Lock. (0453 811644.)

PUBS AND RESTAURANTS

🍺 **Patch Hotel** Opposite the Tudor Arms.
🍺✗ **Tudor Arms** Shepherd's Patch, a few yards from Patch Bridge. (0453 890306). Restaurant and bar snacks, children's room.
🍺 **Berkeley Hunt** Purton, by the lower bridge.
🍺 **Berkeley Arms** Purton. 150yds from the lower bridge. Situated beside the river with an excellent view along it.
🍺 **Severn Bridge & Railway** Sharpness, on a hill to the north east of the docks. The pub sign shows a picture of the former railway bridge.
🍺 **Sharpness Hotel** Sharpness, on a hill to the north west of the docks. A large building on the hill near the Sharpness Marine boatyard.
🍺 **Lammastide Inn** 1 mile east of Sharpness at Brookend. Comfortable pub with 'own brew' beer among others.

An unusual visitor at Sharpness: a Thames Sailing Barge on its way up to Gloucester. *David Perrott.*

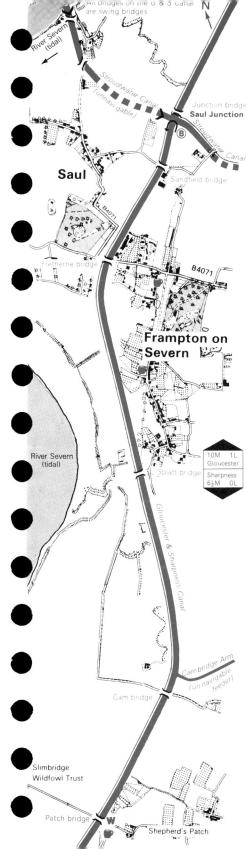

Saul Junction

The Ship Canal continues towards Gloucester,
with the spacious Severn estuary over to the
west. Swing bridges punctuate the canal and at
almost every bridge is a bridge keeper's cottage
(Junction Bridge – 0452 740444, Cam Bridge –
0453 890272). These cottages are peculiar to the
Gloucester & Sharpness Canal and have great
charm – they are only small single-storey
buildings, but each one has a substantial
Classical façade with fluted Doric columns and
a pediment. At Cam Bridge is an unnavigable
arm that feeds the canal with water from the
Cotswolds. At Frampton on Severn the church
is passed on the east side, then after a long
straight the navigation bends to the north east.
Trees encroach here on one side, and several
bridges lead past scattered houses to Saul
Junction. Over to the east the great Cotswold
ridge marches parallel to the canal.

Saul Junction
This unusual waterway 'crossroad' is where the
Stroudwater Canal intersects the Gloucester &
Sharpness Canal. The former canal was an
extension of the Thames & Severn Canal,
which used to run from the Thames at
Lechlade, through the Cotswolds via the great
Sapperton Tunnel and thus to Stroud. Twelve
locks brought the Stroudwater Canal down
from this point to Saul, where it crossed the
Ship Canal and continued to Framilode. Here it
locked down into the tidal River Severn. Like
the Thames & Severn, the Stroudwater Canal
has been disused for many years, and the old
lock by Saul Junction is derelict. However a
300yd stretch to the south east from the
junction to the first bridge (now lowered) is
navigable and in use as a mooring site. At the
junction itself is a swing bridge and a cottage
(previously the Junction Inn) as well as plenty
of boats at the yard. The village of Saul is half a
mile to the west. It is worth walking the mile
from Saul Junction to the River Severn. The
towpath is in good shape and this isolated
section of the Stroudwater Canal is still in
water. There is a pub (the Ship) along the way
and from the riverside church in Framilode a
footpath runs beside the Severn to the Darell
Arms, whose gardens overlook the river.
Restoration of both the Stroudwater and the
Thames & Severn canals is underway.

Frampton on Severn
Glos. PO, tel, stores, garage. A beautiful linear
village notable mainly for its green, which is
about 100yds wide and fully half a mile long.
All manner of attractive houses attach
themselves to the edge of this magnificent
expanse of common land, and the occasional
cars that drive down the middle of it are kept in
their proper scale. Trees and ponds are
scattered along it; the gateway that guards the
Court is on the east side. The Church of St
Mary at the south end of the village, near the
canal, is mainly of the 14thC. The stained glass
and monuments are worth a look, and the
Romanesque lead font is one of only six in
Gloucestershire.

Frampton Court Facing the village green is this
Georgian mansion (1731–33) whose gardens
contain a Gothic Orangery (1745) and an
octagonal dovecote. *Visits by written application
to the owners in residence only.*

BOATYARDS
Ⓑ **R. W. Davis & Son** Junction Dry Dock,
Saul, Gloucester. (0452 740233). Ⓡ Ⓢ Ⓦ Ⓓ
Pump-out, gas, overnight mooring, long-term
mooring, winter storage, crane, dry dock, boat
building, boat sales, engine sales and repairs,
toilets.

PUBS
🍺 **Bell Hotel** Frampton on Severn, ¼ mile
south east of Fretherne Bridge.
🍺 **Three Horseshoes** Frampton, halfway
along the green.

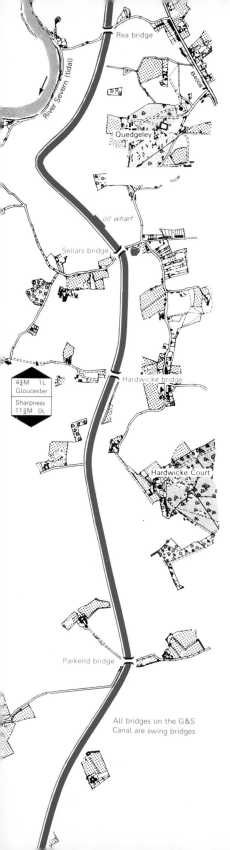

Hardwicke

On from Saul, the canal continues through
undramatic country, which is slightly wooded.
There are no villages on this section, but several
farms are situated near the canal. Towards
Sellars Bridge (0452 720251), the navigation
enters a cutting for the first time since
Sharpness. There is a pub by this bridge, and
just to the north is an oil wharf for small ships.
This is the furthest (northernmost) point which
the oil traffic reaches on the Severn Navigation
– oil used to be carried further on past
Gloucester and right up to Stourport in barges,
but this is all finished now. North of Quedgeley
Wharf the canal approaches the River Severn
(hidden behind a flood bank and far narrower
up here than downstream); turning sharply
eastward, the canal reaches Rea Bridge.

Navigational note
The three bridges, Sellars, Rea and Sims (*see
next page*), have a greater headroom (over 7ft)
than the others on the Gloucester & Sharpness
Canal. Boats normally used on the narrow
canals will find no difficulty in getting under
these three bridges without them being opened,
although they do so at their own risk. Boats
should not pass under these bridges without
receiving a green light from the keeper.

The Severn Bore This famous natural
phenomenon occurs on the section of the river
that is bypassed by the Gloucester & Sharpness
Canal. The Bore is a wave that travels
upstream: it is created by the strong tidal flow
encountering the 'land water' and chasing it
back up the shallow, winding river. One of the
best places from which to see the Severn Bore is
Stonebench, Elmore – only 500yds west of
Lower Rea Bridge on the G & S Canal.
(Another good place is Maisemore Weir, above
Gloucester.) A Bore occurs on the spring tides
but a substantial wave of over 7 to 9ft is a rarer
occurrence. SAE to Area Leisure Officer, BW
Dock Office, Gloucester for annual predictions.

PUBS
Pilot Canalside, at Sellars Bridge.
Anchor Epney (on the river 1½ miles west
of Park End Bridge).

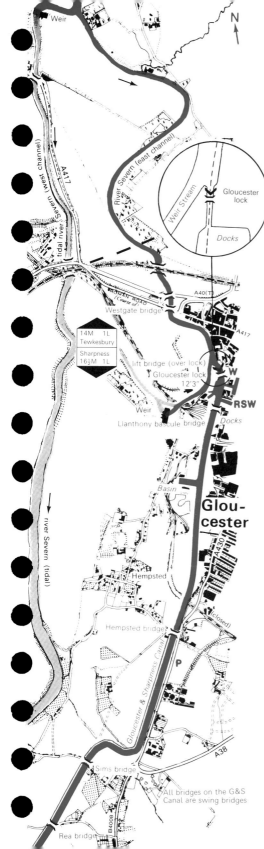

Gloucester

At Rea Bridge the canal enters a cutting and describes a sharp double bend, from which one emerges into a completely different landscape: the quiet countryside has disappeared, its place taken by outlying industrial works on either side of the main road that runs noisily parallel to the navigation. The Ship Canal, strangely enough, plays little part in the generation of wealth that this industry represents, but north of Hempstead Bridge (0452 21880) is a large timber wharf for discharging ships bringing imported wood. Further on is the oil dock, a grain silo and a general cargo quay. Ahead is Gloucester, and the extensive docks that are laid out virtually in the town centre. These are superb docks, for all around are the great warehouses ranged along the quays. Boatmen wishing to moor here – the best place for visiting Gloucester – should go to the office by the lock and seek advice from the BW official. Gloucester Lock (0452 25525) marks the northern end of the Gloucester & Sharpness Canal, and lowers boats back into the River Severn, reminding one that the ship canal is well above the river level. It has to be kept filled with water by pumping up from the river. No boats at the tail of Gloucester Lock should follow the river to the south west, for Llanthony Lock is closed and only a weir awaits them. North of Gloucester Lock, the river is bounded on the town side by a high quay, with moorings more suitable for large vessels than for motor cruisers. Gloucester gaol is nearby. Proceeding upstream, boatmen will find themselves on a dull length of river, narrow and hemmed in by high banks. A sharp bend requires a careful look-out; beyond it are road and rail bridges. The river winds along in its own isolated way, flanked mainly by trees. At one point it approaches a minor road; the former pub here is now a private house. Further upstream is the junction with the big western channel of the Severn, whose separate course between here and Gloucester explains the narrowness of the navigation channel. There is in fact a lock (Maisemore Lock, now closed) just 300yds along the western channel of the Severn. This is a relic of the days before the Ship Canal was built: it used to give access from the upper Severn to the Herefordshire & Gloucestershire Canal (now derelict), which joined the Severn near Gloucester.

Navigational note 1
As with all river navigations, the Severn must be treated with respect, especially after periods of prolonged rain, when the current increases. If you are in any doubt regarding your safety on the river, moor up out of the main stream and seek *expert* advice.

Navigational note 2
All locks on the River Severn are manned. They are open:
08.00–19.15 summer
08.00–16.30 winter
Meal breaks 13.00–13.30, 17.00–17.30. Do not enter a lock unless the green light is showing.

Gloucester
MD: street market Sat, cattle market Mon and Thur. All services. Now a busy manufacturing town, commercial centre and port, Gloucester was once the Roman colony of Glevum. The town was laid out in a cross plan, with north, south, east and west gates. This geography still survives, if only in name. Traces of Roman habitation are much more difficult to find than in other Roman towns in Britain, but when the Bell Hotel was being demolished in recent years, excavations revealed 1000 sq ft of paved courtyard, believed to be the site of the Roman forum. There are a few interesting old buildings in the town centre, notably the 12thC Fleece Hotel and numbers 11–15 Southgate, but otherwise the town centre is of less interest than one might expect. However the glorious cathedral provides an oasis of peace and beauty in the town. The other area of real interest is the docks.

Gloucester Cathedral Founded as an abbey in 1089 by Abbot Serlo, this splendid building is essentially Norman, but extensive remodelling of the choir and transepts between 1330 and 1370 shows fine examples of early Perpendicular architecture. These alterations were authorised by King Edward III, whose father Edward II was murdered at Berkeley (2 miles south of Sharpness). Gloucester Cathedral was the only place that would offer him burial in consecrated ground, and his tomb here became the object of pilgrimage. The new king showed his gratitude to the then Abbot of Gloucester with financial assistance. The great east window is particularly fine – the glass dates almost entirely from 1350, when the window was built, and is one of the first examples of a church window depicting rows of people. But perhaps the most interesting part of the present building is the adjacent cloisters: they feature the earliest known fan-vaulting (mid-14thC). It is still in good condition and is delightfully ornate.

City Museum & Art Gallery Brunswick Road. Exhibits of furniture, glass, silver, costumes and coins; also local archaeology, geology and natural history. *Open weekdays.*

Folklife and Regimental Museum 99–103 Westgate Street. Housed in three Tudor timber-framed buildings known as Bishop Hooper's Lodging and scheduled as an ancient monument. Fine collection of local history and bygones: there is a whole section on the River Severn, its vessels and the salmon and eel fishing industries that it once supported. Relics of the siege of Gloucester (1643) are here, also the collection of the Gloucester Regiment. *Open weekdays.*

Gloucester Docks These extensive docks close to the centre of Gloucester are, to many people, really much more interesting than the town itself. They are at the north end of the Gloucester & Sharpness Ship Canal, where it locks down into the Severn and were built around 1827. Imported timber and grain are two of the main cargoes brought up here – they arrive mostly in big barges from ports down the Bristol Channel, for nowadays only a few coasters a week navigate the length of the canal. One may be sure that if the canal had not the generous dimensions that it has, Gloucester Docks would be disused by now, like the wharves up-river at Worcester and Stourport. The seven-storey dock warehouses are magnificent. Many of the original buildings still stand, lining the waterside-like block houses and concealing it from the town. The docks have now gained an interesting new feature, for the old Llanthony swing bridge carrying a road across the docks has been recently replaced by an elegant steel bascule bridge, which carries heavier traffic and is faster to operate than the old one. Gloucester Docks add up to a fascinating scene and are now the subject of an extensive restoration scheme, which includes the establishment of the National Waterways Museum in the Llanthony Warehouse (*see below*).

The National Waterways Museum Llanthony Warehouse, Gloucester Docks, Gloucester. (0452 307009). Entered through a replica lock chamber, this listed building houses two floors of exhibits illustrating the history of navigation, presented in a lively and interesting way. There are audio-visual displays; historic craft moored outside – including a steam dredger dating from 1925 and the narrowboat *Oak*; a working 'Seagull' vertical compound steam narrowboat engine and demonstrations of traditional canal crafts. Shop, café. *Open 10.00–18.00 every day during British Summer Time (closes 17.00 during winter).* Charge.

Museum of Advertising & Packaging Albert Warehouse, Gloucester Docks, Gloucester. (0452 302309). Contains the fascinating Robert Opie collection, with soap powder and cereal boxes, coffee tins and household cleaners to stir memories of childhood in all who see them. There are also television commercials from the 1950s and 60s, and a wealth of old advertisements. *Open 10.00–18.00, closed Mon.* Charge.

Tourist Information Centre St Michael's Tower, The Cross, Gloucester. (0452 421188).

BOATYARDS

BW Regional Office Llanthony Warehouse, Gloucester Docks, Gloucester. (0452 25524).

PUBS

Walk east from the docks to find these pubs.

📢 **Cross Keys** Cross Keys Lane, Southgate Street, Gloucester. Whitbread and Flowers real ale in an historic old pub. *Lunchtime* food, family room, garden and regular live music.

📢 **County Tavern** Southgate Street, Gloucester. Comfortable hotel with a good choice of real ale, including Eldridge Pope, Ushers and Wadworths. Food *lunchtime and evening.*

📢 **Crown & Thistle** 99–101 Eastgate Street, Gloucester. *Lunchtime* food and a good range of real ale in this busy city centre pub.

The National Waterways Museum, steam dredger No. 4 in the foreground. *BW*.

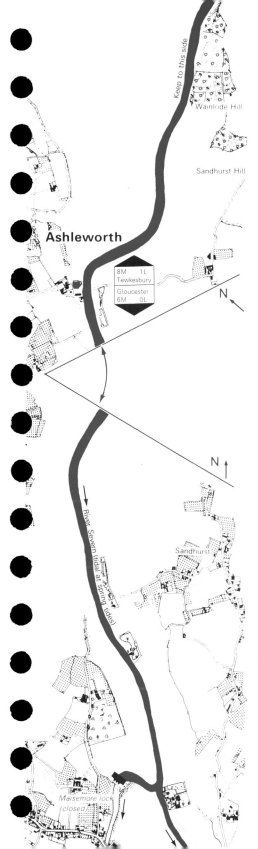

Keep to this side

Wainlode Hill

Sandhurst Hill

Ashleworth

8M   1L
Tewkesbury

Gloucester
6M   0L

N

N

Sandhurst

River Severn (tidal at spring tides)

Maisemore lock
(closed...)

Ashleworth

Leaving the junction (known as the 'Upper
Parting') of the east and west channels of the
River Severn, the river from this point
northwards is predictably wider. Its character
changes very little in all its journey to Stourport
– most of the way it is lined by trees and high
banks. The surrounding countryside that
accompanies the river is quite pretty but
because of the banks, the boater will see little
beyond except for the occasional hills. The
walker along the banks is luckier, in having
good views of the river and the surrounding
countryside; but the towpath has mostly been
eroded away. Away from the centre the river is
often extremely shallow; there are anyway few
mooring places, so access to the villages on
either side is severely limited. After a series of
long reaches, the spire of Ashleworth Church
appears on the left side as the river bends to the
east towards the hills that rise steeply from the
river bank. Unfortunately access to Ashleworth
from the river is poor. The main hill here is
Wainlode Hill, which reaches a height of almost
300ft.

Navigational note
Because of Wainlode Hill's susceptibility to
erosion by the river, old barges have been sunk
in the river near the east bank of the section on
this page, in order to protect the river bank. All
boats should keep to the north side of the river
to avoid the hulks. The area is marked by posts.

Ashleworth Quay
Glos. Behind the tiny isolated pub is a
fascinating group of 15thC buildings, all
virtually intact. Ashleworth Court, a long, low,
stone building, was completed in 1460 and
stands next to the church. (*Open only to parties
on written application to the owner in residence.*)
The church, with its pretty spire, is nearby; but
of greater interest is the big stone tithe barn
(125ft by 25ft). This is owned by the National
Trust but is still used as a working barn by the
farmer – *open daily during daylight hours.*
Ashleworth Manor and the rest of the village
are set well back from the river. The Manor is
contemporary with the Court, and is of
timber-framed construction. (*It is open only by
written appointment to the owner in residence.*)
There used of course to be a jetty at Ashleworth
Quay; but this has vanished now, and boat
crews wishing to get ashore must either ground
their craft and wade ashore through the mud to
the bank or tie up to an overhanging tree where
there is enough water (a few yards downstream
of the pub).

PUBS
Boat Ashleworth. A delightful isolated pub
on the river. Access is difficult (shallow water).
Queen's Arms Village Green, Ashleworth.

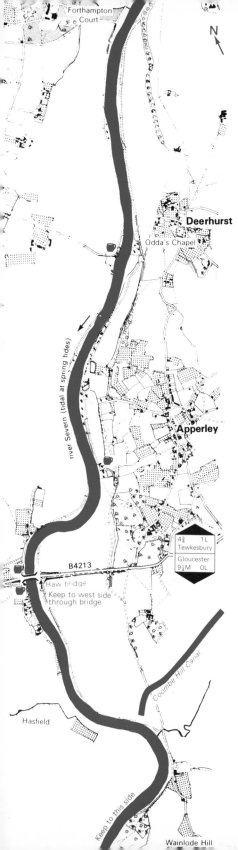

Haw Bridge

The towering mass of Wainlode Hill slowly recedes as the tree-lined river curves round to the north west. The silted-up lock on the east bank is the entrance to the former Coombe Hill Canal, now partly restored, but land-locked. The modern bridge to the north is Haw Bridge. There are pubs and good moorings. Navigators should keep away from the east bank near this bridge – there is a submerged obstruction. The river winds through an S-bend, passing a riverside pub and a line of hills to the east; then it straightens out somewhat as it heads for Tewkesbury. Yet another riverside pub, the Yew Tree Inn, is passed – a half-sunken barge serves as a mooring. A sailing club is based here. Opposite is Odda's chapel, but access is bad because of the rocky banks.

Deerhurst
Glos. Tel, stores. The most important feature of this small village is the beautiful Church of St Mary, parts of which date back to the year 804. The font with its trumpet-spiral motif dates from the late 9thC and for some time the bowl was used as a wash tub in a farm. It was discovered and reunited with the stem in the late 19thC, and is now thought to be one of the best preserved Saxon fonts in England. The church contains some interesting brasses and 15thC stained glass. Access is bad from the river, as the banks are rocky.
Odda's Chapel About 200yds south west of the church. This Anglo-Saxon chapel dates from 1056; for years part of a farmhouse, it was rediscovered for what it is during repairs in 1885. *Open at any reasonable time.*
Haw Bridge The old cast-iron bridge, built in 1824, was knocked down accidentally by a barge in December 1958, when the river was in spate. The replacement bridge was opened in 1961, a few yards downstream of the old one. There are two pubs at the bridge, but little else. The villages of Tirley and Hasfield are a mile to the north west.
Coombe Hill Canal This short canal, running eastwards from the Severn for 2¾ miles, was built in 1796 to facilitate the carriage of coal to Cheltenham. There were two locks. Despite high tolls, the canal never made any money, and changed hands several times during the 19thC. In 1875 the lock gates were swept away by floods, and the canal was formally abandoned the following year. Having lain derelict for many years, it was purchased by the Severn & Canal Carrying Company for £35,000 (seven times the original company's capital). The canal and wharf manager's house, near the basin, has now been restored, and a museum and trips along the canal were planned before the company went into liquidation. It has now been purchased by the Gloucestershire Trust as an important wildlife habitat, and is scheduled as a site of special scientific interest.

PUBS
🍴✗ **Yew Tree Inn** On west bank of river, opposite Deerhurst. (045 278 333). Large pub at the end of a lane. Sailing club based here; food always available. Reasonable temporary moorings. The quiet village of Chaceley (*PO, tel.*) is a mile up the lane.
🍴✗ **Coal House** On east bank of river near Apperley. (045 278 211). Moorings not brilliant, but food is available.
🍴 **New Bridge** Haw Bridge.
🍴 **Haw Bridge Inn** at Haw Bridge. Moorings. Skittle room.

Windmill Tump

(closed)

River Severn (non-tidal)

A38(T)

↗N

(navigable)

N↗

See page 16
for River Avon

Avon

River

B

The Mythe

(closed)

Mythe bridge

A38(T)

A438

Avon
lock

16½M 1L
Worcester

Gloucester
14M 1L

B

Tewkesbury

W

Weir
Upper Lode Lock

Mill Avon

Bloody Meadow

site of battle 1471

River Severn (tidal up to Tewkesbury lock at spring tides)

W

Weir

Upper Lode
lock

Mythe Bridge

The river now passes another pub, facing a
sailing club. There is a private ferry between
them; access to the pub is difficult because of
shallow water. One of the two channels of the
Warwickshire Avon enters here from
Tewkesbury: the Battle of Tewkesbury was
fought just to the east of here in 1471. Marked
by the abbey, Tewkesbury can be seen to the
north east, but the Severn sweeps round to the
west of the town, leaving an enormous expanse
of flat, empty meadow between them. The big
lock (0684 293138) is well concealed on a corner
between the weir and a backwater. (The weir is,
incidentally, the highest point to which normal
spring tides flow.) Upstream of the lock is a
junction with the main (navigable) course of the
River Avon – boats heading for the Lower and
Upper Avon navigations should turn east here,
as should boats intending to visit Tewkesbury.
Beware of the shallow spit projecting south
west from the tip of the junction. Continuing
up the Severn, one reaches the single
170ft-span of the cast iron Mythe Bridge over
the river, built by Thomas Telford in 1828.
Steep wooded hills rise on the east bank by this
bridge, but the river bears off to the north west
and soon leaves them behind. Its character
remains virtually unchanged – it is lined by
high banks and trees, untouched by villages or
towns, and seemingly isolated from the
countryside that its wide course divides so
effectively.

The River Avon in Tewkesbury It is certainly
worth turning off the Severn into the River
Avon – this is the way to Tewkesbury,
Evesham and Stratford-upon-Avon. Boaters
not wishing to buy the short-term pass on to the
Lower Avon Navigation may tie up just below
the big Healing's Mill to visit Tewkesbury, but
those who decide to go through the pretty Avon
Lock (operated by a lock keeper) will find it a
worthwhile diversion. *See page 16* and the River
Avon section for all details and boatyard
services in the town.

PUBS

🍺 **Lower Lode** ¾ mile below Tewkesbury
Lock. 15thC inn with excellent moorings. Bar
meals *lunchtime and evening*, morning coffee
and afternoon teas.

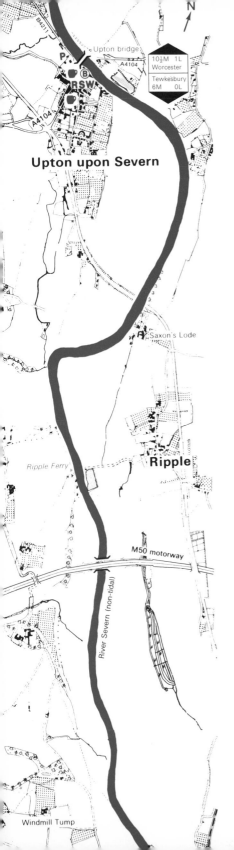

Upton upon Severn

The River Severn continues on its predictable, undramatic course northwards, flanked by wooded banks that prevent any views of the countryside. There are few signs of habitation or human activity apart from boats and anglers. The big steel viaduct carrying the M50 motorway provides a rare feature of interest. The significant-looking pipes sticking out of the ground on the east bank at this point betray the existence of an old underground oil depot, but it is now disused. A mile further on, things improve as the old church tower at Upton upon Severn comes into view, followed by the graceful modern bridge and interesting waterfront of this very attractive small town. Plenty of boats are moored here – there are temporary public moorings on the west bank, just downstream of the bridge.

Upton upon Severn
Hereford & Worcs. EC Thur. PO, tel, stores, garage, banks. This delightful town is well provided with fascinating old timbered and early Georgian buildings, and it is doubly welcome for being situated on the river bank. The best area is nearest the river, where various pubs and venerable hotels beckon; nearby is the prominent 13thC tower with its 18thC copper-covered cupola, all that remains of the church that was demolished in 1937. The tower and the former churchyard have recently been restored as a public garden. The 'new' Church of SS Peter and Paul was built in 1878, on the edge of the town – a good place for it. There are good shops in Upton, including a delicatessen, and it is the best place along the Severn (apart from Worcester) to forsake a boat for a trip to the famous Malvern Hills, which rise to the west. Great Malvern is under 6 miles to the north west, and the hills are visible from the Severn.

Ripple
Hereford & Worcs. PO, tel, stores. Although set back from the river, Ripple is well worth a visit. It is a pretty village, the houses scattered irregularly along the road. The large church is very fine and dates almost entirely from the late 12thC. Only the chancel is late 13thC. The central tower at one time had a spire. Inside are 15thC choir stalls, carved with astrological symbols.

BOATYARDS

ⓑ **Upton Marina** Upton upon Severn. (068 46 3111). Ⓡ Ⓢ Ⓦ Ⓟ Ⓓ Pump-out, gas, overnight mooring, long-term mooring, winter storage, slipway, crane, dry dock, chandlery, books and maps, boat building, boat sales, engine sales and repairs, toilets, showers. Starline Narrowboats is based here.

PUBS AND RESTAURANTS

The only riverside pubs on this section are in Upton.
🍺 **Plough** Riverside, near the bridge. Upton upon Severn. A nicely situated pub, where Marstons real ales are available. Bar meals *lunchtime and evening.*
🍺 **Ye Olde Anchor Inn** High Street, Upton upon Severn. This pub is dated 1601, and is now run as a home-brew house, also offering Uley and Hook Norton real ales. Once the haunt of body snatchers, it now provides meals *lunchtime and evening*, and has a children's room and garden.
🍺✕ **Swan Inn** Waterside, Upton upon Severn. (068 46 2118). Wadworths and Butcombes real ale, bar snacks and restaurant meals (*L & D*). No dogs.

Hanley Castle

Leaving Upton, the river resumes its
high-banked course through the countryside.
On the west bank, but hardly visible from a
boat, is the village of Hanley Castle. Further
up, on the east bank, is a wooded ridge with a
curious turreted house projecting from the
trees. The village of Severn Stoke is to the east;
it is reached by a lane from a jetty on the river.
West of here is an enjoyably romantic stretch of
river, where tall, steep red cliffs rise sharply
from the water to over 100ft. Trees and shrubs
struggle to grow from this treacherous slope,
and somewhere hidden at the top is Rhydd
Court. The steep hill recedes, allowing a large
caravan site to nestle by the river. A scattering
of bungalows appears; then the river leaves
houses and hills and wanders off north east.
Distantly, to the west, can be seen the grey
lumps of the Malvern Hills.

Severn Stoke
Hereford & Worcs. PO, tel, stores. The village is
scattered along the main road, and has no real
centre. The best part is near the pretty half-
timbered pub with its rose garden. Nearby is
the church with its curious 14thC side tower.

Hanley Castle
Hereford & Worcs. PO, tel, stores. The early
13thC castle, built by King John, has now
vanished, leaving only its moat as a memorial.
But the village that grew up around it still
thrives. It is extremely pretty, with a good
collection of half-timbered and brick cottages
around the little green. Overlooking the green
is the church, set in an attractive churchyard. It
is a curious building, half 14thC stone, half
17thC brick, with a squat brick tower. Nearby
are the 17thC almshouses and grammar school,
the whole group a remarkable indication of
village life long ago. A lane leads to the village
from the river, but mooring is difficult. It is not
too far to walk from Upton.

PUBS
Rose & Crown Severn Stoke. Off the main
road near the church.
Three Kings Hanley Castle. In the village
centre. Food, garden.

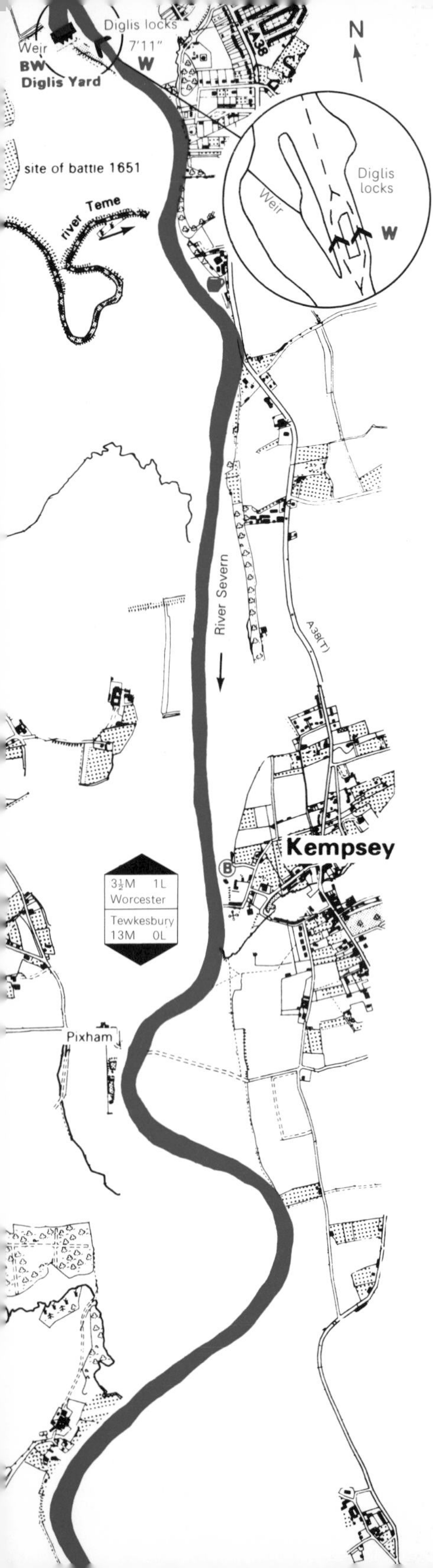

Kempsey

The river winds past the hamlet of Pixham, then the bold tower of Kempsey church appears on the east bank, and a line of moored boats betrays the presence of a boatyard. There are temporary moorings along here for visitors to the village. Upstream, the river straightens out as it makes for Worcester. The Malvern Hills may be glimpsed occasionally, forming the western horizon. Soon the Severn narrows somewhat as a wooded ridge encroaches from the east. The Severn Motor Yacht Club is based here – it is well-named, for the cruisers moored along here are lavish and grand. There is a pub up among the trees near the club. The Battle of Worcester was fought in 1651 near where the little River Teme joins the Severn. Above here is the pair of Diglis Locks (0905 358758), on the outskirts of Worcester. There is a BW maintenance yard and a large freight depot above the locks, so dredgers and tugs are often seen.

Battle of Worcester, 3 September 1651 On 22 August 1651 the young Charles Stuart (later Charles II), having been proclaimed king by the rebels at Scone, reached Worcester with his Scottish army of 17,000. The Roundhead General Lambert was sent off in pursuit with his northern cavalry, and captured the Severn Bridge at Upton upon Severn, cutting off Charles' retreat. Meanwhile another army of 28,000 under Cromwell advanced on Worcester from Nottingham. Charles, realising that he would have to fight at Worcester, organised his defences around the rivers Severn and Teme. After receiving further reinforcements from Banbury, the Roundhead armies advanced across the Severn, using a pontoon made of boats; meanwhile their cavalry crossed by a ford south of Powick Bridge, on the Teme. Heavy fighting broke out, and Charles' Scottish infantry, taken by surprise, were soon driven back. Charles tried to redeem the battle by leading a brave charge out of the east gate of Worcester: supported by cavalry this would have succeeded, but by this time the Scottish cavalry had fled. Cromwell held his ground and forced the Royalists back into the town, killing many in the narrow streets. This Roundhead victory ended the Royalist hopes; Charles fled with a few followers, and after the famous Boscobel Oak episode he made his way back to France.

Kempsey
Hereford & Worcs. PO, tel, stores. A dull village in which acres of new housing have swamped the old. One or two beautiful thatched cottages have survived to defy the invasion of modernity; but it is the church that should be visited, for the enormous scale of this building is matched by interior grandeur. It was constructed to cater for the Bishop of Worcester and his huge retinue – the Bishop's Palace used to stand just a few yards west of the church. Hence the generous proportions of, especially, the chancel and sanctuary. Note the medieval glass in the chancel.

BOATYARDS

BW Diglis Maintenance Yard Diglis Lock. (0905 356264).
Ⓑ ✕ **Seaborn Yacht Company** Court Meadow, Kempsey, Worcester. (0905 820295). R S W D E Pump-out, gas, overnight mooring, long-term mooring, winter storage, slipway, crane, books and maps, boat building, boat sales, engine repairs, toilets, showers, licensed club house, restaurant.

PUBS

Ketch Inn On A38 overlooking the river. Real ale.
Anchor Kempsey. A popular main road hostelry dispensing Ansells real ale and Gaymers real cider. Food *lunchtime and evening*, garden.
Farmers Arms Kempsey Common. Banks real ale, meals *lunchtime and evening*, garden with play area and skittle alley.

Worcester

Just above Diglis Locks is the terminal basin
where the oil tankers used to come to unload
before the traffic finished some years ago. A few
hundred yards on are the disused wharves and
the two locks that lead into Diglis Basin, the
Worcester & Birmingham Canal. (*See page
181.*) Worcester Cathedral is well in view now;
the big square tower commands the town and
the riverside. Two other church towers
contribute to the scene, and the unspoilt nature
of the west bank makes Worcester's riverside a
pretty one. Anglers fish from a path along the
east bank, seemingly just below the great west
window of the cathedral, while 'fours' and
'eights' appear from rowing clubs. There are
two bridges over the river in Worcester – a
five-arched stone road bridge and, just north of
it, a curious iron railway bridge. The best
temporary moorings are north of the railway
bridge. The west bank is built up while the east
bank is green and tree-lined, with the
racecourse right by the river. At its northern
end is a busy waterworks, contrasting with the
bijou houses which adjoin it. North of here the
river moves out into pleasantly wooded
country; the only trace of civilisation is the
glimpse of the occasional farm and a pretty,
secluded riverside pub with good moorings.
There is a field of hops nearby.

Worcester
*Hereford & Worcs. EC Thur. MD Sat. Two
stations. All services.* The 'Faithful City',
Worcester has shown loyalty and devotion to
the Crown for the last 900 years. Hence the
name of Royal Worcester Porcelain, which is
still one of the biggest firms in the town. Other
industries include glove manufacturing and the
making of a certain brown sauce. Worcester has
plenty to offer the visitor, although one's
enjoyment is lessened by the constant flow of
heavy traffic through the town. Foregate Street
has many irregular Georgian buildings with
attractive pediments. A railway bridges the
street, but does not intrude, for the girders are
suitably decorated and trains are infrequent.
However the best area is around Friar Street,
and of course the cathedral.
Worcester Cathedral An imposing building
that dates from 1074 (when Bishop Wulstan
started to rebuild the Saxon church), but has
work representative of the five subsequent
centuries. There is a wealth of stained glass and
monuments to see – including the tomb of King
John, which lies in the chancel. Carved out of
Purbeck marble in 1216, this is the oldest royal
effigy in England. When he was dying at
Newark, King John demanded to be buried at
Worcester Cathedral between two saints: but
the saints have gone now. The best way into the
cathedral is from the Close with its immaculate
lawns and houses, passing through the cloisters
where one may inspect five of the cathedral's
old bells. (Two of these were cast in 1374.) The
gardens at the west end of the building look out
over the Severn and over to the Malvern Hills –
a particularly fine sight at sunset. The Three
Choirs Festival is held annually in rotation at
the cathedrals of Worcester, Gloucester and
Hereford, during the last week in *Aug*. This
famous festival has inspired some fine music,
one notable composer being Vaughan Williams.
For further information about the festival,
contact the Town Clerk in any of the three
cities.
The Commandery By Kings Head Lock, on
the Worcester & Birmingham Canal. This was
founded as a small hospital by Bishop Wulstan
in 1085, but the present timbered building
dates from the reign of Henry VII in the 15thC.
It served as Charles Stuart's headquarters
before the Battle of Worcester in 1651. The
glory of the building is the superb galleried hall
with its ancient windows and the Elizabethan
staircase. Teas. *Open Mon–Sat and Sun
afternoons.*
Tudor House Folk Museum Friar Street. A
new museum of local antiquities, furniture and
porcelain housed in traditional Elizabethan
buildings. (The wattle and daub that make up
the walls can be clearly seen in places.)
Amongst other exhibits are a modern copy of a
traditional coracle, a tiny fishing craft used for
thousands of years on the River Severn, and a

painting of the Waterman's Church in Worcester – a chapel on a floating barge, last used in the 1870s, when it was taken ashore and set up on dry land. *Closed Thur and Sun.*

The Dyson Perrins Museum of Worcester Porcelain The Royal Porcelain Works, Severn Street. (0905 23221). Here, where it should be, is the most comprehensive collection of Worcester porcelain in the world, from 1751 to the present day. *Open Mon–Sat. Tours of the porcelain works can be arranged.*

The Guildhall High Street. Built in 1721–23 by a local architect, Thomas White, this building has a splendidly elaborate façade with statues of Charles I and Charles II on either side of the doorway and of Queen Anne on the pediment. It contains a very fine assembly room.

City Museum and Art Gallery Foregate Street. Collections of folk life material and natural history illustrating man and his environment in the Severn valley. In the Art Gallery are a permanent collection and loan exhibitions. Also museum of the Worcestershire Regiment. *Closed Thur and Sun.*

The Greyfriars Friar Street. *NT property.* Dating from 1480, this was once part of a Franciscan priory and is one of the finest half-timbered houses in the country. Charles II escaped from this house after the Battle of Worcester on 3 September 1651. It is an antique shop now.

Tourist Information Centre (0905) 723471.

BOATYARDS

Ⓑ **Grist Mill Boatyard** Diglis Basin, Worcester. (0905 350814). Craftsmen boatbuilders and fitters, engine repairs.

Ⓑ **Mick Wade** Diglis Basin, Worcester. (0905 763249). Marine engineer.

PUBS

🍺 **Camp House Inn** Camp Lane, Grimley. An isolated riverside pub below Bevere Lock, where the drinking water is electrically pumped from a well. Whitbread West Country and Flowers real ale, Bulmers real cider and excellent bar food *lunchtime and evening*.

🍺 **Wheatsheaf Inn** Henwick Road, Worcester. Marstons real ale and bar food *lunchtime and evening* in a pleasant pub overlooking the racecourse and the river.

🍺 **Crown & Anchor** Hylton Road, Worcester. Lively pub with a skittle alley. Marstons real ale and Bulmers real cider. *Lunchtime* bar meals and snacks.

🍺 **Severn View Hotel** Newport Street, Worcester. Marstons, Wadworths and Banks real ale in a comfortable riverside hotel. Meals *lunchtime and evening*.

DIGLIS BASIN
Enlargement from map page 165

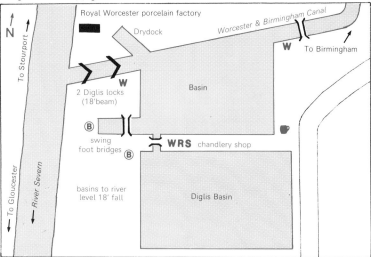

River Severn at Worcester. *Derek Pratt.*

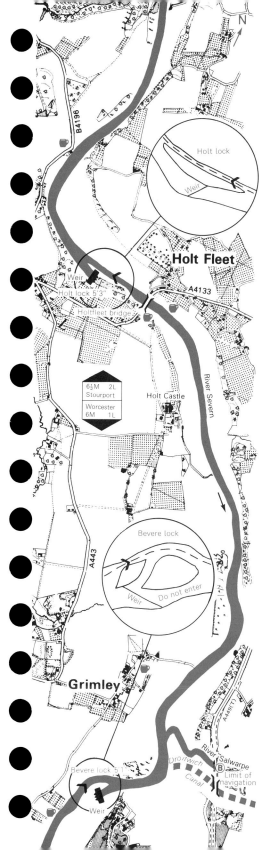

Holt Castle

Just upstream of the Camp House Inn is Bevere Lock (0905 640275), which is certainly one of the prettiest on the Severn. There is a delightful rose garden, tended by the lock keeper and his wife. The island adjoining the lock is connected to the land on the far side by a graceful iron footbridge. Continuing upstream of the lock, the river is approached by wooded hills on its east bank, while on the other side the plain green fields continue, edged by high banks and trees. At one point the little River Salwarpe and the disused Droitwich Canal enter together from the east. The Salwarpe is navigable for craft up to 35ft as far as Judge's Boatyard at Hawford, but there are no visitors' moorings. The canal has yet to be restored. The village of Grimley is at the end of a lane leading up from the river, but it is difficult to distinguish this track, and there are no moorings. The river continues north west now, until Holt Castle is reached, a curious composite building overlooking the river. Beside it is the discreet tower of a small church. Further on is the delicate iron span of Holt Fleet Bridge, and beyond it a steep wooded hillside, with pubs and caravans nearby. Above Holt Lock (0905 620218), the steep wooded hills continue, rising straight up from the river bank. It is a pleasant scene, and there is a riverside pub nearby. The next few miles form an attractive reach, with steep wooded hills rising from the river bank on one side, then on the other. There is a riverside pub close by.

Holt
Hereford & Worcs. PO, tel, stores. Holt is a scattering of assorted settlements, around the river. The elegant narrow bridge here was built by Telford in 1828. Holt Fleet exploits the river in a most unattractive fashion, being composed of a large sprawling caravan site, whose television aerials and wires swamp the riverside. There are two large pubs. Holt Castle is up on the hill, overlooking the river. The 'castle' is a 14thC tower, for the rest of the building is a 19thC battlemented mansion. Nearby, set among the fruit fields, is the church, a fine late Norman building with interesting carving around the doorways, and rich in interior ornamentation.
Grimley
Hereford & Worcs. PO, tel, stores. A small farming village close to, but hidden from, the river. The well-placed church has some Norman work, but has been heavily restored; it has a curious outside staircase by the door. Access from the river is not easy.
The Droitwich Canal This attractive rural waterway, which leaves the Severn ½ mile north east of Bevere Lock, used to go to Droitwich – 5¾ miles and eight locks away. It was then joined by the Droitwich Junction Canal, whose seven locks led it a further 1½ miles to terminate in a junction with the Worcester & Birmingham Canal at Hanbury Wharf (*see page 185*). Both the Droitwich canals have been derelict for most of this century, but they are now reviving. Wychavon District Council and the Droitwich Canals Trust are implementing a scheme to open up the Droitwich Canal from the town to the River Severn by 1992, and it is hoped later to extend the restoration to the Junction Canal. When this happens, it will restore a 22-mile ring of cruising waterways.

BOATYARDS
Ⓑ **George Judge** Mill House, Hawford. (0905 51283). Just east of the A449 bridge on the River Salwarpe. Ⓦ Gas, boat sales and repairs, chandlery, provisions, café, camping and caravan site, long-term mooring. Visitor mooring is very restricted, and craft over 35ft *cannot turn.*

PUBS
Ⓟ **Lenchford** Holt. Riverside, upstream of Holt Lock.
Ⓟ **Holt Fleet Hotel** Holt Fleet, by the bridge.
Ⓟ **Wharf Hotel** Holt Fleet, north bank by caravan site.
Ⓟ✕ **Waggon Wheel** Grimley. (0905 640340). Food.

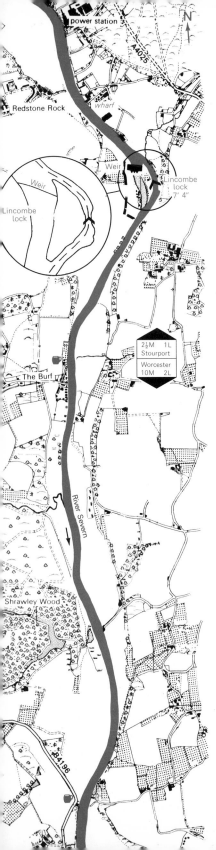

The Burf

The reach from Lenchford to Stourport is one
of the most pleasant on the Severn. Unlike
much of its journey further downstream, the
river runs here through a well-defined valley,
with steep wooded hills never far away from
either bank. The hills on the west bank are the
more impressive and the more thickly wooded,
although the old church at Shrawley can
sometimes be seen peering over the woods.
Roads keep their distance, but at the site of
Hampstall Ferry (The Burf) there is a small
village and a riverside pub, with good
moorings. From here very steep hills encroach
on the east bank of the river, almost hanging
over it at Lincomb Lock (029 93 2887). This
pretty lock is now the northernmost on the
river, for signs of Stourport soon come into
view. First there are the abandoned oil
wharves, whose rusty pipes and terminals are a
sad reminder of the former traffic. On the
opposite side of the river, at the foot of a cliff, is
the Redstone Rock – an unexpected outcrop of
crumbling red sandstone. There was once a
hermitage in caves here. On towards Stourport,
there is a modest restaurant on the east bank
and, beyond it, Stourport Power Station. The
River Stour flows in here.

The Burf
An isolated riverside settlement, comprised
mainly of new housing for retired persons.

PUBS AND RESTAURANTS
🍺 **Hamstall Inn** The Burf, overlooking the
river. Good moorings. Food.

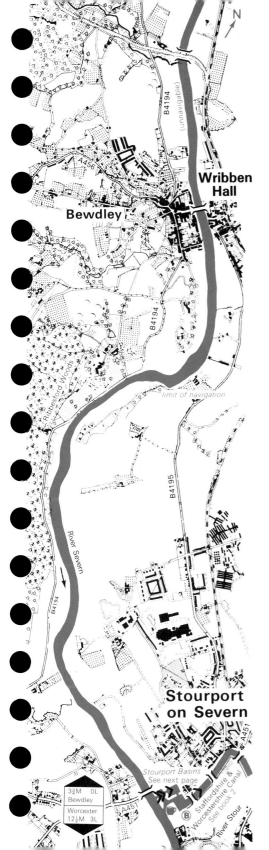

Stourport-on-Severn

At Stourport Power Station the little River
Salwarpe flows in from the east, and just to the
north the Staffordshire & Worcestershire Canal
drops down into the Severn from the unseen
basins. There are two sets of locks – narrow
canal boats should use the upstream set. Just
above these locks is Stourport Bridge, a heavy
iron structure built in 1870. The River Severn
is not officially navigable for more than a couple
of hundred yards above Stourport Bridge, at
which point BW's jurisdiction as navigation
authority ends. However in suitable conditions
small boats not drawing more than 1ft 9in can
penetrate upstream to within a mile of Bewdley
Bridge. A shoal across the river impedes further
progress, and boatmen must tie up or wade
ashore when they reach the shoal. Bradshaw's
Canals and Navigable Rivers, 1904 states that a
few craft, in times of full water, proceed as far
as Arley Quarry, 5 miles above Bewdley,
although the trade is very small. There is a road
into Bewdley on either side of the river (the
B4194 on the west bank being the most direct).
Alternatively, one can avoid all this by leaving
the boat in Stourport and taking a bus to
Bewdley, an excursion well worth the effort.

River Severn above Bewdley
In the 19thC the Severn was fully navigable for
a long way past Stourport: it used to be a vital
trade artery right up into Wales, through
Bridgnorth, Shrewsbury and Newtown. It used
to connect with the Montgomery Canal at
Newtown, the Shrewsbury Canal at
Shrewsbury, and the Shropshire Canal at Hay.
It is unfortunate that this upper section is
unnavigable, for the river is much prettier than
further south: it runs along a narrow valley,
hemmed in by steep and wooded hills.
However, there is a public right of way along
one or both banks up to Bridgnorth and
beyond, and this can form an interesting walk.
Another attraction north of Bewdley is the
Severn Valley Railway, a private railway which
runs a summer service of steam trains between
Bridgnorth, Bewdley and Kidderminster (0299
403816 for details).
Bewdley
*Hereford & Worcs. EC Wed. PO, tel, stores,
garage, bank.* Bewdley is a magnificent small
18thC riverside town, still remarkably intact. It
is blessed with a fine river frontage and elegant
bridge that make the most of the wide Severn,
and a handsome main street that leads away
from the river to terminate at the church. The
scale of the whole town is very pleasing, a
comfortable mixture of old timber-framed
buildings and plainer, more elegant 17th and
18thC structures. Most of the town is on the
west bank, and so Telford's three-arch stone
bridge, built in 1798 to replace an earlier
medieval structure, forms a fitting entrance to
Bewdley.
Stourport-on-Severn
*Hereford & Worcs. EC Wed. PO, tel, stores,
garage, bank.* When the engineer James
Brindley surveyed the line for the Staffordshire
& Worcestershire Canal in the early 1760s, he
intended to meet the River Severn at Bewdley,
which was already an established river port.
But the residents there objected to his plans,
and so he chose instead the hamlet of Lower
Mitton, 4 miles downstream, where the little
River Stour flowed into the Severn. Basins and
locks were built for the boats, warehouses for
the cargoes and cottages for the workmen. The
canal company even built in 1788 the great
Tontine Hotel beside the locks. The hamlet
soon earned the name of Stourport, becoming a
busy and wealthy town. The two basins were
expanded to five (one has since been filled in)
and the locks were duplicated. Nowadays,
plenty remains of Stourport's former glory, for
the basins are always full of boats (there is a
boat club and boatyards). The delightful clock
tower still functions, a canal maintenance yard
carries on in the old workshops by the locks,
and the Tontine Hotel still has a licence. Mart
Lane (on the north east side of the basins) is
worth a look – the original 18thC terrace of
workmen's cottages still stands. Numbers 2, 3
and 4 are listed as ancient monuments. In
contrast with the basin area, the town of

Stourport is not interesting, and although it was built on account of the canal, the town has no relationship at all with the basins now. It seems to have grown up away from the canal.

BOATYARDS

ⓑ **BW Stourport Yard** Stourport Basin, Stourport. (029 93 77661). Ⓡ Ⓢ Ⓦ Dry dock.
ⓑ **Severn Valley Cruisers** York Street Boatyard, Stourport. (029 93 71165). Ⓡ Ⓢ Ⓦ Ⓓ Pump-out, gas, narrowboat hire, overnight mooring, long-term mooring, winter storage, slipway, crane, dry dock, chandlery, books and maps, boat building, boat sales, engine sales and repairs, toilets. Boat shop in Mart Lane.

BOAT TRIPS

Severn Steamboat Company Stourport. (029 93 71177). 40-minute river trips from the bridge *Sun & B. Hols in season.* Also public day trip to Worcester and return *Wed in Jul & Aug.* Two 199-passenger boats available for private charter (with disco).

PUBS AND RESTAURANTS

Bewdley is a town with many fine pubs, including:
🍺 **Angel** Lode Street, town centre, Bewdley. Food *lunchtime Mon–Sun.*

🍺 **Black Boy** Wyre Hill. Garden. (*Not* Black Boy *Hotel*).
🍺 **Cock & Magpies** Severnside North, Bewdley.
🍺 **Mug House** Severnside North, Bewdley.
🍺 **Pack Horse** High Street, Bewdley.
🍺 **Rising Sun** Kidderminster Road, Wribbenhall. Garden.
🍺 **Woodcolliers Arms** Welchgate, Bewdley. *Lunchtime* snacks.
🍺 **Bird in Hand** Stourport. Canalside, south of the railway bridge. Whitbread real ale, garden.
🍺 **Black Star** Stourport. Canalside, by bridge 5. Marstons real ale, snacks.
✕🍷 **Lock, Stock & Barrel** By bridge 5. (029 93 6014). Intimate restaurant. *Closed Sun.*
🍺 **Lord Nelson** York Street, Stourport. M & B real ale.
🍺 **Bell** Stourport, by York Street Lock. Hansons real ale, food, garden.
🍺 **Tontine Hotel** Stourport Basin. Banks real ale and food (*lunchtime Mon–Sat*) in a very large pub built by the canal company in 1788.
🍺 **Old Crown** Stourport, by the Severn Bridge. Banks's real ale.
✕🍷 **Severn Tandoori Restaurant** 11 Bridge Street, Stourport. (029 93 3090). Excellent yet reasonably priced. Take-away service. *L & D.*

STOURPORT BASINS

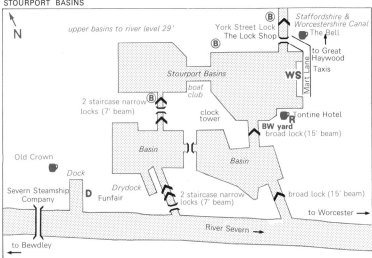

Stourport Basin. *Derek Pratt.*

STRATFORD-ON-AVON

Maximum dimensions

Length: 70'
Beam: 7'
Headroom: 6'

Manager

(0926) 492192

Mileage

KING'S NORTON JUNCTION to
Hockley Heath: 9¾
LAPWORTH Junction with Grand Union
Canal: 12½
Preston Bagot: 16¼
Wootton Wawen Basin: 18½
Wilmcote: 22
STRATFORD-ON-AVON Junction with
River Avon: 25½

Locks: 54

The opening of the Oxford Canal in 1790 and of the Coventry Canal throughout shortly afterwards opened up a continuous waterway from London to the rapidly developing industrial area based on Birmingham. It also gave access, via the Trent & Mersey Canal, to the expanding pottery industry based on Stoke-on-Trent, to the Mersey, and to the East Midland coalfield. When the Warwick & Birmingham and Warwick & Napton Canals were projected to pass within 8 miles of Stratford-on-Avon, the business interests of that town realised that the prosperity being generated by these new trade arteries would pass them by unless Stratford acquired direct access to the network. And so, after the usual preliminaries, on the 28th of March 1793 an Act of Parliament was passed for the construction of the Stratford-on-Avon Canal, to start at King's Norton on the Worcester & Birmingham Canal (itself a long way from completion at that time). The junction was to be less than 3 miles from the junction of the Worcester & Birmingham with the Dudley Canal, and would thus provide a direct route to a major coal producing area without passing through Birmingham.

Progress was rapid at first; but almost the total estimated cost of the complete canal was spent in the first three years, on cutting the 9¾ lock-free miles to Hockley Heath. It took another four years, more negotiations, a revision of the route and another Act of Parliament to get things going again. By 1803 the canal was open from King's Norton Junction to its junction with the Warwick & Birmingham Canal (now part of the Grand Union main line) near Lapworth, with through traffic along the whole of this northern section. Even more delays now followed, with little enthusiasm on the part of private investors to put up more money. Cutting recommenced in 1812, the route being revised yet again in 1815 to include the present

junction with the River Avon at Stratford. (From here, the Avon was navigable down to the Severn at Tewkesbury.)

In its most prosperous period, the canal's annual traffic exceeded 180,000 tons, including 50,000 tons of coal through the complete canal, down to Stratford. By 1835 the canal was suffering from railway competition. This grew so rapidly that in 1845 the Canal Company decided to sell out to the Great Western Railway. There was opposition, however, and it was not until 1st January 1856 that the sale was considered complete. Thus the canal had been in full, independent operation for less than 40 years. Traffic was not immediately suppressed by the new owners, but long-distance haulage was the first to suffer as it was a more direct threat to the railway. In 1890 the tonnage carried was still a quarter of what it had been 50 years before, but the fall in ton-miles was much greater.

This pattern of decline continued in the 20thC, and by the 1950s only an occasional working boat was using the northern section; the southern section (Lapworth to Stratford) was badly silted, some locks were unusable and some of the short pounds below Wilmcote were dry. It is believed that the last boat to reach Stratford did so in the early 1930s but there is evidence that a pleasure cruiser reached Wilmcote during the Easter holiday of 1947.

After the 1939–45 war interest began to grow in boating as a recreation. In 1955 a Board of Survey had recommended sweeping canal closures, including the southern section of the Stratford Canal. Public protest was such that a Committee of Enquiry was set up in 1958, and this prompted the start of a massive campaign to save the canal. The campaign was successful: the decision not to abandon the canal was announced by the Ministry on the 22nd of May 1959. On October 16th of the same year the National Trust announced that it had agreed a lease from the British Transport Commission under which the Trust would assume responsibility for restoring and maintaining the southern section. The transfer took place on the 29th September 1960 and restoration work began in earnest in March of the following year. The terms of the arrangement included a contribution towards the cost of restoration but a very substantial sum was provided by the Trust, which maintained the southern section at its own expense.

The reopening ceremony was performed by Queen Elizabeth the Queen Mother on the 11th of July 1964, after more than four years of hard work by prison labourers, canal enthusiasts, Army units and a handful of National Trust staff. On the 1st April 1988 control of the southern section of the Stratford-on-Avon canal was passed to the British Waterways Board (now British Waterways), finally relieving canal users of the necessity to purchase a separate licence, and the National Trust of a property which, with the best will in the world, it was not ideally qualified to care for.

Natural history

Between the green tunnel of trees near King's Norton and the lily-covered basin at Stratford, there is great scope for seeing the wildlife and plants that frequent this delightful Warwickshire canal. After passing through Shirley, the canal enters the old Forest of Arden and for miles the banks are bordered by sturdy oaks and hazel bushes, which are a great attraction to grey squirrels. Here, the harsh calls of jays and the rattle of magpies are familiar sounds. It is worth making a halt at Earlswood, for it is only a few minutes' walk to the feeder reservoirs which attract naturalists from all over the Midlands. Here, at any time of the year, several pairs of great crested grebes can be seen carrying out their curious courtship ritual; the birds face each other, shake their heads from side to side, then dive and present offerings of weed. In early summer the young grebes can sometimes be seen riding on the parents' backs.

East of the open fields of Hockley Heath, the canal descends through the Lapworth flight. The locks and bridges are interesting as the walls are often covered with profusion of plant life, including the small ferns of the spleenwort family. Further down, in the southern section past lock 29, there is a magnificent display of hartstongue ferns growing near a demolished railway bridge. Past lock 27, the western bank is lined with large alders and pollarded willows, the haunt of tits and warblers. During late summer these trees provide a roosting place for countless swallows.

At Yarningale, the canal crosses a tributary of the River Alne, which flows parallel for several miles. The dipper, which is rather like a blackbird but with a white breast, is sometimes seen around here, skimming over the water or perched on a stone. It is unique in being able to 'fly' underwater, as well as walk on the stream bed in search of insects. From Preston Bagot to Bishopton, the canal passes through one of the richest parts of Warwickshire as far as wildlife is concerned. Badgers are very common in the area and can sometimes be observed from the canal several hours before sunset; with luck, weasels can be seen hunting on the banks. These animals can be observed only when the boat is moored and quiet. It is worth a pause at bridge 51 and a walk up the bridle path to Austy Wood. Apart from numerous warblers, this wood houses a large number of great spotted woodpeckers, whose drumming can be heard during spring. In this area, Canada geese and several species of ducks frequently fly over to Wootton Pool. The harsh 'kwark' of the heron is a familiar sound, for there is a small heronry at the Pool and the birds are busy at their nests from March until August. At least four pairs of kingfisher have their homes on the Stratford Canal, and they may occasionally be seen perched on lock gates as they watch for rising fish. Another interesting bird, which can be heard singing during late afternoon and evening, is the grasshopper warbler; it sounds just like a grasshopper or a fisherman's reel. The moorhen is the most common water-bird on the canal; 57 have been counted in the 5 mile stretch between Lowsonford and Wilmcote. The moorhen nests from early spring to late September, so great care should be taken to avoid clumps of reeds in which a nest may be concealed. Many nests are easy to spot from a boat and, as a rule, they are limited to one side of the canal – opposite the towpath. Moorhens feed on almost anything; they can be seen pecking at blackberries, pulling leaves off plants or foraging in the fields amongst cows. At night they frequently roost in the alder trees lining the bank.

Wild flowers of the canal are too numerous to list. Purple loosestrife is one of the most showy flowers but is not found above Wootton Wawen. It is one of the food plants of the elephant hawkmoth caterpillar, a creature some 3in long with a pair of conspicuous eye spots near the front of its body. The arrowhead is generally considered to be quite rare in the British Isles, but towards Stratford its peculiar arrow-shaped leaves and spikes of white flowers are abundant in summer. The flowering rush is fairly common throughout the canal. Anyone particularly interested in pond life should dip his net at the winding holes where all manner of aquatic insects are to be found among the pink spikes of bistort.

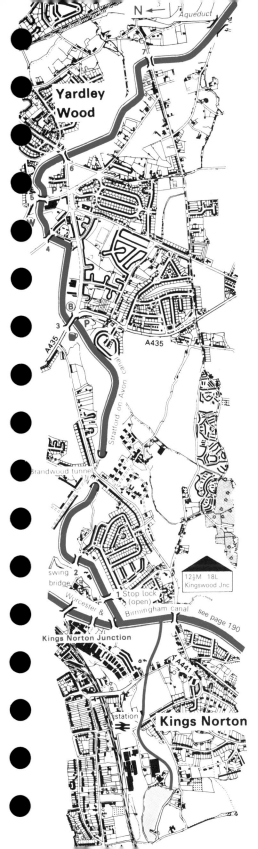

King's Norton

The west end of this delightful canal is at
King's Norton, just outside Birmingham. As
may be guessed from the map, the first 5 miles
of the navigation pass entirely through
residential outskirts of the Birmingham
conurbation. The canal veteran might expect
this to be a dull or scruffy stretch, but he would
be wrong: in fact the Stratford Canal is
bordered all the way with dense but varied
vegetation and, thus protected from the inroads
of the suburbs, forms a quiet, winding ribbon
of green all the way through to the real
countryside. In conjunction with the northern
section of the Worcester & Birmingham Canal,
this is a far more scenically interesting route
between Lapworth and Birmingham than via
the Grand Union Canal. Leaving the Worcester
& Birmingham (*see page 189*) at King's Norton
Junction, the Stratford-on-Avon Canal
proceeds straight to the well-known King's
Norton Stop Lock. In the days of the private
canal companies, stop locks were common at
junctions, as one canal sought to protect its
water supply from any newcomer; but King's
Norton Stop Lock is unusual in having two
wooden guillotine gates mounted in iron frames
balanced by chains and counterweights. The
machinery is now seized up, and boats pass
under the two gates without stopping. The next
bridge is a small swing bridge, then round the
corner is Brandwood Tunnel. Further east is a
beautiful tree-lined cutting, then a bridge with
a pub beside it (*petrol and telephone nearby*) and
the remains of an old arm just beyond it. A
water point is outside a cottage near bridge 5.
The canal continues through pleasant wooded
cuttings – access is bad at most of the bridges,
so the seclusion is virtually complete.

The Patrick Collection Motor Museum 180
Lifford Lane, adjacent to Kings Norton Stop
Lock. (021-459 9111). Cars from 1913 to
present day. Picnic area, souvenir shop,
refreshments, outdoor play area for children
including radio-controlled cars and electronic
games. *Open weekday afternoons and weekends
Easter–Oct.*
Brandwood Tunnel 352yds long, this tunnel
has no towpath. Horse-drawn boats had to be
hauled through by means of an iron hand-rail
on the side. Lengths of this rail can still be seen
in the tunnel.

BOATYARDS

Ⓑ **Lyons Boatyard** Canal Bank, Limekiln
Lane, Warstock. (021-474 4977). At bridge 3
on the Stratford-on-Avon Canal. ⓈⓌⒹ
Pump-out, gas, overnight mooring, long-term
mooring, 7 ton crane, chandlery, groceries
nearby, books and maps, small boat sales,
engine sales and repairs, toilets, showers,
laundry, gifts.

PUBS

🍺 **Horse Shoe** Canalside, at bridge 3. Food.
Telephone and petrol nearby.

Earlswood

Passing over a small aqueduct, the canal reaches a steel lift bridge, which has to be raised and lowered with a windlass. (There are two more of these bridges nearer Lapworth.) Passing under a railway bridge, the canal sheds all traces of the suburbs but maintains its twisting course in wooded cuttings through quiet countryside. The bridges over the navigation are mostly the generous brick arched bridges typical of the canal between King's Norton and Lapworth Locks (in contrast to the much smaller bridges further south), but few roads of any significance come near the canal. At bridge 16 the canal emerges from a long cutting and is joined by a feeder from the nearby Earlswood reservoirs. Several boats are moored along it, for at the junction there is the Earlswood Motor Yacht Club. There are no villages along this rural stretch of canal, but at Salter Street there is a modern school and a strange Victorian church.

Navigational note
Bridge 8 operates hydraulically, using a lock windlass.

Earlswood Reservoir Half a mile south of bridge 16 is this canal-feeding reservoir, surrounded by trees and divided into three lakes: Windmill Pool, Engine Pool and Terry's Pool.

BOATYARDS

Ⓑ 🚤 **Earlswood Marine Services** Lady Lane, Earlswood. (056 46 2552). By the Earlswood feeder. R S W E Overnight mooring, long-term mooring, winter storage, slipway, dry dock, licensed club house. Base of the Earlswood Yacht Motor Club: visitors welcome.

PUBS

🍺 **Blue Bell** Canalside, at bridge 19. Good mooring jetty.
🍺 **Bull's Head** ¼ mile south of bridge 17. Old country pub serving Ansells and Ind Coope (Burton) real ale and Coates real cider. Food *lunchtime and evening (not Sun)*. Live music on *Fri*.
🍺 **Red Lion** 500yds south of bridge 16, near Earlswood Reservoir.
🍺 **Drawbridge** By bridge 8. Davenports and Flowers real ale, *lunchtime and evening* food, canalside patio. Also sells Westons real cider.

Lapworth Locks

The canal continues to wind gently south eastwards through the quiet countryside, sometimes in minor cuttings and often flanked by trees. To begin with, there are no locks, and the bridges – especially those in the cuttings – are still the big brick arches worthy of a broader canal. At Hockley Heath (bridge 25) there is a tiny arm that once served a coal wharf. Nearby the Wharf Inn overlooks the canal. East of here things change dramatically, for the first of the 55 narrow locks down to Stratford is reached. (The top lock is numbered 2, the old stop lock at King's Norton being number 1.) The surroundings of the top lock are indeed pleasant: a white house surrounded by walls and hemmed in by trees stands beside the lock, while a cottage with a delightful garden faces the towpath just below. To the south west can be seen the spire of Lapworth church. After the first four locks is a ½-mile breathing space, then the Lapworth flight begins in earnest, with each of the next nine locks spaced only a few yards from its neighbour. (There is a useful shop by lock 13 selling groceries, home-made bread and cakes, brassware and gifts.) The short intervening pounds have been enlarged to provide a bigger working reservoir of water, so that one side of each lock is virtually an isthmus. The locks have double bottom gates and are not heavy going. They are interspersed with the old cast-iron split bridges that are such a charming feature of the Stratford-on-Avon Canal. These bridges are built in two halves, separated by a 1 in gap so that the towing line between a horse and a boat could be dropped through the gap without having to disconnect the horse. Below lock 19 is Kingswood Junction: boats heading for Stratford should keep right here. A short branch to the left through lock 20 leads under the railway line to the Grand Union Canal.

Navigational notes
1. See note 3, on page 177 regarding lock 15.
2. Bridges 26 and 28 operate hydraulically, using a lock windlass.

Lapworth
Warwicks. PO, tel, stores, garage, station.
Indivisible from Kingswood, this is more a residential area than a village. Two canals pass through Lapworth: the heavily locked Stratford-on-Avon Canal and, to the east, the main line of the Grand Union Canal. These two waterways, and the short spur that connects them, are easily the most interesting aspect of Lapworth. The canalside buildings are attractive and there are two small reservoirs at the junction. The mostly 15thC church is quite separate from the village and is 1½ miles west of the junction; it contains an interesting monument by Eric Gill, 1928.
Packwood House *NT Property.* Lapworth. (0564 782024). ½-mile north of the B4439 road bridge. A 16thC timber-framed house, enlarged in the 17thC by John Fetherstone. It was he who created the clipped yew garden that is held to represent the Sermon on the Mount. The house contains collections of tapestry, needlework and furniture. *Open afternoons only Easter–Sep, Wed–Sun & B. Hols. Also open all day Wed–Sun in Oct.* Charge.
Hockley Heath
Warwicks. PO, tel, stores, garage. A featureless place, but the several shops are conveniently close to the canal bridge.

BOATYARDS

Ⓑ **Swallow Cruisers** Wharf Lane, Hockley Heath. (0564 783442). Ⓡ Ⓢ Ⓦ Ⓓ Ⓔ (by arrangement). Pump-out, gas, day hire craft, winter storage, slipway, groceries, chandlery, books and maps, boat sales, outboard engine sales and repairs, toilets, off-licence.

PUBS

🍺 **Navigation** Lapworth. Canalside, on Grand Union Canal at bridge 65.
🍺 **Boot Inn** Lapworth, near lock 14.
🍺 **Wharf Tavern** Hockley Heath. Canalside, with garden, at bridge 25. Smart pub offering Manns and Marstons real ale, *lunchtime* snacks and *evening* meals (*no food Sun*). Children's room.

A barrel roofed cottage and split bridge, both typical of the Stratford-on-Avon Canal. *Derek Pratt.*

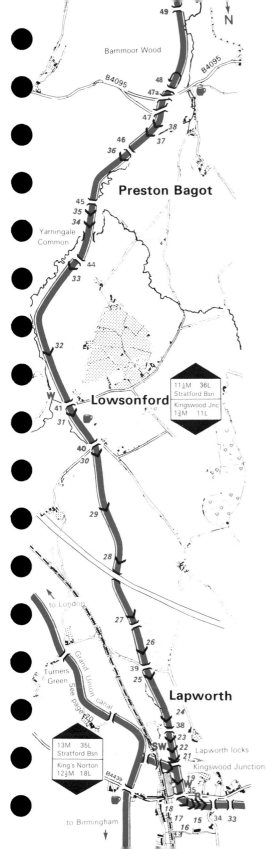

Preston Bagot

At Kingswood Junction the Stratford Canal
continues south, locking steadily downward.
Good moorings are provided by lock 25. These
locks have single gates and very small paddles,
so they are slow to fill and empty. At some of
them are the little iron split bridges over the
lock-tail; and at intervals may be seen the
delightful barrel-roofed lock cottages which are
just as much a hallmark of this canal as are the
bridges. Most of these cottages are inhabited
and well cared for – a great contrast to many on
the canal system. However, the canal itself, and
many of its structures, appear fragile and
overgrown. It is this, and the fact that its course
is secreted amongst folds of pretty wooded
countryside, that gives it such great charm (but
see navigational notes). At Lowsonford is a pub
where boats may moor in among the weeping
willows of the garden; at Yarningale the canal,
having followed a small stream for several
miles, crosses it on a tiny aqueduct adjoining
lock 34. Look out for kingfishers at Preston
Bagot.

Navigational notes
1. The water level in the pound above lock 22
can drop dramatically when the lock is being
filled.
2. Bank erosion is a serious problem on all
canals, and especially so on this one. *Please go
slowly* to minimise your wash.
3. Due to rebuilding, the chamber of lock 15 on
the Lapworth flight is now over 2ft shorter than
the other locks. Those in full length boats
should take extra care when descending.

Preston Bagot
Warwicks. A small, scattered settlement with
attractive, ancient houses here and there,
including the 16thC manor. The Church of All
Saints has a Norman nave and other Norman
details, with Victorian additions.
Lowsonford
*Warwicks. EC Thur. PO, tel, stores (all just west
of lock 30).* Another small and scattered hamlet,
tucked away by the canal. The store is very
pretty.

PUBS AND RESTAURANTS
🍺 **Crab Mill Inn** Preston Bagot. Comfortable
country pub, charging top prices for Hook
Norton, Wadworths, Marstons and Flowers
real ale. Bar meals *lunchtime and evening*,
garden with children's playthings.
🍴 **Haven Tea Rooms & Restaurant** By lock
38. (0926 84 2420). Lunches, grills, salads,
snacks and cream teas. Garden. *Open
10.30–18.00, closed Mon and Tue.*
🍺 **Fleur-de-Lys** Lowsonford, by the canal
north of lock 31. Ancient beamy pub with a
large garden. Flowers and one guest real ale
(changed monthly). Bar meals *lunchtime and
evening.*
🍺 **Tom o'the Wood** Finwood Road,
Rowington. Canalside on the Grand Union.
16thC pub named after one of the three
windmills which used to stand in the village.
Flowers and Samuel Whitbread real ale, bar
meals *lunchtime and evening*, garden, family
room.

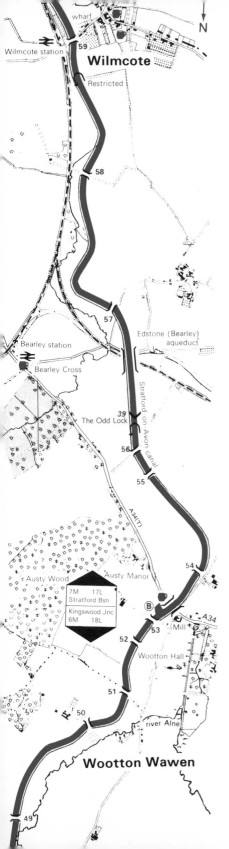

Wilmcote

Lock 38 at Preston Bagot introduces two long
pounds, which are welcome on such a heavily
locked canal. The canal continues through
delightfully quiet country, passing a newly
rebuilt split bridge (number 50) and a farm as
the big Austy Wood looms up on the hill to the
east. (The low stone hall is Austy Manor.)
Beyond bridge 53 the canal widens into a basin
– a boatyard and a pub are here – and then
crosses the A34 road on a cast-iron aqueduct.
Soon it enters a slight cutting – rare on the
southern section of this canal – and then
straightens out at lock 39 – known as the Odd
Lock. Further south the canal rises on an
embankment and is then carried across the
water-meadows, a road and a railway by the
splendid Edstone Aqueduct. At the south end
is a very pretty cottage and garden. The
navigation now winds along a secluded course
to Wilmcote. Just north of the village are the
remains of a bridge – this used to carry a horse
tramway that served nearby quarries. The
winding hole and the cottages on the towpath at
this point were built for the quarry trade.
Wilmcote is close to the canal, and you must
moor north of bridge 59.

Wilmcote
Warwicks. PO, tel, stores, off-licence, garage. A
small and attractive village, typical of this part
of the world. A beautiful lime tree on the green
is the centre of the village: nearby are a fine old
pub, a residential hotel and the most well-
known building in the village – Mary Arden's
Cottage. The school and a vicarage by the
church were built by William Butterfield
c1848. The little railway station is to the east of
the canal: with its trim roses and well-painted
structures it is kept very much in the old
tradition.
Mary Arden's Cottage Wilmcote. This was the
home of Shakespeare's mother, and is a
beautiful 15thC timbered farmhouse. The long,
low house crouches behind luxurious and
well-tended flower beds, and contains a
museum of agricultural implements and local
rural bygones. It is owned by the Shakespeare
Birthplace Trust. *Open daily (closed Sun in
winter).*
Edstone (or Bearley) Aqueduct This major
aqueduct, approaching 200yds in length,
consists of a narrow cast-iron trough carried on
brick piers across a shallow valley. As with the
two other – but much smaller – iron aqueducts
on this canal (at Yarningale and Wootton
Wawen) the towpath runs along the level of the
bottom of the tank, so that towing horses and
pedestrians get a duck's eye view of passing
boats. This feature makes the aqueducts on this
canal very unusual.
Wootton Wawen
Warwicks. PO, tel, stores, garage, station. This
scattered but very pretty village is half a mile
west of the basin. The village has been
designated a conservation area. There are
plenty of timbered houses and the late 17thC
Hall looks superb across the parkland and
pond; but the chief glory is the Church of St
Peter on its rise overlooking the whole village.
This church should certainly be visited. Its
unusual building history has given it a
pleasantly disorderly external appearance, but
inside there are really rare and fascinating
things to see. The church is the only one in
Warwickshire that derives from Saxon times,
and the original sanctuary in the centre of the
11thC church survives intact, still the focus of
the church after over 900 years. The nave is
conspicuously Norman, the chancel is bare but
large, with a superb 14thC east window. The
Lady Chapel is probably the oddest part of the
whole building – it is like a barn in more ways
than one. It is enormous, with a primitive tiled
roof and a completely irregular brick floor.
Birds are often to be found, enjoying the shelter
it provides. All around the walls is a medley of
monuments. It all adds up to an intriguing
building.
Wootton Wawen Basin This wide, embanked
basin was built when construction of the canal
was halted here for a while. A boat hire base –
one of the few on this canal – has been built
here, and was in 1972 awarded a Civic Trust
commendation for its design. With a nearby

pub and petrol station, the wharf is a popular halt with both boaters and motorists. A cast iron aqueduct carries the canal over the A34 by the basin. This aqueduct has often been damaged by lorries hitting the underside, so now a triangular road sign warning motorists of the headroom is mounted on the aqueduct. Unfortunately this sign has been positioned so that it almost completely obscures the original iron plaque that commemorates the opening of the aqueduct in 1813. Just down the hill from the aqueduct is a fine brick watermill, in good repair. This dates from the late 18thC.

BOATYARDS

Ⓑ **Anglo Welsh Narrowboats** The Wharf, Wootton Wawen, Solihull. (0564 793427). Ⓡ Ⓢ Ⓦ Ⓟ Ⓓ Ⓔ Pump-out, gas, narrowboat hire, overnight mooring, long-term mooring, books and maps, groceries nearby, slipway, boat building, boat sales, engine repairs. *Closed winter weekends*.

PUBS

◧✕ **Swan House Hotel** Wilmcote. Comfortable small hotel near Mary Arden's cottage. Hook Norton, Everards, Wadworths and guest real ales, meals (*L & D*), terrace and accommodation.

◧ **Masons Arms** Aston Cantlow Road, Wilmcote. Turn right at the Swan House Hotel. A fine stone-built pub with comfortable bars and a dining room. Flowers real ale and excellent bar meals *lunchtime and evening*.

◧ **Golden Cross** Bearley Cross. Flowers real ale and food *lunchtime and evening*.

◧ **Navigation Inn** Wootton Wawen, at the basin. Flowers real ale and meals *lunchtime and evening*.

Mary Arden's cottage at Wilmcote. *David Perrott*.

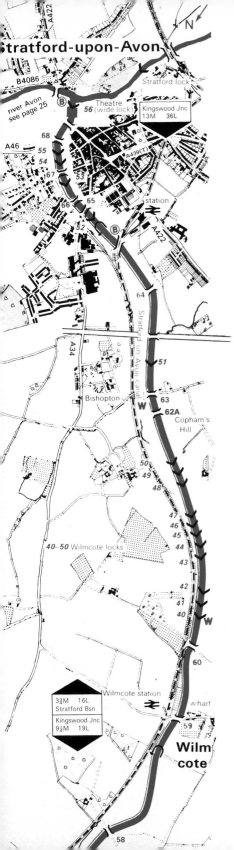

Stratford-upon-Avon

South of Wilmcote, the two long pounds from
Preston Bagot are terminated by a dense flight
of locks – there are 11 in the Wilmcote flight, in
groups of 3, 5 and 3. They are, in the main set
in pleasant open country, in which Stratford
can occasionally be seen to the east although a
rather smelly rubbish tip cannot be ignored by
locks 45 to 47. Meanwhile the countryside
seems flatter, even though there are more locks
to come. At bridge 64, a slight bend suddenly
reveals the nether regions – gas holders and
industrial works – of Stratford. Past two
railway bridges, a grassy wharf on the right is a
boatyard, by an engineering works. At the next
bridge is a winding hole, petrol station and
telephone box; then the canal disappears down
its own private and inaccessible corridor
towards the River Avon. It drops steeply
through several locks, accompanied by the
little-used towpath; then the towpath
disappears altogether, the canal passes through
the lowest bridge since Lapworth and one
suddenly emerges at the splendid great basin in
the middle of the riverside parkland beside the
Shakespeare Memorial Theatre. The contrast is
astonishing – here is an unwalled, public and
attractive basin, constantly surrounded by the
famous Stratford tourists, while only a few
yards away the canal is completely shut away in
a world of its own, forgotten by all except
boaters. If all the moorings in the basin are
taken, a place can usually be found on the river
above Stratford Lock.

Stratford-upon-Avon
See page 25 for details

BOATYARDS

Ⓑ **Stratford-upon-Avon Marina** Clopton
Bridge, Stratford-upon-Avon. (0789 69669).
Ⓡ Ⓢ Ⓦ Ⓓ Ⓔ Pump-out, gas, narrowboat hire,
day boat hire, overnight mooring, long-term
mooring, winter storage, slipway, chandlery,
provisions, books and maps, boat building,
boat and engine sales and repairs, toilet,
showers. *Closed Sat afternoon & Sun in winter.*

PUBS

None on the canal. Plenty in Stratford – *see
page 26.*

WORCESTER & BIRMINGHAM

Maximum dimensions
Length: 71′ 6″
Beam: 7′
Headroom: 6′

Manager
(0527) 72572

Mileage
WORCESTER, Diglis Basin to
Tibberton: 5¾
Dunhampstead: 7½
Hanbury Wharf: 9¼
Stoke Wharf: 12¾
Tardebigge Top Lock: 15½
Bittell Reservoirs: 20½
KING'S NORTON JUNCTION: 24½
BIRMINGHAM Gas Street Basin: 30

Locks: 58

The Bill for the Worcester & Birmingham Canal was passed in 1791 in spite of fierce opposition from the Staffordshire & Worcestershire Canal proprietors, who saw trade on their route to the Severn threatened. The supporters of the Bill claimed that the route from Birmingham and the Black Country towns would be much shorter, enabling traffic to avoid the then notorious shallows in the Severn below Stourport. The Birmingham Canal Company also opposed the Bill and succeeded in obtaining a clause preventing the new navigation from approaching within 7ft of their water. This resulted in the famous Worcester Bar separating the two canals in the centre of Birmingham.

Construction of the canal began at the Birmingham end following the line originally surveyed by John Snape and Josiah Clowes. Even at this early stage difficulties with water supply were encountered. The company was obliged by the Act authorising the canal to safeguard water supplies to the mills on the streams south of Birmingham. To do this, and to supply water for the summit level, 10 reservoirs were planned or constructed. The high cost of these engineering works led to a change of policy: instead of building a broad canal, the company decided to build it with narrow locks, in order to save money in construction and water in operation.

Work on King's Norton Tunnel, described at the time as 'a stupendous undertaking', began in 1794; by 1807 boats could get from Birmingham to Tardebigge Wharf. Here work came to a standstill for several years while the company considered alternative cheaper ways of completing the line down to the Severn. Work eventually started again under a new engineer, John Woodhouse, a great exponent of boat lifts. He proposed reducing the number of locks down to Worcester from 76 to 12, using lifts to descend most of the fall. The company

were less enthusiastic and limited his enterprises to one experimental lift at Tardebigge. This seems to have worked reasonably well but the company were still sceptical. They called in the famous canal engineer John Rennie, who decided that the mechanism would not withstand the rough treatment that it would doubtless receive from the boatmen. Consequently locks were built but reduced in number to 58. The site of the lift became the top lock of the Tardebigge flight – which accounts for its unusual depth.

After this, work progressed steadily and the canal was completed in 1815. In the same year an agreement with the Birmingham Canal proprietors permitted the cutting of a stop lock through the Worcester Bar. The canal had cost £610,000, exceeding its original estimate by many thousands of pounds. Industrial goods and coal were carried down to Worcester, often for onward shipping to Bristol, while grain, timber and agricultural produce were returned to the growing towns of the Midlands. The canal basins in Worcester became important warehousing and transhipment points: Diglis Basin had warehousing for general merchandise, grain and wine, and Lowesmoor Basin specialised in coal and timber. Prosperous businesses were conducted from these wharves and they were an important port of call for the main canal carriers. However the opening of railways in the area in the 1840s and 1850s reduced this traffic considerably and had a profound effect on the fortunes of the canal.

In an attempt to win back salt carrying, the canal company cut the Droitwich Junction Canal in 1852 to connect the Droitwich Barge Canal and the town of Droitwich with their main line at Hanbury Wharf. Toll income and profits continued their relentless decline, however, and after 1864 the company was unable to pay a dividend. In 1874 the canal was bought by the Sharpness New Docks Company. (The words 'Sharpness New Docks and Gloucester & Birmingham Navigation Company' can still be seen on old notices on some of the bridges.) The new management commenced a programme of works to improve the canal in the hope of attracting trade but, in effect, the canal was subsidised by the Gloucester & Berkeley Ship Canal for the rest of its working life.

The animals that used to draw the boats along the Worcester & Birmingham Canal were mainly donkeys worked in pairs instead of the more usual horse. Why this should have been so is not recorded but both horse and donkey were unsatisfactory on the summit level with its four tunnels, for only the short Edgbaston Tunnel has a towpath through it. To overcome the delays caused by the need to 'leg' boats through the other tunnels, steam tugs were introduced in the 1870s and successfully hauled trains of boats through the tunnels for many years.

By the early 1900s the commercial future of the canal was uncertain, although the works were in much better condition than on many other canals. Schemes to enlarge the navigation as part of a Bristol–Birmingham route came to nothing. Commercial carrying continued until about 1964, the traffic being mostly between the two Cadbury factories of Bournville and Blackpole, and to Frampton on the Gloucester & Sharpness Canal. After nationalisation, several proposals were made to abandon the canal but the 1960s brought a dramatic increase in the number of pleasure boats using the waterway thus securing its future use. Now it is part of the popular cruising circuits comprising the River Severn, the Staffordshire & Worcestershire Canal and part of the Birmingham Canal Navigations, and the Rivers Severn and Avon and Stratford-on-Avon route.

Natural history

The Worcester & Birmingham Canal has a rich variety of plant, bird and insect life throughout its length. Apart from its general interest it provides material for more serious study since it flows past extensive salt deposits left by an ancient sea of the Triassic period; consequently the water is quite brackish in some localities. After emerging from the gloom of the West Hill Tunnel it is worth pausing at the exit not only to admire the tree-covered avenue but to examine the variety of ferns and liverworts which grow on the dripping clay of the high banks. A mile or so downstream, a mooring at Bittell is a must, for the reservoirs are among the best-known bird haunts in this part of the country, particularly for wild duck. One large reservoir (Bittell Lower) lies immediately against the west bank

of the canal. There are always great crested grebe and mallard here, but the commonest waterbird is the coot.

The Tardebigge flight of locks gives splendid views over open meadowland where the song of the skylark is usually heard in summer. Here clumps of great willowherb and orange balsam line the banks. The orange balsam was introduced from America, being first recorded in Surrey in 1822; it has now spread along the river and canal system to most of England. When touched, the pods shoot out their seeds to a distance of several feet.

Where the vegetation is dense the harsh scolding of the sedge warbler can be heard; it is particularly frequent in this reach of the canal where caddis flies and other insects are abundant. Two common dragonflies are the large yellow aeshna and the delicate damselfly *ischura elegans*, which has a vivid blue spot on the abdomen. When the locks are emptied the walls can be seen to be covered with thousands of aquatic snails (limnaea). With such an abundance of aquatic organisms it is not surprising that the Worcester & Birmingham Canal is a favourite among anglers.

The calls of redshank and common sandpiper are not unfamiliar at Tardebigge for these waders often fly over on their way to Tardebigge reservoir, which is beside the locks. In addition to waders and waterbirds, herons are usually to be seen feeding in the shallows. In late summer varieties such as the wood sandpiper and the black tern may be occasionally seen at both the Bittell and Tardebigge reservoirs.

At Stoke Prior a subtle change comes over the canal, for the water becomes rather brackish. One interesting waterweed is the enteromorpha – a kind of alga which looks like floating transparent tubes about ½in across. Although the canal is enclosed by brick walls for a short distance, a mass of rosebay willowherb clothes the industrial scars in summer and parts of the waterway are covered with yellow water lilies.

From the Astwood flight to past Hanbury there are many beds of phragmites (reeds) on the west bank. Reed warblers are common in this area as they can only weave their suspended nests in the stems of these plants. Moorhens are common throughout the canal and, in places where bushes and trees hang into the water, families of mallard can usually be seen. Where the bank is low, a grass snake may sometimes be observed swimming in the water hunting for frogs or small fish. The water vole is common everywhere. Being rather short-sighted and slightly deaf it can sometimes be watched from a distance of 3ft for, like many creatures of the canal, it expects intruders only from the towpath.

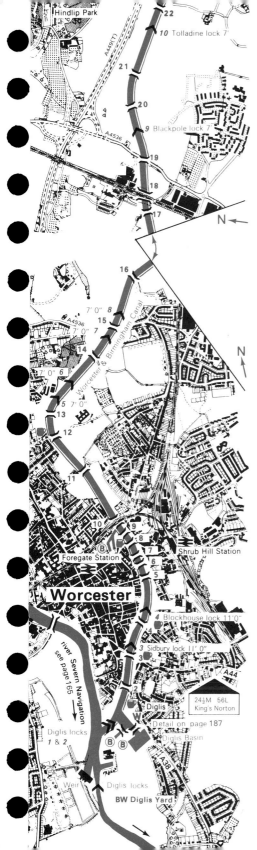

Worcester

The Worcester & Birmingham Canal begins at Diglis, on the south side of Worcester. It leaves the River Severn a few hundred yards north of the Diglis Locks, climbs two wide (18ft) locks and opens out into one of the two Diglis Basins, where a large number of pleasure boats are moored, several of them sea-going: a couple of boatyards and other boating facilities are available here. Past the basin, the canal becomes hemmed in by the town as it enters the first of many deep, narrow locks up to Birmingham. By Sidbury Lock is the Commandery (*see below*). The canal curves round the east side of Worcester, between the town and Shrub Hill station. At one point, near the railway viaduct that leads to Foregate station and the west, the towpath rises over the entrance to the Lowesmoore Basin and wharves. Fish and chips are available in Southfield Street, beyond the viaduct. A series of four locks lifts the canal up and away from the outskirts, then it is crossed by a railway line, with an isolated industrial estate beside it. Worcester is well behind, and the canal is in open country, but the A449 runs parallel. Hindlip Park is to the north.

Worcester
For notes on Worcester, *see page 165.*
Diglis Basin This is a fascinating terminus at the junction of the River Severn and the Worcester & Birmingham Canal. It consists of basins, boatyards, old warehouses and a dry dock. Commercial craft have been entirely replaced by a mixture of pleasure boats designed for narrow canals, rivers and the sea. There are plenty of facilities, a boatyard, and the usual BW services. Permission to use the dry dock should be sought from the BW basin attendant (0905 358758), whose house is at the top of the two locks down into the river. The locks will take boats up to 72ft by 18ft 6in, although obviously only narrowboats can proceed along the canal beyond the first lock. The locks are under the supervision of the basin attendant, who is available *from 08.00–19.30 (16.00 winter) with breaks for meals.* Craft are not permitted to use the locks outside of these times. The locks incorporate a side pond to save water; and near the second lock is a small pump-house that raises water from the river to maintain the level in the basin.
The Commandery By Kings Head Lock. Founded as a small hospital by Bishop Wulstan in 1085, the present timbered building dates from the reign of Henry VII in the 15thC. It served as Charles Stuart's headquarters before the Battle of Worcester in 1651. The glory of the building is the superb galleried hall with its ancient windows and the Elizabethan staircase. Teas. *Open Tue–Sat and Sun afternoons.*

BOATYARDS

Ⓑ **Viking Afloat** Lowesmoor Basin, Lowesmoor Terrace, Worcester. (0905 612707). Ⓡ Ⓢ Ⓦ Ⓓ Pump-out, gas, narrowboat hire, overnight mooring, long-term mooring, books and maps, boat sales, toilets, gifts.

PUBS

🍺 **Cavalier Tavern** Worcester. Canalside, at bridge 12. Comfortable modern pub serving Flowers real ale and *lunchtime* food. Garden.
🍺 **Bridge Inn** Lowesmoor Wharf. A pleasant local serving M & B real ale and *lunchtime* snacks.
🍺 **Bricklayers Arms** Blockhouse Lock. Unspoilt backstreet local. Banks's real ale.
🍺 **King's Head Inn** Near King's Head Lock. Comfortable hotel with a skittle alley. Banks's real ale, regular live music.
🍺 **Red Lion Inn** Adjacent to King's Head Lock. Marstons real ale and *lunchtime* snacks in a busy local.
🍺 **Anchor Inn** Diglis Road, just outside the basin. A pleasant place to enjoy Banks real ale and *lunchtime* snacks.

Dunhampstead

This is a very pleasant stretch of rural canal, entirely typical of the Worcester & Birmingham. Having left the outskirts of Worcester, and accompanied by a minor road, the canal now goes under the A449 and ascends the six Offerton locks, which are set in pleasant pasture land with a pretty cottage by lock 15. The M5 motorway crosses on its skewed steel bridge; it vanishes immediately as the canal enters a short, curving cutting that brings one to the village of Tibberton. There are two pubs nearby, and fruit trees remind one of Worcestershire's orchards. The canal moves towards a ridge of hills to the east, but a railway line intercedes to prevent the canal reaching the side of the valley. This is the main Bristol–Birmingham line, which carries many fast passenger trains, but the only station near the canal is at Bromsgrove. At Oddingley there is a little church and a timbered farm that look out together over the canal; further on are the crowded moorings at Dunhampstead Wharf (popular pub nearby). A wooded cutting leads to Dunhampstead Tunnel, the first of five between here and Birmingham. There is no towpath in the tunnel; horses used to walk over the hill while boatmen pulled the boats through by the handrail (still in place) along each side of the tunnel. It is 230yds long.

Dunhampstead
Hereford & Worcs. Tel. A hamlet consisting of no more than five buildings, including the railway signal box. The only life in the area, apart from the trains that roar past the woods, is provided by the canal and the nearby pub. To the north is the tunnel.

Tibberton
Hereford & Worcs. PO, tel, stores (all to the south of the pubs). A small but expanding canalside village, of little interest. There is a fine old rectory by the Victorian church. Milk is sold by bridge 25.

BOATYARDS

Ⓑ **Brook Line** Dunhampstead Wharf, Oddingley. (0905 773889). Ⓦ Ⓓ Pump-out, gas, narrowboat hire, boat building. Gift shop nearby.

PUBS

🍺 **Fir Tree Inn** Dunhampstead. Very smart and comfortable pub near the canal. M & B, Banks and Bass real ale, and meals *lunchtime and evening*.
🍺 **Bridge Inn** Tibberton. Handsome village local serving Banks real ale. Lots of toys in the garden for the children.
🍺 **Speed the Plough** Tibberton. Attractive cottage pub with small beer garden. Banks real ale, food *Mon–Sat*.

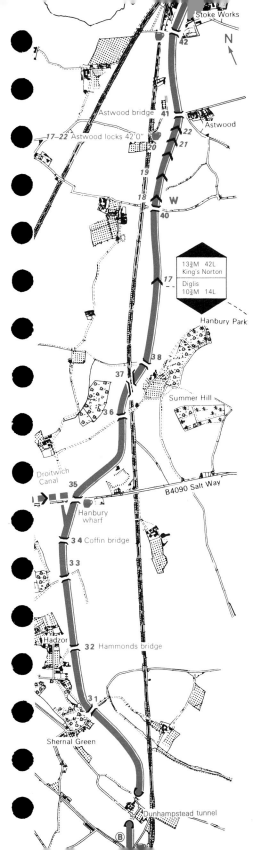

Hanbury Wharf

Leaving Dunhampstead Tunnel, the canal
enters flatter countryside as the hills recede to
the east. The pretty, residential settlement of
Shernal Green flanks the canal, while Hadzor
House (late 18thC in the Classical tradition) is
visible in the trees on the west side of the canal.
This straight stretch is terminated by the very
busy area of Hanbury Wharf, where an old arm
and a new building comprise a boatyard for
small pleasure boats. There is a pub by the
main road bridge – the Droitwich Junction
Canal (unnavigable but undergoing restoration)
joins here. North of here the ridge of hills
approaches again from the east. Navigators
should relish this 5½-mile level – it is easily the
longest pound between Worcester and
Tardebigge Top Lock. But as the canal passes
under the railway to take up an uninterrupted
position on its east side, the ridge of hills nears
again, accompanied by attractive parkland.
Milk, eggs and tea and coffee in jugs are sold
from the cottage at Astwood Bottom Lock, by the
water point. Ahead are the six locks in the
Astwood flight, set in pleasant open
pastureland. Near the top is a pub, beside the
railway line; and beyond the cottages at
Astwood Bridge is a semi built-up area – a
minor road joins the canal, lined by workmen's
terraced cottages. A useful grocery store and
post office here, as well as two more pubs, one
of these having a verandah fronting the canal.
To the north of this settlement is the reason for
its existence – a huge industrial chemical
works. The canal goes through the middle of
this works, much of which is now changing use.

Stoke Works Now closed, this establishment
was built in 1828 to pump brine (salt) from
underground sources for industrial uses, and
provided much of the canal's trade (later gained
by the railways). Now an industrial estate,
where the housing fronts the tree-lined canal,
and all is very tidy.
Hanbury Hall *NT property. (Access via the
public footpath leading south east from lock 17.)*
Set in spacious and well-wooded park, this is a
Wren-style red-brick house built in 1701 and
little altered since then. On show are the long
room and main staircase with painted ceilings
by Thornhill. *Open Wed and Sat afternoons
Apr–Sep.*
Hanbury Wharf An interesting canal
settlement at the junction of the Droitwich
Junction and Worcester & Birmingham Canals.
A short arm leads to the original wharf, but the
old canal cottages here are now overshadowed
by the big new shed that houses a busy modern
boatyard. Construction of the Droitwich
Junction Canal from here down to Droitwich
(2 miles to the west), and of the Droitwich
Canal on to the River Severn, presumably
lessened the usefulness of Hanbury Wharf.

BOAT TRIPS

The Droitwich Canal Trust 1 Hampton Road,
Droitwich. (0905 774225). *Sabrina* is available
for charter for up to 50 persons. Buffet, bar,
music.

PUBS

● **Butchers Arms** Shaw Lane, Stoke Works.
Small village local, with unique decor in the
bar. Davenports real ale.
● **Boat & Railway** Canalside, just south of
bridge 42. Traditional pub with a terrace on to
the canal. Hansons real ale, *lunchtime* food and
skittle alley. There is a temporary mooring
nearby for fish and chips and provisions.
● **Bowling Green** Beside railway bridge,
200yds south west of bridge 41. Small,
attractive and peaceful pub serving Banks real
ale and *lunchtime* food. Garden, bowling green.
● **Eagle & Sun** Hanbury Wharf. Canalside, at
bridge 35. Comfortable, with several cosy
rooms. Excellent food *Mon–Sat*, with *lunchtime*
cold buffet during the summer. Bass real ale.

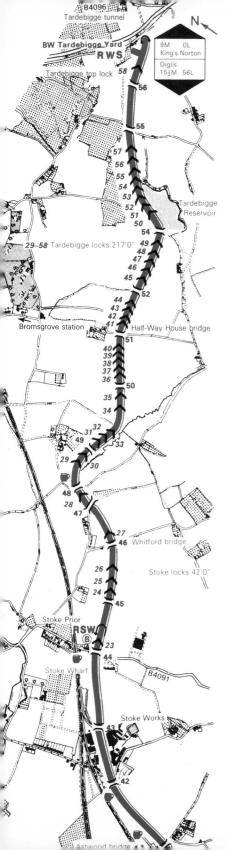

Tardebigge Locks

Approaching Stoke Wharf from the old works, boaters will note the hills to the north east with some misgiving. At Stoke Wharf is the first lock for over a mile; beyond is a crowded mooring site, and then more locks, flanked by trees and pastureland. These locks (numbers 23–28) form the Stoke flight, but in fact there is only a short breathing space of a few hundred yards, with a well-placed pub, before the first of the 30 Tardebigge locks is reached. Forward progress becomes a crawl as this great flight is climbed, but the pleasures of the surroundings make the effort worthwhile. The locks wind up through pretty, folding countryside, leaving the busy railway behind in the west. There are attractive, well-cared-for cottages scattered along the flight, generally near the bridges; their gardens overlook the canal. The locks themselves have great charm, being equipped throughout with traditional wooden gates and balance beams. Large paddles speed up locking, and so a reasonably well co-ordinated crew of two can work through a lock every five minutes. Regrettably, there is no pub at the top, the next being well beyond Shortwood Tunnel. The remote rural course of the canal takes it well wide of Bromsgrove, but Bromsgrove station is only a mile north west of bridge 51. Between locks 50 and 54 Tardebigge reservoir can be seen behind an embankment on the east bank. This feeder reservoir is particularly popular with fishermen. As the reservoir is about 50ft below the summit level, a steam engine was installed to pump water up the hill. The engine-house still stands near the canal, now converted into a restaurant/disco. Tardebigge Top Lock has a fall of 14ft, one of the deepest narrow locks in the country. When the canal was built, there was a vertical boat lift here. Technical problems caused the lift to be replaced by the deep lock, and there is little trace of it now. Above the lock is Tardebigge Wharf, overlooked by the elegant spire of Tardebigge church, up on the hill to the east. At the wharf is an attractive BW maintenance yard, and a large mooring site. Leaving the wharf and its cottages behind, the canal vanishes into a tunnel, passing under a main road (A448) at the tunnel mouth.

Tardebigge
Hereford & Worcs. Stores (on A448, 10 mins' walk from south end of Tardebigge Tunnel). A small farming village flanking the main road. Apart from the settlement near the canal, the best part of the village is up on the hill, around the fine 18thC church with its delicate spire. At the top of the locks a plaque commemorates the founding of the Inland Waterways Association in 1946 by L. T. C. Rolt and Robert Aickman, aboard the narrowboat *Cressy*, moored at this spot.
Stoke Wharf A pretty canal settlement in the best tradition – a lock, a wharf and warehouse, and a pleasant line of houses facing the canal, now housing a boatyard. Stoke Wharf is the only compact element of Stoke Prior – perhaps the heart of the village was drawn to the canal when the latter was built, and has remained there ever since. Stoke Prior church, which is mainly of the 12thC, stands by itself ½ a mile north of the wharf, the other side of the busy railway junction. Stoke Prior is not a good place for shopping: it is better to victual up at the settlement near bridge 42. However there is a pub near the wharf.
Avoncroft Museum of Buildings, Stoke Prior. *1 mile north of Stoke Wharf, off B4091.* Old buildings rescued from demolition are re-erected and displayed here. Exhibits include an 18thC post mill, a local nail and chain works, a 15thC timber-framed house from Bromsgrove, and the 14thC roof of Guesten Hall, Worcester. There is also a reconstruction of an Iron Age hut. *Open mid Mar–mid Oct, Tue–Sun.*

BOATYARDS

Ⓑ **Grist Mill Boatyard** Diglis Basin, Worcester. (0905 350814). Craftsmen boatbuilders and fitters, engine repairs.
Ⓑ **Mick Wade** Diglis Basin, Worcester. (0905 763249). Marine engineer.

Ⓑ **BW Tardebigge Yard** Tardebigge Top Lock. (0527 72572). Ⓡ Ⓢ Ⓦ Overnight mooring, long-term mooring, toilets. Dry dock available.

Ⓑ **Black Prince Holidays** Stoke Wharf. (0527 575115). Ⓡ Ⓢ Ⓦ Ⓓ Pump-out, narrowboat hire, overnight mooring, long-term mooring, winter storage, books and maps, wet dock, boat and engine sales, engine repairs, toilets, gifts.

PUBS AND RESTAURANTS

✕♙ **Engine House** Tardebigge, by lock 57. (0527 35238). Smart restaurant and disco *open Fri and Sat eve*. Suitable only for the well-dressed.

♙ **Queen's Head** Canalside at bridge 48. Busy pub with good food *lunchtime and evening*, and Banks, Sam Smith's and Marstons real ale. Terrace by the water.

♙ **Navigation** Behind Stoke Wharf. A fine spacious pub with a neat smoke room, serving Davenports real ale.

DIGLIS BASIN
Enlargement from map page183

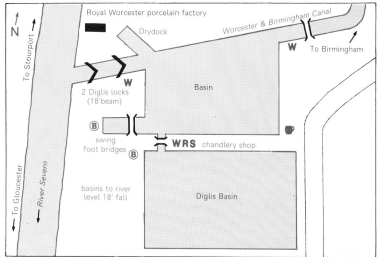

The long haul up Tardebigge Locks. *Derek Pratt*.

Alvechurch

This is a most delightful stretch of canal that winds through the hilly Worcestershire countryside. The flat Severn valley seems very distant as the canal plunges first into Tardebigge and then Shortwood Tunnel. There is a boatyard between the tunnels. East of Shortwood Tunnel and the surrounding fruit plantations, the canal emerges high up on the side of a low wooded hill, overlooking the modest valley of the River Arrow. In the distance is the hum of traffic on the A441. The canal continues northward, winding steadily through this tranquil landscape until the small town of Alvechurch is reached. The town is set below the canal in a hollow, its church up on a hill; the canal winds tortuously along the steep hills round the outskirts, passing a boatyard, a station and a charming canal pub. Then the canal turns abruptly north; ahead in the distance is the ridge of hills that is pierced by King's Norton Tunnel. Unexpectedly, an aqueduct carries the canal over a little lane that leads to Barnt Green and its station (a mile to the west). Past the aqueduct and through bridge 65, Lower Bittell reservoir comes into view, beside and below the navigation. The canal crosses the valley on an embankment; at the north end of this is a very pretty cottage, which stands at the point where the feeder from Upper Bittell reservoir enters the canal. With these on two sides and an overflow weir and the lower reservoir on the third, the house seems to be virtually surrounded by water.

Bittell reservoirs
These two reservoirs were built by the canal company, the upper to feed the canal, the lower being a compensation to local mill owners for the loss of water resulting from construction of the canal. The reservoirs are nowadays popular among anglers and bird watchers.
Alvechurch
Hereford & Worcs. PO, tel, stores, garage, bank, station. A pleasant little town with some fine half-timbered houses, Alvechurch is situated at the bottom of a hollow and surrounded by folds of green hills. However through-traffic on the A441 does not improve the place and there are plans for a southern bypass. The church stands alone on a hill; it is of Norman origin but was largely rebuilt by Butterfield in 1861. There are some interesting monuments within.
Shortwood and Tardebigge Tunnels 613yds long and 580yds long respectively, these are two out of the four tunnels on the 14-mile summit level of the Worcester & Birmingham Canal. Neither contains a towpath, and until the turn of the century a company tug used to pull all boats through Tardebigge, Shortwood and the great King's Norton Tunnel. Navigators will find Shortwood Tunnel extremely wet and walkers will find the path obscured by wheat fields and difficult to follow.

BOATYARDS

ⓑ **Alvechurch Boat Centre** Scarfield Wharf, Alvechurch. (021-445 2909). At bridge 60. ⓡⓢⓦⓓ Pump-out, narrowboat hire, gas, overnight mooring, long-term mooring, slipway, books and maps, boat building and sales, toilets, showers.
ⓑ **Dartline** Old Wharf, Tardebigge. (0527 73898). ⓡⓢⓦⓓⒺ Pump-out, gas, narrowboat hire, day hire craft, overnight mooring, long-term mooring, winter storage, groceries, books and maps, boat sales, engine sales and repairs, toilets.

BOAT TRIPS

Midlander available for private charter. 42 persons. Ring (0527) 73898.

PUBS

🍺 **Crown** Alvechurch. Canalside, at bridge 61. Pleasant country pub serving M & B and Springfield real ale. Seats outside among geraniums.
🍺 **Swan Hotel** Swan Street, Alvechurch. Snacks.

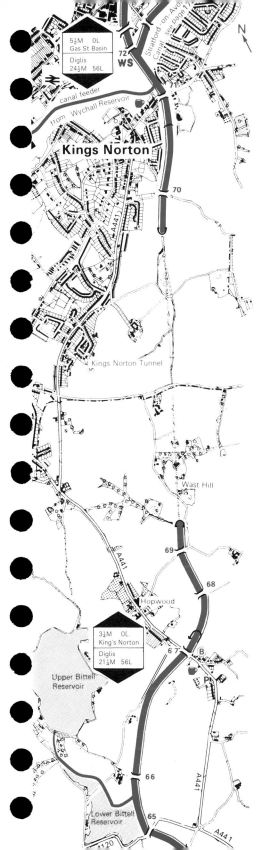

King's Norton Tunnel

Leaving the reservoirs, the canal curves
through a slight cutting to Hopwood, where
there is a pub, a boatyard and a busy main road
crossing. North of here the canal enters a
cutting that leads to King's Norton Tunnel.
The ridge of hills that this tunnel penetrates
serves as an important geographical boundary:
to the south of it is the rolling open countryside
of rural Worcestershire, while north of the
tunnel is Warwickshire, and the southernmost
indications of Black Country industrial
development. The built-up area is revealed as
soon as the canal leaves the cutting at the north
end of the tunnel: to the west is King's Norton,
while all around are new houses and light
industries. At bridge 71 (the best access point
for the village and its shops) is the main
mooring site of the local boat club; just past it is
the old canal cottage at King's Norton
Junction. Here the Stratford-on-Avon Canal
enters at right angles – the guillotine
mechanism of the celebrated King's Norton
Stop Lock can be seen a few hundred yards
along it. Boats heading for the south east should
turn off down the Stratford Canal here (*see page
173*). Meanwhile the Worcester & Birmingham
Canal continues towards Birmingham, under a
roving bridge at the junction, then under an
inelegant steel bridge that connects a canalside
factory with its car park. Another turnover
bridge (73) is encountered: there is a telephone
box near it and a further industrial stretch just
beyond.

King's Norton
*West Midlands. PO, tel, stores, garage, bank,
station.* The village has done well to survive as a
recognisable entity, for the suburbs of
Birmingham have now extended all around it,
and the amount of urban traffic passing through
the village leaves one gasping. But it *is* still a
village, and the small village green, the old
grammar school buildings and the soaring spire
of the church ensure that it will remain so. The
church is set back a little from the green in an
attractive churchyard, and is mainly of the
14thC, although two Norman windows can still
be seen. The grammar school is even older – it
was probably founded by King Edward III in
1344. An interesting puzzle is that the upper
storey is apparently older than the ground
floor. . . . The school declined during the last
century and was closed in 1875. Now restored it
is an ancient monument.
King's Norton Tunnel
Otherwise known as
Wast Hill or West Hill Tunnel, this 2726yd
bore is one of the longest in the country. It is
usually difficult to see right through the tunnel,
and there are plenty of drips from the roof in
even the driest weather. A steam-powered –
and later a diesel – tunnel tug service used to
operate in the days of horse-drawn boats (there
is no towpath). The old iron brackets and
insulators that still line the roof were installed
to carry telegraph lines through the tunnel.
Grandiose bridges (nos 69 and 70) span the
cutting at either end.
Hopwood
West Midlands. Tel, garage. Provisions available
at mobile home site, 200 yds north west of
bridge 67. More a name than a village,
Hopwood is merely a small settlement. There
are buildings near the canal which may be
useful to canal travellers; a pub, a boatyard, a
petrol station. A fast main road bisects the area.

BOATYARDS

Ⓑ **Marine Sales & Services** Birmingham
Road, Hopwood, near Alvechurch. (021-445
2595). Ⓦ Gas, overnight mooring, slipway,
engine repairs. (ⓅⒹ and groceries nearby.)

PUBS

⬤ **Navigation Inn** King's Norton, 100yds west
of bridge 71.
⬤ **Hopwood House** Hopwood. Canalside, at
bridge 67. Food *Mon–Sat*.

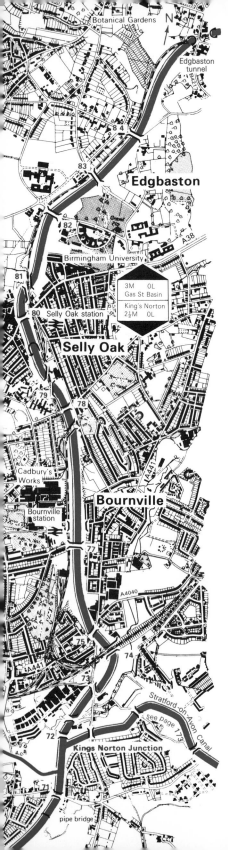

Edgbaston

Just north of King's Norton Junction, the canal enters an industrial area. Access is closed off at most of the bridges. Canal veterans will recognise this as typical of an approach to the great city of Birmingham and will doubtless resign themselves to 10 miles of this kind of scenery. But, thankfully, it does not last, for the canal seems to hold the industries at bay on one side, while a railway line (the main line from Worcester and the south west to Birmingham) draws alongside on its west flank. Canal and railway together drive through the middle of Cadbury's Bournville works, which is interesting rather than oppressive. There is an exhibition, 'Cadbury World', in Linden Road, near the factory, which explains the history of this place. Beyond it is Bournville station, followed by a cutting. Soon the railway vanishes briefly behind the buildings of Selly Oak; the canal goes through this suburb, but access is closed off at the road bridge (80). Between this and the next, skewed, railway bridge is the site of the junction with the Dudley Canal, but no trace remains here now of either the junction or the canal itself. North of here the canal and railway together shrug off industry and town, and head off on an embankment towards Birmingham in splendid isolation and attractive surroundings. Below on either side is the green spaciousness of residential Edgbaston, its botanical gardens and woods. A hospital is on the west side. The University of Birmingham is on the east side; among its many large buildings the most conspicuous is the Chamberlain campanile tower, which was erected in 1900. At one of the bridges near the University, two Roman forts used to stand; but most evidence of them was obliterated by the building of the canal and railway. Only a reconstructed part of the larger fort exists now. Past the University's moorings, canal and railway enter a cutting, in which their enjoyable seclusion from the neighbourhood is complete; the charming old bridges are high, with no access possible, while the cutting is steep, and always lined by overhanging foliage. It is a remarkable approach to Birmingham. The railway is the canal's almost constant companion, dipping away here and there to reappear a short distance further on; but trains are not too frequent, and in a way their occasional appearance heightens the remoteness that attaches to this length of canal. At one stage the two routes pass through short tunnels side by side: the canal's tunnel is the northernmost of the five on this canal and the only one with a towpath through it. It is a mere 105yds long.

The Patrick Collection Motor Museum 180 Lifford Lane, adjacent to Kings Norton Stop Lock. (021-459 9111). Cars from 1913 to present day. Picnic area, souvenir shop, refreshments, outdoor play area for children including radio-controlled cars and electronic games. *Open daily (except Tue) May 6–Oct 26.*
Edgbaston
West Midlands. A desirable residential suburb of Birmingham, Edgbaston is bisected but unnoticed by the canal, and there is little contact between them. However, for those who contrive to be on the 'landward' side of Edgbaston, there are several things to be visited.
Cannon Hill Park Edgbaston, about 1½ miles east of the University. Formal gardens including a Japanese Garden of Contemplation; tropical and sub-tropical plants adjacent. Birmingham Zoo is now housed here.
Cannon Hill Museum Pershore Road, Edgbaston. Designed primarily for children. Illustrated leisure-time pursuits including bird-watching, bee-keeping, fishing and pets. Safari hut around which the sounds, sights and smells of the African bush are recreated. *Open daily. Closed Sun morning.*
Geological Department Museum The University, Edgbaston. Collection of palaeontology, stratigraphy, petrology, mineralogy and physical geology, including the Holcroft collection of fossils and the Lapworth collection of graptolites. *Open daily by arrangement.* (021-472 1301).
Botanical Gardens Edgbaston. Founded over

100 years ago. Alpine Garden, lily pond and a collection of tropical birds. *Open daily.*

Perrott's Folly Monument Road, Edgbaston. Seven-storey tower built in 1758 by John Perrott. One theory as to its origin is that Mr Perrott could, from its height, gaze on his late wife's grave 10 miles away. Since the late 1800s it has been used as an observatory.

The Dudley Canal This canal used to join the Worcester & Birmingham at Selly Oak, thus providing a southern 'bypass' round Birmingham. The eastern end of the canal has been closed for many years, and will certainly remain so. The tremendously long (3795yd) Lappal Tunnel (now collapsed) emerged 2 miles from Selly Oak. This bore was more like a drain pipe than a navigable tunnel – it was only 7ft 9in wide, a few inches wider than the boats that used it, and headroom was limited to a scant 6ft. Boats were assisted through by a pumping engine flushing water along the tunnel, but it must still have been a nightmarishly claustrophobic trip for the boatmen.

Bournville Garden Factory The creation of the Cadbury family, who moved their cocoa and chocolate manufacturing business south from the centre of Birmingham. The Bournville estate was begun in the late 1800s and is an interesting example of controlled suburban development. The old canal wharves can be clearly seen, but nowadays most of the ingredients travel by rail – the shunting engines are painted in the familiar Cadbury's livery.

Cadbury World Linden Road (by the factory and signposted from the canal). (021-458 2000 ex 2843). The story of chocolate. Audio visual, a jungle, and Victorian Birmingham. *Open 10.00–17.30 Mon–Sat, 12.00–18.00 Sun.* Admission charge.

Selly Manor and **Minworth Greaves** Bournville. Two half-timbered Birmingham houses of the 13th and early 14thC re-erected in the 1920s and 1930s in Bournville. They contain a collection of old furniture and domestic equipment. *Open Tue, Wed, Fri afternoons.* Enquiries to the Curator, 44 Mulberry Road, Bournville, Birmingham B30 1TA. *The nearest point of access from the canal is at Bournville station: walk west to the Cadbury's entrance. There is a public right of way (Birdcage Walk) through the works: bear right at the fork, then turn right at the village green. The two houses are close by, on the left.*

The leafy Worcester & Birmingham Canal. *David Perrott.*

Birmingham

The Worcester & Birmingham Canal now
completes its delightful approach to
Birmingham, and in only the last few hundred
yards to Gas Street Basin does it assume the
appearance of a typical Birmingham waterway.
The railway disappears underneath in a tunnel
to New Street station, while the canal suddenly
makes a 90-degree turn left to the basin. The
terminus of the Worcester & Birmingham
Canal is the former stop lock; this is known as
Worcester Bar, for originally there was a
physical barrier here between the Worcester &
Birmingham Canal and the much older
Birmingham Canal. The latter refused to allow
a junction, and for several years goods had to be
transhipped at this point from one canal to the
other. This absurd situation was remedied by
an Act of Parliament in 1815, by which a stop
lock was allowed to be inserted to connect the
two canals. Nowadays the stop gates are kept
open and one can pass straight through, on to
the Birmingham Canal. This canal goes under a
short tunnel (or a long bridge) with a church on
top of it, to Farmer's Bridge Junction. From
here the Birmingham Canal aims off north west
towards the body of the Birmingham Canal
Navigations network (*see book 2*).

*The route described below is the Birmingham &
Fazeley Canal from Farmer's Bridge to Salford
Junction, where it links up with the canals
described in book 2 of this series.*

Turning north east off the main line of the
Birmingham Canal, one arrives shortly at
Cambrian Wharf, a pub, sanitary station and
moorings all overlooked by four big blocks of
flats. There are some well-painted locks too, for
from this point the superb Farmer's Bridge
flight of 13 locks descends steeply into the heart
of Birmingham. Many of the locks were built
very close together and so the intervening
pounds were expanded as much as possible in
every direction. This results in one side of each
lock becoming like a peninsula, flanked by
water. The course of the flight is mainly dark
and mysterious, for over the years the canal has
become frequently crossed by bridges, and
even roofed over by vast buildings, but much
recent work has transformed this once
forgotten area into a tidy and exciting
environment, a popular walking and jogging
route for the city dwellers. After passing the
base of Birmingham's Post Office Tower and
under the great arch of the now closed Snow
Hill station, the canal levels out as the locks
come to an end. But soon comes Aston
Junction, marked by the old iron turnover
bridge, on which is cast 'Horseley Iron Works
Staffordshire 1828'. Here there is an intriguing
mixture of old canal architecture, green open
space and the hi-tech buildings of the
University Science Park. To the north east is the
main line of the Birmingham & Fazeley,
falling through the 11 Aston locks to Salford
Junction. At the second lock from the bottom is
a lock-keeper's cottage: its gate onto the road
gives access to a small grocery, a petrol station
and a pub. Towards Salford Junction itself, the
buildings become fewer and lower as the canal
creeps quietly under a tangle of motorways
which comprise Gravelly Hill, otherwise known
as Spaghetti Junction.

Salford Junction At this unusual junction
the Birmingham & Fazeley arrives from
Birmingham, crossing the River Tame on an
aqueduct and bearing half right (east) towards
Minworth and Fazeley. Meanwhile the short
Birmingham & Warwick Junction Canal
appears from the Grand Union Canal to the
south, also crossing the River Tame on a low
aqueduct. The straight canal entering the
junction from the north west is the Tame
Valley Canal, part of the BCN system. However, this
intersection of waterways is of little significance
compared to what is going on overhead, for this
is the site of the notorious Gravelly Hill
interchange – the most elaborate urban road
junction in Britain. So the whole area of Salford
Junction is completely overpowered by the
mass of concrete pillars and decking carrying
the lines of unseen vehicles in all directions.
The sky is truly filled with roads, while the

canals creep along underneath. The noise is a little disheartening, but it is a fascinating way to see this remarkably lavish piece of civil engineering.

The Digbeth Branch This leaves the Birmingham & Fazeley main line at Aston Junction, and descends through six locks to Bordesley Basin, now disused, where it meets the former Warwick & Birmingham Canal, which became part of the Grand Union Canal when the GUC Company was formed in 1929. There was a stop lock – called Warwick Bar – at the junction by Bordesley Basin. One of the lesser-known tunnels on the canal system is on the Digbeth Branch – Ashted Tunnel. There is a narrow towpath through it, protected by railings and with a corrugated surface for the towing horses to get a good grip on.

Cambrian Wharf The winner of a Civic Trust award in 1970, it is now looking the worse for wear. The construction of four new tower blocks of flats near Farmer's Bridge (very close to the centre of Birmingham) provided the incentive for BWB to dredge out and restore the basins at the beginning of the former Newhall branch canal; for Birmingham City Council to make a pleasing canalside walk and restore two 18thC terraces of cottages in the nearby Kingston Row; and for a local brewery company to build a new canal pub. There are moorings available here. For walkers, it is impossible to go by canal from Cambrian Wharf to Gas Street Basin (*see below*), since the towpath is sealed off at Cambrian Wharf. One must therefore go through the streets, and the route is as follows: Cambrian Wharf, Kingston Row, St Martin's Place, Cambridge Street, straight across Broad Street, down Gas Street and turn left through a small opening. This leads down onto the towpath at the Basin.

Gas Street or Worcester Bar Basin Before the demolition of the surrounding warehouses, this basin had a unique atmosphere. It is still full of colourful narrowboats, but the new buildings show little promise. The basin is shaped like a flat triangle, with a causeway across the middle. *See page 192 for an explanation of the 'Worcester Bar'*

BOATYARDS

Ⓑ**Brummagem Boats** Sherborne Street Wharf, Oozell's Street Loop west of Farmer's Bridge Junction. (021-455 6163). Ⓡ Ⓢ Ⓦ Ⓓ Pump-out, gas, narrowboat hire, day boat hire, wet dock, overnight mooring, winter storage, books and maps, boat building, boat sales and repairs. Toilet.

BOAT TRIPS

Second City Canal Cruises (021-643 4384). Trips from Gas Street Basin to the Black Country Museum and around the BCN *each weekend*. Also trips *some weekday lunchtimes (phone for details)*. Private charter, gift shop, museum.

Brummagem Boats Evening trips for parties of up to 48 people. Details from 021-455 6163.

PUBS

🍺 **Duke of Wellington** near the second lock from Salford Junction, on the Birmingham & Fazeley Canal. The only pub easily accessible from the canal between Farmer's Bridge and Salford.

🍺 **James Brindley** Gas Street Basin. A pleasant modern pub offering seafood at *lunchtime and early evening (Mon–Sat)*.

🍺 **Long Boat** Cambrian Wharf. Canalside, near the top lock. Ansells real ale, food.

🍺 **Prince of Wales** Cambridge Street, 2 minutes from Farmer's Bridge Junction. A fine unspoilt local serving Ansells, Tetley's and Ind Coope (Burton) real ale. Snacks at *lunchtime and early evening*. A better bet than the Long Boat.

Cambrian Wharf, Birmingham. *Derek Pratt*.

A BRIEF HISTORY OF BRITISH CANALS

River navigations, that is rivers widened and deepened to take large boats, had existed in England since the Middle Ages: some can even be traced back to Roman times. In 1600 there were 700 miles of navigable river in England, and by 1760, the dawn of the canal age, this number had been increased to 1300. This extensive network had prompted many developments later used by the canal engineers, for example, the lock system. But there were severe limitations: generally the routes were determined by the rivers and the features of the landscape and so were rarely direct. Also there were no east-west, or north-south connections.

Thus the demand for a direct inland waterway system increased steadily through the first half of the 18thC with the expansion of internal trade. Road improvements could not cope with this expansion, and so engineers and merchants turned to canals, used extensively on the continent.

One of the earliest pure canals, cut independently of existing rivers, was opened in 1745, at Newry in Northern Ireland, although some authorities consider the Fossdyke, cut by the Romans to link the Rivers Trent and Witham, to be the first. However, the Newry is more important because it established the cardinal rule of all canals, the maintenance of an adequate water supply, a feature too often ignored by later engineers. The Newry Canal established the principle of a long summit level, fed by a reservoir to keep the locks at either end well supplied. Ten years later, in England, the Duke of Bridgewater decided to build a canal to provide an adequate transport outlet for his coal mines at Worsley. He employed the self-taught James Brindley as his engineer, and John Gilbert as surveyor, and launched the canal age in England. The Bridgewater Canal was opened in 1761. Its route, all on one level, was independent of all rivers; its scale of operations reflected the new power of engineering, and the foresight of its creators. Although there were no locks, the engineering problems were huge; an aqueduct was built at Barton over the River Irwell, preceded by an embankment 900yds long; 15 miles of canal were built underground, so that boats could approach the coal face for loading – eventually there were 42 miles underground, including an inclined plane – the puddled clay method was used by Brindley to make the canal bed watertight. Perhaps most important of all, the canal was a success financially. Bridgewater invested the equivalent of £3 million of his own money in the project, and still made a profit.

Having shown that canals were both practical and financially sound, the Bridgewater aroused great interest throughout Britain. Plans were drawn up for a trunk canal, to link the four major rivers of England: the Thames, Severn, Mersey and Trent. This plan was eventually brought to fruition, but many years later than its sponsors imagined. Brindley was employed as engineer for the scheme, his reputation ensuring that he would always have more work than he could handle. The Trent and Mersey, and the Staffordshire and Worcestershire Canals received the Royal Assent in 1766, and the canal age began in earnest.

Canals, like the railways later, were built entirely by hand. Gangs of itinerant workmen were gathered together, drawn by the comparatively high pay. Once formed these armies of 'navigators' – hence 'navvies' – moved through the countryside as the canal was built, in many cases living off the land. All engineering problems had to be solved by manpower alone, aided by the horse and the occasional steam pump. Embankments, tunnels, aqueducts, all were built by these labouring armies kept under control only by the power of the section engineers and contractors.

The Staffordshire and Worcestershire Canal opened in 1770. In its design Brindley determined the size of the standard Midlands canal, which of course had direct influence on the rest of the English system as it was built. He chose a narrow canal, with locks 72ft 7in by 7ft 6in, partly for reasons of economy, and partly because he realised that the problems of an adequate water supply were far greater than most canal sponsors realised. This standard, which was also adopted for the Trent and Mersey, prompted the development of a special vessel, the narrowboat with its 30-ton payload. Ironically this decision by Brindley in 1766 ensured the failure of the canals as a commercial venture 200 years later, for by the middle of this century a 30-ton payload could no longer be worked economically.

The Trent and Mersey was opened in 1777; 93 miles long, the canal included five tunnels, the original one at Harecastle taking 11 years to build. In 1790 Oxford was finally reached and the junction with the Thames brought the four great rivers together. From the very start English canal companies were characterised by their intense rivalries; water supplies were jealously guarded, and constant wars were waged over toll prices. Many canals receiving the Royal Assent were never built, while others staggered towards conclusion, hampered by doubtful engineering, inaccurate estimates, and loans that they could never hope to pay off. Yet for a period canal mania gripped British speculators, as railway mania was to grip them 50 years later. The peak of British canal development came between 1791 and 1794, a period that gave rise to the opening of the major routes, the rise of the great canal engineers, Telford, Rennie and Jessop, and the greatest prosperity of those companies already operating. At this time the canal system had an effective monopoly over inland transport: the old trunk roads could not compete, coastal traffic was uncertain and hazardous, and the railways were still a future dream. This period also saw some of the greatest feats of engineering.

An early photograph of the Foxton 'staircase'.

A contemporary view of canal promoters. *Eric de Maré.*

The turn of the century saw the opening of the last major cross-country routes; the Pennines were crossed by the Leeds and Liverpool Canal between 1770 and 1816, while the Kennet and Avon (opened in 1810) linked London and Bristol via the Thames. These two canals were built as broad navigations: already the realisation was dawning on canal operators that the limits imposed by the Brindley standard were too restrictive, a suspicion that was to be brutally confirmed by the coming of the railways. The Kennet and Avon, along with its rival the Thames and Severn, also marks the introduction of fine architecture to canals. Up till now canal architecture had been functional, often impressive, but clearly conceived by engineers. As a result the Kennet and Avon has an architectural unity lacking in earlier canals. The appearance of architectural quality was matched by another significant change: canals became straighter, their engineers choosing as direct a route as possible, arguing that greater construction costs would be outweighed by smoother, quicker operation, whereas the early canals had followed the landscape. The Oxford is the prime example of a contour canal, meandering across the Midlands as though there were all the time in the world. It looks beautiful, its close marriage with the landscape makes it ideal as a pleasure waterway, but it was commercial folly.

The shortcomings of the early canals were exploited all too easily by the new railways. At first there was sharp competition by canals. Tolls were lowered, money was poured into route improvements; 14 miles of the Oxford's windings were cut out between 1829 and 1834; schemes were prepared to widen the narrow canals; the Harecastle Tunnel was doubled in 1827, the new tunnel taking three years to build (as opposed to 11 years for the old). But the race was lost from the start. The 19thC marks the rise of the railways and the decline of the canals. With the exception of the Manchester Ship Canal, the last major canal was the Birmingham and Liverpool Junction, opened in 1835. The system survived until this century, but the 1914–18 war brought the first closures, and through the 1930s the canal map adopted the shape it has today. Effective commercial carrying on narrow canals ceased in the early 1960s, although a few companies managed to survive until recently. However, with the end of commercial operation, a new role was seen for the waterways, as a pleasure amenity, a 'linear national park 2000 miles long'.

Water supply has always been the cardinal element in both the running and the survival of any canal system. Locks need a constant supply of water – every boat passing through a wide lock on the Grand Union uses 96,000 gallons of water. Generally two methods of supply were

The rudimentary tools of the early 'navvies'. *Hugh McKnight.*

Worcester and Birmingham Canal Company toll ticket dated 1816. *Hugh McKnight.*

used: direct feed by rivers and streams, and feed by reservoirs sited along the summit level. The first suffered greatly from silting, and meant that the canal was dependent on the level of water in the river; the regular floods from the River Soar that overtake the Grand Union's Leicester line show the dangers of this. The second was more reliable, but many engineers were short-sighted in their provision of an adequate summit level. The otherwise well-planned Kennet and Avon always suffered from water shortage. Where shortages occurred, steam pumping engines were used to pump water taken down locks back up to the summit level. The Kennet and Avon was dependent upon pumped supplies, while the Birmingham Canal Navigations were fed by six reservoirs and 17 pumping engines. Some companies adopted side ponds alongside locks to save water, but this put the onus on the boatman and so had limited success. Likewise the stop locks still to be seen at junctions are a good example of 18thC company rivalry; an established canal would ensure that any proposed canal wishing to join it would have to lock *down* into the older canal, which thus gained a lock of water each time a boat passed through.

Where long flights or staircase locks existed there was always great wastage of water, and so throughout canal history alternative mechanical means of raising boats have been tried out. The inclined plane or the vertical lift were the favoured forms. Both worked on the counterbalance principle, the weight of the descending boat helping to raise the ascending. The first inclined plane was built at Ketley in 1788, and they were a feature of the West Country Bude and Chard Canals. The most famous plane was built at Foxton, and operated from 1900–10. Mechanical failure and excessive running costs ended the application of the inclined plane in England, although modern examples work very efficiently on the continent, notably in Belgium. The vertical lift was more unusual, although there were eight on the Grand Western Canal. The most famous, built

at Anderton in 1875 (and currently being re-built) stands as a monument to the ingenuity shown in the attempts to overcome the problems of water shortage.

Engineering features are the greatest legacy of the canal age, and of these, tunnels are the most impressive. The longest tunnel is at Standedge, on the Huddersfield Narrow Canal (not navigable throughout, but restored in part). This tunnel runs for 5716yds through the Pennines, at times 638ft below the surface. It is also on the highest summit level, 644ft above sea level. The longest navigable tunnel is now Blisworth, at 3056yds long. Others of interest include the Dudley Tunnel, 3154yds long, which can be seen from the electric trip boat which operates from the Black Country Museum; the twin Harecastle Tunnels on the Trent and Mersey Canal – the first 2897yds long and now disused, the second 2919yds and still in use; Sapperton, which carried the Thames and Severn Canal through the Cotswolds and Netherton on the Birmingham Canal Navigations. This last, built 1855–58, was the last in England, and at a later date by electricity.

The Netherton Tunnel was built wide enough to allow for a towing path on both sides. Most tunnels have no towing path at all, and so boats had to be 'legged', or walked through.

The slowness and relative danger of legging in tunnels led to various attempts at mechanical propulsion. An endless rope pulled by a stationary steam engine at the tunnel mouth was tried out at Blisworth and Braunston between 1869 and 1871. Steam tugs were employed, an early application of mechanical power to canal boats, but their performance was greatly limited by lack of ventilation, not to mention the danger of suffocating the crew.

An electric tug was used at Harecastle from 1914 to 1954. The diesel engine made tunnel tug services much more practical, but diesel-powered narrowboats soon put the tugs out of business: by the 1930s most tunnels had to be navigated by whatever means the boatman

Islington Tunnel during construction. *Hugh McKnight.*

chose to use. Legging continued at Crick, Husbands Bosworth and Saddington until 1939.

Until the coming of the diesel boats, the horse reigned supreme as a source of canal power. The first canals had used gangs of men to bow-haul the boats, a left over from the river navigations where 50–80 men, or 12 horses, would pull a 200-ton barge. By 1800 the horse had taken over, and was used throughout the heyday of the canal system. In fact horse towage survived as long as large-scale commercial operation. Generally one horse or mule was used per boat, a system unmatched for cheapness and simplicity. The towing path was carried from one side of the canal to the other by turnover bridges, a common feature that reveals the total dominance of the horse. Attempts to introduce self-propelled canal boats date from 1793, although most early experiments concerned tugs towing dumb barges. Development was limited by the damage caused by wash, a problem that still applies today, and the first fleets of self-propelled steam narrowboats were not in service until the last quarter of the 19thC. Fellows, Morton and Clayton, and the Leeds and Liverpool Carrying Co. ran large fleets of these boats between 1880 and 1931, by which time most had been converted to diesel operation. With the coming of mechanical power the butty boat principle was developed: a powered narrowboat would tow a dumb 'butty' boat, thereby doubling the load without doubling the running costs. This system became standard until the virtual ending by the late 1960s of carrying on the narrow canals. Before the coming of railways, passenger services were run on the canals; packet boats, specially built narrowboats with passenger accommodation, ran express services, commanding the best horses and the unquestioned right of way over all other traffic. Although the railways killed this traffic, the last scheduled passenger service survived on the Gloucester and Berkeley Canal until 1935.

The traditional narrowboat with its colourful decoration and meticulous interior has become a symbol of English canals. However this was in fact a late development. The shape of the narrowboat was determined by Brindley's original narrow canal specification, but until the late 19thC boats were unpainted, and carried all male crews. Wages were sufficient for the crews to maintain their families at home. The increase in railway competition brought a reduction in wages, and so bit by bit the crews were forced to take their families with them, becoming a kind of water gipsy. The confines of a narrowboat cabin presented the same problems as a gipsy caravan, and so the families found a similar answer. Their eternally wandering home achieved individuality by extravagant and colourful decoration, and the traditional narrowboat painting was born. The extensive symbolic vocabulary available to the painters produced a sign language that only these families could understand, and the canal world became far more enclosed, although outwardly it was more decorative.

As the canals have turned from commerce to pleasure, so the traditions of the families have died out, and the families themselves have faded away. But their language survives, although its meaning has mostly vanished with them. This survival gives the canals their characteristic decorative qualities, which make them so attractive to the pleasure boater and to the casual visitor.

FISHING

Many anglers start their fishing careers on the canals and navigable rivers, mainly because our system of waterways has always offered excellent opportunities for the thousands of angling enthusiasts throughout Great Britain.

Most of these cross-country waterways have natural reed-fringed and grassy banks, and in addition to the delightful surroundings the fishing is generally good. In most areas there has been a steady improvement in canal fishing in recent years and in many places new stocks of fish have been introduced. The popular quarry are roach, perch and bream, but the canals also hold dace, tench, chub and carp in places, in addition to pike and other species in particular areas.

Canals afford good hunting grounds for those seeking specimen fish (that is, fish above average size) and these are liable to be encountered on almost any water. The canals also make good venues for competition fishing, and in most places nowadays matches are held regularly at weekends throughout the season.

The Statutory Close Season for coarse fish is March 15 to June 15 inclusive, but in some areas, notably the Yorkshire River Authority, the Close Season is from February 28 to May 31. The Close Season for pike in some areas is March 15 to September 30.

Permits and fishing rights

Most parts of the waterways system are available to anglers. The big angling associations – eg the London AA, Birmingham AA, Reading & District AA, Coventry & District AA, Nottingham AA plus many smaller clubs – rent fishing rights over extensive areas on the system. In most cases, day tickets are available.

On arrival at the waterside it is always advisable to make enquiries as to who holds the fishing rights, and to obtain a permit if one is required *before* starting to fish. Remember, also, that a River Authority rod licence is usually required in addition to a fishing permit. It is essential to obtain this licence from the relevant River Authority *before* starting to fish. Some fishing permits and licences are issued by bailiffs along the bank, but local enquiry will help to determine this.

A canalside pub or a local fishing tackle shop are good places to enquire if permission or day tickets are required for the local stretch of water. Canal lock keepers are usually knowledgeable about the fishing rights in the immediate locality, and often a lock keeper may be found who issues day tickets on behalf of an angling association, or owner. It is likely that he will also know some of the better fishing areas, as well as local methods and baits which may be considered most successful.

The fishing rights on most canals are owned by British Waterways and many miles of good fishing are leased to clubs and angling associations. They also issue day tickets on certain lengths, so it is worth enquiring at the local British Waterways office when planning a trip. Special arrangements are made for fishing from boats, again, enquire with the BW locally.

'Private fishing' notices should *not* be ignored. If the owner's name and address is on the board then application can be made for permission for a future occasion. Once permission has been obtained it would be advisable to find out if there are any restrictions imposed, since some clubs and associations ban certain baits, or have restrictions on live-baiting for pike: and on some fisheries pike fishing is not allowed before a specified date.

Other restrictions may concern size-limits of fish, and this certainly applies to the London AA canal fisheries. Some River Authority by-laws prohibit the retention of under-sized fish in keep nets. A local club holding the fishing rights may have imposed their own size-limits in order to protect certain species. Such restrictions are generally printed on permits and licences.

Tackle

In the slow moving, sluggish waters of canals the float tackle needs to be light and lines fine in order to catch fish. When fishing for roach and dace lines of 1½lb to 2lb breaking strain are the maximum strength normally needed in order to get the fish to take a bait – particularly when the water is clear, or on the popular reaches that are 'hard-fished'.

Fine tackle also means small hooks, sizes 16 and 18 – or even as small as 22 at times. Such light gear is also effective when fishing for the smaller species, such as gudgeon and bleak. This tackle will require a well-balanced float to show the slightest indication of a bite.

Bait

Baits should be small, and maggots, casters (maggot chrysalis), hempseed, wheat, tiny cubes of bread crust, or a small pinch of flake (the white crumb of a new loaf) may take fish. It always pays to experiment with baits; bait that is effective on one occasion will not necessarily prove to be as effective the next. With slight variations, similar fishing methods can be used effectively on the majority of waterways.

Northern anglers who regularly compete in contests on canals use bloodworms as bait. They have become extremely skilful in using this tiny bait and often take fish on bloodworms when all other baits fail. Bloodworms are the larvae of a midge, and are a perfectly natural bait. The anglers gather the bloodworms from the mud and, apart from a wash in clean water, the baits are ready for use.

A popular groundbait that has had great success is known as 'black magic'! This is a mixture of garden peat and bread crumbs mixed

Barbel

Bleak

Common Bream

Bullhead

Common Carp

Chub

Dace

Freshwater Eel

Gudgeon

River Lamprey

Perch

Minnow

Roach

Pike

Ruffe

Rudd

Stickleback

Tench

Brown Trout

dry and carried to the water. When dampened and mixed it can be thrown in in the usual way. The basis of most groundbaits is bread, and many other materials may be added, although stodgy mixtures should be avoided when canal fishing. Canals are not waters which respond to heavy groundbaiting tactics. It is far better to use a cloudbait, and this can be purchased ready for use. Some successful Midland anglers wet their cloudbait with milk instead of water to increase the cloud effect.

Methods

Once the swim – that is the area of water to be fished – has been decided upon, and the tackle set up, use a plummet to find the depth and adjust the float, but be cautious when doing so in clear waters. At times it may be best to find the depth by trial and error. Often most fish will be caught from around mid-water level, but always be prepared to move the float further up the line in order to present the bait closer to the bottom, where the bigger fish are usually to be found. At frequent intervals toss a few samples of the hook-bait into the top of the swim to keep the fish interested.

Fish in different waters may vary in the way they take a bait and this creates a different bite registration. It may be found that fish take the hook-bait quickly, causing the float to dip sharply or dive under the surface. The strike should be made instantly, on the downward movement. On some canals the fish are even quicker – and perhaps gentler – not taking the float under at all, and in this case the strike should be made at the slightest unusual movement of the float.

Roach and dace abound in many lengths and although working the float tackle down with a flow of water takes most fish, better quality fish – including bream – are usually to be taken by fishing a laying-on style, with the bait lying on the bottom. This method can often be best when fishing areas where there is no flow at all. This is done with float tackle, adjusted to make the distance from float to hook greater than the depth of water, so that when the float is at the surface the bait and lower length of line are lying on the bottom.

The alternative method of fishing the bottom is by legering, the main difference in the methods being in the bite indication. Without a float a bite is registered at the rod-tip where, if need be, a quiver-tip or swing-tip may be fitted. These bite detectors are used extensively on Midland and Northern waters. Legering is a method often used in the south, where in some southern canals barbel and chub are quite prolific. These species grow to good sizes in canal waters – chub up to 7lb and barbel up to 14lb have been taken – but these are exceptional and the average run of fish would be well below those weights. Nevertheless, both species are big fish and big baits and hooks may be used when fishing for them.

Many bigger than average fish – of all species – have been taken by fishing the bait on the bottom. Whatever the style of leger fishing, always choose the lightest possible weight, and position it some 12 to 18in up from the hook. There are no hard and fast rules governing the distance between weight and hook, so it pays to experiment to find the best to suit the conditions.

Anglers who regularly fish the Northern and Midland canals invariably use tiny size 20 and 22 hooks, tied to a mere ¾lb breaking strain line, and when float-fishing use a tiny quill float – porcupine or crow quill. A piece of peacock quill is useful because it can be cut with scissors to make it suit prevailing conditions. Such small floats only need tiny weights to balance them correctly, and usually the Midland anglers position this on the line just under the float so that the bait is presented naturally. Once the tackle has been cast out, the bait falls slowly through the water along with hook-bait samples, which are thrown in at the same time. This is called 'fishing on the drop'. A fine cloudbait is also used with this style.

Canals which have luxuriant weed growth harbour many small fish, which are preyed upon by perch. These move in shoals and invariably the perch in a shoal are much the same size. Usually the really big perch are solitary, so it pays to rove the canal and search for them. They are to be caught from almost any canal and although they may be caught by most angling methods, the most effective is usually float-fishing. The fishing depth can vary according to conditions, time of year, and actual depth of the canal, so it pays to try the bait at varying depths. The usual baits for perch are worms, small live-baits (minnows etc) and maggots. Close by wooden lock gates is often the haunt of large perch.

In certain places canals and rivers come together and take on the characteristics of the river (ie with an increased flow) and different methods are needed. These places are often noted for splendid chub (and sometimes barbel) in addition to roach and other species. Trotting the stream is a popular and effective fishing style.

Weather

Weather conditions have to be taken into consideration. Canals usually run through open country and catch the slightest breeze. Even a moderate wind will pull and bob the float, which in turn will agitate the baited hook. If bites are not forthcoming under such conditions then it may be best to remove the float and try a straightforward leger arrangement.

When legering, the effects of the wind can be avoided by keeping the rod top down to within an inch or two of the water level – or even by sinking the rod-tip below the surface. Anglers in the North and Midlands have devised a wind-shield for legering that protects the rod-tip from the wind and improves bite detection. Nevertheless, in some circumstances a slight wind can be helpful because if a moderate breeze is blowing it will put a ripple on the water, and this can be of assistance in fishing in clear waters.

Where to fish

Most canals are narrow and this makes it possible to cast the tackle towards the far bank, where fish may have moved because they had been disturbed from the near bank. Disturbance will send the fish up or downstream and often well away from the fishing area. So always approach the water quietly, and remember to move cautiously at all times. When making up the tackle to start fishing it is advisable to do so as far back from the water as possible to avoid scaring the fish. It pays to move slowly, to keep as far from the bank as possible, and to avoid clumping around in heavy rubber boots. If there is cover along the bank – shrubs, bushes, tall reeds and clumps of yellow flag iris – the wise angler will make full use of it.

There are some canals that are no longer navigable, and these are generally weedy. At certain times in the season the surface of the water disappears under a green mantle of floating duckweed, which affords cover and security for the fish. It is possible to have the best sport by fishing in the pockets of clear water that are to be found.

Some canals have prolific growths of water lilies in places, and are particularly attractive for angling. They always look ideal haunts for tench, but they can also be rather difficult places from which to land good fish. Tench are more or less evenly distributed throughout the canals and the best are found where weed growth is profuse. It may be best to fish small areas of clear water between the weeds. Groundbait can encourage tench to move out from the weed beds, and to feed once they are out. Sometimes it is an advantage to clear a swim by dragging out weeds or raking the bottom. This form of natural groundbaiting stirs the silt, which clouds the water and disturbs aquatic creatures on which the fish feed.

Bream seem to do well in canals and some fairly good fish up to 5lb may be taken. Any deep pools or winding holes (shown as ⤳ on map) are good places to try, particularly when fishing a canal for the first time.

Other places worth fishing are 'cattle drinks' regularly used by farm animals. These make useful places to fish for bream, roach and dace. The frequent use of these drinking holes colours the water, as the animals stir up the mud, and disturb various water creatures. The coloured water draws fish into the area – on the downstream side of the cattle drink when there is the slightest flow.

Pike are to be found in every canal in the country – they are predators, feeding on small fish (which gives a sure indication of the most effective baits). Any small live fish presented on float tackle will take pike. The best places to fish are near weed beds and boats that have been moored in one place a long time.

Many of our canals are cut through pleasant and peaceful countryside, and this enables anglers to spend many delightful hours along the banks – and always with the chance of making a good catch. As a general rule, never fish in locks on navigable canals, or anywhere that could obstruct the free passage of boats. Remember that you will inconvenience yourself as well as the boatman if you have to move in a hurry, or risk a broken line. Never leave discarded line or weights on the bank, and never throw these items into the water. Waterfowl become entangled in the line, and are poisoned by the lead shot, which they swallow when grubbing for food, so use non-lead weights only. All responsible anglers take their spoilt tackle and litter home with them, where it can be disposed of properly.

British Waterways produce a 'Waterways Code for Anglers', which can be obtained from local BW offices, or from Customer Services, Greycaine Road, Watford, Herts WD2 4JR. (0923 226422). All who intend to fish on BW's waterways are strongly advised to obtain a copy, as it contains information regarding safety, health and pollution.

BRITISH WATERWAYS OFFICES

CUSTOMER SERVICES

British Waterways, Greycaine Road, Watford, Herts WD2 4JR. (0923 226422).

AREA OFFICES

Will deal with enquiries regarding stoppages, long-term moorings and specific problems on a particular canal. The canal manager's telephone number is given on the introductory page for each waterway.

Birmingham Area British Waterways, Auchinleck House, Broad Street, Five Ways, Birmingham B15 1DL. (021-633 3666).
Grand Union Canal (north)
Oxford Canal (north)
Stratford-on-Avon Canal (north)
Worcester & Birmingham Canal

Gloucester Area British Waterways, Llanthony Warehouse, The Docks, Gloucester GL1 2EH. (0452 25524).
Kennet & Avon Canal
Monmouthshire & Brecon Canal
Gloucester & Sharpness Canal
River Severn

South East Area British Waterways, Wynyard House, 99 Langley Road, Watford WD1 3PE. (0923 31363).
Grand Union Canal (south)
Lee & Stort Rivers
Oxford Canal (south)

For assistance from operational staff outside normal office hours, and at weekends, dial 100 and ask for FREEPHONE CANALS.

Other navigation authorities are listed in the appropriate place in the text.

Lock mechanism, Worcester & Birmingham Canal. *Derek Pratt.*

INDEX